## THE CAMBRIDGE COMPANION TO
## AMERICAN NOVELISTS

This *Companion* examines the full range and vigor of the American novel. From the American exceptionalism of James Fenimore Cooper to the apocalyptic post-Americanism of Cormac McCarthy, these newly commissioned essays from leading scholars and critics chronicle the major aesthetic innovations that have shaped the American novel over the past two centuries. The essays evaluate the work, life, and legacy of influential American novelists including Melville, Twain, James, Wharton, Cather, Faulkner, Ellison, Pynchon, and Morrison, while situating them within the context of their literary predecessors and successors. The volume also highlights less familiar, though equally significant writers such as Theodore Dreiser and Djuna Barnes, providing a balanced and wide-ranging survey of use to students, teachers, and general readers of American literature.

Timothy Parrish is Professor of English at Florida State University. Author of *Ralph Ellison and the Genius of America* (2012), he has published widely in journals such as *Contemporary Literature* and *Studies in American Literature*. He is editor of *The Cambridge Companion to Philip Roth* (2007).

*A complete list of books in the series is at the back of this book.*

THE CAMBRIDGE
COMPANION TO

# AMERICAN NOVELISTS

# THE CAMBRIDGE
# COMPANION TO
# AMERICAN
# NOVELISTS

Edited by

## TIMOTHY PARRISH
*Florida State University*

**CAMBRIDGE**
UNIVERSITY PRESS

CAMBRIDGE UNIVERSITY PRESS
Cambridge, New York, Melbourne, Madrid, Cape Town,
Singapore, São Paulo, Delhi, Mexico City

Cambridge University Press
32 Avenue of the Americas, New York, NY 10013-2473, USA

www.cambridge.org
Information on this title: www.cambridge.org/9781107600973

First published 2013

Printed in the United States of America

*A catalog record for this publication is available from the British Library.*

*Library of Congress Cataloging in Publication data*
The Cambridge companion to American novelists / [edited by] Timothy Parrish,
Florida State University.
pages   cm – (Cambridge companions to literature)
Includes bibliographical references and index.
ISBN 978-1-107-01313-1 (hardback) – ISBN 978-1-107-60097-3 (paperback)
1. American fiction – History and criticism.   2. Novelists, American.   I. Parrish,
Timothy, 1964– editor of compilation.
PS371.C35   2012
813.009–dc23          2012033808

ISBN 978-1-107-01313-1 Hardback
ISBN 978-1-107-60097-3 Paperback

# CONTENTS

# Contents

Contents

# CONTRIBUTORS

VICTORIA AARONS is O. R. & Eva Mitchell Distinguished Professor of Literature and chair of the English Department at Trinity University. She is the author of *A Measure of Memory: Storytelling and Identity in American Jewish Fiction* and *What Happened to Abraham? Reinventing the Covenant in American Jewish Fiction*, each a recipient of the *Choice* Award for Outstanding Academic Book. Her work on American Jewish and Holocaust literatures has appeared in a number of scholarly venues, including *Studies in American Jewish Literature, Modern Jewish Studies, Contemporary Literature, Literature and Belief,* and *Shofar*. Aarons has published essays and book chapters in a variety of volumes and reference works, including *The Call of Memory: Learning about the Holocaust through Narrative* and the two-volume compendium *Holocaust Literature: An Encyclopedia of Writers and Their Work*. Aarons is on the editorial board of the *Saul Bellow Journal* and *Philip Roth Studies*.

LEONARD CASSUTO, Professor of English at Fordham University, New York, is the author of *Hard-Boiled Sentimentality: The Secret History of American Crime Stories* (2009), which was nominated for the Edgar and Macavity Awards. Other books include *The Inhuman Race: The Racial Grotesque in American Literature and Culture* (1997) and four edited volumes, including *The Cambridge History of the American Novel* (2011), of which he was General Editor. Cassuto is also an award-winning journalist, writing about subjects ranging from sports to the scientific search for room-temperature semiconductors. He writes a regular column, "The Graduate Adviser," for the *Chronicle of Higher Education*.

JULIAN W. CONNOLLY is Professor of Slavic Languages and Literatures at the University of Virginia. He is the author of *Ivan Bunin* (1982), *Nabokov's Early Fiction: Patterns of Self and Other* (1992), *The Intimate Stranger: Meetings with the Devil in Nineteenth-Century Russian Literature* (2001), and *A Reader's Guide to Nabokov's Lolita* (2009). He also edited the volumes *Nabokov's Invitation to a Beheading: A Course Companion* (1997), *Nabokov and His Fiction: New Perspectives* (1999), and *The Cambridge Companion to Nabokov* (2005). He has written more than seventy articles on nineteenth- and twentieth-century Russian literature.

# Contributors

CLARK DAVIS is a professor of English and chair of the Department of English at the University of Denver. He is the author of *After the Whale: Melville in the Wake of* Moby-Dick and *Hawthorne's Shyness: Ethics, Politics, and the Question of Engagement.*

TODD DAVIS teaches creative writing and American literature at Penn State University's Altoona College. He is the winner of the Gwendolyn Brooks Poetry Prize and the author of four books of poetry, most recently *The Least of These* (Michigan State University Press, 2010) and *Some Heaven* (Michigan State University Press, 2007). In addition to his creative work, Davis is the author or editor of six scholarly books, including *Kurt Vonnegut's Crusade, or How a Postmodern Harlequin Preached a New Kind of Humanism* (State University of New York Press, 2006) and *Postmodern Humanism in Contemporary Literature and Culture: Reconciling the Void* (Palgrave Macmillan, 2006).

WILLIAM DOW is Professor of American Literature at the Université Paris-Est (Marne-la-Vallée) and teaches at the American University of Paris. He is the Managing Editor of *Literary Journalism Studies* (Northwestern University Press) and has published articles in such journals as *Publications of the Modern Language Association,* the *Emily Dickinson Journal, Twentieth-Century Literature, ESQ: A Journal of the American Renaissance, Critique,* the *Hemingway Review, MELUS, Revue Française D'Etudes Américaines, Actes Sud, Prose Studies,* and *Etudes Anglaises.* He is the author of the book *Narrating Class in American Fiction* (Palgrave Macmillan, 2009) and coeditor of *Richard Wright: New Readings in the 21st Century* (Palgrave Macmillan, 2011). He is currently completing a book-length study on American modernism and radicalism entitled *Reinventing Persuasion: Literary Journalism and the American Radical Tradition, 1900–2000.*

CLARE EBY is a professor of English at the University of Connecticut. She has written *Dreiser and Veblen, Saboteurs of the Status Quo*; edited the Dreiser Edition of *The Genius* and *The Norton Critical Edition of Upton Sinclair's* The Jungle; and coedited *The Cambridge Companion to Theodore Dreiser* and *The Cambridge History of the American Novel.* She is completing an additional book, *Until Choice Do Us Part: The Theory and Practice of Marriage in the Progressive Era,* forthcoming with University of Chicago Press.

BRIAN EVENSON is the chair of the Literary Arts Department at Brown University. He is the author of ten books of fiction, most recently *Fugue State* (Coffee House Press, 2009), as well as a critical study on Robert Coover.

EUGENE GOODHEART is the Edytha Macy Gross Professor of Humanities at Brandeis University. He is the author of eleven books of literary and cultural criticism, including *The Reign of Ideology: Does Literary Studies Have a Future?* and *Darwinian Misadventures in the Humanities,* as well as a memoir, *Confessions of a Secular Jew*. His essays and reviews have appeared in many journals, including *Partisan Review*, the *Sewanee Review*, *Critical Inquiry*, *Daedalus*, and *New Literary History*.

ALEX GOODY is Reader in Twentieth-Century Literature at Oxford Brookes University and the author of *Modernist Articulations* (2007) and *Technology, Literature and Culture* (2011). She has also coedited *American Modernism: Cultural Transactions* (2009) and is the author of numerous chapters and articles on modernist women, New York Dada, modernist drama, contemporary poetry, and the work of Djuna Barnes and Mina Loy. Her forthcoming books are *Modernism and Feminism* and *Machine Amusements: Gender, Technology and Modernist Poetry*.

SARAH GRAHAM is Lecturer in American Literature at the University of Leicester. Her research focuses on American texts from the modernist period to the contemporary. Her main publications to date have focused on the works of H. D. (Hilda Doolittle) and J. D. Salinger, and she has ongoing research interests in American novels and short stories, 1940s to the present, particularly representations of adolescence and of the AIDS epidemic. She has published essays on H. D. and is the author/editor of *J. D. Salinger's* The Catcher in the Rye (Routledge, 2007) and author of *Salinger's* The Catcher in the Rye (Continuum, 2007). She is currently writing a study of Salinger's short fiction (Continuum, 2013) and is the Series Editor for Studies in Contemporary North American Fiction (Continuum).

THOMAS HEISE is an Associate Professor of English at McGill University, where he teaches post–World War II American literature, creative writing, and critical theory. He is the author of two books, *Urban Underworlds: A Geography of Twentieth-Century American Literature and Culture* (Rutgers University Press, 2010) and *Horror Vacui: Poems* (Sarabande, 2006). His essays have been published in *African American Review*, *Arizona Quarterly*, the *Journal of Popular Culture*, *Modern Fiction Studies*, and *Twentieth-Century Literature*.

LOVALERIE KING is an Associate Professor of African American Studies and Women's Studies at Penn State University, where she teaches courses in African American literature and culture and Women's Studies and serves as Director of the Africana Research Center. She is the author or coeditor of seven volumes on African American literature and culture, including *James Baldwin and Toni Morrison: Comparative Critical and Theoretical Essays* (Palgrave, 2006); *Race, Theft, and Ethics: Property Matters in African Literature* (LSU, 2007); *The Cambridge Introduction to Zora Neale Hurston* (2008); *African American Culture and Legal Discourse* (Palgrave, 2009); and *Contemporary African American Literature: The Living Canon* (Indiana, 2012). Her current projects include a handbook of African American fiction and a book-length critical examination of *The Wire* through the lens of ethics. She coordinates Penn State's conference series on African American literature, is a lifetime member of the College Language Association and a founding member of the George

Contributors

Moses Horton Society for the Study of African American Poetry, a member of the Toni Morrison Society, and a member of the Wintergreen Women Writer's Collective.

PAMELA KNIGHTS is an Honorary Senior Lecturer at Durham University. She is the author of *The Cambridge Introduction to Edith Wharton* (2009) and, with Janet Beer and Elizabeth Nolan, *Edith Wharton's* The House of Mirth (2006); other publications on Wharton and her contemporaries include chapters in *The Cambridge Companion to Edith Wharton* (1995), *Edith Wharton's* The Custom of the Country (2010), and *"This Strange Dream upon the Water": Venice and the Cultural Imagination* (forthcoming); introductions to *The House of Mirth* and *Ethan Frome*, and an edition of *Kate Chopin: The Awakening and Other Stories* (Oxford World's Classics, 2000). In a different field, she is currently working on a book, *Reading Dance and Performance Narratives for Children: Critical Moves* (Palgrave Macmillan).

JOSHUA KUPETZ has taught at the University of Michigan, the University of Colorado at Boulder, and Dickinson College, and he holds an M.F.A. from Columbia University and is currently a Ph.D. student at the University of Michigan. He has written the introduction "'The Straight Line Will Lead You Only to Death'" for *Jack Kerouac's On the Road: The Original Scroll* (2007).

PETER MESSENT is Emeritus Professor of Modern American Literature at the University of Nottingham, UK. He has written four books on Mark Twain, of which the most recent is the award-winning *Mark Twain and Male Friendship* (Oxford, 2009). He has also written books on narrative theory and the American novel and on Ernest Hemingway. He is presently completing *A Handbook of Crime Fiction* for Wiley Blackwell.

ROBERT MILDER, Professor of English at Washington University in St. Louis, has published widely on American Renaissance authors and has contributed to the Cambridge Companions to Melville and Emerson. His books include *Reimagining Thoreau* (Cambridge, 1995), *Exiled Royalties: Melville and the Life We Imagine*, and *Hawthorne's Habitations*.

THOMAS J. OTTEN teaches English at Boston University. He is the author of *A Superficial Reading of Henry James* (2006) and of essays in *ELH, American Literature, Yale Journal of Criticism*, and *PMLA*. "Hawthorne's Twisted Letters," an essay on the history of ekphrasis, recently appeared in *MLQ* (2009).

TIMOTHY PARRISH is Professor of English at Florida State University. He is the author of *Walking Blues: Making Americans from Emerson to Elvis* (2001), *From the Civil War to the Apocalypse: Postmodern History and American Fiction* (2008), and *Ralph Ellison and the Genius of America* (2012). He is also the editor of *The Cambridge Companion to Philip Roth* (2007). He has published widely on contemporary American literature in such journals as *Contemporary Literature*,

*Modern Fiction Studies, Prospects, Studies in American Fiction, Texas Studies in Literature and Language,* and *Arizona Quarterly,* among others.

RUTH PRIGOZY is former Chair of the English Department at Hofstra University and is the Executive Director of the F. Scott Fitzgerald Society, which she cofounded in 1990. She has published widely on F. Scott Fitzgerald as well as on Ernest Hemingway; J. D. Salinger; the Hollywood Ten; film directors Billy Wilder, D. W. Griffith, and Vittorio De Sica; the detective film and the short story; and a biography of actor/singer Dick Haymes. She has edited three of Fitzgerald's novels and written an illustrated life of Fitzgerald. She is completing a biography of the actor/singer Gordon MacRae.

STEPHEN RAILTON teaches American literature at the University of Virginia. The author or editor of ten books and numerous articles (including the Barnes & Noble edition of *Last of the Mohicans*), he has spent much of the last dozen years in virtual reality, where he has created major online Web sites devoted to *Uncle Tom's Cabin* and American Culture, Mark Twain, and William Faulkner.

ARTHUR RISS teaches U.S. literature before 1900 at Salem State University. The author of *Race, Slavery, and Liberalism in Nineteenth-Century American Literature* (2006), he is currently writing a book on Reconstruction.

JOAN SCHENKAR is the author of the widely praised biography *Truly Wilde: The Unsettling Story of Dolly Wilde, Oscar's Unusual Niece,* as well as a collection of award-winning plays, *Signs of Life: Six Comedies of Menace.* She edited and introduced *Patricia Highsmith: Selected Novels and Short Stories,* and her celebrated, award-winning literary biography *The Talented Miss Highsmith: The Secret Life and Serious Art of Patricia Highsmith* is regarded as the definitive work on the subject. She lives and writes in Paris and Greenwich Village.

JAMES SCHIFF is Associate Professor of English at the University of Cincinnati, where he teaches American literature and edits the *John Updike Review.* He is the author or editor of five books on contemporary American fiction, including *John Updike Revisited* and *Understanding Reynolds Price.* His essays have appeared in *American Literature, Critique,* the *Southern Review,* and elsewhere.

DAVID SEED is Professor of American Literature at the University of Liverpool. He has published studies of Joseph Heller and Thomas Pynchon, and his other publications include *American Science Fiction and the Cold War* (1999) and *Brainwashing* (2004). He edited the Blackwell *Companion to Science Fiction* (2005) and the Blackwell *Companion to Twentieth-Century United States Fiction* (2010).

DEBRA SHOSTAK is Professor of English at the College of Wooster, in Wooster, Ohio. She is the author of *Philip Roth – Countertexts, Counterlives* (2004) and the editor of *Philip Roth – American Pastoral, The Human Stain, The Plot against America* (2011).

Her articles on contemporary American novelists, including Paul Auster, Jeffrey Eugenides, John Irving, Maxine Hong Kingston, and Philip Roth, have appeared in *Contemporary Literature, Critique, Modern Fiction Studies, Shofar, Studies in the Novel,* and *Twentieth Century Literature.* She also writes on film and is currently working on cinematic adaptations of three contemporary American novels.

VALERIE SMITH is Dean of the College, Woodrow Wilson Professor of Literature, and Professor of English and African American Studies at Princeton University. Her research and teaching interests include African American literature and culture, black feminist theory, autobiography, black film, and twentieth- and twenty-first century U.S. literature. She is the author of *Self-Discovery and Authority in Afro-American Narrative; Not Just Race, Not Just Gender: Black Feminist Readings;* and the forthcoming *Toni Morrison: Writing the Moral Imagination* as well as numerous articles on African American literature and visual culture and black feminist theory. Her edited volumes include *African American Writers; Representing Blackness: Issues in Film and Video; New Essays on Song of Solomon;* and a special issue of *Signs* (coedited with Marianne Hirsch) on gender and cultural memory. At present, she is completing a book on the civil rights movement in cultural memory.

PHILIP WEINSTEIN, Alexander Griswold Cummins Professor of English at Swarthmore College, served as president of the William Faulkner Society from 2000 to 2003. He has written extensively on modern fiction, and his most recent books attend in a sustained way (when not exclusively) to Faulkner: *Faulkner's Subject: A Cosmos No One Owns* (Cambridge, 1992), *What Else but Love: The Ordeal of Race in Faulkner and Morrison* (1996), *Unknowing: The Work of Modernist Fiction* (2005), and *Becoming Faulkner* (2010). The Society for the Study of Southern Literature chose *Becoming Faulkner* as the best book on southern literature written in 2010, bestowing on it their Hugh Holman Award.

HANA WIRTH-NESHER is the Samuel L. and Perry Haber Chair on the Study of the Jewish Experience in the United States in the Department of English and American Studies at Tel Aviv University. She is also the Director of the Goldreich Family Institute for Yiddish Language, Literature, and Culture. She is the author *of Call It English: The Languages of Jewish American Literature* (Princeton University Press, 2005) and *City Codes: Reading the Modern Urban Novel* (Cambridge, 1996). She has edited *New Essays on Call It Sleep* (Cambridge, 1996) and *What Is Jewish Literature?* and coedited *The Cambridge Companion to Jewish American Literature* (Cambridge, 2003).

DAVID YAFFE is a professor of English at Syracuse University. He is the author of *Fascinating Rhythm: Reading Jazz in American Writing* (2005) and *Bob Dylan: Like a Complete Unknown* (2011). He is currently at work on *Reckless Daughter: A Portrait of Joni Mitchell* (forthcoming).

# INTRODUCTION

*Timothy Parrish*

The novel existed before the United States of America, but American history has been peculiarly conducive to the novel's formal possibilities. When Miguel de Cervantes wrote arguably the first novel, the globe was still terra incognita. The story of *Don Quixote* (1605, 1615) was largely the story of antiquated assumptions about culture, history, and identity being subjected to and in a sense destroyed by new ways of perceiving, knowing, and imagining that ever since that period have persistently been called "modern." Even as the form of the novel spread throughout Europe and on to America and elsewhere, its persistent preoccupation has been the question of individual identity. The novel has charted the relationship between an individual consciousness and the world around it. To Cervantes, Quixote's quest to assert the will of his self, though, was unsettling and fundamentally comic. Previous heroes such as Achilles, Odysseus, or Aeneas fulfilled their destiny; they did not create it. The prospect that an individual could fashion himself as a protagonist, a hero, without the consent or even the interest of the gods and despite the prevailing wisdom of social institutions such as the church was the beginning of a new conception of identity. "In the absence of a Supreme Judge," Milan Kundera suggests, the world of *Don Quixote* "suddenly appeared in its fearsome ambiguity" as the "single divine Truth decomposed into myriad relative truths parceled out by men. Thus was born the world of the Modern Era, and with it the novel, the image of and model of that world" (6).[1]

From a broad perspective, the story of the American novel comes out of two historical developments: the invention of the novel and the invention of America. These two inventions have always been intertwined. The core subjects of the Cervantean novel – innocence, idealism, violence, human depravity, and corruption; a boundless faith in possibilities that are betrayed by reality; a poignant and trenchant sadness; the desire for adventure motivated by the belief that you can invent your own identity and that your identity may be at odds with those surrounding you – are at the core and compose the history of the American novel. Arguably, *Don Quixote* as both a hope and a delusion predicts the main line of the American (and Latin American) novel much more than it does the English novel, since Quixote's quest is rooted in the creation of a reality opposed to the one he encounters. Classic American characters such as James Fenimore Cooper's Natty Bumppo, Mark Twain's Huckleberry Finn, Willa Cather's Antonia Shimerda, F. Scott Fitzgerald's Jay Gatsby, and J. D. Salinger's Holden Caulfield would not be lost or out of place on the plains of Quixote's windmills. The self-consciousness that characterizes many classic American novels emerges precisely out of a tension existing between expectations that one is discovering something already existing out there and the intuition that one is inventing that something through one's imagination. The history of the American novel tells us over and over that America has never been discovered but is ceaselessly being invented.

Kundera says that "the sole *raison d'être* of a novel is to discover what only the novel can discover," and as a form the novel has been mostly preoccupied with the relationship between individual perception and formal innovation (*Art* 5). Looking back through the history of the novel as a form we can see how Quixote's faltering individuality anticipates the sustained novelistic investigations and formal experiments concerning individual consciousness that will come with writers as different as Samuel Richardson, Leo Tolstoy, and Marcel Proust. The history of the form connects these writers to one another, even if their works were fashioned from different vernaculars and cultural assumptions. Without disputing Kundera's point that the novel is at heart a formal practice, one may also say that the novel inevitably reflects the society and the history of the society in which it is being written. The picaresque form of *Don Quixtote* illuminates the society of early seventeenth-century Spain, just as Richardson's novels illuminate the emergent middle-class consciousness of eighteenth-century England. Novels are at once a specific literary form and a living place that readers inhabit through their shared imaginations, cultures, and histories. "America" is one such living place that the novel has inhabited and tried to imagine. The American novel is an ongoing literary practice that engages a material reality, but it is more fundamentally an imaginary construct, an invention.

*The Cambridge Companion to American Novelists* begins with Fenimore Cooper, but it would be as naïve to insist that Cooper literally begins the American novel as it would be to insist that America itself has a definite point of origin. When the Spanish "discovered" America and tried to domesticate it according to their ideals, they brought with them not only guns (technology), maps (science), and the Bible (religion), but *Don Quixote* too. Whole print runs of *Don Quixote* were completed in Seville to be loaded on ships headed to the New World, and there is the sense that for the Spanish conquistadores the New World existed as an epic novel to be written. A work such as Bernal Díaz's *The Conquest of New Spain* (1632), which told the story of adventurers trying to possess a world that seemed to them as strange as it was magical, can be read as the first New World or American novel, just as it might be read as the kind of book Quixote would have written had he been a *conquistador*. In North America the most readily available books during the seventeenth and early eighteenth centuries were the Bible, almanacs, and *Pilgrim's Progress* (1678). *Don Quixote* and *Pilgrim's Progress*, which Willa Cather remembers as a staple of her reading in the late nineteenth century, assume different types of heroes, yet it is not too difficult to see how these works would speak to readers making their way in a new land as adventurers who also wanted to believe that their stories were the consequence of having been chosen to pursue them.

Rather than identifying the precise origin of the American novel, it is worth recalling that the novel evolved as a literary form for expressing a new sense of the individual consciousness at roughly the same historic moment in which America, or the United States, was evolving as a material form for expressing new European understandings about science, political theory, and religion. In the Old World the novel was written over existing literary forms; in the New World, the novel was an indigenous form, born with and alongside America itself. As a genre, the novel arises out of the particular and carries the particular with it, a generic fact that has been fundamental to the way in which the American novel has developed and flourished. Despite the inevitable and important differences among American novelists, there remains the feeling that American novelists self-consciously engage the invention of their own national story in ways that classic English or French novels do not. In this respect, American novelists are always in conversation with each other through their competing inventions of American reality.

In its inception during the eighteenth century, the United States was understood to mark a radical departure from existing forms of government. Its government was an experiment that promised to do away with antiquated forms of authority and would instead place its power in the hands of the many rather than the few. Its society was conceived less as an experiment in community than as something that would protect and further the possibilities of individual Americans. Consistent with the prevailing assumption that the United States of America was a departure from European forms of government was the expectation that out of this "new nation" would evolve a distinctive and original culture. Perhaps the most famous exposition of this perspective was in Ralph Waldo Emerson's 1837 address "The American Scholar," in which he explicitly called for the creation of an American culture as radical and as exceptional in its practice as the American Revolution was in its break from England. What forms these cultural expressions might take Emerson could only grandly point toward, but his assumption was that, regardless of how they manifested themselves, the "new" American culture would somehow reflect what he took to be the nation's epic origins. Although Emerson was a near neighbor of Nathaniel Hawthorne, he did not anticipate that the American novel would provide the form in which his questions would receive their most thorough analysis and most lasting expression.

More than one hundred and fifty years after Emerson first outlined his exceptionalist view of American culture, scholars rightly point out the contradictions inherent in an exceptionalist understanding of American history. While the new American nation was predicated upon congeries of contradictions that disguised the fundamental inequality of American society, it is equally important that we recognize that as a historical and political entity the United States of America came into being as a type of human invention. The ubiquitous phrase "Founding Fathers" implies a definite point of origin for the existence of the United States of America, but the term "America" is only imaginary since its enabling premise is that its arrangement might have been otherwise but for this or that political conception. Clearly, the form that the novel has taken in America inevitably emerges from the shifting cultural, geographic, and material reality that is America, but it does so to pose American reality as its own invention. The inevitable term "the Great American Novel" persists in our literary imagination because American literature is bound by the quixotic wish that the essence of America might be perfectly embodied in a single aesthetic artifact. American material reality makes this wish impossible, but the living desire to fuse an ideal of America with the aesthetic possibilities of the novel gives the American novel its aura of continuity.

"If the novel had not existed at the time the United States started becoming conscious of itself as a nation," Ralph Ellison observed, "it would have been necessary for Americans to invent it."[2] The sense of being American, or not being American, endures in American novels, whether the hero is Henry Roth's David Schearl or Maxine Hong-Kingston's Wittman Ah Sing, yet most classic American novels are framed according to characters or stories resisting the definition of the American society in which they find themselves. "In the beginning was not only the word, but its contradiction," Ellison further notes (*Collected* 702). American heroes such as Natty Bumppo, Hester Prynne, Melville's Ishmael, Huckleberry Finn, Ellison's invisible man, Sal Paradise, Holden Caulfield, and the kid of *Blood Meridian* (1985) stand opposed to or outside the status quo of conventional American society. They become quintessentially American heroes to the extent that they stand in opposition to some existing notion of Americanness and propose their own vision to replace what they oppose. Herman Melville praised Hawthorne because his works shouted "NO – in thunder," and this shout can be heard from Harriet Stowe's *Uncle Tom's Cabin* (1852) to Toni Morrison's *Song of Solomon* (1977).

Any critical anthology of American novelists can only be a snapshot of always changing literary practices and cultural orientations. Critical tastes shift violently. There is always a battle between what the past seemed to say about itself and what the present has determined it needs to say about the past. As I write this Introduction, many scholars argue that a model for understanding literature that is based on "nationality" makes little sense in a world where geographic boundaries seem permeable and the identities of nations and peoples fluid. Where words such as "English" or "American" once were perfectly obvious descriptive terms to place before the word "novel," many now prefer to use terms such as "postcolonial" or "transnational" to describe novels. Certainly, *Absalom, Absalom!* (1936) is a postcolonial novel, just as *The Ambassadors* (1903) is a transnational one. One can be too precise about one's terminology, though, in that definitions always work to render in discrete forms experiences that may be otherwise continuous. Terms such as "postcolonial" and "transnational" are indeed useful, but rather than replacing a nationalist logic they may redirect that logic along a different axis. The most basic point about a novel is that it constitutes a literary form that can be practiced potentially by any person of any nationality and as a work of art need not be known by labels of nationality. As Roberto Bolaño suggests in a remark that echoes the quest initiated by *Don Quixote*, "every writer becomes an exile simply by venturing into literature, and every reader becomes an exile simply by opening up a book."[3]

Following *The Cambridge Companion to English Novelists* (2009) this *Companion* is organized around chapters dedicated to individual authors, and in all cases the literary merit of the author's work is part of the author's story. The narrative innovations of these authors helped to define the history of the form, while their stories have remained persistently relevant to readers and would-be writers of new versions of the American literary and cultural tradition their works embody. Variety of aesthetic preoccupation and cultural experience is to be expected of a form that has been tested by artists of different historical periods and aesthetic temperaments over a long period. Writers such as Djuna Barnes or Vladimir Nabokov clearly occupy different spaces as "American novelists" than do Willa Cather or William Faulkner. John Updike and Kurt Vonnegut lived through roughly the same era, but their works are so different that the champions of one author may not recognize the achievement of the other. The two most influential nineteenth-century American novelists, Mark Twain and Henry James, could not read each other's works, yet the American novel, however defined, is inconceivable without both of them. While the writers in this *Companion* clearly respond to the history of the novel as a particular form and ongoing possibility, their works achieve a certain collective resonance when read against each other as the work of *American novelists*.

The proverbial Great American Novel has many incarnations, by more novelists than this volume can contain. The reader of this book should be engaged in an ongoing conversation that has been enacted by each novelist, a conversation that evolves not only through his or her works but also through readers' historical encounters with these works. Some readers may be disappointed not to find a chapter devoted to a favorite and deserving author, living or dead, but the absence of that author should not be construed as a lasting literary judgment. Living authors (born before World War II) have been included to indicate and make accessible to readers, students, and experts the continuing vitality and the living continuity of the American novel. The purpose of this book is not to entomb the tradition of the American novel. What matters is that even as new writers and voices, dead or living, enter or fall out of the conversation that constitutes the tradition of American novelists, the conversation does exist and it continues.

Five hundred years ago, Don Quixote set out on a comic quest to explore the limits of his own identity against the changing world of his time. Quixote never left Spain, but the new narrative form that contained his story traveled to the New World, where it was taken up by American novelists seeking to define the limitations and possibilities of their American world.

James Fenimore Cooper was arguably the first American novelist to be understood as a representative "American" novelist. As the author of the five novels that constitute the Leatherstocking Tales, Cooper created a mythology of American identity and history that revealed, in D. H. Lawrence's famous formulation, "the very-intrinsic most American." Stephen Railton points out, though, that it was "much harder for Cooper to make American literature new" than Emerson's stirring statements on the "American Scholar" had seemed to suggest. Cooper's "unflinchingly autonomous" heroes, as Railton terms them, enacted a story in which one becomes American by turning one's back on America. This gesture would be taken up by Melville and Twain, just as Cooper's romances about what occurs when civilized whites collide with the frontier and the racialized Other appear again in the works of Cather, Faulkner, and Cormac McCarthy.

If Cooper suggests an American identity in flight from itself, Nathaniel Hawthorne's novels – what he called "romances" – created a psychological profile that located an American consciousness within an ongoing – and terrifying – Puritan present. As Robert Milder demonstrates, Hawthorne's development of the American romance-novel is persistently concerned "with versions of the conflict between the 'I want' and the 'thou shalt.'" Faulkner's later sense that the past is never past is already evident in Hawthorne, just as his nuanced portraits of an individual's psychology anticipate the novels of Henry James. In *The Human Stain* (2001) Philip Roth finds the spirit of Hawthorne in the impeachment of President Bill Clinton. To read Hawthorne is to understand that the American is not necessarily blessed and that one's American optimism comes at the terrible, perhaps exorbitant, psychological cost of repressing sins that remain unacknowledged.

Herman Melville dedicated *Moby-Dick* (1851) to Nathaniel Hawthorne, and, like *The Scarlet Letter* (1850), it stands as an unquestioned American masterpiece. Although Ahab's monomaniacal quest for the white whale makes the novel a thrilling adventure story for beginning readers, Melville also portrayed the imperial will to power that drove Americans along with the subjugation of blacks and Indians that this will demanded. As powerful as Melville's political imagination was, though, so was his commitment to experimenting with the form of the novel. As Clark Davis notes, Melville was drawn to Shakespeare as what he called a "thought-diver" – a writer whose language made it possible to achieve "those short, quick probings at the very axis of reality." At its best, Melville's writing exemplifies this ideal, and among Melville's many achievements in *Moby-Dick* was to instill a Shakespearian majesty in the language of the American novel. Virginia Woolf recognized *Moby-Dick* (which she admired over *Ulysses* [1922]) as a kind of protomodernist novel in which the voice of the narrative was an achievement beyond the novel's plot. Likewise, *The Confidence Man* (1857), with its emphasis on the "inventedness" of identity, betrayed an experimentalism that made Melville a forerunner to the symbolists, the surrealists, and the modernists.

Ralph Ellison argued that the moral tradition of the American novel begins with the recognition that a society that was forever proclaiming its commitment to equality and freedom nonetheless was rooted in the practice of slavery. This paradox, as Arthur Riss makes clear, is at the heart of Harriet Beecher Stowe's *Uncle Tom's Cabin*. On the one hand, Stowe's novel was perhaps the most important text in "helping transform slavery from a debatable political question into an absolute moral issue about which compromise was impossible." Yet, having sold 2.5 million copies in its first year of publication and with perhaps as many as ten readers to each copy, *Uncle Tom's Cabin* may also have been responsible for perpetuating racial stereotypes among its readers, a marker, as Riss notes, of the ways in which "race and slavery ... were indivisible, mutually sustaining terms, not independent concepts." Riss's Stowe reveals how inextricably bound the fact of race is with so many classic American novels, while setting the stage for the replies to Stowe by Richard Wright and Toni Morrison.

Mark Twain is often understood as a quintessential American moralist despite his famous warning at the beginning of *Huckleberry Finn* (1885) that "persons attempting to find a moral in it will be banished." Indeed, as Peter Messent argues, the novel is structured around a series of moral oppositions, "and the very instability they reveal ... taps into a common ground that goes far beyond the audiences and historical conditions of Twain's own period." More self-consciously than Stowe, Twain portrayed the moral ambivalence of white Americans' relationships with black Americans. Equally important, as Messent makes clear, one of Twain's great achievements was to introduce an "American vernacular" into the novel that was "readily accessible and comprehensible to a national and international English-speaking audience." Ellison would hear a black American dialect embedded in Huck's speech, while Hemingway found the beginning and future of the American novel. The biting moral ironies of Twain's voice would find their echo in the postmodern novels of Kurt Vonnegut. Perhaps more obviously than any other American writer, Twain marks the intersection where other American novelists have found direction and meaning.

One essential American writer who did not stand at Twain's crossroads was Henry James. Of all American novelists, perhaps none has been so self-consciously concerned with the question of literary form. Early works such as *The American* (1877), *Daisy Miller* (1878), and *Washington Square* (1880) defined American identity as something markedly different from the wise primitives of Twain or Cooper. Not unlike Hawthorne, James was preoccupied with the self's limitations rather than with a sense of its unlimited grandeur. As Thomas J. Otten argues, "the American novel's ways of managing meaning changes radically with James." For James, the definition of character was a consequence of seeing, of literary form. Otten suggests that James's works best demonstrate the nineteenth-century shift from "stable" characters embodying (or not) an inherent moral worth, to "personality-driven" characters with an "emphasis on flux, growth, and the vicissitudes of desire." James thus points the way toward the modernists' radical narrative experiments in which character is the function of an often-volatile perceptivity. This "endlessly experimental James," as Otten says, so playful in his characterizations and formal innovations, is still our contemporary, and even today we are catching up with, in Wallace Stevens's words, the keener voices and ghostlier demarcations of the Jamesian way of seeing.

Often misleadingly compared to her friend Henry James, Edith Wharton had a vision of society that was more encompassing than his for she was more truly a historian of manners and a specific social caste. As Pamela Knights suggests, her works "provoke questions about the nature of emotion, the psyche, language, creativity and belief, within cultures driven by the forces of finance, consumerism and technological innovation, and divided by gulfs of privilege and inequality." In novels such as *House of Mirth* (1905), *The Custom of the Country* (1913), and *The Age of Innocence* (1920), Wharton perceived that James's sense of form was a mechanism for portraying the complex social relations that determine identity. Moreover, in her depictions of the shifting plights of female characters, her works predict contemporary understandings of the performance of gender.

Transcendentalists spoke of the need for the self to be transformed, but Theodore Dreiser portrayed Americans seeking self-transformation through an engagement with the seemingly infinite sense of material possibility. As Clare Eby explains, "Dreiser is the consummate chronicler of that mythic American ascent narrative because he understands to his core the allure of money ... [and] uses the quest for money to examine the meaning of America." In *Sister Carrie* (1900), the heroine embodies the transition away from an agrarian society. For Carrie the city is the repository of desire, the place where the self might be endlessly transformed. The transcendental American soul that James imagined in Isabel Archer takes on in Carrie a corporeal and material form. Dreiser's novels, especially *Sister Carrie* and *An American Tragedy* (1925), portrayed the American capacity for living in a state of endless desire that would make F. Scott Fitzgerald's Jay Gatsby into a representative American hero.

Contrasting with Dreiser's urban novels of the American self in perpetual transformation is Willa Cather's historical vision of a pastoral America that epitomized the virtues of civilization. Infusing the epic into the novel and mixing history with fiction, Cather created works that challenged the conventional boundaries of the novel. Cather's novels looked to Virgil's example to create a founding narrative of an America perfectly balanced between the virtues of European civilization and the extraordinary natural landscape that had housed pre-European civilizations. Cather's America, like Virgil's Roman Empire, is the product of a variety of civilizations. In novels such as *Death Comes for the Archbishop* (1927) and *Shadows on the Rock* (1931) Cather located the origins of American civilization in the work of Spanish missionaries in the Southwest and French missionaries in Quebec. In *Song of the Lark* (1915) and *My Antonia* (1918) Cather created female characters capable of possessing worlds ordinarily dominated by men, just as she portrayed characters who need not find a conventional heterosexual marriage in order to be fulfilled. In challenging many conventions of the American novel while creating her own landscape of America beyond New England or the South, Cather's works occupy a singular place in the American canon.

Although F. Scott Fitzgerald is known as the writer of the Jazz Age, the short, lyrical *The Great Gatsby* (1925) is for many readers the ultimate American novel. Something as prosaic and as typically American as Benjamin Franklin's guide to becoming a better person becomes in the figure of Jay Gatsby a twentieth-century myth more entrancing than Twain's Tom Sawyer or Cooper's Leatherstocking Saga. As Ruth Prigozy notes, upon its publication T. S. Eliot, Gertrude Stein, and Edith Wharton recognized the novel's importance, recognition that has not faded. Bob Dylan once suggested that in American culture there is no success like failure and failure is no success at all. *Gatsby*'s doomed grandeur enacts the logic of this aphorism even as it suggests why, for instance, Dreiser's heroes were willing to immolate themselves in their quest for the elusive American dream.

Ernest Hemingway earned his reputation as the epitome of the American machismo, a pure and male heroic. At the core of both Hemingway's appeal and the feeling among some readers that his work is now dated may well be Hemingway's ongoing interest in exploring the notion of heroism in a world in which the heroic was no longer possible. Emphasizing that Hemingway is "inescapably a modern writer," Eugene Goodheart suggests that "at his best, Hemingway takes us behind the scenes of courage and heroism, where we find psychic wounds, fear, anxiety, depression and the threat of nothingness." As a close student of Ezra Pound and, especially, Gertrude Stein, Hemingway created works that stand up because of their extraordinary prose – a style of writing that might be referred to as the American vernacular and one that is essential to the history of the American novel. "No American writer of the twentieth century has had so great an influence on our literature and culture as Hemingway," Goodheart adds, an influence evident in the later writers Norman Mailer, Joan Didion, and Raymond Carver.

Other than Henry James, William Faulkner has written more novels considered to be masterpieces than any other American writer. He said that not until he realized that the "postage stamp" of his Mississippi might house a universe of fiction as rich and diverse as the world created by Balzac was he able to begin to realize his talent as a novelist. This is as much a tribute to Faulkner's extraordinary experiments in literary form as his much discussed historical vision. Faulkner's novels evoke a mythic view of the southern past, but as Philip Weinstein argues here, "his great work – the work that reveals Faulkner *as* Faulkner – sees strenuously through this myth. Indeed, the act of seeing through this myth enables Faulkner to become the most powerful white novelist of race relations this country has yet produced." Although

Faulkner's novels can be read as critiques of the myth of the Confederate past, for many readers they memorialize that past as if it were the lost Troy of American literature. In exploring this myth, Faulkner's novels experimented radically with narrative form and point of view and, as in Twain's works, often gave lyrical voice to characters whose lives were uneducated and thus whose narrative complexity was startling to encounter in a work of literature.

Like Ralph Ellison and Djuna Barnes, Henry Roth is known for one novel. *Call It Sleep* (1934) was initially dismissed as a Depression-era Joycean indulgence, but in 1964 the critic Irving Howe reclaimed it as a classic American novel. In a nation of immigrants, *Call It Sleep* is arguably the definitive American novel since no other American novel so profoundly captures the simultaneously exhilarating and alienating experience of becoming American. It is also an unparalleled portrayal of childhood as well as being one of the few American novels to depict the grittiness and complexity of urban life. Hana Wirth-Nesher suggests, though, that its true appeal as a "modernist masterpiece" is "through its articulation of loss conveyed through word play that negotiates a web of accents, dialects, and languages" and that ultimately Roth "makes a space for the drama of Jewish American literature and culture in the making." Sixty years after his first novel Roth completed another long work, *Mercy of a Rude Stream* (1994–8), that arguably did justice to and in a sense completed his earlier achievement, one that is unique within American literature.

Despite the critical imprimatur of T. S. Eliot and despite being arguably the most impressive and demanding work of American modernist prose, Djuna Barnes's *Nightwood* (1936) remains famously unknown. In its structure and language, the novel reflects the logic of her remark that "there is always more surface to a shattered object than its whole." Even as she is read and reread, Alex Goody suggests, Barnes "remains inassimilable, a writer who made a profoundly singular but nonetheless profound contribution to the history of the novel." Like other modernist landmarks such as *Ulysses* or *The Waves* (1931), *Nightwood* shatters the whole of the realist novel and reconfigures it as a constellation of narrative fragments in which each piece seems to comprise its own infinite reflecting surface. At the same time, the novel enacts a relentless exploration of sexuality that serves as a point of departure for contemporary debates regarding the relationship between sexuality and identity.

Before becoming a novelist, Zora Neale Hurston worked with the eminent Columbia University sociologist Franz Boaz and as a researcher documenting black folk customs in the American South and in Haiti for the Library of Congress. Hurston had an extraordinary verbal facility that allowed her to realize a central aim of the Harlem Renaissance: to translate into literary form the vernacular language and folk consciousness of postslavery blacks. Although Hurston's work was largely rejected by the major figures of the Harlem Renaissance, her achievement anticipates Ellison's in *Invisible Man*, and her novels would inspire subsequent writers such as Alice Walker and Toni Morrison. As Lovalerie King emphasizes, "Hurston's outstanding work in the woman-centered narrative is an important link between African American women's literary production in the second half of the twentieth century and beyond to African American women's literary production in the nineteenth century."

In *Black Boy* (1945) Richard Wright had described the almost unimaginable journey he had completed from being born a poor black boy in racist Mississippi to becoming the Pulitzer Prize–winning author of *Native Son*. When the sociologist Robert Park met the author of *Native Son* (1940), he reportedly asked, "Where in the hell did you come from?" Wright's searing portraits of blacks suffering the material and social degradation of their place in American society destroyed forever the image that American blacks could be content with a subordinate place in American society. Wright's work became a critical point of departure for writers as diverse as Ellison, James Baldwin, and Toni Morrison. As William Dow argues, "Wright was the first to portray a distinctively black psychology," one that emphasized ghetto life from the perspective of the poor and the self-consciously undereducated. Wright's novels, however, were not merely sociology but also acts of literary philosophy. The existentialism of his work earned the admiration of Jean Paul Sartre and Simone de Beauvoir and his experimentation with identity and narrative earned the approval of Gertrude Stein.

While recasting Raymond Chandler's novel *The Big Sleep* (1939) into a movie (with the assistance of screenwriter William Faulkner), the film director Howard Hawks was uncertain about the plot so he wired Chandler to clear it up. To Hawks's question of "What happened?," Chandler famously responded, "NO IDEA." As Leonard Cassuto demonstrates, a novel like *The Long Goodbye* (1953) is "fueled not so much by plot as by Marlowe's emotions" as he confronts a world in which "surface glitz spreads a thin veneer over pervasive hollowness within." Cassuto further suggests that Chandler was committed to "using genre fiction as a platform for unique artistic achievement." In Chandler's works plots never serve to reveal an ultimate truth (in part because there is no ultimate truth to be revealed): the texture of conveyed experience matters more than the action. In this respect, Chandler is as "modernist" as he is "hard-boiled."

Ralph Ellison's *Invisible Man* (1952) endures as one of the most read and taught of American novels. Because it engages major authors such as Fyodor

Dostoevsky, Emerson, Hawthorne, Melville, Twain, James, Faulkner, James Joyce, and Richard Wright, among seemingly countless others, *Invisible Man* is arguably the most self-consciously canonical novel in American literature. The novel is also richly African American in that much of its narrative vitality depends on Ellison's scholarly though always deft use of black folk culture – slave tales as well as blues and jazz. His ultimate achievement as an artist, though, was not to demonstrate his comprehensive knowledge of the American literary history and the African American folk and intellectual tradition, but to write a novel that confirmed the basic premise of literature: that readers may make imaginative affiliations across cultural lines. Thus, in a gesture of American inclusiveness, Ellison affirmed – against the stacked odds of history – the democratic ideals of the American republic by presenting his African American hero as the voice of all readers willing to recognize him. As David Yaffe's essay suggests, "We are still living in a country imagined by Ralph Ellison."

J. D. Salinger's *The Catcher in the Rye* (1951) is perhaps the most well-known twentieth-century American novel. Its hero, the skeptical adolescent Holden Caulfield, recalls Huckleberry Finn as he questions the mindless conformity of his society. Sarah Graham points out that the "phoniness" that Holden discerned in an American society "mired in self-serving superficiality" can be read as Salinger's protest against white Americans' cheerful willingness "to settle for the consolations of post-war prosperity." Salinger's work thus tried to unsettle a too comfortably settled America as it enacted an "openness to experience and a commitment to finding enlightenment." In this respect, Salinger's work marks an intersection between the spiritual quests found in Jack Kerouac's "beat" novels and Ellison's challenge to the moral complacency of white Americans in *Invisible Man*.

Like Chandler, Patricia Highsmith is known as a writer of genre fiction, but as Joan Schenkar argues, her works were "corralled into categories that couldn't begin to account for their depth." After Henry James, whom she read closely, Highsmith's novels refuse the assumptions of conventional heterosexuality. *The Price of Salt* (1952) was one of the first American novels to depict an openly lesbian relationship, and it made waves because its protagonists were given a satisfying and mostly happy relationship. In works such as *Strangers on a Train* (1952) and *The Talented Mr. Ripley* (1955), "Highsmith is as unconscious a 'gay male novelist' as Ernest Hemingway, and as gifted an anatomist of male sexual anxiety as Norman Mailer," Schenkar suggests. Her most famous creation, Tom Ripley, recasts Tom Sawyer and Gatsby with a sense of charming menace while his story is also a rich and subversive rewriting of James's American abroad novels. A deeply original writer, Highsmith created works that patiently turn inside out the assumptions of many classic American novels and are in their way more truly revisionist than those of more praised authors such as Don De Lillo and Thomas Pynchon.

Born in St. Petersburg the son of a Russian nobleman during the time of the tsars, Vladimir Nabokov made himself over as an American writer unlike any other in the canon. Nabokov liked to joke that in order to become an American writer he first had to invent America, a task he fulfilled in *Lolita* (1955), one of the extraordinary novels of the twentieth century. His novels are verbal mirror games, dense with textual illusion, and very much literary palimpsests that emerge out of a dazzling array of sources. Works such as *Pale Fire* (1962) and *Ada* (1969) refract modernist innovations in ways that are unrecognizable in Faulkner, though taken up by other American writers such as John Barth, Robert Coover, and Thomas Pynchon. As Julian W. Connolly suggests, though, Nabokov's works cannot be restricted to nationality, and he is probably American literature's most obviously transnational novelist.

Along with Saul Bellow, Jack Kerouac was the major prose poet of the American self in the twentieth century. Influenced by Thomas Wolfe and Marcel Proust, Kerouac's subject was the self and its relation to time and experience. In Proust and Faulkner, the reader encounters dense narratives in which a single incident is understood to be central to understanding a character's existence. Their intricate narratives ceaselessly venture away from and return to that single moment: a whole life in the bite of a madeleine or the chiming of bells. Kerouac's novels, however, arise out of a new postwar experience of subjectivity as "fragmented and indeterminate." As a result, Joshua Kupetz suggests, "Kerouac's protagonists are invariably dashed against the rocks of an unknowable internal coast, a liminal space where the multiplicity of possibilities for one's personality refuses to adhere into a unified identity knowable to either the reader or to the protagonist." Kerouac's famous "bop prosody" was a carefully wrought prose style fashioned to negotiate his sense that "universal assumptions of nationhood and citizenship" were breaking down. Perhaps his greatest achievement, though, was to adapt the modernist narrative imperative that Virginia Woolf identified as "moments of being" into a jazzy, American voice in opposition to the mechanized, post–World War II American cultural landscape.

Saul Bellow occupies a peculiar place in post–World War II American literature. His most ebullient works can be said to celebrate the self in all of its contradiction. In *Herzog* (1964), his most famous creation, Moses Herzog, discerns all around him what he calls the "wastelander" outlook, which he understands to be a commitment to alienation. Nonetheless, Herzog insists upon his quest to become a "marvelous" Herzog. His defiant assertion of self in the face of social incomprehension recalls Emerson, and Bellow's novels can be read through an Emersonian lens. Yet, as Victoria Aarons argues, as a Jewish writer Bellow in his work acknowledges "a post-Holocaust universe" in which one must always confront "a crime so vast that it brings all Being into Judgment." In 1976 Bellow was awarded the Nobel Prize in Literature for his "human understanding," but for Bellow it was precisely the "human" that was at stake in the late twentieth century. Aarons suggests that Bellow's engagement with the Holocaust and general sense that civilization was collapsing after the world wars of the twentieth century deepen the usual accounts of Bellow's comic optimism and place him on the stage of world literature.

Because of his sense of humor and gift for plain speech, Kurt Vonnegut linked his own work with that of Mark Twain. Todd Davis characterizes Vonnegut as "his generation's supreme moralist"; "Vonnegut's legacy as an American novelist might best be characterized by his persistent belief in the best humanity might aspire to, while at the same moment laughing at the ridiculousness of such a thought." Vonnegut's novels mimic "nonliterary" genres such as science fiction (*Cat's Cradle* [1963]) or espionage (*Mother Night* [1962]) and also challenge "realist" conceptions of order. They anticipate Don DeLillo and Thomas Pynchon even as they share common ground with the work of Philip K. Dick. Among Vonnegut's many gifts as a writer was his ability to clarify succinctly the intrinsic absurdity of a situation. In *Slaughterhouse-Five* (1969) Vonnegut took what for many Americans had been a clear, unambiguous, morally uplifting story, victory in World War II, and rendered it impossibly vexed. In a novel that mixes fact with fiction and confuses chronology more effectively than any modernist novel, all that is certain is that enormous and efficient machines of mass death have been invented and are being efficiently deployed by their human agents. Moreover, Vonnegut's works are cherished by contemporary readers not yet born when *Slaughterhouse-Five* was published but who recognize that the world Vonnegut imagined is the one they have inherited.

Of the writers in this book, John Updike creates works that are arguably the least oppositional and the most satisfied with what William Dean Howells, a clear precursor to Updike, called the smiling aspects of American life. Updike, as James Schiff notes, "did not seek isolation or exile, did not feel mistreated or marginalized by his country or culture, did not feel inclined to protest politically or personally, and was not interested in pursuing the romantic persona of the solitary, troubled artist. Rather, Updike generally embraced and celebrated his culture and nation, finding a comfortable place near the center from which he could witness domestic, local, and national events." While Updike's novels serve as a kind of cultural history of the social mores of white American Protestants of his time, his often dazzling prose is inspired by Nabokov. As Schiff explains, Updike's "writing becomes a performance, with language taking precedence over action and scene." Writing during a period in which antiexceptionalism characterized American intellectual life, Updike stands as the twentieth-century author tacitly willing to portray and defend an exceptionalist America.

Thomas Pynchon's novels describe the postmodern moment but are situated in a Euro-American cultural-intellectual context that looks back to the time before America's origins. His short novels (*The Crying of Lot 49* [1966], *Vineland* [1990], and *Inherent Vice* [2009]) explicitly recall the American Edenic mythology perhaps best evoked at the end of *The Great Gatsby*. As David Seed makes clear, Pynchon both identifies and critiques this national tradition, assuming "throughout his work that no one can stand outside history, with the result that his characters to varying degrees are always embedded within the situations they are trying to understand." His encyclopedic novels (*Gravity's Rainbow* [1973], *Mason & Dixon* [1997], and *Against the Day* [2006]) portray postmodern America as a necessary consequence of European history – its science, in particular. These novels are about technology and the extent to which humans are the agents – and victims – of the machines and the knowledge systems they have invented to control their environment. At their darkest, these novels suggest that the legendary experiment of American democracy is in practice a delivery system for the potential death of humanity unleashed by the genius of Euro-American science and the technological systems of control engendered by that genius. Nonetheless, as a stylist, Pynchon is a tender, lyrical writer and his voice is one of the most distinctive and compelling in the tradition of the American novel.

Toni Morrison's work has drawn comparison with writers of many different nationalities and traditions: Thomas Hardy, James Joyce, Virginia Woolf, Gabriel García Márquez, Chinua Achebe, and Faulkner. Her novels reveal her complex understanding of modernist prose aesthetics, but the true achievement of her fiction has been to give voice to an African American point of view previously unrepresented in American literature. Her novels engage and critique the American literary tradition that runs from Twain to Faulkner. As Valerie Smith suggests, Morrison's work is preoccupied with "African American language" and "the impact of racial patriarchy upon the lives of black women during specific periods of American history." Like Hurston and Ellison, she transforms the vernacular black voice of music and oral tradition – so crucial to American experience – into literature.

After Bellow and Updike, Philip Roth has had perhaps the most storied career among post–World War II American novelists. Roth's ambition is evident in the novelists his work invokes: Beckett, Joyce, and Proust, not to mention Hawthorne, James, and Faulkner, among the Americans. Roth's subject is almost always the self, a question that he may often pose in terms of "late twentieth-century post-immigrant Jewish sensibility," but that, as Debra Shostak points out, emerges out of "Roth's engagements with enduring preoccupations of American literature: how history floods into – or washes away – the Emersonian self engaged in its own making." While Roth often seems to pursue the self defined in terms of an American teleology of infinite possibility, he also worries that a self that lives up to "the individuality and agency promised by the American democratic ideal" is no more than a fiction. Exploring the tension in being at once "ethnic" (Jewish) and "American," Roth's novels explore the contradictions inherent in a national identity composed of many nationalities. No American novelist has pursued such contradictions with the imaginative vitality that Roth's works demonstrate.

Don DeLillo's fictions anatomize postmodern American culture. As Thomas Heise makes clear,

> DeLillo has shown himself to be an unflinching chronicler of the whole of the American scene, a writer of difficult fiction at the edge of mystery and despair whose novels charting familial breakdown, spiritual crises, compromised privacy, terrorism, assassination, and war are made more rich by the fact that they do not lose sight of the redemptive qualities of art and language that provide consolation, order, and dignity to a precarious national life whose shared consensus is only, ironically, its uncertainty.

Despite his range of subjects (advertising, football, mathematics, Wall Street, Hitler, terrorism, the Kennedy assassination), DeLillo's consistent interest is in the ways in which media define the world as a fiction in which Americans live. Film, television, radio, video, and the Internet are the media through which his novels are inflected. Recognizing that the authority of these narratives resides in the ubiquity of their presence, DeLillo's books are attempts to change the channel, to articulate a human voice distinct from the "white noise," to use one of his novel's titles, of multinational, postmodern American culture. DeLillo is the novelist of postmodernity whose works insist on the continuing vitality of the novel as a cultural form.

Before the best-selling *All the Pretty Horses* (1992), Cormac McCarthy was regarded as an obscure, though distinguished, southern writer in the tradition of Faulkner and Flannery O'Connor. The well-meaning comparisons were unfair because McCarthy's works were concerned not only with a specific cultural history but also with the question of universal human depravity. Like Highsmith, McCarthy exposes the dark shadow of the American innocent. *Blood Meridian* (1985) actually marked McCarthy's shift to that recognizably American form, the western. Yet, to call *Blood Meridian* and the novels that followed it "western" novels is nearly as misleading as to call *Ulysses* a Dublin travel guide. *Blood Meridian* cannibalizes virtually all works of classic American literature before it, but its scope looks back to the moment when Europeans first arrived on the continent. McCarthy's last published novel, *The Road* (2006), recalls a postapocalyptic *Don Quixote* as it imagines both the end of America and the end of the novel as a form. As Brian Evenson suggests, "McCarthy's best books function almost as the subconscious of American literary history" and at times seem to offer "violence severed from the possibility of redemption." There will be other American novels and novelists, though, and there is no reason yet to think that McCarthy has found the end of the American novelists' road.

## NOTES

1 Milan Kundera, *The Art of the Novel*, trans. Linda Asher (New York: Grove Press, 1988) p. 6. Hereafter cited as *Art* in the text.
2 Ralph Ellison, *The Collected Essays of Ralph Ellison*, ed. John F. Callahan (New York: Modern Library, 1995), p. 701. Hereafter cited as *Collected* in the text.
3 Roberto Bolaño, *Between Parentheses: Essays, Articles and Speeches, 1998–2003*, ed. Ignacio Echevarría, trans. Natasha Wimmer (New York: New Directions, 2011), p. 51.

# I

# James Fenimore Cooper

STEPHEN RAILTON

James Fenimore Cooper (1789–1851) published his first novel in 1820, and his last, thirty-second novel in 1850. During most of his three-decade career he was among the world's most famous and, particularly in the 1820s, widely read writers. By the twentieth century he was best known as the author of The Leather-Stocking Tales, five novels about Natty Bumppo, a hunter, woods-man, and frontier warrior whose closest friendship is with Chingachgook, a chief of the dispossessed Delaware tribe. Variously called Leather-stocking, Hawkeye, Pathfinder, and Deerslayer, Natty has often been cited as the first quintessentially American literary hero, and the Tales, set against historical contexts that range from the pre-Revolutionary fighting between England and France to the Lewis and Clark Expedition, have struck many as a kind of prose epic of early American life. Natty's adventures in the woods are often drenched in violence and suspense. Cooper's own heroism is harder to see, especially so long after the fact. We are used to thinking of the United States as the world's great superpower, but when Cooper began writing the nation was still struggling with its status as a former colony of Great Britain, the superpower of that era. Cooper was the first American author to earn a living writing fiction, yet his work also reveals how much a postcolonial culture has to contend with in its quest for nationality.

Cooper's first Leather-Stocking Tale was his third novel, *The Pioneers*, published in 1823. The story it tells begins on Christmas Eve, that moment on which for Christians human history pivots from the old world defined by Adam's fall and Mosaic law to the new one brought forth by the birth of a savior who opens up the possibility of redemption. The setting is an upstate New York village called Templeton, which is based very closely on Cooperstown, the settlement founded by the novelist's father in the 1780s and the scene of his own childhood. Natty appears in the book's first chap-ter. This initial appearance gives little hint of the role he ended up play-ing in either Cooper's career or American literature: he is an old man who soon disappears into the woods, while the narrative moves forward into the town where "the pioneers" are busy civilizing the wilderness. The story of that process is the one Cooper initially tells, as readers are taken past the stumps of the trees that have recently been cut down to make room for fields, buildings, and roads and introduced to the various characters who inhabit a new settlement, from the landlord in his "Mansion House" to the shiftless Yankee emigrant to the Episcopalian minister who preaches a Christmas Eve sermon in the village's one-room schoolhouse to Baptists and Presbyterians and Chingachgook, here the aged remnant of a vanished tribe whom the settlers call Indian John. The town already has two taverns, but the pioneers are still building a church, and its unfinished state is a reminder that in this new world "civilization" is very much a work in progress.

Cooper describes Templeton in elaborate detail, but his tone is more satiric than nostalgic. Take his account of Judge Temple's mansion, the town's most imposing building. Designed from models found in books of European architecture, it has a "portico" complete with columns, but the frosts of a frontier winter have shifted the base so that the columns are now being held up by the roof they are supposed to support. This pattern of incongruities is repeated, both symbolically and literally, inside the house, where the decor in the main hall includes imported wallpaper "that represented Britannia weeping over the tomb of Wolfe."[1] General Wolfe, of course, was the hero of the 1759 British victory over the French at Quebec, but so ineptly have the rolls of wallpaper been installed that over and over again around the room his arm is cut off from the rest of his body. What we see in both examples is how slavishly and badly the pioneers are trying to construct a new world civilization out of the misaligned pieces of old world culture. Even as the settlers clear-cut the woods, Temple ornaments his grounds with "poplars brought from Europe" (45) – trees are carried across an ocean and into the American forest because, according to old world standards, manor houses must be equipped with Lombardy poplars as well as columns.

Cooper's narrative also reckons the moral implications of the way "civilization" is being imposed on the American environment. Here the most powerful instance is the extermination of the Indians, who the narrator reminds us were "the original owners of the soil" (83). Except for Chingachgook, the Indians are already gone by the time Cooper's story begins, but when in a later chapter he describes the settlers waging war, with rifles and even a cannon, on a "feathered tribe" of pigeons they are determined to drive away from their cultivated fields (246), readers get a glimpse of the violence that underlies the march of progress across the continent. These birds are in fact passenger pigeons, the first native species that was made extinct by overhunting. Unlike Henry Thoreau, Cooper is not often associated with environmentalism, but *The Pioneers* speaks directly to the concerns of modern ecocritics. Another scene in the novel describes the settlers overfishing the lake. The forest fire that almost claims the novel's heroine's life at the book's climax was started by the same settlers' carelessness and exacerbated by the wasteful way they harvest fuel from the woods. Late in the novel the sheriff of Templeton arrests a "gang of counterfeiters that had ... buried themselves in the woods, to manufacture their base coin" (347). By that point the ironies have piled up sufficiently to suggest that "American civilization" itself is a kind of counterfeit, a base imitation of a European original that, like the real counterfeiters' fake money, "circulated from one end of the Union to the other."

*The Pioneers* brilliantly dramatizes the cultural inferiority complex that, far more than local circumstances or the possibilities of a new world, provides the blueprint for the society the pioneers are building in the woods. At the same time, as a novel it displays advanced symptoms of the same postcolonial malaise. While the setting and subject are American, most of the novel's formal properties derive from the same place Temple got the plans for his house: English books. Cooper knew that American readers, who had as yet had few chances to read American novels, were conditioned to defer to the authority of British literature. His first novel, *Precaution* (1820), was set in England, depicted exclusively English characters, and was reviewed as the work of an English author. To determine that book's length, Cooper computed the number of words in one of Sir Walter Scott's books and wrote to that limit. By setting his second novel, *The Spy* (1821), in the midst of the American Revolution, even including George Washington as a character, Cooper sought to reclaim his American identity, but as a historical romance *The Spy* is heavily indebted to the conventions of Scott's Waverley novels, the best-selling fictions of that time in the United States as well as in England. Throughout his career Cooper was frequently referred to as "the American Scott." One reason for his success with the American reading public was his ability to combine the "novel" with the familiar, to develop stories about American settings and subjects using the kinds of character and narrative archetypes his audience had learned to expect from reading imported books. In *The Pioneers*, for example, Oliver is very much one of Scott's "wavering" heroes, just as Ben Pump, a member of Temple's household staff, is one of Scott's "bores." As the hero, Oliver is matched by Elizabeth Temple as the heroine, and contemporary readers would have been extremely surprised, and displeased, if these two characters did not marry in the book's last chapter. As in Scott, each of Cooper's novel's forty-one chapters begins with an epigraph from a work of poetry, and nearly all of the quoted authors are British – Shakespeare, Goldsmith, Scott himself, and so on. While various characters speak colloquially, the narrator's own voice is similarly derived from foreign models; it is formal and literary and often deploys words like "swain" or "wight," words, that is, that one would never hear in American speech but could only find in British books.

The two other most acclaimed pioneers of American literature in the 1820s – Washington Irving in prose and William Cullen Bryant in poetry – succeeded by performing the same kind of cultural cross-dressing act: clothing American materials in British literary conventions. Although *The Pioneers* doesn't subject its own imported aesthetics to the same ironic scrutiny that it bestows on Templeton's neocolonial posturing, it becomes increasingly difficult to ignore the inauthenticity of this practice. The book's only American epigraph appears in chapter 7, which focuses on Chingachgook, the book's only Native American character. The quotation – from Philip Freneau's "Indian Student" – refers to its Native American protagonist as "the shepherd of the forest" (83). There is no reality in which that description could make any sense, for Indians had no herds of sheep, and sheep in any case would starve in a forest for lack of food. Behind Freneau's trope is the classical European genre of the pastoral, where shepherds are the symbol for a life in harmony with nature. Freneau's concern to fit his work and his hero into that old world tradition carries his art away from its new world source. Like Wolfe's "severed" arm on the walls of Temple's house, European forms and American experience fail to connect.

This can bring us back to the fact that *The Pioneers* begins on Christmas Eve, for both the counterfeit society it depicts and the imitative art it uses to render that society seem very much in need of redemption. As the novel goes on, moving through almost a year in the life of a frontier settlement, a potential savior appears, though he seems at first a very unlikely candidate for the role. In his first narrative appearances, Natty Bumppo is, as even his name suggests, more a comic than a heroic figure, a grumpy relic of the days before settlers entered the woods. One of the most fascinating sights in American literary history is watching how over the course of the narrative Natty's character commandeers more and more of Cooper's attention. His grumpiness, for example, is transformed into a kind of prophetic wrath against what he calls "the wicked and wasty ways" of civilization (356). When he is put on trial by society for breaking one of its laws, the reader has no trouble seeing how the proceeding actually exposes the guilt of a community that lives by legal forms rather than the spirit of justice, or (as Natty puts it) "what's right between man and man" (202). He even takes over the job of the romance hero, twice rescuing the heroine from death. Natty has absolutely no conventional credentials for the role of hero: he is old, unmarriageable, propertyless, illiterate. When the novel arrives at its structurally predestined conclusion, the wedding of Oliver and Elizabeth as the promise of more enlightened national future, there is no narrative place for Natty. But when the book ends with him disappearing one last time into the woods, leaving the newlyweds in, of all symbolical places, a cemetery, he takes the reader's sympathy with him. In 1823 there were no literary historical precedents for novelistic sequels, any more than for novelistic heroes who looked, talked, and acted like Natty, but given the power Natty has acquired by that ending, it might have been predicted that Cooper's imagination would soon have to return to this character.

He turned back to Natty four times, twice in the 1820s and then twice more in the early 1840s. The next Leather-Stocking Tale written was *The Last of the Mohicans* (1826), in which Natty and Chingachgook are young warriors fighting for the British in the French and Indian War. Against this historical backdrop Cooper writes a tale of relentless gothic terror and violent action. *Mohicans* was one of the nineteenth century's very best-selling novels, and of all Cooper's stories the one that has had the longest popular life in its television and movie adaptations. Some critics cite the book as his masterpiece. Certainly anyone interested in how Cooper's fiction helped his culture construct its ideas about race – red, black, and white – and an idea of American nationhood that excluded all but the last of those three colors should read the novel, but to me it lacks the thematic richness of *The Pioneers*. Natty dies of old age at the end of *The Prairie* (1827) but is again young in the last-written tales, *The Pathfinder* (1840) and *The Deerslayer* (1841). To D. H. Lawrence, the twentieth-century British modernist, the antichronological sequence of the five Tales, "from old age to golden youth," is why they constitute "the true myth of America," the "sloughing of the old skin."[2] Lawrence's phrase helps link Cooper to Ralph Waldo Emerson, the transcendentalist who began his first book, *Nature* (1836), by also going into the woods, where, he wrote, is "perpetual youth," where "a man casts off his years, as a snake his slough."[3] Emerson took a much more explicit stance against the authority of British literature, protesting that the "American Scholar" has "listened too long to the courtly muses of Europe" in his 1837 address at Harvard that the American poet Oliver Wendell Holmes called "our intellectual Declaration of Independence."[4] But while the Leather-Stocking himself can defy the forms of civilization to inhabit a world that seems perpetually fresh, it was much harder for Cooper to make American literature new. In those last two Tales, for example, he pushes a bit against fictional conventions by involving Natty directly in the novels' romantic plots. He loves in *The Pathfinder* and is beloved in *The Deerslayer*. But while Natty never marries, his creator's imagination remains wedded to such conventional elements as those romantic plots. Cooper's cultural insecurities led him to try revising Natty's possible role in the narrative, rather than recreating novelistic narrative to develop Natty's possibilities.

Thus as an American hero, Natty is a subversive rather than a transformative figure. He exposes the vitiating effect of the derivative formal gestures by which both society and literature in the new world organize themselves but cannot himself reconstruct either. Cooper left it to Mark Twain's *Huckleberry Finn* (1885) to become the book that, according to Ernest Hemingway, makes "all modern American literature" possible.[5] Hemingway is referring mainly to the voice of Twain's novel, which is Huck's unmistakably American voice, a colloquial, un-"literary" voice that remains in direct contact with American reality. While obviously an overgeneralization, there is some truth to Hemingway's claim. But if it is clear that Cooper's narrator, like Huck's friend Tom Sawyer, has read too many European books, or at least defers too much to them, it's equally clear how much Huck's own character owes to Natty, and not just in the fact that both "light out for the Territory"[6] or have their most meaningful friendships with nonwhite characters. As *The Pioneers* goes on, Cooper discovers more and more eloquence in Natty's vernacular voice. When the novel's narrator describes the beauty of Elizabeth's "Grecian" nose, "spotless" forehead, and cheeks "burning with roses," we hear the echo of those courtly muses (66). Even when he praises her dark hair, "shining like the raven's wing," we are likely to think more about other raven-haired heroines in books than birds in nature. However, when Natty elsewhere says of Elizabeth that "I won't mistrust the gal; she has an eye like a full-grown buck" (336), he points the way toward Huck, whose diction is similarly drawn from his own life, from American experience.

And as a subversive figure, even today Natty has power that can still transcend the dated formal elements of the texts that tell his story. In some respects, he actually seems to thrive on the tension between his stubbornly inviolable selfhood and the compromised social and aesthetic settings in which he finds himself. He is one of the great No-sayers in literature. Literally, his first words in *The Pioneers* are "No–no–Judge" (21), and a great many of his speeches begin with that one word, usually repeated for emphasis. Thematically, morally, and even emotionally, Natty's rejection of just about every way in which American society pursues happiness – wealth, status, marriage, education, this list could go on for a long time – becomes the point of view from which American society itself is judged and found wanting. The wilderness that Natty keeps disappearing into in that novel, a much newer world than the one the settlers are making in the village, becomes a place of radical renunciation and fulfillment. One contemporary reader reported to Cooper that as he watched Natty walk away from society, "I longed to go with him."[7] Natty has had a lot of company out there, beyond culture, and not just the many generations of American readers who have gone vicariously with him into the woods. Many of the most memorable characters in American literature can be seen as descended from his unflinchingly autonomous stance: Herman Melville's eponymous "Bartleby" (1853), Thoreau's *Walden* (1854) persona, Huck of course (1884), Kate Chopin's Edna in *The Awakening* (1899), William Faulkner's Ike McCaslin in "The Bear" (1942). If the Templeton pioneers represent "sivilization," as Huck calls it, these figures are its most intransigent "discontents."

Many of Cooper's other twenty-seven novels describe, and in various ways interrogate, the project of creating the new nation. Eight of them are set in new settlements, from colonial New England (*The Wept of Wish-ton-Wish*, 1829) to the Old Northwest, as the Upper Midwest used to be called (*The Oak Openings*, 1848); to a volcanic atoll in the Pacific Ocean (*The Crater*, 1847). None of these books contains a character as original as Natty, but all raise the same question posed by his very existence: how sustaining and sustainable are the social structures that Americans are building in this new world? Early in his career, even as Natty absented himself from the scene of American progress, Cooper himself mainly celebrated his country's achievements. Flush with the popularity of novels like *The Spy* and *The Pioneers*, he even planned a series of thirteen novels, one for each of the colonies, set during the Revolution. When the first of these, *Lionel Lincoln* (1825), was not a commercial success, he abandoned that scheme, but not his posture as a patriot. In 1826, like Irving before him and many American authors afterward, Cooper moved to Europe, but the novels he wrote on that side of the Atlantic were still more overtly committed to republican values like freedom and representative government. On the other hand, his later writings put satiric and often bitter quotation marks around the idea of "American progress." *Home As Found* (1838) returns to the site of Cooper's own life, "Templeton." The village is forty years older than in *The Pioneers*. The evil it now suffers from has nothing to do with a postcolonial deference to European culture, but rather is a rampant case of American egalitarianism; at the end of this later novel, it is the descendants of Oliver and Elizabeth who are planning to light out for a different territory, and this time that territory is Europe. At the end of *The Crater*, the settlement that American colonists have created on the atoll has an apocalyptic end: the eruption that erases it from the face of the earth is treated, by implication at least, as a righteous and divine judgment against the sins of government by the mob that calls itself "the people."

By the time he wrote *Home As Found*, Cooper had returned from Europe and was living in Cooperstown. But as that novel makes clear, Cooper's homecoming had been anything but triumphant. The first text he published after his return, *A Letter to His Countrymen* (1834), was intended to be the last he ever published. In this pamphlet he declares his independence from the people by announcing his retirement from writing. He was "lay[ing] aside the pen," he told his audience, because he was convinced that no American writer could count on the support of the American reading public.[8] Behind this action were two different sets of events: when he shifted the setting of his fiction to European history in three novels published 1831–3, his American sales suffered, though not drastically, and as one of the country's most prominent figures, he was often the target of partisan attacks in the fiercely political American press. His feeling of betrayal by his country was clearly an overreaction, but while it says a lot about the thinness of Cooper's own skin, it also helps us remember how vulnerable and exposed early American writers could feel as they explored that new frontier called American literature. Charles Brockden Brown in the previous generation and Herman Melville in the following one were among the other American novelists who quit writing fiction when it seemed to them that their audience had let them down.

Cooper's announcement, it turned out fairly soon, was premature. Economic realities, as well as a psychic need to keep talking to "his countrymen" – which he rationalized as the belief that his countrymen needed a stern talking-to – soon compelled him to pick up the pen again. Eighteen of his novels, along with eleven other books, were published after his "retirement," and among them were some of his best: not just the final two Leather-Stocking Tales, but, for instance, *Satanstoe* (1845), a thoroughly charming story of the colonial Dutch, in "New Amsterdam" (as New York City was originally called), in Albany, and in the wilderness not far from Cooperstown. This is the first volume of The Littlepage Manuscripts, a trilogy in which Cooper takes a last long look at the process of introducing civilization to the new world. The final volume in that series, *The Redskins* (1845), which advances the story of America up to the present in which Cooper is writing, is probably the angriest book he ever wrote. The "Redskins" are not the Native Americans who had to be dispossessed from the land, but the modern American rabble, who are possessed with a grasping populism that threatens to make society more savage than the wilderness ever was.

Cooper has other claims on students of literature than the ones we have considered here. He is generally considered the creator of the genre known as "sea fiction." This began with his fourth novel, *The Pilot* (1824), which characteristically had *its* origins in a Walter Scott novel, *The Pirate* (1822). Cooper, who had served in the U.S. Navy a dozen years earlier, became impatient with the praise he heard heaped on Scott for *The Pirate*'s nautical elements and decided to show the world a more accurate representation of ships and seafaring. The success of that novel led to nine additional tales of the sea. These include *The Red Rover* (1828), probably second among his fictions in international popularity, though more for its Byronic hero than for the realism of its nautical details, and *The Sea Lions* (1849), about a cruise toward the South Pole in quest of furs that, by the time the Antarctic winter sets in, anticipates the symbolist uses to which Melville puts ocean voyaging in *Moby-Dick* (1851). Both Melville and Joseph Conrad, the two great masters of the genre, acknowledged Cooper's own mastery of it. To make his fictions marketable, Cooper provided them all with marriage plots; love, however, never inspired his imagination as profoundly as the vast settings of ocean and wilderness.

That first sea fiction suggests how throughout his career Cooper's artistic motivations intermixed the personal, the professional, and the patriotic: the "Pilot" is John Paul Jones, the hero of the Revolutionary War who also took on the might of Great Britain and, against long odds, won. The story of Cooper's three decades as a novelist is larger and possibly more dramatic than any of the stories he tells in those thirty-two novels. It is the story of an American author writing in the long shadow cast by European culture, wrestling with America itself – as both his subject matter and his audience. That story has both its comic and its tragic aspects, but in the end, as both a popular and an unpopular figure, Cooper emerges as one of the founders of that complexly begotten thing we call American culture. When he died, in Cooperstown in 1851, his "countrymen" – and women – were probably relieved as well as saddened. Yet they were also grateful and proud for all he had done to put that new world called "American fiction" on the map.

## FURTHER READING

Adams, Charles Hansford, *The Guardian of the Law: Authority and Identity in James Fenimore Cooper*, University Park, Pennsylvania State University Press, 1990.

Baker, Martin, *The Lasting of the Mohicans: History of an American Myth*, Jackson, University Press of Mississippi, 1995.

Beard, James Franklin (ed.), *The Letters and Journals of James Fenimore Cooper*, Cambridge, Mass., Belknap Press of Harvard University Press, 1964–9.

Dekker, George, *James Fenimore Cooper: The American Scott*, New York, Barnes & Noble, 1967.

Dennis, Ian, *Nationalism and Desire in Early Historical Fiction*, New York, St. Martin's Press, 1997.

Fiedler, Leslie, *Love and Death in the American Novel*, New York, Stein & Day, 1966.

Franklin, Wayne, *James Fenimore Cooper: The Early Years*, New Haven, Conn., Yale University Press, 2007.

Kelly, William P., *Plotting America's Past: Fenimore Cooper and the Leatherstocking Tales*, Carbondale, Southern Illinois University Press, 1983.

Person, Leland S. (ed.), *A Historical Guide to James Fenimore Cooper*, Oxford, Oxford University Press, 2007.

Railton, Stephen, *Fenimore Cooper: A Study of His Life and Imagination*, Princeton, N.J., Princeton University Press, 1978.

Smith, Henry Nash, *Virgin Land: The American West as Symbol and Myth*, Cambridge, Mass., Harvard University Press, 1950.

Tompkins, Jane, *Sensational Designs: The Cultural Work of American Fiction*, New York, Oxford University Press, 1985.

Wallace, James D., *Early Cooper and His Audience*, New York, Columbia University Press, 1986.

## NOTES

1 James Fenimore Cooper, *The Pioneers* (New York, Penguin, 1988), p. 64; additional references to this novel will be cited in parentheses in the text.

2 D. H. Lawrence, *Studies in Classic American Literature* (1923; rpt. New York, Viking, 1964), p. 54.

3 Emerson, *Nature*, in *Ralph Waldo Emerson: Essays and Lectures*, ed. Joel Porte (New York, Library of America, 1983), p. 10.

4 Emerson, "American Scholar Oration," in *Ralph Waldo Emerson: Essays and Lectures*, ed. Joel Porte (New York, Library of America, 1983), p. 70; Holmes, qtd. in Wilson Sullivan, *New England Men of Letters* (New York, Macmillan, 1972), p. 235.

5 Ernest Hemingway, *The Green Hills of Africa* (New York, Scribners, 1935), p. 22.

6 Mark Twain, *Adventures of Huckleberry Finn*, ed. Stephen Railton (Peterborough, Broadview Press, 2011), p. 365.

7 Richard Henry Dana, letter to Cooper, qtd. in Marcel Clavel, *Fenimore Cooper and His Critics: American, British and French Criticisms of the Novelist's Early Work* (Aix-en Provence, Imprimerie Universitaire de Provence, 1938), p. 149.

8 Cooper, *A Letter to His Countrymen* (1834), qtd. in Stephen Railton, *Fenimore Cooper: A Study of His Life and Imagination* (Princeton, N.J., Princeton University Press, 1978), pp. 142–3.

# 2

# Nathaniel Hawthorne

ROBERT MILDER

Nathaniel Hawthorne (1804–64) is at the very center of the American novel tradition, not only because so many students read *The Scarlet Letter* (1850) in high school or college, but also because the issues the book raises – sex and religion, liberation versus repression, gender and the position of women, the nature of the human personality and the prospects for remaking the social order – are enduringly part of American culture. Hawthorne's special insight, like Faulkner's, is his understanding of how individuals are at once timeless in their basic impulses and inflected by and enmeshed in history, often tragically. We must read him with something of this same understanding. Hawthorne is different from us, a man of the mid–nineteenth century even when he writes of the mid–seventeenth, and he is also like us, addressing versions of the conflict between the "I want" and the "thou shalt" (social, moral, religious, psychological) that besets people in all ages and cultures.

Hawthorne came to the novel late, at forty-five, in what might be called the third phase of his career. The first phase was the period of near-seclusion he spent mainly in his family house in Salem between his graduation from Bowdoin College in 1825 and the publication of *Twice-Told Tales* in 1837, years in which he wrote and anonymously published many of his best and nearly all of his darkest tales. The second phase began with his marriage to Sophia Peabody in July 1842 and their settling at the Old Manse in transcendental Concord, and it extended through the fall of 1845 when a combination of events returned Hawthorne to Salem and presently installed him as surveyor of customs in the Salem Custom House.

The Salem period was formative in establishing the literary habits that would eventuate in Hawthorne's practice of romance. Deprived of the fiction writer's fund of social experience, Hawthorne was forced back upon himself with "nothing but thin air to concoct [his] stories of" and the attendant difficulty of "giv[ing] a lifelike semblance to such shadowy stuff" (15:251–2).[1] Was such rarefied fiction a distillation of the real in the service of a deeper truth or was it an evasion of the real? Hawthorne could never decide. In either case, by the early 1830s in tales like "Young Goodman Brown" (1835), "My Kinsman, Major Molineux" (1832), and "Roger Malvin's Burial" (1832) he already had fashioned the "neutral territory, somewhere between the real world and faery-land" (1:36), that he would later identify as the site of romance.

In his preface to *Mosses from an Old Manse* (1846), his second collection, Hawthorne voiced dissatisfaction with his output of "idle stories" and confessed his hope of the Manse years that he might "achieve a novel, that should evolve some deep lesson, and should possess physical substance enough to stand alone" (10:4, 5). He achieved nothing of the sort. Save for the early, suppressed *Fanshawe* (1828), his longest works before *The Scarlet Letter* had been "The Gentle Boy" (1832) and "Rappaccini's Daughter" (1844), each occupying fewer than forty pages in the Centenary edition. Even *The Scarlet Letter* was not originally intended to "stand alone" but to comprise "the most prolix among the tales" in a volume to be titled "Old-Time Legends" and to be introduced by an autobiographical preface, "The Custom–House" (1:4; 16:306).

Aside from "explaining how" the materials of *The Scarlet Letter* "came into [his] possession, and … offering proofs of [their] authenticity" (1:4) – a claim credited by no one, nor intended to be – "The Custom-House" served several functions for Hawthorne. It filled out a narrative he continued to find skimpy; it established its author's familial and cultural credentials as a chronicler of Puritan times; it tonally balanced what he called "positively a h-ll-fired story, into which [he] found it almost impossible to throw any cheering light" (16:312); and it allowed him to avenge himself on the political enemies who had ousted him from his surveyorship, much to his humiliation and economic loss. The heart of the preface is Hawthorne's purported discovery of the threadbare scarlet letter along with Surveyor Pue's narrative of Hester Prynne, his futile attempts to write the story in off-hours from his official duties, and his evocation of a physical scene – a chamber whose homely artifacts are spiritualized by silvery moonlight and humanized by the rosy warmth of a coal fire – that symbolizes at once the state of mind in which the romancer creates, the generic status of his creation (a romance, not a novel), and the mood of imaginative receptivity required of its readers.

Hawthorne introduced each of his four completed romances with a preface in which he pointedly identified the work *as* a romance, claiming, as he said in *The House of the Seven Gables* (1851), "a certain latitude" for his narrative "both as to its fashion and material." By "fashion" he meant technique or mode of literary representation; the novel was realistic (noonday light), the romance elevated and evocative (moonlight). By "material" he meant content; the novel dealt with "the probable and ordinary course of man's experience," the romance with the *extra*ordinary, whether in the form of "the Marvellous" (2:1) or of an intensity of psychic inwardness.

The irony of Hawthorne's distinction in *Seven Gables* is its imperfect correspondence to the books he actually wrote. Apart from *The Scarlet Letter*, in which "the Actual and the Imaginary" do indeed "meet, and each imbue[s] itself with the nature of the other" (1:36), his romances tend to be hybrids, oscillating between what Richard H. Brodhead calls the "solidly verisimilar" (the novel) and the "dreamily emblematic" (romance).[2] As developed in the prefaces, Hawthorne's notion of "romance" is less a coherent aesthetic theory making for a consistent practice than an attempt to explain and justify the marginally realistic character of his fiction and shape reader expectations for works that might seem artificial or absurd if set beside familiar experience.

Hawthorne himself vacillated between confidence in his art and deprecation of it. In painting he preferred the homely realism of the Dutch Masters to the idealizations of the Italians; in fiction he enjoyed the novels of the British novelist Anthony Trollope, which seemed to him "just as real as if some giant had hewn a great lump out of the earth and put it under a glass case, with all its inhabitants going about their daily business, and not suspecting they were made a show of" (18:229). Toward his own more ethereal fiction he was chronically ambivalent. When the glow of creation faded, he tended to wonder whether his art of moonlight was one of genuine revelation or simply of moonshine. He wondered until the very end.

It is apt that the titles of Hawthorne's first romance (*Fanshawe* [1828]) and his near-last (the uncompleted *Grimshawe* [1861]) should be plays upon his surname, for, while not directly autobiographical, his fictions often involve displacements of personal concerns. The *fan*tasy of *Haw*thorne enacted in *Fanshawe* is a romanticization of Hawthorne's youthful plight as an aspiring man of letters estranged from his provincial New England world and torn between a desire for fame and a hunger for human communion. *Fanshawe* never represented more than a side of the young Hawthorne, and as he outgrew its morose, alienated mood and literary crudeness, he came to regret writing the romance, destroyed whatever copies of it he could, and later in life never publicly acknowledged the work.

It would be twelve years before he published another romance. In unrelated notebook entries of earlier years, he had anticipated each of *The Scarlet Letter'* s major characters and several of its themes; for example: "The life of a woman, who, by the old colony law, was condemned always to wear the letter A, sewed on her garment, in token of her having committed adultery";

"To symbolize moral or spiritual disease by disease of the body; – thus, when a person committed any sin, it might cause a sore to appear on the body"; "A story of the effects of revenge, in diabolizing him who indulges in it"; "Pearl – the English of Margaret – a pretty name for a girl in a story" (8: 254, 227, 278, 242). By what process these materials came together and were transmuted into *The Scarlet Letter* we can never know.

Hawthorne might have called his book *Hester Prynne; or, A Fallen Woman*; by titling it *The Scarlet Letter* he identifies its subject as the ramifications of Hester's adultery for all concerned, Puritan society included. Structurally, the book is organized around three scaffold scenes that stand as markers of the characters' relationships to one another and of their state of soul as they struggle to come to terms with the transgression that set events into motion. Whether that transgression is a sin (a violation of divinely instituted moral law) or a crime (a violation of a time-bound civil statute extenuated or even sanctified by love) is a question that divided readers from the outset and seems inscribed in the text itself. From one point of view, the book is an allegorical romance whose characters enact a pattern of sin and repentance that extends beyond themselves as individuals or as representatives of time and place. From another point of view, the book is a psychological novel testifying less to moral absolutes than to human impulses as warped by the social and mental structures of a particularly repressive age. In the first case, Hester and Dimmesdale are sinners who must work out their redemption for themselves without help from God or society; in the second, they are victims of a historical situation within which (Dimmesdale) or against which (Hester) they struggle but from which they cannot finally escape. Hawthorne's achievement in the book is to make these rival perspectives, a potential either/or, into an obligatory both/and. One cannot read *The Scarlet Letter* ideologically within a Christian moral framework or a radical liberationist one without doing violence to the ambiguity that Hawthorne builds into the text, even when as intrusive narrator he seems most judgmental.

The situation of Dimmesdale, tormented by secret guilt, harks back to that of Reverend Hooper in "The Minister's Black Veil" (1836), a tale from the Salem period. What is new in *The Scarlet Letter*, or a delayed fruition of the Concord years and Hawthorne's contact with the romantic individualism of Emerson and the feminism of Margaret Fuller, is Hester Prynne. As Hester grows from a defiant but overmatched girl to a formidable, free-thinking woman, she develops a critique of Puritan society, of woman's position in Western society generally, and of inhibited, sin-obsessed Christianity itself. The plan of beginning life anew she proposes to Dimmesdale in the forest involves more than their personal escape from Boston; symbolically, it amounts to a refounding of America on the basis of a law of love, or the free and harmonious development of the self as it engenders a new morality and corresponding social forms. It is a prospect Hawthorne found enormously attractive but also, in its threat to moral order and trust in the impulses of human nature, deeply unsettling.

Hawthorne would return to this theme with two subsequent dark-haired heroines, Zenobia in *The Blithedale Romance* (1852) and Miriam in *The Marble Faun* (1860), unable to embrace the vision they represented or to put it out of mind. In *The Scarlet Letter* he mediates his hopes and fears by postponing the "coming revelation" (1:273) to a remote historical future even as he has Hester defer to moral law by returning to Boston in the book's "Conclusion" and voluntarily reassuming the scarlet letter. In one way or another, each of Hawthorne's four romances will flirt with the possibility of cultural regeneration, then work to contain it by punishing, killing off, or neutralizing its proponent. It might almost be said that beneath the books' overt and particular themes, the tension between these rival visions is Hawthorne's inciting subject and a defining factor in his management of characterization and plot.

Uncomfortable with his gloomy themes and with the genre of romance itself, Hawthorne had thought to move toward a sunnier, more contemporary, and more realistic art even before he wrote *The Scarlet Letter*. *The House of the Seven Gables* is his experiment with a balance of past and present, shadow and sunlight, tragedy and comedy, stern moralism and sentiment, and as such it is the book he liked to believe was most representative of his nature. Its donnée is an aboriginal sin of avarice and class injustice perpetrated by the founder of the Pyncheon dynasty and extending down to the present, ostensibly as a curse upon the house but in fact as a flaw in family character that leads descendants to replicate the initial act. The historical causality is obscure and not of serious interest to Hawthorne except as a means for importing into his narrative of contemporary life an aura of the wondrous and quasi-supernatural. His more genuine engagement is with New England history, culture, and character types: the movement from Puritan to modern times and from aristocracy to middle-class democracy; the reformist impulse as it bids to sweep away the inheritance of the past versus the cheerful, domestic neoconservatism that would retain the moral fiber of the old shorn of its morbidness and fanaticism; the situation of the aesthete in a world of commercial philistines; and, above all, perhaps (as Hawthorne recalls the idyll of his courtship and early married life at the Old Manse), the power of love to awaken the soul and renew the ossified forms of tradition and social organization without radical reform.

The vitality of *Seven Gables* lies in its portraits of the grotesque but devoted Hepzibah; Phoebe the plebeian household angel; Holgrave the transcendentally tinged reformer; the smiling, treacherous Judge Pyncheon; and the victimized and enfeebled Clifford, an artist-nature into whom Hawthorne projected both his sensitivities and his lifelong suspicion of their lurking sensuality and selfishness. The plot of the book is rudimentary – virtually nothing happens, then, in a rush, everything happens – and has importance chiefly as a schematic resolution of the cultural elements embodied in its characters. The book "darkens damnably toward the close," Hawthorne told his publisher, unhappily, "but I shall try hard to pour some setting sunshine over it" (16:376). Pour he did. The ending of the narrative is an improbable fabrication: Holgrave marries Phoebe, disowns his radical opinions, and rides off with the other characters to live at the deceased Judge Pyncheon's country estate. The book seemed to Hawthorne "better than the Scarlet Letter" (16:406), it delighted his wife, and through the entrepreneurial labors of the publisher James T. Fields it sold reasonably well and enhanced his emerging reputation.

Encouraged by success, Hawthorne soon began another work, *The Blithedale Romance*, set in the 1840s at a utopian community modeled after Brook Farm, at which he spent a few months in 1841. Blithedale itself is only cursorily described in the book, which soon resolves itself into the personal and ideological relationships among its four major characters, Hollingsworth, Zenobia, Priscilla, and the first-person narrator Miles Coverdale. Indirectly, however, *Blithedale is* about "Blithedale" in that its exploration of human motives and behavior comprises a test in miniature of the viability of reformist dreams. Apropos of socialism, Freud remarked that "aggressiveness was not created by property" and that if "personal rights over material wealth" were removed, "there still remains prerogative in the field of sexual relationships, which is bound to become the source of the strongest dislike and the most violent hostility among men who in other respects are an equal footing."[3] He might almost have been describing the erotic tangle at Blithedale. Unifying the book's apparently centrifugal themes – utopianism, feminism and gender relations, prison reform, mesmerism, and the relationship of matter to spirit – is Hawthorne's inquiry into the forces of self-aggrandizement and sexuality driving human interactions. The willful, erotic Zenobia is the Eve and Pandora of this would-be paradise, but responsibility for its "fall" and for her own personal tragedy rests chiefly with the surrounding male world, which vocationally and sexually confines her passionate womanhood to the straitened paths of convention. Like *The Scarlet Letter*, *Blithedale* closes with an appeal for gender reform but defers it to an unspecified future even as it consolidates the status quo by exorcising the disruptively prophetic woman.

Henry James called the vibrant Zenobia Hawthorne's "nearest approach ... to the complete creation of a *person*" and found *Blithedale* "the lightest, the brightest, the liveliest" of his fictions.⁴ It might also have been his best had he been able to sustain the scenic presentation of its earlier chapters in an unbroken narrative rather than a fractured one impaired by gaps in Coverdale's knowledge and by the unreliability of his telling, warped by sexual jealousy and petty malice. As Hawthorne's only effort at first–person romance, *Blithedale* raises the question of whether such a subgenre is even possible, since first-person narrative typically reflects back on the character and situation of the speaker while romance aims at a more archetypal characterization independent of such skewing. At one point, Coverdale addresses this issue directly, conceding that his perspective is flawed and his portraits reductive and overdrawn but asking that they be taken as fundamentally accurate nonetheless. This seems Hawthorne's own stance in *Blithedale*: "Read my book as a romance about gender relations among its socially representative characters *and* read it as a psychological novel about a narrator who deals with his exclusion from intimacy with his friends by casting himself as the interpreter of their lives." At the heart of *The Blithedale Romance* is an ambiguity about who its romancer is, Coverdale or Hawthorne himself, and whether it is a romance at all.

The year of *Blithedale*'s publication, 1852, also saw the election of the Democrat Franklin Pierce, a Bowdoin classmate for whom Hawthorne wrote a campaign biography and who rewarded him with the lucrative consulship at Liverpool. As it turned out, Hawthorne would spend more than seven years in Europe, including about a year and a half in Italy, divided chiefly between Rome and Florence. His first literary project in Italy was "The Ancestral Footstep," a romance about an American claimant to an English title begun in April 1858. In that same month, however, he saw a copy of Praxiteles' Faun and began to imagine "a little Romance about it" (14:191), which superseded the English book and evolved into *The Marble Faun*. As first conceived, the story was to have "all sorts of fun and frolic in it" (14:178), but the mood and theme were soon eclipsed by Hawthorne's decision to focus upon the Fall of Man – mythically, the fall from Eden; culturally, the fall from rustic simplicity to modern civilization; and morally and psychologically, the fall from an innocence that was ignorance to a depth of being achieved through the struggle with sin and pain.

The element of "romance" in *The Marble Faun* centers on the rustic Donatello as his story paradigmatically enacts "the riddle of the Soul's growth" (4:381). Donatello, however, is the least interesting and least intimately explored character in the book, whose more vital concern is with how its other figures (Miriam, Kenyon, Hilda, the narrator himself) negotiate the challenges of experience in the postlapsarian world of Rome. With its vast and layered history and mingled grandeur and squalor, Rome struck

Hawthorne as a compendium of Western experience, and as such it defied assimilation to New World ideas of morality, Providence, and historical design. Above all, Rome and its history seemed to proclaim what Miriam calls "that pit of blackness" that lies beneath the "thin crust" of familiar life, "spread over it, with just reality enough to bear up the illusive stage-scenery amid which we tread" (4:162).

*The Marble Faun*'s "story of the fall of man" amounts to old business for Hawthorne, who had been writing variations on this theme for thirty years. Passages like that on blackness, uttered by the characters or intruded meditatively by the narrator, reflect a more emergent self as Rome drew forth and intensified doubts Hawthorne had felt throughout his career. Through the romance of Donatello's development from faun to man, Hawthorne tries to contain his book within the framework of Christian theodicy (the mystery of a wise and benevolent God's permitting evil), but the power and authenticity of *The Marble Faun* lie in its heterodoxies: in Hilda's feeling of moral and spiritual bereftness in "The Emptiness of Picture-Galleries," drawn heavily from Hawthorne's notebooks; in Kenyon's existential despair in "The Flight of Hilda's Doves"; and in reflections of the narrator that expose a nihilism at odds with the book's benign construction of the "fortunate fall." In none of his romances does Hawthorne reveal more of himself than in this ostensibly moralistic one. Toward the close of the book, his freethinker Kenyon confesses his bewilderment and asks the priggish Hilda to "guide me home!" (4:461) – to America, to domesticity, and to the safety of absolute morality and convention. Bewildered by Rome, Hawthorne, it seems, would also be guided home, and after drafting *The Marble Faun* in Italy and rewriting it in England, he did, in mid-1860, return to America, now alien to him and on the brink of epochal catastrophe.

Hawthorne's last years are a record of literary frustration and declining health. Two projects absorbed him – first, in 1860–1, "Etherege" and "Grimshawe," developments of what his editors call "The American Claimant Manuscripts" that had begun with "The Ancestral Footstep"; and, second, in 1861–4, "Septimius Felton," "Septimius Norton," and "The Dolliver Romance," romances about the quest for a potion conferring immortality. Hawthorne's novelistic strength was never as a plot maker, but having begun the claimant manuscripts with an intention to contrast England and America and "The Elixir of Life Manuscripts" with an inquiry into the meaning of lives aborted by death, he lost hold of his themes and found himself wandering through increasingly intricate, improbable, and tedious labyrinths of plot, as if by wildly exfoliating his story he might discover what it meant. Most memorable in his unfinished narratives is the portrait of the misanthropic Doctor Grimshawe ("grim Hawthorne"?), as charismatic a figure as any in his work and the projection of a side of him suppressed in life and seen only by flashes in his published writing.

Hawthorne did not, toward the end, lose his power to write. Even as he struggled with his fictional projects, he elaborated notebook materials into the sketches of England published as *Our Old Home* (1863), a work of insight and grace that Henry James considered stylistically the best of his writings. His problem was that he continued to regard himself as a romancer long after he had exhausted his materials, his enthusiasm, and his belief in the genre. At the urging of his publisher, Fields, he submitted three chapters of the fragmentary "Dolliver" to the *Atlantic Monthly*, then resisted Fields's pleas for more, knowing the project would never be satisfactorily completed. He died in May 1864.

Thanks largely to the promotional activity of Fields, Hawthorne became a classic author even in his lifetime and, to the world, an exemplar of American literary genius. Since then, through fluctuations of literary taste and ideological fashion, his reputation has continued relatively unscathed. Such favor is owing partly to his institutionalization in schools and colleges but also to the particular character of his writing, which is subtle and ambiguous enough to speak, or be taken to speak, to the concerns of disparate cultural generations.

Hawthorne's canonization assumed special academic prominence with Richard Chase's *The American Novel and Its Tradition* (1957). Responding to the British critic F. R. Leavis and his own Columbia colleague Lionel Trilling – the former identifying the "great tradition" of English fiction with the social novels of Jane Austen, George Eliot, Henry James, and Joseph Conrad; the latter arguing that such fiction "has never really established itself in America"[5] – Chase converted an absence into a more than compensatory presence. Against "the solid moral inclusiveness and massive equability" of a novel like Eliot's *Middlemarch* (1874), Chase set the "freer, more daring, more brilliant fiction" of what he called the American romance, or romance-novel.[6] Suddenly, in this postwar decade of American nationalism and the burgeoning of American Studies programs, the United States had a literary tradition as "great" as, and more imaginative than, Leavis's English tradition. At the center of this tradition was Hawthorne, without whom any such configuring of American fiction would have been impossible. Once Hawthornean romance was in place as a point of reference, other writers and writings, even elements from more realistic works, might be grouped around it to form a distinctive national "tradition." The glass that had appeared half-empty now seemed wondrously full. Although a product of its times, Chase's argument long outlived those times, and while approaches to Hawthornean romance have altered with shifts in critical theory and practice, they have tended to operate within the assumptions about genre established by Chase.

Fiction writers have also worked under the influence of Hawthorne, whether in affection and gratitude, in revision, in rebellion, or in some combination of these. The writings of Henry James are the most obvious, complex, and oft-discussed case. The Ohioan William Dean Howells grew up revering Hawthorne, managed as a young man to meet him, and later as the champion of realism reacted against his example with no diminution of his personal fondness for his work. The naturalist Harold Frederic's *The Damnation of Theron Ware* (1896) is a fascinating recasting of *The Scarlet Letter*, as is John Updike's *Roger's Version* (1986), one of three Updike novels inspired by Hawthorne's book. Twentieth-century southern writers sharing Hawthorne's absorption in regional history and sense of original sin (Faulkner, Robert Penn Warren, Walker Percy) have been especially responsive to his work, as have those cultivating the strangeness of the gothic (Carson McCullers, Truman Capote). In "Some Aspects of the Grotesque in Southern Fiction" (1960), Flannery O'Connor records her affinity with Hawthorne, and in one of her finest stories, "The Artificial Nigger" (1855), she comically/pathetically rewrites "My Kinsman, Major Molineux." "Without Hawthorne," Joel Porte remarked, "there could no firm theory of American romance."[7] There would also be a quite different and much diminished fictional practice.

## FURTHER READING

Baym, Nina, *The Shape of Hawthorne's Career* Ithaca, N.Y., Cornell University Press, 1976.

Bell, Michael Davit, *The Development of American Romance*, Chicago, University of Chicago Press, 1980.

Bercovitch, Sacvan, *The Office of the Scarlet Letter*, Baltimore, John Hopkins University Press, 1991.

Brodhead, Richard H. *Hawthorne, Melville, and the Novel*, Chicago, University of Chicago Press, 1976.

Brodhead, Richard H., *The School of Hawthorne*, New York, Oxford University Press, 1986.

Budick, Emily Miller, *Engendering Romance: American Women Writes and the Hawthorne Tradition*, New Haven, Conn., Yale University Press, 1994.

Carpenter, Frederic I., "Scarlet A Minus," *College English*, 5 (1944): 173–80.

Crews, Frederick, *The Sins of the Fathers: Hawthorne's Psychological Themes*, 1966; rpt. Berkeley, University of California Press, 1989. New York, Oxford University Press, 1966.

James, Henry, Hawthorne, 1879; rpt. Ithaca, N.Y., Cornell University Press, 1956.

Long, Robert Emmet, *The Great Succession: Henry James and the Legacy of Hawthorne*, Pittsburgh, Pa., University of Pittsburgh Press, 1979.

Matthiessen, F. O., *American Renaissance*, New York, Oxford University Press, 1941.

McCall, Dan, *Citizens of Somewhere Else: Nathaniel Hawthorne and Henry James*, Ithaca, N.Y., Cornell University Press, 1999.

Mellow, James R., *Nathaniel Hawthorne in His Times*, Boston, Houghton Mifflin, 1980.

Milder, Robert, *Hawthorne's Habitations: A Literary Life*, New York, Oxford University Press, 2013.

Millington, Richard H., *Practicing Romance*, Princeton, N.J., Princeton University Press, 1992.

Rahv, Philip, "The Dark Lady of Salem," *Image and Idea*, New York, New Directions, 1949.

Waggoner, Hyatt H., *Hawthorne: A Critical Study*, rev. ed., Cambridge, Mass., Harvard University Press, 1963.

## NOTES

1 All citations of Hawthorne's writings are to the *Centenary Edition of the Works of Nathaniel Hawthorne*, ed. William Charvat et al., 23 vols (Columbus, Ohio State University Press, 1962–93), and are indicated by volume and page number. The volumes cited are as follows: 1. *The Scarlet Letter*; 2. *The House of the Seven Gables*; 3. *The Blithedale Romance* and *Fanshawe*; 4. *The Marble Faun*; 8. *The American Notebooks*; 9. *Twice-Told Tales*; 10. *Mosses from an Old Manse*; 11. *The Snow-Image and Uncollected Tales*; 14. *The French and Italian Notebooks*; 15. *The Letters 1813–1843*; 16. *The Letters 1843–1853*; *The Letters 1853–1856*; 18. *The Letters 1857–1864*.

2 Richard H. Brodhead, *Hawthorne, Melville, and the Novel* (Chicago, University of Chicago Press, 1976), p. 41.

3 Sigmund Freud, *Civilization and Its Discontents*, trans. James Strachey (1929; rpt. New York, Norton, 1962), pp. 60–1.

4 Henry James, *Hawthorne* (1879; rpt. Ithaca, N.Y., Cornell University Press, 1956), pp. 106, 105.

5 See F. R. Leavis, *The Great Tradition* (London, Chatto and Windus, 1948); and Lionel Trilling, "Manners, Morals, and the Novel," *The Liberal Imagination* (1948; rpt. London, Mercury Books, 1961), p. 212.

6 Richard Chase, *The American Novel and Its Tradition* (Garden City, N.Y., Doubleday, 1957), p. viii.

7 Joel Porte, *The Romance in America* (Middletown, Conn., Wesleyan University Press, 1969), p. 95.

# 3
# Herman Melville

CLARK DAVIS

> Though I wrote the Gospels in this century, I should die in the gutter.
> Melville to Nathaniel Hawthorne, 1851

In 1849, as he was arranging for the publication of his third novel, *Mardi*, Herman Melville (1819–91) wrote to his friend Evert Duyckinck, editor of the *Literary World*. The topic of discussion was Melville's reaction to hearing Emerson lecture at the Freeman Place Chapel in Boston. "Emerson is more than a brilliant fellow," the young author explained. "To my surprise I found him quite intelligible." Emerson might be a fool, "full of transcendentalisms, myths & oracular gibberish," but he was at least a fool who "dives": "I love all men who *dive*. Any fish can swim near the surface, but it takes a great whale to go down stairs five miles or more; & if he dont [*sic*] attain the bottom, why, all the lead in Galena can't fashion the plummet that will."[1] "Thought-divers" – this was the term Melville reserved for the writers who impressed him as unrestrained in their pursuit of difficult truths. Shakespeare stood at the head of the class as "the profoundest of thinkers," capable of "those occasional flashings-forth of the intuitive Truth in him; those short, quick probings at the very axis of reality."[2] But even Shakespeare could feel the pressures of political or cultural restraint. If only he had been an American:

> I would to God Shakspeare [*sic*] had lived later, & promenaded in Broadway. Not that I might have had the pleasure of leaving my card for him at the Astor, or made merry with him over a bowl of the fine Duyckinck punch; but that the muzzle which all men wore on their souls in the Elizebethan [*sic*] day, might not have intercepted Shakspere's [*sic*] full articulations. For I hold it a verity, that even Shakspeare, was not a frank man to the uttermost. And, indeed, who in this intolerant Universe is, or can be? But the Declaration of Independence makes a difference. (*C*, 122)

This fantasy is at once a personal manifesto and a cultural vaunt. The writer willing to say, "No! in Thunder" has more freedom to do so in 1849 New York than in Elizabethan London, but he must think of writing as a stripping away of compromise and half-truth, a tearing off of the social mask to speak "the sane madness of vital truth."[3]

Melville began his career essentially as a travel writer. Both *Typee* (1846) – his racy account of time spent in the Marquesas Islands – and *Omoo* (1847), its sequel, were sold as narratives of fact. That these commercially successful books were actually complicated mash-ups of autobiography, "borrowed" source material, and outright fantasy was not absolutely clear until the 1920s. But in the 1840s they served to establish Melville as a writer daring enough to capitalize on his experience with a vivid imagination and a prose style of surprising flexibility and comic energy. If he pushed the boundaries of believability, so much the better to create a combined sense of scandal and Barnumesque bravado. Did he really cavort so freely and happily with undressed native women? Did the beautiful, blue-eyed Fayaway, who must have seemed even then a white man's unthreatening fantasy, really exist? And did she, as depicted in the book's most famous scene, use her nude body as a mast to extend the sail of a canoe on a small inland lake?: "With a wild exclamation of delight, she disengaged from her person the ample robe of tappa which was knotted over her shoulder (for the purpose of shielding her from the sun), and spreading it out like a sail, stood erect with upraised arms in the head of the canoe."[4] True or not – and the scene had as many doubters as believers – such romantic dash could not help but entice readers, particularly when it was paired with darker ruminations on the origin of evil. In his first attempt at full-length fiction Melville proved that he could tell a rousing story, but it was in the digressive spaces around the plot that he seemed most energized by the freedom to pose difficult, perhaps impossible, questions.

It was during the development of *Mardi* that he finally cast off all pretense to sailor memoir and began to measure the full potential of his imagination. It was 1849, and along with writing his third major narrative, Melville had been reading – intensely. He was drawn to Renaissance writers, dramatists like Shakespeare of course but also unclassifiable literary philosophers like Thomas Burton and Sir Thomas Browne. Burton's *The Anatomy of Melancholy* (1621) is the sort of book Melville loved: ostensibly a medical treatise on depression, it gathers quotations from a wide variety of writers on such topics as "Of Witches and Magicians, how they cause Melancholy" and "Perturbations of the Mind Rectified." And Burton tied his remedies and nostrums together with a baroque style capable of accommodating almost any offhand remark that might occur to its author. A similar freedom of subject and digression defined Browne's masterpiece *Religio Medici* (1643). After borrowing the book from Duyckinck's extensive and handy library, Melville reported on his reading by christening Browne a "kind of crack'd Archangel," just the sort of heaven-reaching, rule-defying voice the young author was looking for.

The difficulty of course was that the marketable Herman Melville, known still as the "man who lived among the cannibals," was the author of travel books about the South Seas. But that was about to change. In March of 1848 he wrote to his English publisher John Murray to announce that *Mardi* would be a "Romance of Polynisian [*sic*] Adventure" (*C*, 106). Though he had begun, as he claimed, a "narrative of *facts,*" he had soon found reportage too limiting: "I began to feel an invincible distaste for the same; & a longing to plume my pinions for a flight, & felt irked, cramped & fettered by plodding along with dull common places" (*C*, 106). After a hundred or so pages of sea tale, *Mardi* sailed straight off the map of marketable travel writing and into one of the most peculiar allegorical romances ever concocted – a sort of "crack'd" book in its own right, with islands that stand for countries or philosophies and Polynesians who engage in Platonic dialogues. (One is even possessed by an extremely talkative demon.)

However strange *Mardi* may be, it marks a crucial moment in Melville's career. By casting off the admittedly loose shackles of travel writing for the comparative freedoms of the romance, he took the bold step of risking his lucrative readership by positioning himself above or outside generic consistency. The romance may have seemed like an alternative to the novel or travelogue, but a declared allegiance to its possibilities could also serve as an escape valve, a way to pursue thought and imagination beyond the constraints of expectation or plausibility. Hawthorne used it this way, though within a much more limited range, claiming that the romance granted the author "a license with regard to every-day Probability" that could create "an atmosphere of strange enchantment, beheld through which the inhabitants have a propriety of their own."[5] Realism implied a collective vision of everydayness, a world most people could agree upon and recognize. The romance made room for eccentricity and the idiosyncratic wanderings of the individual imagination. In Melville's youthful hands it also permitted a kind of generic insouciance, a shameless hybridity that made the truth telling he sought less beholden to inherited forms and other potential "muzzles" on the soul.

Calling *Mardi* a romance thus made Melville neither a novelist, strictly speaking, nor a "romancer" but a writer of *books*. The romantic book, Melville's kind of book, is its own creature, its shape and meaning growing from the impulses that animate the driving mind: "What I feel most moved to write, that is banned, – it will not pay," he wrote to Hawthorne in 1851, recognizing the market's preference for familiar stories and his own for more feral explorations. "Yet, altogether write the *other* way I cannot. So the product is a final hash, and all my books are botches" (*C*, 191). To write a book on these terms – to conceive of the struggle so – was less to participate in a tradition of formal development than it was to subordinate all forms to the driving impulse to speak. The mixing of genres within the romantic book tended to negate the sovereignty of genre itself. Rules were not merely made to be broken; they were not rules at all, since to believe in such boundaries on the romantic artist's voice was to endorse a sense of limitation Melville abhorred, even in so bold a writer as Shakespeare.

*Mardi* was the first such experiment, and not surprisingly it had a hard time with critics. "If this book be meant as a pleasantry," wrote the reviewer for the *London Athenaeum*, "the mirth has been oddly left out – if as an allegory, the key of the casket is 'buried in ocean deep' – if as a romance, it fails from tediousness – if as a prose-poem, it is chargeable with puerility."[6] But having caught a glimpse of the depths that drew him, Melville was even less likely to be satisfied with wading familiar shallows. He published two strong, sea-based narratives (*Redburn* [1849] and *White-Jacket* [1850]), written he said for tobacco money, and then embarked on another *Mardi*-like, genre-busting voyage. *Moby-Dick* (1851) is both famous and infamous for its encyclopedic and essayistic digressions. This time, however, the curious, ever-probing, and often comic narrative voice belonged to a character who may come closest of all to embodying the idea of Shakespeare as New Yorker. Ishmael, though certainly the exile or "isolato" that his chosen name implies, combines the "unmuzzled" promenader of Broadway with the romantic thinker capable of marshaling any and all forms of expression to meet his imagination's need. If the romantic book was meant to seem the spontaneous production of a grand spirit, Ishmael's was the mind and soul large enough to reach beyond literary limits. All forms seem to do his bidding: dictionaries, the short story, biological and anthropological textbooks, staged drama, bawdy satire, and even, astonishingly, operetta. His confessed subject is the whale and the business of whaling, but in reality he reaches for everything, hoping to render the infinite plenitude of experience. As a result his book, the romantic book par excellence, can never be completed and as a massive fragment speaks to the inability of all forms to contain the real: "But I now leave my cetological System standing thus unfinished, even as the great Cathedral of Cologne was left, with the crane still standing upon the top of the uncompleted tower. For small erections may be finished by their first architects; grand ones, true ones, ever leave the copestone to posterity. God keep me from ever completing anything. This whole book is but a draught – nay, but the draught of a draught."[7]

Ishmael's embrace of the unfinished finds its counterpoint, though not precisely its opposite, in Ahab's refusal to accept limits of any kind. The mad captain embodies Melville's fervent need for a Shakespearian speaker, at every entrance dragging with him the declamatory conventions of

Elizabethan tragedy. In full-throated address to the crawling St. Elmo's fire, Ahab is Lear, his rhythms treading close to steady iambics: "I own thy speechless, placeless power; but to the last gasp of my earthquake life will dispute its unconditional, unintegral mastery in me. ... But war is pain, and hate is woe. Come in thy lowest form of love, and I will kneel and kiss thee; but at thy highest, come as mere supernal power; and though thou launchest navies of full-freighted worlds, there's that in here that still remains indifferent" (*MD*, 507). Ahab's dark truths – his minor Satanism and adolescent defiance – seem trapped inside the narrative machinery of the prophecy play. He may be the vehicle for integrating American acquisitiveness with probing thought, but he is also a case study in what it means to be hemmed in by an insistence on completeness or closure. Unlike his creator, Ahab is unable to see around the constraints of generic thinking, and his rage indicates a recognition of the walls that contain him. Infamously he tells his crew that one must "strike, strike through the mask!" of reality, but he is never able to accept, as Ishmael clearly does, that the mask is a product of his own imagination and therefore an object of skepticism rather than anger. By momentarily balancing his own relentless questioning against a comic acceptance of "this strange mixed affair we call life" (*MD*, 226), Melville was able to reach a level of personal expression consistent with his ideal of a darkly inflected, democratically liberated American Shakespeare.

*Moby-Dick* is thus a remarkable, and extremely tenuous, solution to Melville's intensifying dilemma: how to liberate his preferred brand of American frankness in a marketable narrative product. "I have written a wicked book, and feel spotless as the lamb," he wrote to Hawthorne, registering the momentary satisfaction of having had his unfettered say (*C*, 212). It was a rush of artistic satisfaction he would apparently never feel again. *Pierre; or, the Ambiguities* (1852), his seventh full-scale production in as many years, he perhaps jokingly called a "rural bowl of milk," but it was in fact an attempt, in the words of *Moby-Dick*'s Father Mapple, to "preach truth to the face of Falsehood!" by means of the domestic novel. It remains unclear whether Melville was seeking to parody the form from the beginning, but it is abundantly evident that he chafed at its conventions from the moment he set his pen to the page. The enervated idyll of Saddle Meadows, Pierre's country home, is nearly hallucinatory in its forced cheer and ill-concealed perversity, and Melville's style immediately assumes a neurotic intensity that suggests pent-up violence:

> But a reverential and devoted son seemed lover enough for this widow Bloom; and besides all this, Pierre when namelessly annoyed, and sometimes even jealously transported by the too ardent admiration of the handsome youths,

who now and then, caught in unintended snares, seemed to entertain some insane hopes of wedding this unattainable being; Pierre had more than once, with a playful malice, openly sworn, that the man – gray-beard, or beardless – who should dare to propose marriage to his mother, that man would by some peremptory unrevealed agency immediately disappear from the earth.[8]

Caught in an incestuous shadow play with his hypermasculine mother, the young idealist sets out to shatter the world by committing himself to what seems its darkest secret: the rumored presence of his illegitimate half sister. Fittingly he takes refuge in the city and becomes an author, laboring on a book suspiciously similar to the very one in which he appears. But his path, like Ahab's, leads purely to self-destruction, a maddening involution in which he begins to question the basis for his rebellion. And this time there is no Ishmael to lead the reader out of the chaos. Pierre's book fails as *Pierre* itself collapses inward, the end of the novel and its heaven-bent hero foreshadowing the death of Melville's struggle with fiction itself. "You are a swindler," Pierre's rapacious publishers write in the letter that sends him to his death. "Upon the pretense of writing a popular novel for us, you have been receiving cash advances from us, while passing through our press the sheets of a blasphemous rhapsody, filched from the vile Atheists, Lucian and Voltaire."[9] Melville had anticipated readers' objections in earlier works, but the conclusion of *Pierre* amounted to a preemptive strike on what were sure to be angry responses to so outrageous a drama. (More than one reviewer, like Charles Gordon Greene in the *Boston Post*, questioned Melville's sanity: "What the book means, we know not. To save it from almost utter worthlessness, it must be called a prose poem, and even then, it might be supposed to emanate from a lunatic hospital rather than from the quiet retreats of Berkshire."[10]) As the soon to be published "Bartleby, the Scrivener" (1853) suggests, a writer's energies, his will to work, can come to end. Melville had written and offered to the public seven novels in seven years. If nothing else, *Pierre* forecasts the possibility that Melville's turbulent relationship with fiction was entering its final phase.

But if *Pierre* sounded a muted death knell, one astonishing postmortem remained. After producing a number of short stories and the refreshingly light *Israel Potter* (essentially a retelling of a revolutionary soldier's reminiscences), Melville began in 1856 to assemble a sequence of stark dramatic scenes said to take place on a phantom riverboat called the *Fidèle*. The almost plotless action of *The Confidence-Man* (1857) takes place on April Fools' Day and begins with the appearance of a flaxen-haired deaf mute beside the Mississippi River at St. Louis. This "lamb-like" figure holds a small chalkboard on which he scrawls quotations from First Corinthians about the nature of charity. The flowing crowd of passengers ignores him, and only a barber's nearby placard – the image of a hovering razor with the words "No Trust" inscribed beneath – suggests the nature of the book's coming debate. Onboard dialogues follow, thinly staged, ironic conversations between disguised versions of the so-called confidence-man and potential believers. Trust is sought, sometimes given, and just as quickly disregarded and destroyed. By the book's end the world of the *Fidèle*, like the doomed *Pequod*, seems little more than a burnt out husk. The book makes it clear that no one in this transitory society is genuinely trustworthy, and those capable of believing in their fellow passengers are shown to be little more than fools.

Belief is a social necessity in a democratic society. In a capitalist economy trust makes possible a circulating currency. But the riverboat is known for its counterfeiters, both literal and figurative, and among these, according to the parodic voice of this book's narrator, is the novelist himself. *The Confidence-Man* is studded with chapters that make ironic and half-serious arguments for leniency toward the writer of fiction. In chapter 14, the narrator makes his case that true characters are never consistent, and so the audience for fiction should not expect consistency in his characters any more than they should expect a flying squirrel to be like other squirrels. And in chapter 33 the same defensive voice tells us that the world of his book must be unrealistic in order to seem real: "And as, in real life, the proprieties will not allow people to act out themselves with that unreserve permitted to the stage; so, in books of fiction, they look not only for more entertainment, but, at bottom, even for more reality, than real life itself can show."[11] In other words, fiction, like bank notes and acts of charity, requires trust. For both private and public reasons, Melville saw America in 1857 as a society incapable of such social or artistic faith. People who could not believe other's stories seemed doomed, afloat on an antebellum ship of fools. The passengers on the *Fidèle* are thus fittingly left with little more to protect themselves than useless counterfeit detectors and "life-preservers" that double as chamber pots.

Melville continued to write after the unsuccessful publication of *The Confidence-Man*, but his engagement with prose fiction essentially came to an end. Except for a few short sketches meant to serve as preludes to various poems and the unfinished manuscript of *Billy Budd* (1924) found at his death, he dedicated himself to verse from the late 1850s until 1891. There are several theories for the shift. To some he seems spent after ten years of almost constant labor on ten remarkable books. In 1851 he had hinted to Hawthorne that he was developing so fast he would soon exhaust himself: "Until I was twenty-five, I had no development at all. From my twenty-fifth year I date my life. Three weeks have scarcely passed, at any time between then and now, that I have not unfolded within myself. But I feel that I am now come to the inmost leaf of the bulb, and that shortly the flower must fall to the mould" (C, 193). To others, the expressive possibilities of fiction, particularly given the demands of the market, had failed him. His uneasiness with the novel, the frequent dissatisfaction with its constraints and demands, may have given way to a simpler desire to speak in a voice more directly personal. And yet just as poems had appeared in early works such as *Mardi*, novelistic elements did not entirely disappear from Melville's most fully formed poetic productions. The volume of Civil War poems, *Battle-Pieces and Aspects of the War* (1866), is much more than a collection of lyric pictures or first-person observations. Carefully structured to reflect the entire range of action and argument throughout the conflict, it avoids the emotions recollected in tranquility of the romantic individual and offers instead the dramatized voices of participants or distant observers of battles. It stresses historical perspective and tragic vision rather than isolated or partisan experience. In a similar vein, though far more ambitious, the epic philosophical poem *Clarel* (1876), born of Melville's trip to the Holy Land in 1857, combines *Mardi*'s fondness for Platonic dialogue with the restless search for metaphysical certainty that drives *Moby-Dick* and *Pierre*. Stuffed with quasi-allegorical characters who tend to be spokesmen for various religious and philosophical points of view, its more than eighteen thousand lines constitute what is arguably the most novelistic major poem of the nineteenth century.

"Though I wrote the Gospels in this century, I should die in the gutter," Melville wrote to Hawthorne in 1851 (C, 192). In the midst of writing *Moby-Dick*, he was almost certainly exaggerating his dilemma, and yet the hint that he thought of his work, no matter how mockingly, as akin to scripture is revealing. In his letters Melville often accused himself of preaching, and it is true that he sometimes took on the role of the prophet when his enormous energies ranged freely. *Moby-Dick*'s Father Mapple may be his truest fictional double, a commentator on the darker shadows of the Old Testament and dedicated disturber of the peace. Father Mapple's faith may have been surer than Melville's ever was, but his sense of mission and its terrible costs – as well as his depiction of a fallen and unheeding audience – echo his creator's personal plaints. Father Mapple is a kind of Jonah, and Jonah a kind of novelist, at least as Melville thought of the role for the midcentury American:

> And now how gladly would I come down from this mast-head and sit on the hatches there where you sit, and listen as you listen, while some one of you reads *me* that other and more awful lesson which Jonah teaches to *me*, as a

pilot of the living God. How being an anointed pilot-prophet, or speaker of true things, and bidden by the Lord to sound those unwelcome truths in the ears of a wicked Nineveh, Jonah, appalled at the hostility he should raise, fled from his mission, and sought to escape his duty and his God by taking ship at Joppa. But God is everywhere; Tarshish he never reached. (*MD*, 47)

The "pilot-prophet" is the thought-diver returned to the surface, and with his overriding sense of mission, he speaks less as the practitioner of a given form in a given tradition than as the urgent messenger of an inner drive to awaken and to warn. The confidence games of antebellum America demanded such dark-eyed urgency, despite the near-certainty of commercial failure. Melville, in essence, used his remarkable literary career to grow *into* this kind of failure. Learning to disturb rather than please, he became what he imagined – an exile speaking "sane madness" to a nation approaching crisis.

## FURTHER READING

Brodhead, Richard, *Hawthorne, Melville, and the Novel*, Chicago, University of Chicago Press, 1977.

Bryant, John, and Robert Milder (eds.), *Melville's Evermoving Dawn: Centennial Essays*, Kent, Ohio, Kent State University Press, 1997.

Davis, Clark, *After the Whale: Melville in the Wake of Moby-Dick*, Tuscaloosa, University of Alabama Press, 1995.

Delbanco, Andrew, *Melville: His World and Work*, New York, Knopf, 2005.

Dillingham, William B., *Melville's Later Novels*, Athens, University of Georgia Press, 1986.

Dryden, Edgar A., *Monumental Melville: The Formation of a Literary Career*, Palo Alto, Calif., Stanford University Press, 2004.

Hayford, Harrison, *Melville's Prisoners*, Evanston, Ill., Northwestern University Press, 2003.

Levine, Robert S. (ed.), *The Cambridge Companion to Herman Melville*, Cambridge, Cambridge University Press, 1998.

Leyda, Jay, *The Melville Log: A Documentary Life of Herman Melville 1819–1891*, New York, Harcourt, 1951.

Milder, Robert, *Exiled Royalties: Melville and the Life We Imagine*, Oxford, Oxford University Press, 2006.

## NOTES

1 Herman Melville, *Correspondence*, ed. Lynn Horth (Evanston, Ill., Northwestern University Press and the Newberry Library, 1993), p. 121. Hereafter *C*.

2 Melville, "Hawthorne and His Mosses," in *The Piazza Tales and Other Prose Pieces, 1839–1860*, ed. Harrison Hayford, Alma A. MacDougall, and G. Thomas Tanselle (Evanston, Ill., Northwestern University Press and the Newberry Library, 1987), p. 244.

3  Melville, "Mosses," p. 244.
4  Melville, *Typee: A Peep at Polynesian Life*, ed. Harrison Hayford, Hershel Parker, and G. Thomas Tanselle (Evanston, Ill., Northwestern University Press and the Newberry Library, 1968), p. 134.
5  Nathaniel Hawthorne, *The Blithedale Romance*, ed. William Charvat, Roy Harvey Pearce, and Claude M. Simpson (Columbus, Ohio State University Press, 1965), p. 1.
6  Henry Fothergill Chorley, "*Mardi*" (review), *London Athenaeum* (March 24, 1849), pp. 296–8.
7  Melville, *Moby-Dick; or, The Whale*, ed. Harrison Hayford, Hershel Parker, and G. Thomas Tanselle (Evanston, Ill., Northwestern University Press and the Newberry Library, 1988), p. 145. Hereafter *MD*.
8  Melville, *Pierre; or, The Ambiguities*, ed. Harrison Hayford, Hershel Parker, and G. Thomas Tanselle (Evanston, Ill., Northwestern University Press and the Newberry Library, 1971), p. 5.
9  Melville, *Pierre*, p. 356.
10  Charles Gordon Greene, "*Pierre*" (review), *Boston Post* (August 4, 1852).
11  Melville, *The Confidence-Man: His Masquerade*, ed. Harrison Hayford, Hershel Parker, and G. Thomas Tanselle (Evanston, Ill., Northwestern University Press and the Newberry Library, 1984), p. 182–3.

# 4

# Harriet Beecher Stowe

ARTHUR RISS

In April 1857, Maryland authorities arrested Samuel Green, a free African-American minister, charging him with two crimes: first, possessing a map of Canada, a railroad schedule to Canada, and letters Green's son had written from Canada; second, "knowingly having in his possession a certain abolition pamphlet called 'Uncle Tom's Cabin' or 'life among the lowly.'" These items, according to the indictment, were "of an inflammatory character calculated to create discontent amongst the colored population of this State." Although the court concluded that the letter, map, and railroad schedule were not conclusive proof of Green's intention to help slaves escape, it ruled that Green's possession of *Uncle Tom's Cabin* was clearly a crime.[1] In May, Green was sentenced to ten years in the Maryland State Penitentiary for having a copy of Harriet Beecher Stowe's (1811–96) novel. *Uncle Tom's Cabin* (1852) was never merely phenomenally popular; it was fundamentally dangerous.

The novel remains dangerous. If at one time *Uncle Tom's Cabin* was thought to be the single most powerful instrument for destroying slavery – an understanding illustrated by Abraham Lincoln's notorious yet apocryphal comment upon meeting Stowe: "So you're the little woman who wrote the book that made this great war" – more recently, readers have regarded the novel as an insidious mechanism for solidifying demeaning stereotypes about African Americans (a position crystallized by the way that the incendiary epithet Uncle Tom has become shorthand for the cowardly obsequiousness of a race traitor).[2] As one critic has rather dramatically declared, "The devil himself could have forged no shrewder weapon" to oppress African Americans than *Uncle Tom's Cabin*.[3]

So what exactly is the danger that Stowe's novel poses? Should *Uncle Tom's Cabin* be praised for ending slavery? Condemned for encouraging racism? This chapter on Harriet Beecher Stowe will focus primarily on how to understand the influence and importance of what Langston Hughes called "the most cussed and discussed book of its time," the novel commonly regarded as the most influential and important book ever written by a U.S. author. Although *Uncle Tom's Cabin*'s status as a significant "aesthetic" artifact has been uneven (some, such as Leo Tolstoy, have called it the greatest novel ever written, while others, such as James Baldwin, have asserted that it is "a very bad novel," a political tract disguised as an overwrought melodrama), its status as a monumental political achievement remains undisputed. Rather than try to determine whether *Uncle Tom's Cabin* was a catalyst for abolition or a vehicle for proliferating racial stereotypes, I want to suggest that Stowe's novel has been held responsible both for ending slavery and for enabling racism because it did do both. Stowe's novel authorized both abolitionism and racial stereotypes. The question is how to understand the relationship that Stowe establishes between racial essences and slavery.

Harriet Beecher Stowe was born in Litchfield, Connecticut, into one of the most remarkable families of the nineteenth-century United States, a family, it was said, who felt they were born to save the world. In 1832, her father, Lyman Beecher, one of the most famous Presbyterian ministers in New England, moved his family to Cincinnati, a free city bordering the slave state of Kentucky, when he was appointed the first president of Lane Theological Seminary, a school almost immediately embroiled in debates over slavery. All of Lyman Beecher's seven sons became ministers; Henry Ward indeed became a national figure – a celebrity preacher, social crusader, abolitionist, and, in 1875, a party in the most sensational scandal of the century when he was accused of committing adultery with a friend's wife (the Beecher-Tilton affair). Harriet's older sister, Catharine (one of six daughters from two marriages), would become a pioneer in the new field of home economics. Another sister, Isabella, became an important advocate of women's rights and the only member of the family to support Elizabeth Tilton's allegations against Henry Ward.

In 1836 Harriet married Calvin Ellis Stowe, a widower and Lane professor. Between 1836 and 1850, she gave birth to seven children and suffered at least two miscarriages. When not debilitated by her pregnancies or by the physical demands of her domestic obligations, Stowe wrote. She wrote, in part, to supplement Calvin's small income and, in part, because her deep religious faith inspired an intense sense of public duty. In 1850, the Stowes moved to Bowdoin College in Brunswick, Maine. It is there that she, outraged by the Fugitive Slave Law provision of the Compromise of 1850, composed *Uncle Tom's Cabin*. First serialized in the antislavery newspaper *The National Era* (1851–2) and then published by John P. Jewett & Company, a rather minor Boston publisher specializing in texts by the evangelical wing of Congregationalism, *Uncle Tom's Cabin* changed everything. Stowe began a long career as the most celebrated and often best paid writer in the United States.

Though Stowe has come to be thoroughly identified with *Uncle Tom's Cabin*, it is far from the only significant, controversial, or influential text she wrote. Stowe was a highly productive author, publishing more than thirty books and countless shorter pieces in a professional career spanning more than half a century, books as varied as geography primers, numerous historical romances of New England, a landmark handbook (coauthored with her sister Catharine) on "domestic science," biblical studies, travel narratives, as well as a controversial feminist defense of Lady Byron in which she accused Lord Byron of incest with his sister. Moreover, *Uncle Tom's Cabin* is neither Stowe's only nor her most radical novel against slavery.[4] It is, however, the text that has come to define her (without it she probably would be remembered primarily as a local colorist or religious writer), the work against which all her other work inevitably is read.

It is difficult to exaggerate the extraordinary immediate success of *Uncle Tom's Cabin*. Readership of the *National Era* jumped from 17,000 to 28,000 during the story's serialization. In the first week of its publication in book form, *Uncle Tom's Cabin* sold 10,000 copies; in its first year, it outsold the Bible, sales figures reaching 310,000 in the United States and more than one million in England, where the book was regularly pirated since it was not protected by international copyright law.[5] In that first year, total sales of *Uncle Tom's Cabin* are estimated at 2.5 million copies, making it the first megahit of modern publishing.[6] Indeed, the sales figures only hint at the number of readers, for at the time, books were understood as communal property, shared among families, read aloud in groups, and borrowed from lending libraries. One reviewer speculated that *Uncle Tom's Cabin* "has probably ten readers to every purchaser."[7] Its audience, moreover, was everyone; as Emerson averred, it was the "only book that found readers in the parlor, the nursery, and the kitchen in every house-hold." By 1854, the novel had been translated into thirty-seven languages, and it remains the world's second most translated book (behind only the Bible).

The novel's success, of course, was more than simply commercial. Many newspapers and journals in both North and South saw *Uncle Tom's Cabin* as a turning point in the mobilization of antislavery feeling in the North. A striking sign of the novel's unprecedented political impact is that it incited a veritable explosion of counternarratives. In 1852 alone, defenders of slavery published at least eight anti-*Tom* novels. Scholars have found thirty-four novels written before the Civil War in response to *Uncle Tom's Cabin* and the number keeps growing. *Uncle Tom's Cabin* established that literature would play a critical role in the political debate over U.S. slavery. Indeed, to a large extent the national debate over slavery became an argument over whether Stowe's account of the "peculiar institution" was accurate or the product of an uninformed and overly passionate imagination.[8] *Uncle Tom's Cabin* polarized the nation, helping transform slavery from a debatable political question into an absolute moral issue about which compromise was impossible.

Because it was immediately commercialized, *Uncle Tom's Cabin* gained a cultural power that exceeded its explicitly political and religious origins. The novel was mined for merchandise to a degree that George Lucas and J. K. Rowling might covet. Images from the novel – images that Stowe had no legal control over and would not profit from – quickly became ubiquitous, attached to any- and everything that could be sold: there were Uncle Tom poems, songs (most famously Stephen Foster's "My Old Kentucky Home, Good Night," originally called "Poor Uncle Tom, Good Night"), dioramas, figurines, candles, plates, mugs, busts, ash trays, wallpaper, handkerchiefs, embossed spoons, painted scarves, needlepoint, and innumerable games, including one in which players competed to reunite the families of separated slaves. There were Uncle Tom's Shrinkable Woolen Stockings, Uncle Tom's Improved Flageolets, Uncle Tom's Pure Unadulterated Coffee, and eventually even Uncle Tom's Spool Cotton. Many of these products, often depicting a caricatured and smiling Uncle Tom, continued to be produced well into the twentieth century, long after the novel's sales slowed considerably.

Many more people interacted with images and representations of the novel than read the novel itself. *Uncle Tom's Cabin* may have been the best-selling novel of the nineteenth century, but the primary way audiences came to know the story of Tom and Eva was through the innumerable theatrical productions based (however loosely) on Stowe's novel. As Henry James explained the phenomena, if other books were like fish swimming in water, *Uncle Tom's Cabin* was like a "wonderful leaping fish," and "one of the first things it did was thus to flutter down on every stage, literally without exception, in America and Europe." In these productions, Stowe's novel was "taken up and carried further, even violently to the furthest."[9]

Even before its serialization was complete, *Uncle Tom's Cabin* began to be adapted for the theater. Stowe herself initially refused to write or approve any dramatization because she suspected the morality of theater (she eventually did write *The Christian Slave* [1855], not a full staging of her novel but a one-woman performance written specifically for the African-American actress Mary Webb). Because copyright laws did not grant authors control over adaptations of their work, playwrights could tell the story in any way they wanted. Unauthorized theatrical productions multiplied quickly. What connected these quite diverse versions was that they organized their variety acts, sketches, and tableaux around a single story, something that U.S. audiences were not accustomed to at the time. These Tom Shows rapidly took on a life of their own, each attempting to exceed the other in melodrama and spectacular stagecraft. In one version, Eliza and her baby cross the Ohio River chased not only by bloodhounds (not in the novel) but by elephants and camels. These various productions increasingly departed from Stowe's novel (proslavery versions of Tom's story were often staged). After the Civil War, touring companies (known as "Tommers") began to spring up with exponential frequency. By 1870 there were fifty, by 1890 more than five hundred such companies were staging productions in countless cities and small towns, and these Tom Shows continued well into the 1940s. Historians estimate that fifty people saw a Tom Show for every reader of the novel.

It is these Tom Shows that have most often framed modern understandings of a novel as contributing to antiblack racism. These adaptations foregrounded minstrel conventions, exaggerated the farcical aspects of Stowe's novel, and often incorporated nostalgia for the plantation. These shows rewrote the abused child Topsy into a slapstick figure of song and dance and transformed Tom from a "broad-chested, powerfully-made man" who dies protecting fellow slaves into the shuffling and happily subservient old man of popular discourse. These Tom shows, Duke Ellington explained as he tried to stage a musical about African-American identity in 1941, "taught" the American audience "to expect a Negro on stage to clown and 'Uncle Tom.' That is, to enact the role of a servile, yet lovable, inferior." The task of an African-American artist, according to Ellington, was to "take Uncle Tom out of the theatre" and "bury" the Uncle Tom image "exploited by Hollywood and Broadway." It is, thus, imperative to distinguish Stowe's novel from the way her novel was altered as it moved into other media. Indeed, since Stowe neither authorized nor had legal means to regulate appropriations of her novel and its characters, one cannot hold Stowe responsible for the abject gray-haired Uncle Tom and the cartoonish Topsy figures created in the marketplace and by the theater.

To distinguish between the novel and its various incarnations, however, does not mean that we can immediately dismiss the charge that Stowe's novel created and perpetuated damaging stereotypes of African Americans.[10] We cannot so simply absolve Stowe because the book unmistakably is written in the idiom of racial essences. Stowe, for example, explains that Africans have "naturally fine voices" and an "indigenous talent" for cooking, that "the negro mind" is innately "impassioned and imaginative," and that there "is no more use in making believe be angry with a negro than with a child."[11] Africans are "ever yearning toward the simple and childlike" and "are not naturally daring and enterprising, but home-loving and affectionate," easily enchanted by bright colors and ornate displays because they possess "a passion for all that is splendid, rich, and fanciful" (93, 205, 161).

Indicting Stowe for antiblack stereotypes may not be false, but it is incomplete. This charge leaves unexamined the particular way that Stowe deploys the notion of racial essences. It neglects how Stowe most persuasively argues against slavery by arguing for a particular account of the Negro's nature: the Negro, according to Stowe, is the ideal Christian precisely because of the way that the race is biologically constituted. Negroes, as Tom most clearly demonstrates, have "a natural genius for religion"; "in their gentleness, their lowly docility of heart, their aptitude to repose on a superior mind and rest on a higher power, their child-like simplicity of affection and facility of forgiveness ... they will exhibit the highest form of the peculiarly *Christian life*" (*UTC*, 183, 178, original emphasis). According to Stowe, the "principle of reliance and unquestioning faith," "the foundation" of Christianity," is "more a native element" in the African race (*UTC*, 393). Of "all races of the earth," Stowe repeatedly tells her readers, "none have received the Gospel with such eager docility" (*UTC*, 449). And as she elaborates in *The Key to Uncle Tom's Cabin* (1854), "the divine graces of love and faith, when in-breathed by the Holy Spirit, find in [the Negro's] natural temperament a more congenial atmosphere" (41).

The Negro's inherent affinity with Christian submission is what marks Negro slavery as particularly unconscionable, according to Stowe. Although chattel slavery is an intrinsically blasphemous institution because it grants human beings an absolute and "wholly irresponsible power" that only God is worthy of holding, this blasphemy becomes even more unforgivable when, as is the case with U.S. slavery, it takes as its subject a race born with a wonderfully docile and pious nature. A horrific parody of Christian worship, slavery perverts a Negro's natural subservience, twisting the race's intrinsically devotional spirit by putting profane masters in the place of God. The fundamental idolatry of the slave system is made most explicit in the slave owner Simon Legree. Legree sees himself as a rival to the Almighty, telling Tom, for example, "I am your church now." Tom emphasizes the profanity of Legree's claim that he owns Tom "body and soul," declaring "No! no! no! my soul ain't yours, Mas'r! You haven't bought it, – ye can't buy it! It's been bought and paid for by One that is able to keep it" (356).

The genius of Stowe's argument against U.S. slavery is that she does not challenge the idea that the African is uniquely suited to be a slave; rather she rewrites such bondage as the defining quality of the true Christian, as a divine rather than degraded condition. Stowe shifts the burden of the slavery problem onto the masters. Rather than attacking the idea of racial essences, she contrasts the racial essence of the Anglo-Saxon to that of the Negro. If the African race is naturally religious, the "hard and dominant Anglo Saxon race," Stowe announces at the beginning of the novel, is distinguished by an "instinct" for cold, abstract logic, an instinct that is simultaneously opposed to the spirit of Christianity and the spirit of the African race (*UTC*, xvii). The Anglo-Saxon, unlike the Negro, has to work to be Christian. If not moderated by Christianity, the Anglo-Saxon, being "a more coldly and strictly logical race," will, Stowe explains, produce things like the American slave code, a set of laws that "*coolly* classes" human beings with "bundles, and bales, and boxes" (*UTC*, 128). Indeed, U.S. slavery is "more atrocious than any ever before exhibited under the sun" precisely because the Anglo-Saxon race innately possesses the "unflinching courage to ... work out an accursed principle, with mathematical accuracy, to its most accursed result."

The Christic lexicon that Stowe establishes culminates in the apocalyptic warning concluding the novel. There are signs that the Day of Judgment (what Stowe calls the "last convulsion") looms near, and if the United States continues to mock divine authority by sanctioning the absolute authority of the slave master, such "injustice and cruelty," the closing words of the novel declare, "shall bring on nations the wrath of Almighty God!" (*UTC*, 511). It is within this apocalyptic logic that one must understand the novel's endorsement of colonization – an endorsement that Stowe herself realized could be misunderstood as an endorsement of the American Colonization Society and thus soon repudiated.[12] Stowe sends off her surviving black characters to Africa not because she scorns them as fellow citizens, but because she values them as ideal Christian missionaries. These Christianized Africans will formally convert Africans so that Africa can finally take its place as God's favored land. As Stowe explains, God "hath chosen" to make "poor Africa" the "highest and noblest in that kingdom which he will set up, when every other kingdom has been tried and failed" (*UTC*, 204). The novel's Negroes are not exiled to make the United States white but sent to Africa to prepare for "the kingdom of Christ" that is about to "come on earth" (*UTC*, 451). Colonization is not Stowe's solution to this nation's slavery problem but a consequence of it: the United States, no longer God's covenantal nation, now faces imminent divine retribution.

One, in short, cannot deny that Stowe passionately promotes racial essentialism, however, at the same time, one does not necessarily need to condemn or apologize for this fact. There is little question that Stowe's text certainly helps install and perpetuate the notion that there are distinct races; for example, its catalog of successful Negroes specifies the percentage of "Blackness" each possesses, thereby treating black and white "blood" as absolute and quantifiable biological substances that never actually mix. But it is precisely because one cannot understand Stowe's representation of the submissive Negro as marginal, as something that simply can be segregated from the novel's foundational antislavery argument, that Stowe's commitment to racial essences should not simply be written off as racist. To axiomatically assert that Stowe's racial theory is racist too quickly conflates racialism (the belief that distinct races exist) with racism (a pernicious social hierarchy based on racial differences), too quickly discounts the extent to which Stowe's moral censure of slavery depends upon racial essentialism. Such a charge fails to appreciate how Stowe's representation of Negro identity effectively undercuts the most powerful defense of slavery: the belief that the Negro is uniquely constituted and born to be a slave. Any reflexive denunciation of Stowe as a racist ultimately assumes that all instances of racial essentialism (whether, for example, Stowe's or Thomas Dixon's) are equally destructive, thereby collapsing any and every instance of racialism into ahistorically equivalent instances of racism.

That we continue to be uncomfortable with Stowe's representation of "the Negro" is, of course, understandable; it is a symptom of how difficult it is for modern readers to recover the religious framework that organized her argument (for example, we often treat her claim that *Uncle Tom's Cabin* was written by God as merely rhetorical). And such discomfort recognizes that in the current historical context the attribution of racial essences probably would work to authorize invidious social hierarchies. But there is another reason that we remain troubled by the way that *Uncle Tom's Cabin* champions immediate abolition as it simultaneously disseminates notions of essential racial difference: we imagine that the discourse of slavery and the discourse of race are distinct (albeit logically connected) arguments. Any discussion of Stowe's account of race and slavery as paradoxical or contradictory, after all, is premised on the assumption that slavery and race are discrete social formations. One wonders, however, whether one of the lessons of *Uncle Tom's Cabin* is that race and slavery, at least during the antebellum period, were indivisible, mutually sustaining terms, not independent concepts. If such is the case, then we must reconsider our confidence that we know what *race* truly is. Indeed, it is perhaps because we have so thoroughly absorbed Stowe's certainty that slavery is this nation's original sin that we tend to forget that Stowe was speaking to a radically different historical moment, one in which slavery and race might have been imagined in fundamentally different ways. That *Uncle Tom's Cabin* still provokes us to ask basic questions about race and slavery perhaps best demonstrates why it still deserves to be called "the Great American Novel."[13]

## FURTHER READING

Baldwin, James, *Notes of a Native Son*, Boston, Beacon Press, 1955, rpt., 1984.

Berlant, Lauren, *The Female Complaint: The Unfinished Business of Sentimentality in American Culture*, Durham, N.C., Duke University Press, 2008.

Best, Stephen Michael, *The Fugitive's Properties: Law and the Poetics of Possession*, Chicago, University of Chicago Press, 2004.

Brown, Gillian, *Domestic Individualism: Imagining Self in Nineteenth Century America*, Berkeley, University of California Press, 1990.

Douglas, Ann, *The Feminization of American Culture*, New York, Alfred A. Knopf, 1977.

Fisher, Philip, *Hard Facts: Setting and Form in the American Novel*, New York, Oxford University Press, 1985.

Gossett, Thomas, *Uncle Tom's Cabin and American Culture*, Dallas, Southern Methodist University Press, 1985.

Hedrick, Joan D., *Harriet Beecher Stowe: A Life*, New York, Oxford University Press, 1994.

Meer, Sarah, *Uncle Tom Mania: Slavery, Minstrelsy, and Transatlantic Culture in the 1850s*, Athens, University of Georgia Press, 2005.

Pelletier, Kevin, *Apocalyptic Sentimentalism: Love and Fear in U.S. Antebellum Literature*, Athens, University of Georgia Press, forthcoming.

Railton, Stephen, director, *Uncle Tom's Cabin and American Culture: A Multi-Media Archive*, University of Virginia, www.iath.virginia.edu/utc.

Reynolds, David S., *Mightier than the Sword: Uncle Tom's Cabin and the Battle for America*, New York, Norton, 2011.

Riss, Arthur, *Race, Slavery, and Liberalism in Nineteenth-Century American Literature*, New York, Cambridge University Press, 2006.

Tompkins, Jane, *Sensational Designs: The Cultural Work of American Fiction, 1790–1860*, New York, Oxford University Press, 1985.

Weinstein, Cindy, ed., *The Cambridge Companion to Harriet Beecher Stowe*, New York, Cambridge University Press, 2004.

Williiams, Linda, *Playing the Race Card: Melodramas of Black and White from Uncle Tom to O. J. Simpson*, Princeton, N.J., Princeton University Press, 2001.

## NOTES

1 Richard Blondo, "Samuel Green: A Black Life in Antebellum Maryland," MA thesis, University of Maryland (1988).

2 It has become obligatory to relate this anecdote, but the only sources confirming it were written after Stowe's death by family (Charles Edward Stowe's revised version of his biography of his mother, written with his son Lyman Beecher Stowe) and by friends (Annie Field's "Days with Mrs. Stowe"). The difficulty establishing a reliable source, however, is not the only reason to suspect this remark. When Stowe met Lincoln in December 1862, the Emancipation Proclamation was not yet signed (the Preliminary Emancipation Proclamation was announced on September 22) and thus it was not yet clear that the War would be understood as a war against slavery. Indeed, Stowe sought to meet Lincoln to urge him to officially issue the Emancipation Proclamation.

3  J. C. Furnas, *Goodbye to Uncle Tom* (New York: William Sloane, 1956), p. 50.

4  *Dred: A Tale of the Great Dismal Swamp* (1856) is a radically apocalyptic vision of potential slave violence written during the brutal battles between Free Soilers and pro-slavery forces in the Kansas-Nebraska territories.

5  At the time, a book only had the protections of international copyright law if it was published in England before the United States.

6  Claire Parfait, *The Publishing History of Uncle Tom's Cabin, 1852–2002* (Burlington, Vt.: Ashgate, 2007).

7  "The Uncle Tom Epidemic," *The Literary World* (4 December 1852): 355.

8  The novel's centrality in debates over the slave question incited Stowe to publish *A Key to Uncle Tom's Cabin* (1853), a nonfiction compendium of the factual sources for the novel's major characters and events.

9  Henry James, *A Small Boy and Others* (New York: Charles Scribners Sons, 1913), pp. 159–60.

10 In Robert Alexander's play *I ain't yo' uncle: the new Jack revisionist 'Uncle Tom's Cabin'* (1990/1995) Stowe's characters put Stowe on trial for "perpetuating negative stereotypes" and for "failing to 'get their story right'."

11 Harriet Beecher Stowe, *Uncle Tom's Cabin; or Life among the Lowly* (1852), ed. Alfred Kazin (New York: Bantam, 1981), pp. 32, 234, 83. All further references to this edition will be cited parenthetically in the text.

12 In the May 1853 minutes of the American and Foreign Anti-Slavery Society, Dr. Leonard Bacon, a close friend of Stowe, states that Stowe told him that if "she were to write *Uncle Tom's Cabin* again, she would not send George Harris to Liberia." In *Dred* no characters go to Liberia, and the African-American characters form interracial communities in New York and Canada.

13 The Reconstruction novelist John William De Forest coined this term and first applied it to *Uncle Tom's Cabin*. See De Forest, "The Great American Novel," *The Nation* 6 (January 9, 1868), pp. 27–29.

# 5

# Mark Twain

PETER MESSENT

Mark Twain (1835–1910) first made an impact on the American literary scene with "The Jumping Frog of Calaveras County," published in 1865, the year the Civil War ended. The dates are not just coincidental, for sectional animosity among its readers could be put aside in this comic story of the American frontier, written by an adopted westerner in a distinctively "American" style. As soon as Simon Wheeler starts to speak, any idea of a standardized national "literary" language crafted according to a model of eastern cultural propriety effectively falls away. Wheeler's opening statement, "There was a feller here once by the name of Jim Smiley, in the winter of '49 – or may be it was the spring of '50 – I don't recollect exactly, somehow" (*JF*, 9), is the first step in a literary journey that leads straight to *Adventures of Huckleberry Finn* (1884) – "You don't know about me, without you have read a book by the name of 'The Adventures of Tom Sawyer,' but that ain't no matter," (*HF*, 17) – and from there to Salinger's *The Catcher in the Rye* (1951) and Russell Banks's *Rule of the Bone* (1995).

Hemingway's pronouncement that "all modern American literature comes from one book by Mark Twain called Huckleberry Finn" may be both overquoted and exaggerated, but the novel stands nonetheless as a crucial intervention in the nation's literary history.[1] The radical impact of Twain's use of the vernacular as he gives Huck, his ill-educated and disreputable first-person narrator, control of his novel cannot be underestimated. The American vernacular had of course seen literary use before the "Jumping Frog" story. But Twain's avoidance of the phonetic techniques of other humorists and remarkable ability to represent vernacular (and, in *Adventures of Huckleberry Finn*, African-American) speech in a way that was readily accessible and comprehensible to a national and international English-speaking audience make his work distinctive. Indeed, from the start of his career, Twain was able to cross regional and national barriers with ease, so much so that his early popularity in England rivaled that in America.

Perhaps no American author, before or since, has held such transatlantic and transnational appeal.

Twain's humor is at the very center of writing. "The Jumping Frog" is a brilliantly constructed tale built around the hoax. The genteel and educated frame narrator is hoaxed first by Artemus Ward, who has apparently suggested the call on Wheeler, and then (possibly) by Wheeler himself – who is either a naive simpleton or a skillful trickster deliberately frustrating the (presumably eastern) first narrator by means of his long-winded, digressive, and absurdist anecdotes. Jim Smiley, the gambler, is hoaxed by the stranger, who fills Dan'l Webster, his jumping frog, with quail shot. Finally, the reader is hoaxed by Twain as s/he looks for some proper conclusion to the first narrator's encounter with Wheeler, and some final point both to Wheeler's stories and to the wider narrative. In a text circling around motifs of trickery, unexpected reversal, misplaced trust, community and the insiders and outsiders that compose it, the reader is shuttled among interpretive positions, left only with the sense of comic indeterminacy that Twain (no doubt) intended.

But it is perhaps the comic touches built around the attribution of human characteristics to the animals in Wheeler's tales that have guaranteed the story's continuing vitality. So the fighting bull-pup Andrew Jackson, for example, beats his opponents by seizing them by the joint of the back leg and "freez[ing] to it ... till they threw up the sponge." On coming across a dog, though, whose hind legs had "been sawed off by a circular saw":

> he come to make a snatch for his pet holt, [and] he saw in a minute how he'd been imposed on, ... and then he looked sorter discouraged-like.... He give Smiley a look, as much to say his heart was broke, and it was his fault, for putting up a dog that hadn't no hind legs for him to take holt of, ... and then he limped off a piece and laid down and died. (*JF*, 13)

Twain's comic repertoire was extensive. He delighted in the visually grotesque humor of the American frontier – see, for brief example, Miss Wagner and her borrowed and ill-fitting glass eye in *Roughing It* (1872; 385–6). He was, too, a sharply honed satirist. So Huck Finn describes the Shepherdsons and Grangerfords taking "their guns along to church" shortly before Buck is killed as part of the families' long-standing feud, and adds: "It was pretty ornery preaching – all about brotherly love, and such-like tiresomeness; but everybody said it was a good sermon" (*HF*, 148). He ranged through burlesque, ludicrous exaggeration, and black humor to biting irony: "There are many humorous things in the world; among them the white man's notion that he is less savage than the other savages" (*FE*, 213). He was also a master of the aphorism and the casual witticism. His May 1897 reply to a

London newspaper man on rumors of his demise, that "the reports of my death have been greatly exaggerated," is still commonly recalled more than a century on.[2] Twain was also a highly successful lecturer, best known for his drawling and deadpan manner and highly effective use of the comic pause. There are very few who have matched him before or since for sheer comic brilliance.

Twain's range and influence as a writer, across genres, were also quite extraordinary. His first book-length commercial success was the travel narrative *The Innocents Abroad* (1869), where he more or less defined the comedy inherent in the cultural clash between New and Old World. Extending his previous use of the "Mark Twain" persona – a constructed and often humorously naïve comic figure, but one who shares at times the opinions and values of the author, Samuel L. Clemens – Twain opens up the Old World to freshly independent and clear-sighted inspection, to "suggest to the reader how he would be likely to see Europe and the East if he looked at them with his own eyes instead of the eyes of those who travelled in those countries before him" (*IA*, preface). The book's early predominant note is of a comic irreverence toward Europe's "courtly muses": Twain prefers copies of Da Vinci's *The Last Supper* to the original (*IA*, 191), and when he and "the boys" are shown a "magnificent bust" of "ze great Christopher Columbo," they undermine any assumption of awe or cultural respect through deadpan – "Christopher Columbo – pleasant name – is – is he dead?" (*IA*, 292). Such respect is partly replaced, too, by criticism of the material squalor he finds in Europe, malodorousness (Italians and their "garlic-exterminating mouth[s]," *IA*, 184) and religious and political backwardness.

But this is only one side of a more complex picture. For the more we read, the more such assumptions of confident superiority are undermined. The author is clearly aware of the often-blinkered and bigoted attitude of his narrator and holds it at an ironic remove. So, too, the "pilgrims" who compose the majority among these Americans abroad are pilloried for their mean-mindedness, self-righteousness, and hypocrisy. And respect and reverence for Old World culture constantly vie with the protagonist's bumptious iconoclasm. As so often in Twain's work, there is a relativistic and ambivalent stance toward his materials that refuses the black-and-white comparisons that may at first appear to be the case.

What is perhaps most interesting about *The Innocents Abroad*, though, and sets the pattern for the travel books that follow is the way Twain refashions the genre, and in a profoundly influential way. W. D. Howells, the most respected American literary figure of his time, wrote of his close friend's literary methods that "he was not enslaved to the consecutiveness in writing which the rest of us try to keep chained to.... [H]e wrote as he thought,

... without sequence, without an eye to what went before or should come after. If something beyond or beside what he was saying occurred to him, he invited it into his page."[3] If this is an exaggeration, it captures something of the essence of the travel books where Twain uses his first-person protagonist (himself, often recast as quasi-fictional comic persona) as the hook on which to hang his narrative – one that wanders in an apparently improvised way from topic to topic: through description, present thought and experience, past memory, reported dialogue, related anecdote, guidebook information, and the like. He links these various moves through what Richard Bridgman calls "mechanisms of association," one topic providing a trigger (a thought, word, or image) that calls up its – often unexpected – successor.[4] The travel journey itself provides the book's loose ongoing structure. And much of the spark and sporadic brilliance of Twain's narratives lies in exactly this alternating focus, with fluid boundaries between the performing subject and the objects of his attention, between fictional invention and nonfictional reportage. Twain anticipated what Tom Wolfe would, in 1973, call "New Journalism" and provided a model of the greatest importance for the future of the travel writing genre.

Twain's impact on American literary history goes far beyond this, though. In his first novel, *The Adventures of Tom Sawyer* (1876), he wrote what would become one of America's defining boyhood texts and one that has had a profound impact on the whole national psyche, as the long-established presence and popularity of "Tom Sawyer Island" at Disneyland suggests. The official Walt Disney World Web site welcomes its visitor thus: "Sitting alongside the Rivers of America on the porch of Aunt Polly's Dockside Inn, sipping on a glass of lemonade, you can soak up a real glimpse of the idyllic world of yesteryear that Mark Twain and Walt Disney loved."[5] Twain's novel – like Disney's representation of its world – appeals to children and to adults. Its setting, the village of St. Petersburg in the 1830s or 1840s (a close approximation of Twain's own boyhood Hannibal, Missouri) provides a step backward from post-Civil War America, and the massive changes and anxieties then associated with the fast-modernizing country – anxieties that have only increased in the time since. This step back, to boyhood and to a tight-knit and apparently premodern rural community – with the "Delectable Land [of Cardiff Hill], dreamy, reposeful, and inviting" (*TS*, 26), and the similarly utopia-charged Jackson's Island, just beyond – explains much of the book's appeal. But the ambiguities and contradictions of the text – as Twain contrasts childhood play, boyhood "pure freedom" (*TS*, 28), personal charisma, and romantic individualism with conformity, domesticity, discipline, capitalist achievement, and model citizenship – also root the book firmly back in the time of Twain's writing and the pressures and problems already then apparent (and indeed already emerging in an antebellum world). The famous whitewashed fence is the symbolic barrier separating the extremes of these two realms of romantic adventure and disciplined conformity, realms that Tom Sawyer, significantly, agilely crosses more or less at will.

But another character, curiously twinned with Tom, also bridges these worlds – the cruel and violent "murderin' half-breed" (*TS*, 89), Indian Joe. Utopian escapism meets its nightmare opposite in this gothic figure. Freedom from social restraint, Twain suggests, has two sides to it. And whitewashing takes on a metaphoric connotation as Joe's renegade savagery, racial difference, and physical and sexual threat are eventually obliterated through the actions of Judge Thatcher, the representative of community law and order – who (unintentionally) imprisons Joe in the underground and labyrinthine McDougal's cave and so condemns him to death. Just as this book more or less ignores antebellum slavery, so the whitewash here lies in the consignment of all that is truly antisocial in the novel to this figure of the racial and moral "other," for Tom's own actions are always recuperable and he ends up a community hero. There are many evasions and compromises in the book, nowhere more so than in its "hero," the initially subversive figure who ends up as the traditional American success story – with a "simply prodigious" income and planned attendance at the "best law school in the country" (*TS*, 269). Twain has his cake and eats it, and so does his audience, as the gap is closed between antebellum past and postbellum present, boyhood rebellion and domestic and community belonging, iconoclastic individualism and deep conformity. Twain could half-see this – thus his decision not to take Tom Sawyer any further as a main protagonist. But it is in its very fudging of such issues, its failure to resolve deep ideological contradictions, that the book achieves its memorable success. The reading of Twain's book and all the lemonade sipping in the world cannot, however, remake the past as an idyll; cannot divorce it from the pressures and problems of the present. Both worlds are, in fact, symbiotically codependent.

So much of Twain's work has had profound literary and cultural impact that selective commentary fails to do it justice. But a number of texts must at least be mentioned. With *A Connecticut Yankee in King Arthur's Court* (1889), Twain turned in the direction of time travel and fantasy, relocating his nineteenth-century Yankee protagonist, Hank Morgan, in sixth-century Arthurian England. Twain would become an insistent opponent of Western imperialism later in his life and, here, what seems initially to be a straightforward celebration of modern American civilization in fact anticipates later reservations about its expanding scope and influence. Hank is "head superintendent" of "the great arms factory" (the Colt Firearms Manufactory) in Hartford, Connecticut, and his reference to the making of ' "guns, revolvers, cannon, ... all sorts of labor-saving machinery" (CY, 20) strikes an early ironic, and threatening, note. Twain milks considerable humor from the contrasts between the (apparently) "progressive" and primitive worlds that Morgan traverses. But as the book continues – and in a move typical of the author – the reader is left increasingly uncertain about their relative value. Hank's vulgar materialism and opportunistic enterprise appear in an increasingly negative light, and in the Battle of the Sand Belt that (almost) ends the book, his technological expertise produces only mass slaughter – with Gatling guns, dynamite torpedoes, and electric fences destroying the army of twenty-five thousand men facing him. Hank, finally transported back to his modern world, ends up mourning his premodern "lost land" (CY, 26). And Twain questions conventional Victorian beliefs in progressive evolution in a novel that takes us from dark ages to dark ages and ends in battle scenes anticipating the slaughter of 1914–18. This is a book that veers from comedy to tragedy and, despite its unevenness in tone and focus, has powerfully influenced the American (and Western) imagination.

*Pudd'nhead Wilson* (1894) is a much sparer novel than *Connecticut Yankee* and relies on plot and irony rather than character development for its effect. Twinned themes of race and slavery – subjects that permeate Twain's writings – dominate the book. The apparently idyllic landscape of Dawson's Landing is subverted by its status as a "slaveholding town" (*PW*, 20) and the miscegenation, owning of human property, destruction of family relationships, and dehumanization this entails (Percy Driscoll was "a fairly humane man toward slaves and other animals," *PW*, 35). Much of the seriousness of the novel, as is so often the case with Twain, is masked by its humor. Twain, though, launches a sharp attack here on conventional assumptions about what we might call deep subjectivity, our claims to unique character and identity. For when two individuals, Tom and Valet, are swapped at birth and each adapts to his new socially and racially defined role, the one in effect becomes the other, with no way of distinguishing between them apart from their fingerprints (for this is a type of detective novel too). But even more searing is his critique of racial essentialism, where the very idea of a (southern) social reality based on a firmly defined base of racial difference is hollowed out. Fixed racial identity is shown to be a lie in an America where the slaves Roxy and Tom are just as white (in terms of skin color) as any member of the ruling racial group, defined as "black" simply by fiat of southern legal codes. When Twain writes that Tom is "by fiction of law and custom a negro" (*PW*, 33) – a result of the one-thirty-second part of him that is "black" – he exposes the label ("blackness") that defines racial inferiority in the South as entirely artificial, a constructed category that bears no relation to actual human difference, nor (necessarily) to the color of one's skin. However masked by its fictional form, such an understanding acted as powerful resistance to the prevalent racial assumptions of the time. And Susan Gillman's comment is well earned: "Of the major US authors of the late nineteenth century, none is more identified with the struggle to claim the national memory of slavery than Mark Twain."[6]

As Twain's literary and cultural reception has changed over time, so – in recent years – there has been a surge of interest in Twain's late works, and particularly in *Following the Equator* (1896), *The Mysterious Stranger* manuscripts (1890–1910), and the *Autobiography* (1906–7). *Following the Equator* is more serious than Twain's other travel books, with race, colonialism, and imperialism as the linked subjects binding the book together. The best of *The Mysterious Stranger* manuscripts work by way of rapid and defamiliarizing moves through both time and (transnational) space. Thus in *No. 44, The Mysterious Stranger*, No. 44 manipulates both elements as he conveys August, the young narrator, (in time) from "Adam's predecessors" and the "Missing Link" to Twain's own present-day world, and (in space) from Austria, America, and China, to "the starred and shoreless expanses of the universe" (*MS*, 403, 332). Such moves stand as an almost-allegorical illustration of the range and comparative nature of Twain's own expanding and expansive artistic imagination at his career end. The first of three volumes of the definitive version of Twain's *Autobiography* has only just been published, following a number of earlier partial versions. Twain here rewrote the rule book for the genre, anticipating postmodernist challenges to coherent linear narrative and centered subjectivity. Ranging to and fro across his life, and following the dictates of the mental associations accordingly made, Twain eschews chronological sequence and discursive uniformity to move at will between personal reminiscence and public history, using travel notes, literary fragments, biographical jottings, and social, philosophical, and political commentary in an unpredictable and "freewheeling spoken narrative" (for the work was a dictated one) of quite extraordinary interest.[7]

I leave Twain's most significant and contentious work, *Adventures of Huckleberry Finn* (1885), till last. This is his best-known and most influential book by far. Its cultural resonance lies in a number of complex factors: partly in its use of a vernacular narration – that of a socially powerless boy who contains and represents within his story all the other (and with the exception of Jim) more powerful voices of this southern world; partly in its thematic focus on race and color (then, and still, the most fraught issues in American social life). The book's effect is rooted, too, in the pairing of its two social outcasts (ill-educated boy and escaped slave) and its contrasts between moral integrity, silence, and solitude (Huck alone in nature; Huck ready to "light out for the Territory ahead of the rest," *HF*, 366) and the shams, hypocrisies, and pressures of the surrounding social world. But there is much more to the novel than this.

The book has – as with any text of lasting cultural value – been interpreted differently over the years. Critics still argue over the structural and thematic success or failure of its final "evasion" sequence. But this is generally now historicized in terms of the racial conditions of the period in which Twain wrote. Thus Tom's complicity in Jim's imprisonment as an escaped slave (despite his knowledge that Jim has in fact been freed) and the indignity and torment he has Jim suffer as he looks to "free" him all over again are seen as the mirror of a historical situation where the Emancipation Proclamation and the positive changes in African-American lives that followed had been effectively disabled in the webs of renewed oppression (economic, political, and social) of the post-Reconstruction years. As Shelley Fisher Fishkin comments: "Scholars are increasingly coming to understand the evasion as a satire on the way the United States botched the enterprise of freeing its slaves."[8] We must, however, step tentatively here, for – as so often with Twain – serious social and political meanings remain oblique and opaque, concealed behind a (mainly) comic surface.

The novel, though, has recently been subject to as much negative critique as praise. Jonathan Arac in particular, in 1997, challenged its status as a national literary icon, seeing it as overvalued and "hypercanonized," awarded a kind of "idolatry" or literary sainthood – one of those "very few individual works [that] monopolize [an undeserved] curricular and critical attention."[9] Both white and African-American readers and critics, too, have expressed discomfort with the number of times the racially abusive term "nigger" appears in the book. The fact that Twain uses the term ironically to highlight its failure to measure Jim's human value and identity has been outweighed here by the massively negative connotations of the very appearance of the word itself.

I would accept Arac's contention that this one book has been asked to bear more cultural and national weight than any one book can, both as the epitome of American ideological value (with Huck's presumed ability to find a personal integrity and "freedom" in the face of a constricting society) and as distinctive literary form. But I would nonetheless argue that we cannot discount the evidence of the novel's 20 million plus (past and present) readers: that the text has been – and will remain – of great literary and cultural importance, as long as it continues to engage its national and international audience so deeply. And perhaps – though I tread warily here – such a constant and widespread readership suggests that there is something about the oppositions that structure the novel (black and white, instinct and impulse versus social belonging and learned language, river and shore and raft versus permanent "home," civilization and wilderness, childhood and adulthood, male and female, slavery and freedom), and the very instabilities they reveal, that taps into a common ground that goes far beyond the audiences and historical conditions of Twain's own period. We might perhaps start to explain this in the context of that rapid modernization occurring as he wrote – that profound change in social conditions that established some of the basic ongoing anxieties and problems of the modern and postmodern age. Thus we can see within the novel an awareness of the problematic nature of individual agency and moral autonomy, increasingly apparent in a period of increasing reification and monadization, and in a society where forms of economic and social control were became ever more pressing. We can see too that the novel's celebration of space for the libidinal body and its expressive freedoms counters a historical situation where these were increasingly compromised. The desire for interracial community, too, linked in the novel to such threatened or vanishing "freedoms," stands as a utopian counter to the stratified social and racial forms of late nineteenth-century America, stratifications that existed before Twain wrote and still exist today. But whatever the reason for *Huckleberry Finn*'s hold on the national imaginary, and its international popularity, it is unlikely – and even despite the refashioning of approaches to American literature of recent years and the criticism that the book has faced – that its importance and influence will be very much diminished any time soon. Toni Morrison's description of the novel as "an amazing, troubling book," her praise for its "language cut for its renegade tongue and sharp intelligence," and her judgment of it as a work of "classic literature, which is to say it heaves, manifests and lasts," seem likely to hold its ground for some time yet to come.[10]

## FURTHER READING

Budd, Louis J. and Messent, Peter (eds.), *A Companion to Mark Twain*, Oxford, Blackwell, 2005.

Camfield, Gregg, *The Oxford Companion to Mark Twain*, New York, Oxford University Press, 2003.

Fishkin, Shelley Fisher (ed.), *A Historical Guide to Mark Twain*, New York, Oxford University Press, 2002.

Messent, Peter, *Mark Twain and Male Friendship*, New York, Oxford University Press, 2009.

Michelson, Bruce, *Mark Twain on the Loose: A Comic Writer and the American Self*, Amherst: University of Massachusetts Press, 1995.

Powers, Ron, *Mark Twain: A Life*, New York, Simon & Schuster, 2005.

Robinson, Forrest, *The Cambridge Companion to Mark Twain*, Cambridge, Cambridge University Press, 1995.

Scharnhorst, Gary, *Mark Twain: The Complete Interviews*, Tuscaloosa, University of Alabama Press, 2006.

## NOTES

1 Ernest Hemingway, *Green Hills of Africa* (1935) (New York, Scribner's, 1963), p. 22.
2 His exact initial words were "The report of my death was an exaggeration," but as they were retold and refined so they took this form.
3 William Dean Howells, *My Mark Twain: Reminiscences and Criticisms* (New York, Harper, 1910), p. 17.
4 Richard Bridgman, *Traveling in Mark Twain* (Berkeley, University of California Press, 1987), p. 9.
5 http://disneyworld.disney.go.com/parks/magic-kingdom/attractions/tom-sawyer-island/ (accessed 10 November 2010). Here and elsewhere, arguments in this essay appear in expanded form in Peter Messent, *Mark Twain* (Basingstoke, Macmillan, 1997) and *The Cambridge Introduction to Mark Twain* (Cambridge, Cambridge University Press, 2007).
6 Susan Gillman, "Is He Dead?" *Times Literary Supplement*, 4 June 2010. To say this is to remain aware of the troubling sense of paradox and inconsistency that seems to inhabit the racial (and identity) politics of this text. I address this issue in Messent 1997 and Messent 2007.
7 Harriet Elinor Smith, "Introduction" to the *Autobiography of Mark Twain: Volume 1* (Berkeley, University of California Press, 2010).
8 Shelley Fisher Fishkin, *Was Huck Black? Mark Twain and African-American Voices* (New York, Oxford University Press, 1993).
9 Jonathan Arac, *Huckleberry Finn as Idol and Target: The Function of Criticism in Our Time* (Madison, University of Wisconsin Press, 1997), pp. 11 and 133.
10 Toni Morrison, "Introduction" to Mark Twain, *Adventures of Huckleberry Finn*, Oxford Mark Twain, New York, Oxford University Press, 1996), pp. xxxi, xli.

# 6

# Henry James

THOMAS J. OTTEN

Shortly after the Civil War, when Henry James (1843–1916) began publishing fiction, the endings of American novels changed. Whereas William Hill Brown's *The Power of Sympathy* (1789), Susanna Rowson's *Charlotte Temple* (1791), Hannah Webster Foster's *The Coquette* (1797), Catharine Maria Sedgwick's *A New-England Tale* (1822), James Fenimore Cooper's *The Pioneers* (1823), Nathaniel Hawthorne's *The Scarlet Letter* (1850), and Harriet Beecher Stowe's *Uncle Tom's Cabin* (1852) all end with tombstones, James's *The Portrait of a Lady* (1880–1), William Dean Howells's *The Rise of Silas Lapham* (1885), and Abraham Cahan's *Yekl* (1896) and *The Imported Bridegroom* (1898) end with troubled marriages. This shift from public memorial to the dynamics of a largely private relation between persons is not absolute, of course, and it is hard to make the immensely varied body of late nineteenth-century fiction fit any pattern at all. Nevertheless, it seems that a formula that once shaped fiction with extraordinary consistency has broken down and the sense of an ending has changed. In turn, a new sense of the novel emerges, one that Henry James, more than any other writer, brought into being.

At the close of *Charlotte Temple*, Charlotte's father gestures toward her tomb as he addresses her seducer: "Look on that little heap of earth…. Look at it often, and may thy heart feel such true sorrow as shall merit the mercy of heaven."[1] The tomb – here only a mound of earth, since Charlotte has just been buried – creates a public monument out of a personal story; as tombstones so often do in early American novels, this grave has the effect of pulling outward and making legible a private story that nevertheless requires interpretation. Novels that graphically reproduce epitaphic inscriptions on the page – *The Coquette*, *The Scarlet Letter* – make out of their characters' lives a text literally open to all; these figures pass on to the reader the task of interpreting, reflecting on, and remembering. Like the "brighter period" when "a new truth would be revealed" that Hester foresees at the end of *The Scarlet Letter*, or like the antislavery resolution that George Shelby makes at Uncle Tom's grave in Stowe's novel, or like the grave of Chingachgook in *The Pioneers* – with a misspelling that needs to be corrected and so a suggestion that the Native American legacy is left unresolved – all these novels end with monuments to the nation's unfinished business: the reader's subjective response to the text is entwined with matters of national identity, an identity that comes into being *through* the reader's imagination, as Benedict Anderson has argued.[2]

Henry James will write this plot just once, toward the beginning of his career, in *Daisy Miller* (1878); adopting the pattern of classic American fiction of the preceding generations, he will also in this novella empty that plot of its customary significances. Daisy's endless energy for amusements, for the company of "gentlemen friends," for "going round" in a social whirl, fails to conform to the code of modesty – and to the dictates of the courtship plot that heavily depends on that code.[3] When Daisy dies of malaria, infected at the Coliseum in Rome, her death is abrupt and arbitrary: she has died not for giving in to the wiles of the seducer as did the heroines of *Charlotte Temple* and *The Coquette*, but instead for doing the same thing others do, visiting the great sites of Roman antiquity as an American tourist in search of the picturesque. More specifically, Winterbourne, the passionless overly Europeanized American who views Daisy with fascinated disdain, has gone to the Coliseum at the same moment. He intends to stay only briefly while Daisy has spent the whole evening there. Daisy dies, then, not for doing something wrong but for doing the conventional thing in the wrong way; while the ending of *Daisy Miller* allows for many different readings, it is hard to believe that when the other characters gather around the heroine's grave in the Protestant cemetery in Rome they do so in order to memorialize for the reader the communal value of tact or refinement or a certain feminine diffidence. Daisy is "an American girl," as her little brother Randolph tells Winterbourne – and as the whole novella repeatedly informs the reader – and the novella's insistence on its heroine's nationality suggests that James is here ironically following the dictates of an earlier plot while draining it of its power to create a national imaginary (18:7). That James wrote his perennially controversial – and somewhat condescending – critical study of his great American forebear, Nathaniel Hawthorne, at the same time further suggests that in this moment in the late 1870s he is consciously distancing himself from a national tradition.

The American novel's ways of managing meaning change radically with James, then. The tombstones that would in an earlier era have attached personal stories to a wider community are (in most instances) gone, and in their place appear relationships – often marriages but also friendships – that are unfathomable, ongoing, in flux, and deeply idiosyncratic. At the end of

*The Portrait of a Lady*, when the aggressively American Henrietta Stackpole
engages herself to the clubby Englishman Mr. Bantling, she tells her friend
Isabel Archer, "I think I know what I'm doing; but I don't know as I can
explain." Henrietta seems to look to Isabel expecting to see her looking
for an explanation of this attraction of opposites, but no, Isabel observes
that no explanation is possible here: "One can't explain one's marriage,"
she answers (even though she and Henrietta go on trying out provisional
explanations) (4:399). When Isabel abruptly returns to Rome and her own
extremely unhappy marriage at the novel's end, this inexplicability is taken
to a new level of bewilderment: readers are left to fill in for themselves the
heroine's motivations in a radically open-ended conclusion that undermines
the promise of the novel's title that this long book will ultimately arrive at
the stasis associated with the genre of the visual portrait. Instead of believing they are regarding "a painted picture," readers fully attuned to Jamesian
ambiguity may well feel that they are trying to hit a moving target (4:375).
The last time we see Isabel (although many elements of the novel quietly
undermine that equation of reading and seeing) she is standing in a doorway, a point of transition. It is as if Daisy Miller's energy, ultimately buried
by generic constraint in that novel's ending, is now set free.

The dynamism, the opacity, the inscrutability we find in the ending of
*Portrait* are at work in every level of the text. "You won't, I think, in any
way, be easily right about her," Isabel's aunt says of her early in the novel
(3:58). "You're changed; you've got new ideas over here," Henrietta tells
Isabel soon after their arrival in England (3:138). "You're unfathomable,"
Madame Merle tells Gilbert Osmond (3:411). "I can't understand, I can't
penetrate you!" Caspar Goodwood says to Isabel (4:138). Perhaps no other
novel or novelist so convincingly demonstrates the usefulness of Warren
Susman's daring hypothesis that the nineteenth century's definition of the
self shifts from a model of character – one emphasizing stability and moral
worth – to one of personality – with its emphasis on flux, growth, and the
vicissitudes of desire.[4] This new dynamism helps to explain why James is not
only a great novelist of troubled marriage but also a great novelist of friendship, a relationship that, in the words of the sociologist Anthony Giddens,
has at its "core" a ceaseless "reflexive questioning."[5] In other words, the
theory of friendship Isabel learns from Madame Merle is trustworthy, even
if so much else about that duplicitously worldly character is not: "Madame
Merle ... declared her belief that when a friendship ceases to grow it immediately begins to decline – there being no point of equilibrium between liking more and liking less. A stationary affection ... was impossible – it must
move one way or the other" (4:40). Another term for this movement might
be simply the Jamesian plot.

From the beginning of his career, readers recognized that James was developing a new kind of fiction; from the beginning of his career, that fiction has inspired strong reactions. In an 1875 issue of the *Atlantic Monthly*, in what may be the first review of James (unsigned but possibly by William Dean Howells), the critic wrote, "Since his earliest appearance ... people have strongly liked and disliked his writing."[6] Another unsigned review in the *Atlantic* in 1879 observed that James's writings are "fine-spun" to the point of being "deficient in incident," so much so that while they reward studious "reperusal," they can hardly be comprehended in serial publication, which, presumably, depends on dramatic incident for readers to remember a novel from month to month.[7] A British review from 1880 – a complimentary one – pointed out that James "does not much trouble himself to contrive intricate plots, or to imagine strange situations; but he cuts a slice out of life almost at haphazard, and then goes about to reveal and analyse its constituent parts."[8] Take it as a historical fact, then, that for all the illuminating comparisons one can make between James's novels and a tradition that includes Hawthorne or Jane Austen or Honoré de Balzac, readers from the beginning have recognized the Jamesian novel as revisionary – and have found it difficult to regard that revision neutrally. Where did this newness come from?

One powerful explanation can be developed by thinking of James's fictions and techniques as part of a larger evolution within American culture – the emergence of a self-consciously refined, aesthetically polished, highbrow literary art written in opposition to the tastes appealed to by mass culture. As Lawrence Levine has demonstrated in his fascinating study of this cultural shift, reading became at the end of the nineteenth century a far more studious enterprise, a potentially daunting challenge that served as an occasion for demonstrating one's expertise, one's cultivation. This was the era of Browning Societies (devoted to explications of a notoriously difficult poet); it was the era when Shakespeare made the transition from stage (a public entertainment open to all social strata) to page (a difficult writer requiring serious study and a full apparatus of editorial helps).[9] In this context, James's subtle concentration on unity, maintenance of point of view, and care in registering minute shifts in consciousness, and his belief that fine modulations in relationships between characters constitute a sufficient plot emerge as a corrective to or even an elite critique of "vulgarity." As James wrote to a friend in 1881, "You say that literature is going down in the U. S. A. I quite agree with you.... I suspect the age of letters is waning, for our time. It is the age of Panama Canals, of Sarah Bernhardt, of Western wheat-raising, of merely material expansion. Art, form, may return, but I doubt that I shall live to see them."[10] Faced with an era defined by the growth of big business and the celebrity of mass media, James might be said to develop such novels as *Washington Square* (1880) – where nothing seems to happen – or *The Turn of the Screw* (1898) or *The Golden Bowl* (1904) – where even very good readers cannot always say exactly *what* happens – as antidotes to and latent critiques of a widespread loss of the sense of "art," of "form." The drama of *Washington Square* depends on Dr. Sloper's watching his daughter, Catherine, even as she becomes newly preoccupied with her own emotional life: Catherine "had an entirely new feeling ... a state of expectant suspense about her own actions. She watched herself as she would have watched another person, and wondered what she would do."[11] The inward turn of plot here becomes the vehicle for a study in form in which James challenges the reader to become absorbed in a story in which very little happens and in which the expectations of genre are defeated (*Washington Square* sets itself up as a courtship novel and then leaves Catherine sitting alone, "for life, as it were," in the end).[12] A study of consciousness provides the occasion for an escape from an age of commerce and debased tastes.

This argument is useful – up to a point. There is a lot of evidence to support the thesis that Jamesian formalism evolves as a defense against a rapidly expanding mass literary market. Indeed, one reviewer – for the highly nationalistic and highly moralistic Boston-based *Literary World* – found *Washington Square* incomprehensible: "If any of our more penetrating readers can say what Mr. Henry James's last story amounts to, we shall be happy to publish the estimate."[13] And yet the interpretation of James's formal preoccupations as constituting a rarefied flight from lowbrow culture leaves out a great deal and begs at least as many questions as it answers. For one, it leaves out James's fascination – delighted, satirical, sometimes repelled – with actresses (and their managers), with newspaper reporters, with art collectors, with advertising, with poseurs and decadents, with a culture of celebrities and commodities. As Ross Posnock has powerfully argued, James is at once "contemplative" and "spontaneous," given both to "hoarding" meanings so that his texts seem to be forbidding palaces of art in which their author holds himself apart from an unruly social world and "permeable," open to social change, even if that openness means risking his identity as a high priest of aesthetic refinement.[14] For Posnock, James's vulnerability to and curiosity about the dislocations of the modern era – especially its casting away of the anchorage of tradition – make him endlessly experimental, playfully ironic, something like our postmodern contemporary. Perhaps there is no better instance of James's capacity for this kind of mobility than "The Figure in the Carpet" (1896), where the sort of rarefied reading the *Literary World* failed to produce in its review of *Washington Square* is itself subjected to parody. The characters in this story are adept at "grim reading," to use Richard Poirier's term for the determination modernist literary difficulty requires; they take up the collected works of the fictional novelist Hugh Vereker in dogged pursuit of a hidden pattern that unites all the texts.[15] Self-consciously elite readers, they are in search of something that "isn't for the vulgar" as they read Vereker "page by page, as they would take one of the classics, inhal[ing] him in slow draughts and let[ting] him sink all the way in" (15: 237, 243). Yet in their pursuit of esoteric knowledge, they lose the ability to delight in Vereker's writing, which ultimately comes to seem boring: not keeping their attention free-floating and ambulatory, the characters miss whatever pleasures the novels have to offer. As in "The Real Thing" (1892), where the opposition between high and low culture seems to dissolve, James treats with an ironic sense of play the highbrow conception of art he himself cultivated.

And yet at some level, none of this – neither the high-cultural thesis about James nor its critique – fully captures what the novels can mean for us as readers now. "Do you *like* Henry James?" The person who asked me that, as I was in the midst of writing a book about the author, was a university press editor, superbly educated and who, as an editor in charge of acquiring manuscripts in the humanities, might be expected to have an intuitive feel for the subtle and the sophisticated (as he usually did). Yet James was a strange taste he had not managed to acquire. This distaste carries an irony of its own, for James's revision of the novel actually remakes the genre into one that more closely reflects our own emotional lives than any novel that came before. As in the examples cited previously from *Washington Square*, where Dr. Sloper watching his daughter watch herself is enough to constitute a plot, James's fiction lowers the threshold of narration until the merest shift in one person's perception of another is itself an action of considerable dramatic interest. As in such late novels as *The Golden Bowl*, where Maggie Verver powerfully reimagines the world her father, her husband, and her stepmother live in, what comes to seem most real in the texts is the pressure of one consciousness on another. The insecurity we feel over the Jamesian text is not an abstruse study in epistemology, then, but a study in problems deeply familiar to us from the everyday life those problems might be said to constitute: What is between us? Does this friendship – or romance, or marriage – create a sense of well-being or constriction? Is this friendship – or romance, or marriage – real? Such questions have no end; as James famously observed in the preface to *Roderick Hudson* (1875), "Really, universally, relations stop nowhere" (1: vii). Endless self-questioning, the perpetually interpretable ambiguities of relations between selves: that is why James's fictions are so often so open-ended, and those are the preoccupations that make reading them seem to me such a moving experience. As the many

Jamesian novels that end with problematic marriages make especially clear, such narratives project a future of endless renegotiation between selves, and that is why the tradition of terminating a story with a tombstone itself comes to an end with James's fiction.

But what of "The Beast in the Jungle" (1903), that late, notoriously inscrutable tale that ends with John Marcher "fl[inging] himself, face down, on the tomb" of May Bartram? (17:126). Such an ending may seem a return to the plot of earlier nineteenth-century fiction, but the apparent resemblance to the endings of *The Coquette* or *The Pioneers* serves to highlight what a different kind of fiction James wrote. The "bond," the "intimate community" between Marcher and May, is made up of ceaseless questions: their friendship remains open to interpretation to the end because it so thoroughly resists formalized meanings (17:75, 86). Marcher's presentiment of a coming terror – "something or other [that] lay in wait for him, amid the twists and the turns of the months and the years, like a crouching beast in the jungle" – forestalls his adopting any socially recognized role in relation to May; building a friendship by pondering together the ambiguous identity of that nameless "something" is what the two put in place of a more traditional relationship (17:79). Hence when May lies dying, Marcher is excluded from her sickroom, and when she is buried, he is given no part to play in her funeral: he bears to May "no connexion that any one seemed" obliged "to recognize" (17:115). Neither her husband nor her lover nor her brother nor her heir, Marcher's relation to May develops outside preexisting definitions. Hence the illegibility of the text depends in large measure on the lack of social traditions that would give its plot some ground rules, a recognizable genre, a classification. While Marcher sees May's tombstone as "an open page" that gives him a sense of "identity," he also sees her memorial – from the outside, as it were – as a "blankness" (17: 121, 120). What gives the modern self its "identity" (the text is explicit about that word) is its strange, unclassifiable relations with others.

That is one way of reading "The Beast in the Jungle" and of explaining something of where the sheer weirdness of the text – and of many of James's later fictions – comes from. It is not quite the way Marcher reads his own story in the end, however. In the tale's last scene, Marcher catches a glimpse of another mourner at another grave, and sees in this grief-ravaged face a sign of all the sexual intimacy he himself passed up in not marrying May. Marcher's sense of loss in this closing scene is the loss of "deep" "passion": failing to court May means for Marcher that his "life" has been a "void" (17:125, 124). Yet this belated appeal to (or refuge in) the relatively firm structures of the heterosexual plot has itself fallen under critical suspicion. In "The Beast in the Closet," perhaps the most influential essay on

James of the last quarter-century, Eve Kosofsky Sedgwick reads the text's incessantly indirect naming of Marcher's secret – "his predicament," "his inevitable topic," "the abyss," "his queer consciousness," "the great vagueness" – as a "quasi-nominative, quasi-obliterative structure" that simultaneously expresses and expunges Marcher's desire for other men.[16] Reading the tale in the triple-layered context of the emergence of a recognizably gay identity in the 1890s, the erotic pull James felt toward other men in his own life, and the long Western traditions of homophobia (especially the rhetorical tradition of naming homosexual acts and desires as "the unspeakable"), Sedgwick gives to the traditional critical topic of Jamesian ambiguity a new specificity and a new urgency. "Queer" is, in fact, one of James's favorite words—a word by which he names at once gay desire and the strangeness of modern relationships. Here "there is really too much to say," as James himself said at the end of the preface to *The Portrait of a Lady* (3:xxx), but it *is* clear that the ambiguities of James's new novel have kept it current long after the work of many of his contemporaries has faded from view.

## FURTHER READING

Bersani, Leo, "The Jamesian Lie." *A Future for Astyanax: Character and Desire in Literature*, Boston, Little Brown, 1976, pp. 128–55.

Blair, Sara, *Henry James and the Writing of Race and Nation*, Cambridge, Cambridge University Press, 1996.

Freedman, Jonathan, *Professions of Taste: Henry James, British Aestheticism, and Commodity Culture*, Stanford, Calif., Stanford University Press, 1990.

Holland, Laurence B., *The Expense of Vision: Essays on the Craft of Henry James*, Princeton, N.J., Princeton University Press, 1964.

McGurl, Mark, *The Novel Art: Elevations of American Fiction after Henry James*, Princeton, N.J., Princeton University Press, 2001.

Otten, Thomas J., *A Superficial Reading of Henry James: Preoccupations with the Material World*, Columbus, Ohio State University Press, 2006.

Posnock, Ross, *The Trial of Curiosity: Henry James, William James, and the Challenge of Modernity*, New York, Oxford University Press, 1991.

Rivkin, Julie, *False Positions: The Representational Logics of Henry James's Fiction*, Stanford, Calif., Stanford University Press, 1996.

Sedgwick, Eve Kosofsky, "The Beast in the Closet: James and the Writing of Homosexual Panic." *Epistemology of the Closet*, Berkeley, University of California Press, 1990. pp. 182–212.

Yeazell, Ruth Bernard, *Language and Knowledge in the Late Novels of Henry James*, Chicago, University of Chicago Press, 1976.

## NOTES

1 Susanna Rowson, *Charlotte Temple*, ed. Cathy N. Davidson (New York, Oxford University Press, 1986), pp. 117–18.

2  Nathaniel Hawthorne, *The Scarlet Letter*, ed. Brian Harding and Cindy Weinstein (Oxford, Oxford University Press, 2007), p. 204; Benedict Anderson, *Imagined Communities: Reflections on the Origin and Spread of Nationalism*, rev. ed. (London, Verso, 1991), pp. 24–34.

3  Henry James, *Daisy Miller*, in *The Novels and Tales of Henry James*, New York Edition, 24 vols. (New York, Scribner's, 1907–9), 18: 5, 9. Hereafter by volume and page number.

4  Warren Susman, *Culture as History: The Transformation of American Society in the Twentieth Century* (New York, Pantheon, 1984), pp. 271–85.

5  Anthony Giddens, *Modernity and Self-Identity: Self and Society in the Late Modern Age* (Stanford, Calif., Stanford University Press, 1991), p. 91.

6  Unsigned review of *A Passionate Pilgrim and Other Tales*, *Atlantic Monthly* 35 (April 1875): 490, in Roger Gard (ed.), *Henry James: The Critical Heritage* (London, Routledge & Kegan Paul), 1968), p. 31.

7  Unsigned review of *The Europeans*, *Atlantic Monthly* 43 (February 1879): 169, in Gard, p. 73.

8  Unsigned review of *Confidence*, *Spectator* 53 (1880): 48–49, in Gard, p. 84.

9  Lawrence W. Levine, *Highbrow/Lowbrow: The Emergence of Cultural Hierarchy in America* (Cambridge, Mass., Harvard University Press, 1988), pp. 52–73.

10  Virginia Harlow, *Thomas Sergeant Perry: A Biography and Letters to Perry from William, Henry, and Garth Wilkinson James* (Durham, N.C., Duke University Press, 1950), pp. 309–10.

11  Henry James, *Washington Square*, ed. Brian Lee (Harmondsworth, Penguin, 1986), p. 106.

12  James, *Washington Square*, p. 220.

13  Unsigned review, *Literary World* 12 (January 1881): 10, in Gard, p. 91.

14  Ross Posnock, *The Trial of Curiosity: Henry James, William James, and the Challenge of Modernity* (New York, Oxford University Press, 1991), p. 21.

15  Richard Poirier, "The Difficulties of Modernism and the Modernism of Difficulty," *Humanities in Society* 1 (1978): 273. Mark McGurl quotes this phrase and provides a highly intelligent discussion of these issues in *The Novel Art: Elevations of American Fiction after Henry James* (Princeton, N.J., Princeton University Press, 2001), pp. 10–19.

16  Eve Kosofsky Sedgwick, *Epistemology of the Closet* (Berkeley, University of California Press, 1990), p. 203.

# 7
## Edith Wharton

PAMELA KNIGHTS

For readers across the United States in 1905, "The novel of the year, with the emphasis on the 'The,'"[1] was Edith Wharton's (1862–1937)*The House of Mirth*: "Above the level of our modern novels it towers head and shoulders high." Wharton was "alone in her own class ... among that handful of English-speaking novelists ... whose books are the chief literary events of our day."[2] While some considered her subject (fashionable high life) too narrow and modish, prophecies of her future standing proved just. After a slight dip of reputation, in the mid-twentieth century after her death in 1937, Wharton has continued to command a wide following and maintained her established status as one of the most important American novelists. No single text could possibly encapsulate her career (in forty years, she published more than forty volumes, any one of which rewards discussion), but with this novel as an entry point, this chapter will attempt simply to give a sense of her remarkable scope and diversity.

Launched in January 1905, as a monthly serial in the popular *Scribner's Magazine*, Wharton's story of the high-maintenance Miss Bart, a husband-hunting socialite, flirting, gambling, and, in private, smoking, her way through the Manhattan smart set, captured its audience from the start, and published as a book, in October, with the much-anticipated final installment looming, it became an instant bestseller, breaking all *Scribner's* records, and making Wharton famous. *The House of Mirth* was Wharton's second novel, and she herself would come to view it as her much delayed, professional breakthrough (the first episode appeared in the month of her forty-third birthday). Seeing her early chapters in print, when she was still working out the later ones, forced her, so she claimed, into the discipline essential to a writer; she learned how to bring complex materials under control, and to steer a work to its close. Her declaration, "My last page is always latent in my first,"[3] seems borne out in her novel's strong narrative arch, and a compelling pace that gripped readers at every step of Lily's passage. Many felt moved to write to Wharton, some to express desolation at the ending, others unbounded enthusiasm: "I love ... every period and comma."[4] The press charted the rising sales figures (as did Wharton in her notebook), as her novel jostled with Thomas Dixon's racist tract, *The Clansman*, and a new rival, Upton Sinclair's *The Jungle*, in early 1906; the stage adaptation and *Revue de Paris* serialization (both 1906) stirred further waves. Wharton's photograph (aloof, aristocratic, costumed in furs) appeared above exclamatory columns debating her portrayal of the machinations of the rich, the morals of her heroine, and the motivation of Lawrence Selden, Lily's closest, but most vacillating, admirer. Mrs. Wharton's own unimpeachable New York upper-class credentials and independent fortune gave frisson to interpretation. The knowledge that the author wrote from a born insider's view of "The Four Hundred" (Manhattan society's exclusive inner circle) roused speculation about the identity of originals, and irritable letters in *The New York Times* argued over the accuracy of Wharton's representations, and her fairness, or lack of it, in painting the world of wealth at its worst.

The epicenter of gossip in Wharton's narrative, Lily Bart, as parasite and victim of the rich, became a reference point in wider conversations about the twentieth-century woman. Lily had "individual traits" but was "above all things, a daughter of her place and time, a girl of modern New York."[5] Her name features in the press in an array of contexts. A pleasantry about her opportunistic interest in "Americana," to hook the millionaire hobbyist Percy Gryce, enlivens an item on two archaeologists' engagement: in courtship, shared specialisms could be an advantage. She appears in warnings about extravagant expectations ("the poor girl with rich tastes ... is always in an unnatural and demoralizing position"); in anxieties over current fiction ("Is the Good Woman Too Tame for Art?");[6] and as a touchstone for other protagonists. Wharton's publishers maintained the buzz, promising with each latest heroine the prospect of yet keener debate.

Through even a single figure, Wharton opens inquiries into changing social forms, their impact upon the self and upon the relations between individuals. Characters and readers pursue "the real Lily" through a narrative of rapidly dissolving scenes, where metaphors of stage machinery and tropes of optical illusion unsettle any certainty. The text's ambiguous surfaces, from Lily's "art of blushing" to the "spectacular effects"[7] of the rich, in the tableaux vivants centerpiece, destabilize fixed identities. Wharton projects fictional equivalents of the sociologist Thorstein Veblen's *The Theory of the Leisure Class* (1899), illuminating the signs of the power elite. Anticipating late twentieth-century accounts of the performance of self or gender, Lily vanishes into her own objectification: "Why could one never do a natural thing without having to screen it behind a structure of artifice?" (*HM*, 22). In her next, industrial problem novel, *The Fruit of the Tree* (1907), Wharton mirrors Lily's decorative inutility in Bessy, another hothouse product, but she employs as her case for scrutiny Lily's opposite, the high-principled nurse Justine Brent. Again "action" and "artifice" blur, as with Justine's deed of mercy killing, the controversial act at the heart of the story, Wharton turns reading into autopsy.

All her narratives provoke questions about the nature of emotion, the psyche, language, creativity, and belief, within cultures driven by the forces of finance, consumerism, and technological innovation, and divided by gulfs of privilege and inequality. Lily's astonishingly varied line of successors, to give a severely abbreviated list, included Mattie Silver in *Ethan Frome* (1911) and the equally mercurial Sophy Viner in *The Reef* (1912); Undine Spragg, career divorcée, in *The Custom of the Country* (1913); Charity Royall, suffocating in the desiccated New England village of *Summer* (1917); Susy, in *The Glimpses of the Moon* (1922), whose experiment in marriage reworks Lily's and Selden's story; sexually suspect Ellen Olenska and Kate Clephane, in *The Age of Innocence* (1920) and *The Mother's Recompense* (1925), returning from Europe to the ambiguous security of their native New York; the frenetic managerial hostess, Pauline, in *Twilight Sleep* (1927); fifteen-year-old Judith, the object of disturbing forms of attention in the international pleasure grounds of *The Children* (1928); or, in *Hudson River Bracketed* (1929) and its sequel *The Gods Arrive* (1932), sensitive Hero, companion to a self-obsessed artist, suffering, as one reviewer described, "what the married life of Agnes Wickfield might have been, if the last chapters of *David Copperfield* [1849] had been written eighty years later;"[8] and the quintet of young American aspirants who raid Europe for husbands in Wharton's final, unfinished *The Buccaneers* (1937). All these continue to stimulate discussion into the twenty-first century.

Even in the dazzle around Lily in 1905, many recognized that Wharton's gifts went beyond her deadly way with gossip, or her insights into how parvenus spent their millions. With allusions to the perennial laments over the lack of ambition of current American fiction, reviewers praised her novel, as, at last, a literary treatment of the contemporary United States that did justice to the dynamics of a new century. Although Wharton presented herself as an apprentice, readers had admired her previous work for qualities that, now fully developed, would make her work endure: her style, psychological acuity, and brilliant social analysis. Over the previous decade, building a name as a cultural observer and travel writer, as for a significant body of fiction, she had published nine books: among them, a critique of American taste, *The Decoration of Houses* (1897), in collaboration with the architect Ogden Codman Jr.; a translation of a German tragedy; and two volumes of Italian travels, drawing on her passions for European architecture, landscape, and gardens. These interests would inform all her fiction, passing into the minutiae of her analysis.

In fiction, her wit, verbal polish, and nuance often (to Wharton's annoyance) prompted comparisons with her friend and mentor Henry James, particularly the explorations of the moral and aesthetic sensitivities of well-to-do Americans, in her three recent collections of short stories, and two novellas, *The Touchstone* (1900) and *Sanctuary* (1903). Differences that complicate simple statements of affiliation come into the foreground with *The House of Mirth*. After her first novel, *The Valley of Decision* (1902), an erudite chronicle of eighteenth-century Italy, she was contemplating subjects nearer home, a move reinforced by James's encouragement to avoid his own etiolated experience of "exile," and *"Do New York!"*(*EW*, 27).Turning her traveler's eye towards the metropolis and its outposts, Wharton scrutinized tiers whose specifics could only be guessed at by the hoards of "society novelists" (now long forgotten) and that serious novelists had left alone. In Lily's ventures on the social heights, from the luxury of a Hudson estate, to the "studied tropicality" (*HM*, 293) of Monte Carlo, Wharton explores orbits above the milieu of William Dean Howells's middle classes, inaccessible to Theodore Dreiser's showgirl, Carrie, and unthinkable in the streets of Stephen Crane's Maggie. While Wharton's narrative keeps Lily, in her decline, on the edge of gentility, the "abyss" (the text's all-purpose image for obliterating poverty, disease, social extinction) remains an ever-present threat. In her first extended fiction of the city, the novella "Bunner Sisters" (1892; published 1916), Wharton had located her entire narrative on this line, presenting, as in Lily's straits, the shifts and accommodations in lives with no margin beyond subsistence.

Now, her stratum for investigation was that of the privileged, all-consuming few: the influx of vast unregulated fortunes that were transforming New York into a city that stunned observers and galvanized social comment. Although in 1900, an *Arena* article asserted, "It is unfortunate for the novelist that the question of money enters so largely into our social life; for it is death to poetry and romance,"[9] Wharton makes money her medium; as Selden exclaims of the rich, to Lily, "'take them into another element, and see how they squirm and gasp!'" (*HM*, 111). In *The House of Mirth*'s social ecosystem, constructed in references to tides, rock pools, microorganisms, the wealthy remain buoyant, destructively secure in their entitlement. But Wharton keeps the reader aware of societal infrastructures, the efforts of housekeeping of all kinds that maintain the show: smells from the kitchen, the labor of servants, the silent witnesses to the posturing of the rich (even as Lily's father announces ruin, Mrs. Bart furiously hides the scene from the butler). A lexis of evolutionary sacrifice, of the numerous hordes of "dingy" people, used up to create one perfect bloom, keeps the costs in view. While Wharton does not write Lily directly in terms of desire, as Kate Chopin did Edna in *The Awakening* (1899), characters are sexually embodied. Lily recoils from Gus Trenor's touch, the horror of rape ("Her heart was beating all over her body"[*HM*, 236–7]). (Later novels, such as *The Reef*, or Wharton's revelatory "love-diary," "The Life Apart,"[1907] would take sensuality further.)

Readers noted other distinctions. Enjoining a friend to buy the latest *Scribner's*, "on account of a tale in two parts called the 'Touchstone' by Mrs. or Miss Wharton," the artist Susan Hale, in 1900, gives a glimpse of first impressions:

> We have only read the first part, and are impatiently awaiting the end in the April number. It is very clever; she is more James-y than James himself, epigrammatic in every line; but her style thus far has the merit that you can understand what she means on account of her finishing her sentences which her master had long since ceased to do.[10]

Clarity and commitment to story (aspects of the craft that, at the turn of the century, seemed remote from James's interests) are inseparable from Wharton's deepest novelistic concerns. She observes with an eye informed by biological and social sciences, disciplined by precision with detail and data. Her library included Charles Darwin and his followers, Herbert Spencer's sociology, and anthropological studies (such as Edward B. Tylor's *Primitive Culture*, 1871), which would shape her fictional analyses and color central characters' perspectives. In ultimately devastating effects of estrangement, Ralph Marvell, in *The Custom of the Country*, and Newland Archer in *The Age of Innocence* come to view their own rule-bound New York as akin to a primitive tribe. In *Ethan Frome*, a modern engineer speculating about the frozen life of a failed hill farmer sees, for an instant, a volume of new biochemical research bridge the gap between his sphere and his subject's.

In her autobiography, Wharton recalls a painful exchange over James's own recent fictions. Puzzled by his experimental severity, in *The Golden Bowl* (1904), his "idea in suspending the four principal characters … in the void," she wondered about the hinterland: "'What sort of life did they lead when they were not watching each other, and fencing with each other? Why have you stripped them of all the *human fringes* we necessarily trail after us through life?'"(*ABG*, 191). More important here than James's nonplussed response ("'My dear – I didn't know I had!'"), or than the fidelity, or not, of an anecdote recalled after three decades, is Wharton's image of entanglement, of fabric and furnishing. Her fiction posits problems of personal identity and consciousness as possibly, in themselves, material compositions, intertwined with, even generated from, the properties of their habitat: rooms, clothes, houses, artifacts, dinner settings, modes of transport, streets, and cities. Henry James himself had aired such propositions (as Isabel Archer debates with Madame Merle in chapter 19 of *The Portrait of a Lady*, 1881), and his brother, the psychologist William James, in *The Principles of Psychology* (1890) had advanced a systematic conceptualization of the "Material Me," and related forms of interior mental space. But Wharton takes her inquiry into the substance of her texts, where it shapes her constructions of character and her representations of the environments where they live and move. She denounced modernist excursions into the subconscious: for her, James Joyce's *Ulysses* (1922) was "unformed & unimportant drivel" (*EW*, 442). She viewed novelistic form as wrought out of awareness of a continuum: that "the bounds of a personality were not reproducible by a sharp black line, but that each of us flows imperceptibly into adjacent people and things."[11] So a character wonders, in *Twilight Sleep*, "Where, indeed ... did one's own personality end, and that of others, of people, landscapes, chairs or spectacle-cases, begin?"[12]

In her seventies, in autobiographical self-review, Wharton turns her lens from the turbulent 1930s to her origins in the sheltered upper classes of mid-nineteenth-century New York:

> But we must return to the brownstone houses, and penetrate from the vestibule (painted in Pompeian red, and frescoed with a frieze of stencilled lotus-leaves, taken from Owen Jones's *Grammar of Ornament* [1856]) into the carefully guarded interior. What would the New Yorker of the present day say to those interiors, and the lives lived in them? Both would be equally unintelligible to any New Yorker under fifty.[13]

Wharton was distanced from her milieu early, by family migrations in Europe, her linguistic fluency, reading, and intellectuality, and, after following the conventional forms of a debut, and marriage to a leisure-class gentleman, she would eventually make her own life, in a secret affair, and as a divorced, independent, expatriate writer in France. She construes her 1870s world throughout her writings, as a lost civilization, as far from modern experience as the cities of Pompeii, Troy, or Atlantis so fascinating to late nineteenth-century antiquarians. At times in fiction, as in lifewriting, her narrative voice presents itself as a recorder, labeling and cataloging remnants of extinct cultures. Such notes have risked confining her, in turn, to the class of novelist of manners; or to be dismissed more generally as a custodian of white patrician nostalgia, racially and culturally conservative.

Yet more dynamic than vessels of conservation, in Wharton's larger realist project her novels lay bare the deeper structures of a culture, underpinned by a naturalist, objective effort of scientific understanding. Leading us through a "vestibule," a deep red tunnel, she figures her role as archaeological investigator, opening a long-sealed tomb, or ancient labyrinth. Her narratives seek, similarly, to "penetrate" the "guarded interiors" of imaginations and moral visions, coterminous with the airless rooms that sequester them. Guiding readers into other grammars of ornament, they unlock language codes and customs now gone, or on the cusp of destruction. This is the "hieroglyphic world" that Newland Archer, lost in New York's "labyrinth," in *The Age of Innocence* in the 1870s, disastrously fails to interpret.[14] In *The Custom of the Country*, set in the early 1900s, Undine Spragg finds herself constrained by social classifications now "obsolete as a medieval cosmogony."[15] The obverse of this culture, but always interdependent, are interiors, outside the hothouse. As Charles Cook, her chauffeur, drove Wharton and James out from her summer mansion, The Mount, in the early 1900s, she speculated about the lives in the isolated hill farms of the Berkshires. Her cautious approach, through the frame narrative of *Ethan Frome*, offers another trope of entry, the survey from the perspective of privilege of the culture of the disadvantaged.

Little in Wharton seems more lethal than the poison of stagnation. Specters rise from stillness and enclosure in her extraordinary ghost stories, felt by indirection, like the omnipotent "Mr. Jones" in the English country estate, or the snowbound silence in her final tale, "All Souls'."[16] It emanates in the longer fictions from figures cast in images of freezing or petrifaction: the stiff Mrs. Peniston, who stifles Lily Bart; the venomous Zeena, in *Ethan Frome*; the glacial van der Luydens at the pinnacle of *The Age of Innocence*; or in *Old New York* (1924), the calcified Miss Raycie, sitting "above stairs in a large cold room," who "seemed a survival of forgotten days, a Rosetta Stone to which the clue was lost."[17] As the critic Kathy Fedorko has argued, in an influential study, Wharton disturbs realism with other genres, the gothic, fantastic, or mythic. Such nonrealist tremors in the text (with the jolt of the uncanny) illuminate the unspeakable in the culture and the psyche: sex, social exploitation, financial guilt.

As the novelist Tim Parks writes of ghosts, more generally: "Every ghost story is two stories: the story of how the ghost came to be a ghost, the story of our encounter with the ghost."[18] Wharton was always interested in greater tectonic movements of historical transition. In *The Valley of Decision*, and in her celebrations of overlooked details in Italian paintings in *Italian Backgrounds* (1905), she registers wider stories through the pulse of the everyday. So, where she shows hauntings, she hints at histories: when the repressed rises, the horrors lead to reflection on how selves and cultures are made and broken. In Wharton's terrifying pictures of New England in economic decline – of those, entrapped, in *Ethan Frome* and *Summer*, with no chance of release, through love or work – even Zeena Frome or Lawyer Royall seem less monstrous specters than victims. In *The Custom of the Country*, Undine Spragg seems soulless as the nymph her name evokes. Wharton presents her in images of dangerously unstoppable energy: soaring "skyward in a mirror-lined lift, hardly conscious of the direction she was taking" (*CC,* 116), but in this most expansive meditation on cultural meanings, Undine is nonetheless an apparition bred from the culture that created her.

Writing her Pulitzer Prize–winning *The Age of Innocence*, from her Paris home in 1919, Wharton reached in memory to reconstruct the deeper past, across the catastrophic gulf of World War I. Exhaustive lists crisscrossed the Atlantic as her friend and onetime sister-in-law, Mary Cadwalader Jones, checked dates and details woven into their shared social and family histories. Transmuting her research, to compose the fabric of Newland Archer's unsettled consciousness, Wharton reanimates this era. Through Newland's eyes, she stages the rituals of his clan in a series of great scenes, framed, as if in display cases: by the opera-house proscenium or the bright lawns against which ladies pose in graceful archery. At the climax, a careful barricade of lamps and a bay window jardinière convert a drawing-room into an arena for a killing: a "rally around a kinswoman about to be eliminated from the tribe" (*AI,* 337). Bringing the discourses of threatened systems into focus with self-reflexive hints throughout the text (from archaeological ruins to worries about digestive tracts), Wharton exhibits a society intent on self-preservation. She steps back, in the final pages, to reveal its passing, and to open up a new phase of history, the fresh air, free lines of communication, and exuberant mobility of young Dallas Archer's generation of the early 1900s. Yet as the novel's first readers knew, in a further world cycle, that generation would be short-lived, now already lost in the wreck of war.

Wharton, who had lived in Paris throughout the conflict, struggled with these ghosts in her novella *The Marne*, of 1918, and her disturbing novel, *A Son at the Front*, published in 1923, but begun, and set aside, in the immediate aftermath. In the shadow of terrible knowledge, *The Age of Innocence* revalues the stasis of the old order. Wharton's novels of the 1920s, in the tangles of modernity, represent all codes in confusion, suggesting uncertainty, now, of how any civilization might survive. She recoiled from mass culture and American globalization: "Ford motors and Gillette razors have bound together the uttermost parts of the earth" (*UCW,* 156), she wrote in 1927. In the homogenizing reach of movies, jazz, and a degenerate language, her fictions present the erasure of any rich European inheritance and a world reduced to "a playing-field for our people" (*UCW*, 156). In *The Children* and *The Mother's Recompense*, blighted childhoods, intergenerational rivalries, incest, and blocked forms of reproduction are pervasive tropes, as Wharton, with apocalyptic notes, suggests historical impasse. Even beauty (unlike Lily's) is standardized, stamped out of magazine templates. In *Twilight Sleep*, memorabilia of Old New York are ghosts of a dead age, lifeless people, protected from "the plebeian intrusion of light and air" (*TS*, 236); and Nona, named in proleptic terms of negation, sees no assurances in the past, and no shape to her future.

Wharton has been reread in multiple ways throughout the last century and remains an animating presence. Characters return in sometimes surprising ways. Recent sightings include Newland Archer, as one model for the hero of *Twilight*; Ellen Olenska, as Serena van der Woodsen, of Cecily von Ziegesar's *Gossip Girl*; and Wharton's Lenox estate, The Mount, in "Ghost Hunters," as a Sci-Fi Channel docusoap. The novelist and Wharton critic Lev Raphael has revived *The House of* Mirth, in *Rosedale in Love* (2011), from the perspective of Lily's Jewish financier suitor, and Jeffrey Eugenides, in *The Marriage Plot* (2011), made play with a student's passion for Wharton and Roland Barthes: "*Bart*. So that was how you pronounced it."[19] The view of Lily, on her way to a house party, drifting into the gaze of Lawrence Selden in the afternoon rush at Grand Central Station, in her novel's opening paragraph, is still, for many readers, one of their first encounters with Wharton's writings – a richer and more complex body of fictions than perhaps any revenant can suggest.

## FURTHER READING

Beer, Janet and Avril Horner, *Edith Wharton: Sex, Satire and the Older Woman*, Basingstoke, Palgrave Macmillan, 2011.

Beer, Janet, Pamela Knights and Elizabeth Nolan, *Edith Wharton's* The House of Mirth, London, Routledge, 2007.

Bell, Millicent, *The Cambridge Companion to Edith Wharton*, New York, Cambridge University Press, 1995.

Benert, Annette, *The Architectural Imagination of Edith Wharton: Gender, Class and Power in the Progressive Era*, Madison, N.J., Fairleigh Dickinson University Press, 2007.

Boswell, Parley Ann, *Edith Wharton on Film*, Carbondale, Southern Illinois University Press, 2007.

Fedorko, Kathy, *Gender and the Gothic in the Fiction of Edith Wharton*, Tuscaloosa, University of Alabama Press, 1995.

Joslin, Katherine, *Edith Wharton and the Making of Fashion*, Lebanon, University of New Hampshire Press, 2009.

Kassanoff, Jennie A., *Edith Wharton and the Politics of Race*, Cambridge, Cambridge University Press, 2004.

Knights, Pamela, *The Cambridge Introduction to Edith Wharton*, Cambridge, Cambridge University Press, 2009.

Lee, Hermione, *Edith Wharton*, London, Chatto, 2007.

Montgomery, Maureen M, *Displaying Women: Spectacles of Leisure in Edith Wharton's New York*, New York, Routledge, 1998.

Olin-Ammentorp, Julie, *Edith Wharton's Writings from the Great War*, Gainesville, University Press of Florida, 2004.

Rattray, Laura (ed.), *Edith Wharton in Context*, Cambridge, Cambridge University Press, 2012.

Singley, Carol J. (ed.), *A Historical Guide to Edith Wharton*, Oxford, Oxford University Press, 2003.

Waid, Candace, *Edith Wharton's Letters from the Underworld: Fictions of Women and Writing*, Chapel Hill, University of North Carolina Press, 1991.

Wright, Sarah Bird, *Edith Wharton's Travel Writing: The Making of a Connoisseur*, Basingstoke, Macmillan, 1997.

## NOTES

1 W. P. Kirkwood, "Problems of the Day as Seen thru the Eyes of Authors," *Minneapolis Journal*, December 9, 1905, 5. Library of Congress, "Chronicling America: Historic American Newspapers," http://chroniclingamerica.loc.gov/. Hereafter, "CA."

2 "The Latest Books under Brief Review," *Times-Dispatch* [Richmond], November 5, 1905, 28, "CA."

3 Edith Wharton, *A Backward Glance* (New York, Appleton-Century, 1934), p. 208. Hereafter, *ABG*.

4 Quoted in R. W. B. Lewis, *Edith Wharton* (London, Constable, 1975), p. 152. Hereafter, *EW*.

5 *New-York Tribune*, October 14, 1905, 8, "CA."

6 "Specialities and Marriage Chances" *Evening World*, December 30, 1905, 8; "What Money Is Doing," *Columbus Journal*, May 23, 1906, 6; "Is the Good Woman Too Tame for Art?" *North Platte Semi-Weekly Tribune*, January 28, 1910, 7, All "CA."

7 Edith Wharton, *The House of Mirth* (New York, Scribner's, 1905), pp. 218, 8, 212. Hereafter, *HM*.

8 Elmer Davis, "History of an Artist," *Saturday Review of Literature* 9 (October 1, 1932): 145.

9 Annie Stegner Winston, "America as a Field for Fiction," *Arena* 23.6 (June, 1900): 656.

10 Letter from Susan Hale to Caroline Weld, March 25, 1900, in *Letters of Susan Hale*, ed. Caroline Atkinson (Boston, Marshall Jones, 1919), p. 359.

11 Edith Wharton, *The Writing of Fiction* (1924; New York, Octagon, 1966), p. 7.

12 Edith Wharton, *Twilight Sleep* (New York, Appleton, 1927), p. 237.

13 Edith Wharton, "A Little Girl's New York" (1934; published posthumously, 1938); in Frederick Wegener (ed.), *Edith Wharton: The Uncollected Critical Writings* (Princeton, N.J., Princeton University Press, 1996), pp. 276–7. Hereafter, *UCW*.

14  Edith Wharton, *The Age of Innocence* (New York, Appleton, 1920), p. 42. Hereafter, *AI*.
15  Edith Wharton, *The Custom of the Country* (New York, Scribner's, 1913), p. 193. Hereafter, *CC*.
16  Collected by Wharton; published posthumously in Edith Wharton, *Ghosts* (New York, Appleton, 1937).
17  Edith Wharton, "False Dawn: (The 'Forties)," in *Old New York* (New York, Appleton, 1924), p. 69.
18  Tim Parks, "Ghosts," in *Adultery and Other Diversions* (London, Secker, 1998), p. 88.
19  Jeffrey Eugenides, *The Marriage Plot* (London, Fourth Estate, 2011), p. 27.

# 8

# Theodore Dreiser

CLARE EBY

One of the most famous, though possibly apocryphal, conversations in American literary history took place between Ernest Hemingway and F. Scott Fitzgerald. According to legend, Fitzgerald remarked, "The rich are very different from you and me," to which Hemingway replied, "Yes – they have more money." Theodore Dreiser (1871–1945) fuses those contradictory attitudes. Few have written more probingly about wealth than Dreiser, and his perspective ranges from awestruck to outraged. The power of his writing results from his completely understanding – and having lived – the most familiar iteration of the American Dream: a young man from a poor, socially marginal family transcends his origins by hard work and singular talent, leading ultimately to success and even, in Dreiser's case, international celebrity. Dreiser is the consummate chronicler of that mythic American ascent narrative because he understands to his core the allure of money – while also providing unsurpassed critical analysis of it. Loving chronicler and fierce critic of the national obsession with wealth, Dreiser uses the quest for money to examine the meaning of America.

In a famous scene in Dreiser's debut novel *Sister Carrie* (1900), the title character strolls down Broadway with her friend Mrs. Vance. A "showy parade" of people "going purposely to see and be seen" all wear "the latest they could afford." Even the not-particularly-well-dressed "Carrie found herself stared at and ogled," suggesting the close relationship between displaying what one owns and attracting the opposite sex (another important Dreiserian theme, to which we will return), a point magnified by her sensing around her a "heavy percentage of vice," implying that prostitutes are strutting on Broadway along with the wealthy and the wanna-bes. Dreiser ends the chapter by swooping down from this wide-angled panorama to a close-up: Carrie "felt that she was not of it." A sense of personal inadequacy reawakens her slumbering ambition: "She longed to feel the delight of parading here as an equal. Ah, then she would be happy!" Equality is determined by having enough money to exhibit oneself effectively. As Dreiser's contemporary, the economist Thorstein Veblen, explained what he called "conspicuous consumption," impressing observers requires a display in such large, bold strokes that "he who runs may read."[1]

Dreiser illustrates the display of wealth as the arbiter of personal worth, but he also places a searchlight on the more disturbing spectacle of poverty. It is far more comforting to treat the poor as invisible, as do Carrie and Hurstwood when a Chicago beggar asks them for change. But Dreiser forces readers actually to *see* the poor. In a very disturbing scene late in *Sister Carrie*, Hurstwood, the onetime affluent manager reduced to beggary, becomes a public spectacle on a street in the Bowery. A philanthropist called simply "the Captain" implores passing citizens to donate a few cents to help a group of homeless men. "Spectators" of the mass misery quickly grow into a "pushing, gaping crowd" (453). Even after the Captain has accumulated enough to march the men off to dinner, the show continues, for "midnight pedestrians and loiterers stopped and stared" (457). The similarities of this sequence with the showy parade on Broadway make Hurstwood's indigence all the more disturbing. Dreiser suggests there must be some underlying connection between Carrie's and Hurstwood's stories, between the displays of wealth and of poverty.

One way of understanding that connection is to consider Carrie's and Hurstwood's different experiences in the "walled city" of New York. As Hurstwood realizes he has lost his investment in a neighborhood bar, "He began to see as one sees a city with a wall about it. Men were posted at the gates. You could not get in." Money provides access to the social order: "Those inside did not care to come out to see who you were. They were so merry inside there that all those outside were forgotten, and he was on the outside" (317). Once Carrie succeeds as an actress (off-Broadway, but still very much on display), her salary of $150 a week ($3,700 in today's dollars) gives her a different vantage point: "Ah, she was in the walled city now! Its splendid gates had opened, admitting her from a cold, dreary outside" (432).[2] Money provides the key to the city as well as to social interaction within it. And keys can lock one person out while letting another one in.

Readers often conclude Dreiser's message to be that money does not buy happiness. But if Carrie's trajectory seems to support that conclusion, Hurstwood's saga shows that lack of interest in money does not buy happiness, either. When we hold together in our mind's eye the outcomes of both characters – particularly if we ask why both turn out as they do – then the message starts looking more complicated and less comforting.

Throughout *Sister Carrie*, characters either strive or atrophy. They move forward and upward, or they move backward and downward. But some sort of movement is always necessary, as symbolized by the two train rides that set everything in motion (Carrie's to Chicago in the beginning, Carrie and Hurstwood's to New York in the middle). Movement is also, Dreiser suggests, part of the biological process. Hurstwood's decline is framed with the generalization that "a man's fortune or material progress is very much the same as his bodily growth. Either he is growing stronger, healthier, wiser, as the youth approaching manhood, or he is growing weaker, older, less incisive mentally, as the man approaching old age" (315).

While Dreiser references geography and biology, the movement that matters most is socioeconomic. Characters who react keenly to economic stimulus seek self-improvement in the only terms that, according to Dreiser, U.S. culture recognizes: acquisition of money. Those who react sluggishly decay. If Carrie's motto could be that consumer objects "touched her with individual desire," Hurstwood's might be seeing "nothing remarkable in asking [Carrie] to come down lower" (21, 418). Although Carrie and Hurstwood demonstrate most spectacularly the climb up and descent down the social ladder, they are hardly unique. Drouet, Julia and Jessica Hurstwood, and Mrs. Vance are, like the ingénue actress, strivers. They are, as we say, on the move. Bob Ames may appear to provide an alternative, but even the character who declares he would not care to be rich dines at the lavish Sherry's restaurant, another site of "exhibition," this time of "showy, wasteful, and unwholesome gastronomy" (308). Ames simply allows his wealthy relatives to pick up the check. Criticizing people for materialism is pointless when the city provides a ceaseless parade of things to want. In that environment, desire for acquisition becomes, the narrator says, "the innate trend of the mind" (46). And so the external world profoundly shapes – even determines – individual consciousness.

If the official promise of the United States is to ensure life, liberty, and the pursuit of happiness, then Dreiser suggests that while pursuit does indeed matter, happiness is not the point. Happiness entails contentment – whether in who one is, what one has, or whom one lives with – thus marking a state of quiescence, even stasis. Happiness, in other words, does not move. Dreiser repeatedly shows that when a person acquires something (whether the perfect dress, a "name," a trophy girlfriend), then that garment, status, or relationship loses its charm. Pursuit thrills us; attainment stultifies. Thus while Drouet ceases to prize Carrie soon after she moves in, when he reencounters her as a starlet, the object of the desire of hundreds of men, the salesman wants her again – precisely "because she was now so far off" (463). Likewise, after Hurstwood has begun his downward spiral and looks back on his former affluence, "the significance of the realm he had left" suddenly hits: "It did not seem so wonderful to be in it when he was in it ... but now that he was out of it, how far off it became" (317). In *Sister Carrie*, if neither money nor indifference to money buys happiness, then happiness does not buy happiness, either.

*Sister Carrie* provides a further disturbing message. The complementary, interlocking trajectories of Carrie's ascent from nonentity to celebrity and Hurstwood's from affluent manager to "nothing" (281) suggest that a culture of acquisition requires failure in order to sustain success. In a passage early in the New York section discussing Hurstwood's decline, the narrator remarks that "the great create an atmosphere which reacts badly upon the small" (281). There will always be "the great"; their tastes and whims will always shape the walled city; their displays of wealth will always wound the "small," who feel, precisely as they are supposed to feel, personal inadequacy because of it.

Dreiser's observations about the income gap in a 1920 collection of essays illuminate a discrepancy between national ideals and practice. The average U.S. citizen believes himself better off than elsewhere, but also faces "the very irritating spectacle of thousands upon thousands who have so much more than he has or can get." Particularly important is the concluding phrase, "or can get," for as Dreiser also notes, 5 percent of the nation's population owned 95 percent of the total wealth. (Recent data show the top one-one-hundredth of a percent [0.0001] of households average $27,000,000 a year while the bottom 90 percent earn $31,224.) Dreiser describes the United States as officially "dedicated to so-called intellectual and spiritual freedom," while "actually devoted with an almost bee-like industry to the gathering and storing ... of purely material things."[3]

Dreiser pursues that discrepancy between national ideals and practice in his aptly named masterpiece, *An American Tragedy* (1925). Published the same year as *The Great Gatsby*, the *Tragedy* also charts the course of a youth born to humble parents who dreams of wealth (inextricably associated with attainment of a particular woman) – and whose dream, tainted from the start with criminality, becomes the cause of his death.

The humiliating poverty of Clyde Griffiths's childhood is palpable. Like Hurstwood, Clyde is made into a shameful public spectacle: evangelical parents drag him onto the streets of Kansas City as they preach to the unconverted. Within the first few pages of an eight-hundred-page novel, it becomes clear that Clyde, "ashamed, dragged out of normal life, to be made a show and jest of," seeks escape. Two things motivate him: to "better himself" socially and to gratify the "sex lure." It turns out that those two drives are inextricable.[4]

Clyde's first step away from poverty, working as bellhop at the Green-Davidson Hotel, establishes the fusion of money and sex. Thanks to tips from hotel guests, "Clyde was impressed by the downpour of small change that was tumbling in upon him and making a small lump in his right-hand pants pocket" (49). The "lump" of coin suggests the adolescent's emergent sexuality, also aligning successful masculinity with earning money. Appropriately, Clyde becomes aware of illicit sex at the Green-Davidson; in addition, coworkers take him to a prostitute. In the culmination of this education in hotel culture the young men borrow a car and end up accidentally killing a girl. Clyde goes on the run, to reinvent himself, like many another Dreiser character, in Chicago. More importantly, the car accident that concludes book one weaves the motif of accidental criminality into the pattern of money and sex.

The sexy, shallow Hortense Briggs also advances Clyde's education. She lusts after a fur coat, which she addresses with annoying baby talk: "Oh you pity sing ... if I could only have 'oo" (102). Figuring she can manipulate Clyde into buying it for her, Hortense tries on the coat for him in front of a three-way mirror. This triple display of the coat (reminiscent of Carrie's Broadway stroll) magnifies Clyde's desire for the woman in it. His lust tangible, he speculates "as to the probable trading value, affectionally speaking, of such a coat" (102). Although Clyde never gets Hortense, he is starting to see the equivalence of sex and money.

If Clyde thinks (with good reason) that Hortense can be bought, his desire for the glamorous Sondra Finchley links romance and money in a different way. The daughter of a wealthy manufacturer, Sondra belongs to the "fast set" (149). Her on-the-move friends drive fancy cars that make Clyde feel "a keen sense of a deficiency" (327). While Sondra (another baby talker) seems "the most adorable feminine thing he had seen in all his days," Clyde desires her, surprisingly, "without lust" (378). Rather, we hear in a surprising simile, the young man "dreamed into her eyes as might a devotee into those of a saint" (379). Clyde's chaste longing indicates that social aspiration trumps even sexual conquest. Sondra, quite simply, "arous[ed] in him a curiously stinging sense of what it was to want and not to have" (225). If that reaction sounds familiar to readers of *Sister Carrie*, then so should Sondra's consummate desirability precisely because she lies just out of reach. As Fitzgerald's Daisy Buchanan does for Gatsby, Sondra "materialized and magnified for [Clyde] the meaning of that upper level" (319).

Clyde's relationship with the factory worker Roberta Alden is initially as passionate as his desire for Sondra is sexless. And Roberta's own desire mirrors Clyde's social ambitions. Like almost everyone else in Lycurgus, Roberta "imagined he moved" in a "superior world" of wealth. This mistaken assumption contributes to her becoming "seized with the very virus of ambition and unrest that afflicted him" (257). And as Roberta sees in her boss the better social position to which she aspires, he sees in her the shameful poverty that he has fled. Clyde's agonizing over how to get rid of Roberta (which begins almost as soon as their sexual relationship commences) reaches crisis point when, out on a drive with his rich pseudofriends, Clyde realizes they have stopped, coincidentally, right in front of the "extremely dilapidated old farm-house" where Roberta grew up. Instinctively, Clyde wants to "turn and run" from his deepest fear: that "this other world from which he sprang might extend its gloomy, poverty-stricken arms to him and envelop him once more, just as the poverty of his family had enveloped and almost strangled him from the first" (444–5). Implausible as a plot device, the coincidence nevertheless illuminates the psychology of a person who feels he has "made it" – but instinctively understands the precariousness of his status.

Without question, Clyde's most contemptible desire is to get rid of the girlfriend he has impregnated. But where did he get that ugly notion of poor people as expendable? We need look no further than to the upright, ultrasuccessful Samuel Griffiths. The uncle who represents everything Clyde wants informs his family right after he has hired Clyde, "If he doesn't [make good], we will have to toss him aside, of course" (160). In addition to believing his own relative is disposable, Griffiths finds class hierarchy delightful, believing "there had to be higher and higher social orders to which the lower social classes could aspire" (178). Yet by instructing his family to ignore their cousin while telling Clyde not to fraternize with factory hands, Griffiths places Clyde in a social no-man's-land. If Hurstwood regretted his invisibility to partygoers in the walled city, then Clyde has no sanctioned community at all.

Samuel Griffiths's attitudes concretize why Dreiser did not title the novel "A Young Man's Tragedy" but *An American Tragedy*. In an essay about the genesis of the novel, Dreiser explains that he had traced for decades a criminal pattern: young men of impoverished backgrounds killed pregnant girlfriends when there was a wealthier, more glamorous girlfriend in the wings. Dreiser extensively researched one such 1906 murder case, Chester Gillette's drowning of his pregnant girlfriend Billy Brown. (The accused man's initials became those of Dreiser's protagonist Clyde Griffiths, while "Billy" reappears as the girlfriend nicknamed "Bert.") Poring over this case, Dreiser became "convinced that there was an entire misunderstanding ... of the conditions or circumstances surrounding the victims of that murder *before* the murder was committed." Born to "street preachers" who were "pariahs," Gillette "had obviously been over-impressed by what he considered the superior state of others"; he believed affiliation with a wealthy uncle would make him "naturally pass from a lower to a higher social and financial state." The critical point for Dreiser is that Gillette's ambition was to attain precisely what American culture had taught him mattered: wealth and status. Thus, Dreiser concluded, Gillette did not have "an *anti-social* dream as Americans should see it, but rather a *pro-social* dream."[5]

That perspective illuminates the exhaustive (and exhausting) account of the prosecution of Clyde in book three. All the novel's main action completed, Dreiser concentrates on implication, analysis, and social commentary. (A great admirer of Dreiser, Richard Wright would adopt this tripartite structure to similar ends in *Native Son* [1940].) Ironically, Clyde attains in the public eye the status he had always sought – only it turns out that perception has nothing to do with reality. To the prosecuting attorney, Clyde personifies the arrogance of "Wealth! Position!" His drowning Roberta was "part and parcel of a rich and sophisticated youth's attitude toward a poor girl" (540). A second arm of the legal system, the jury perverts the justice they are supposed to serve because all were "convinced of Clyde's guilt before ever they set down" (671). Their verdict disregards the judge's explicit instructions that if Roberta fell from the boat "accidentally or involuntarily" and Clyde "made no attempt to rescue her," then he was not guilty (774). The media ensure that all citizens follow the jury in betraying the premise that everyone is innocent until proven guilty. Cashing in on the tragedy's "national news value," the press disseminates half-truths that are then repackaged as pamphlets for sale – along with peanuts, popcorn, and other tasty snacks. Book three of the *Tragedy* takes Dreiser's interest in the spectacle of social position to a devastating conclusion.

Three novels from the middle of Dreiser's career, *Jennie Gerhardt* (1911), *The Financier* (1912), and *The "Genius"* (1915), continue to examine the discrepancy between national ideals and practice. Still involved with money and status, these novels also expose how the official values of U.S. culture concerning sex and marriage lead people to prejudge others who are stronger, better, and, in some cases, more moral than those who place themselves in the role of jury.

The title character in *Jennie Gerhardt*, who is from a family even poorer than Clyde Griffiths's, finds herself unwed and pregnant when her lover, an older senator, unexpectedly dies. It will take her father years to forgive Jennie for her sin, and she suffers class-based judgment from the wealthy family who hires her as a maid and considers her in all ways their inferior. When a love affair with the well-connected Lester Kane develops, Jennie hides her illegitimate child from him even while she and Lester both hide their relationship from his family. When Lester discovers Jennie's child, he condemns her – astoundingly, as he is sleeping with her himself. During all this, the Kane family agitates for Lester to marry the heiress Letty Pace – not because he loves her but because she seems the "ideal wife" and "ideal social figure."[6]

*Jennie Gerhardt* pits authentic goodness (represented by Jennie) against conventional morality (represented by the Kane family and Letty Pace). Passages throughout the novel assert Jennie's decency, integrity, and even moral superiority. Likewise, Jennie's common-law marriage with Lester appears as the novel's legitimate, authentic relationship because, quite simply, they love each other. Lester considers Jennie his "soul-mate or affinity," the "only woman" for him (185, 410). Conventional morality, however, dictates that marriage is a legal, religious, and social institution and valid only in those terms. When the Kanes discover Lester's liaison with a social inferior, they increase their "coercion" (278), using the threat of disinheritance to compel him to marry Letty. When Lester finally "sacrifice[s] … the virtues – kindness, loyalty, affection – to policy," he knows that leaving Jennie for Letty, while socially correct, is "spiritual[ly]" wrong (365, 369). And so correctness triumphs over goodness.

Frank Cowperwood of *The Financier* is as self-centered and ruthless as Jennie is other-directed and considerate. Young Cowperwood's outlook crystallizes when he abstracts from the spectacle of a lobster devouring a squid a Social Darwinian message – "Things lived on other things.… Lobsters lived on squids" – and men must therefore live on other men. Cowperwood's code, "I satisfy myself," serves him well in the stock market, where he excels in selling short.[7] Betting that the price of stock will fall, particularly during panics, the short seller makes millions from others' losses, demonstrating in another way the structural dependence of wealth on poverty.

Cowperwood's amoralism extends from the boardroom into the bedroom. When his wife started having babies, the financier "liked it, the idea of self-duplication. It was almost acquisitive" (57). However, Cowperwood quickly tires of his dull, conventional wife and falls for Aileen Butler, the fiery-haired daughter of a key business associate. As in *Jennie Gerhardt*, the relationship marked by love, passion, and compatibility – the relationship that seems truly authentic – exists outside marriage. While "society lifts its hands in horror" at sex out of wedlock, while "dogma may bind some minds; fear others," the narrator admires the "freer basis of relationship" he delineates between the financier and Aileen. The retaliation against Cowperwood once the affair is discovered dwarfs anything endured by Lester Kane. The rage of Aileen's father combined with a general climate of self-righteousness sets in motion a complicated series of events culminating in the trial and imprisonment of Cowperwood. (He emerges phoenixlike at the end, and Dreiser continues the Cowperwood saga in *The Titan* [1914] and *The Stoic* [1947].)

Frank Cowperwood is often compared to the protagonist of Dreiser's most autobiographical novel, *The "Genius."* Eugene Witla also dreams big and has a constitutional aversion to monogamy. But Witla is an artist, and *The "Genius"* traces two interlocking trajectories: his zigzagging ascent as an Ashcan painter and the steady descent of his marriage. Sex lies at the center of both plots. Inspired by the fleshy, sensuous nudes of the nineteenth-century French painter Bouguereau, Witla believes that art represents an alternative to conventional morality. (A connoisseur and collector, Cowperwood also loved painting.) Witla revels in art that is "anathema to the conservative and puritanical in mind, the religious in temperament, the cautious in training or taste." An antipuritan "pagan to the core," Witla paints boldly, much as he pursues women, before, during, and after his marriage. His wife, Angela, who believes "as it was written socially and ethically upon the tables of the law, so was it," represents the force of the conventional that Witla must keep at bay in order to produce original art.[8]

"True art," Dreiser himself maintained, "speaks plainly." He meant by that, first, that writers should use direct, unvarnished words. But he also meant that writers had a moral obligation to depict reality – particularly when reality had been obscured by wish fulfillment, hypocrisy, or convention. For Dreiser, that obligation meant spotlighting the dark side of the American Dream, the fact that spectacular wealth required abject poverty, the frequent irrelevance of official morality to doing the right thing. Dreiser's notion of "true art" redirected the course of U.S. literary history. Sinclair Lewis, in his speech accepting the Nobel Prize for literature, paid tribute to Dreiser as having "cleared the trail from Victorian and Howellsian timidity ... to honesty and boldness and passion of life. Without his pioneering," Lewis continued, "I doubt if any of us could, unless we liked to be sent to jail, seek to express life and beauty and terror."[9]

### FURTHER READING

Cassuto, Leonard and Clare Virginia Eby, *The Cambridge Companion to Theodore Dreiser*, Cambridge, Cambridge University Press, 2004.

Fleissner, Jennifer, *Women, Compulsion, Modernity: The Moment of American Naturalism*, Chicago, University of Chicago Press, 2004.

Howard, June, *Form and History in American Literary Naturalism*, Durham, N.C., Duke University Press, 1985.

Kaplan, Amy, *The Social Construction of American Realism*, Chicago, University of Chicago Press, 1988.

Michaels, Walter Benn, *The Gold Standard and the Logic of Naturalism*, Berkeley and Los Angeles, University California Press, 1987.

Pizer, Donald (ed.), *Critical Essays on Theodore Dreiser*, Boston, G. K. Hall, 1981.

Pizer, Donald (ed.), *New Essays on Sister Carrie*, Cambridge, Cambridge University Press, 1991.

## NOTES

1 Theodore Dreiser, *Sister Carrie* (New York, Signet Classic, 2000), pp. 298, 299; Thorstein Veblen, *The Theory of the Leisure Class* (New York, Modern Library, 1934), p. 87. Subsequent references to *Sister Carrie* will be made parenthetically.

2 Calculation based on Consumer Price Index on measuringworth.com.

3 Theodore Dreiser, "Some Aspects of Our National Character," in *Hey Rub-a-Dub-Dub* (New York, Boni and Liveright, 1920), p. 46; Dave Gilson and Carolyn Perot, "It's the Inequality, Stupid," *Mother Jones,* accessed online http://mother-jones.com/politics/2011/02/income-inequality-in-america-chart-graph; Theodore Dreiser, "Life, Art, and America," in *Hey Rub-a-Dub-Dub*, p. 258.

4 Theodore Dreiser, *An American Tragedy* (New York, Signet Classic, 2000), p. 4, 8, 13. Subsequent references will be made parenthetically.

5 Theodore Dreiser, "I Find the Real American Tragedy," rpt. in *Theodore Dreiser: A Selection of Uncollected Prose*, ed. Donald Pizer (Detroit, Wayne State University Press, 1977), pp. 296, 297, Dreiser's emphasis. Woody Allen's *Match Point* (2005) updates this American plot with a distinctive twist.

6 Theodore Dreiser, *Jennie Gerhardt*, ed. James L. W. West III (Dreiser Edition: Philadelphia, University Pennsylvania Press, 1992), p. 310, 312. Subsequent references will be made parenthetically.

7 Theodore Dreiser, *The Financier* (New York, Meridian, 1995), pp. 8, 121. Subsequent references will be made parenthetically.

8 Theodore Dreiser, *The "Genius"* (New York, Boni and Liveright, 1923), pp. 52, 734, 65.

9 Theodore Dreiser, "True Art Speaks Plainly," *Documents of Modern Literary Realism*, ed. George Becker (Princeton, N.J., Princeton University Press, 1963), p. 154; Sinclair Lewis, "The American Fear of Literature," rpt. in *The Man from Main Street*, ed. Harry E. Maule and Melville H. Cane (New York, Pocket Books, 1953), pp. 7–8.

# 9
## Willa Cather

TIMOTHY PARRISH

Willa Cather (1873–1947) is one of a handful of undeniably "classic" American authors. Where many of the most cherished American novelists are known primarily for having written one novel that is read again and again, Cather wrote several. The Prairie Trilogy of *O Pioneers!* (1913), *The Song of the Lark* (1915), *My Antonia* (1918), along with *A Lost Lady* (1923), *My Mortal Enemy* (1926), and *Death Comes for the Archbishop* (1927) compose a list of works that would be the envy of virtually any other twentieth-century novelist. Among American novelists, only Henry James and William Faulkner can be said to have written a greater number of novels of enduring value than Cather. *My Antonia* and *Death Comes for the Archbishop* stand beside *The Scarlet Letter* (1850), *Moby-Dick* (1851), *Huckleberry Finn* (1884), and *Invisible Man* (1952) as essential literary works that seem to ask and definitely answer the question of what it has meant to try to be American. Cather may be the most truly "national" writer in the American literary tradition, though as a literary artist her work was uncompromisingly original. Were we to imagine that all of American literature had been bound and contained within a single library and that by some terrible misfortune that library had been set ablaze, the survival of Cather's works perhaps more than those of any other American writer would speak to future readers and allow them to imagine the challenges and disappointments faced by strangers come together from foreign lands to wrest from nature and each other a civilization that was itself the pursuit of an ideal. She was America's elegist and, as a novelist, its epic poet.

Cather is known as the writer of Nebraska, a master of the native tongue that became the language of the American plains. Equally important, Cather was profoundly writing within the larger tradition of the novel of James and Hawthorne as well as Tolstoy, Flaubert, and Balzac. The conjunction of a particular setting embedded within a larger literary tradition marks the terrain of her achievement: a perfect instance of how the American novel at its best reinvents the form under the pressure of a new location. Sometimes miscast simply as a local colorist, Cather's imagination was epic as well as novelistic. A deeply cultured writer, Cather drew on Virgil's *Georgics* and *Aeneid,* poetic narratives of farming and nation building that she recast in her frontier stories. As in the work of Cormac McCarthy, her most obvious inheritor, Cather's Americans find themselves on the border where the Old World of Europe confronts the strange New World of America. Thus, her fiction looks back to the peoples who inhabited the North American continent before the Europeans arrived even as it portrays how those Europeans were transforming the legacies of those peoples. Cather's writing, with its insistence on the primacy of nature, portrays both the transience of human endeavor and humans' will to leave a record of their noblest intentions. William Faulkner's famous declaration that writers must write against the certainty of doom is an apt description of Cather's work as well.

Cather was born in Virginia in 1873 but her family relocated to Red Cloud, Nebraska, when she was nine. The move decisively shaped how she perceived the world and her place in it. In her words, she was "jerked away" from a "child's life" that was "bound up in the woods and the hills around it" and thrown "into a country that was as bare as a piece of sheet metal." "I felt," she said, "as if we had come to the end of everything – it was a kind of erasure of personality."[1] From this desolate feeling of being exposed before nature with "no place to hide," exiled with only the sky and the plains for company, Cather fashioned her aesthetic vision.

The "erasure of personality" she experienced upon moving to the prairie she would give to Jim Burden, the narrator of *My Antonia*, who also arrives in Nebraska lost beneath "the complete dome of heaven, all there was of it." Jim recalls being "jolted" by the wagon that carries him. Stranded between an equally vast earth and sky, he feels "erased, blotted out."[2] Eventually, the Czech immigrant Antonia will inspire him to appreciate his surroundings. In a famous passage, Antonia points to the sky and asks Jim to provide the English word for what she sees. After Jim tells her the word he thinks that she wants to hear, Antonia points to the sky and to Jim's eyes. He repeats the word, which Antonia pronounces as "ice." At first Antonia's language confuses Jim, but together they determine that Antonia is trying to say that the sky and Jim's eyes are the same color. The phrase "blue sky, blue eyes" is almost the only English that Antonia knows but it deftly conveys Cather's aesthetic vision: humans cannot see except in the context of the natural world that surrounds them. The emptiness that Jim initially experiences under the vast Nebraska sky is redeemed by his encounter with Antonia. Jim's eyes express the beauty of the sky as they also reflect the beauty of Antonia as she struggles to make a place for herself on the prairie.

Cather's characters struggle to fashion a living space within the vast blankness that threatens Jim Burden. The story of Willa Cather is of someone who came from nowhere and from humble origins fashioned a career for herself as one of America's greatest writers. Like the opera singer Thea Kronberg in *Song of the Lark*, Cather benefited from unusual friendships with talented adults. In her twenty-five-hundred-person town, Cather befriended immigrant adults from Norway, Germany, and England who taught her music, shared their libraries, and helped her to read Greek and Latin. With William Ducker, a clerk in a dry goods store, Cather not only studied Homer, Virgil, and Ovid, but also learned to conduct scientific experiments in his laboratory and even practiced vivisection. She hoped to become a doctor. When she was preparing to enter the University of Nebraska as one of its few female students, however, she wrote an essay on Thomas Carlyle that so impressed her instructor that he submitted it without her knowledge to the *Nebraska State Journal*. Upon seeing her work in print, Cather decided to give up medicine for writing.

Twenty years would pass before Cather would begin to make a name for herself with her first novel, *Alexander's Bridge* (1912), a work that reviewers labeled as being derivative of Henry James. In between she worked as a teacher and journalist, publishing numerous stories and poems. She knew Stephen Crane and met Sarah Orne Jewett, who urged her to write about the places and people she knew from childhood. Meeting Crane and Jewett confirmed her sense that she could be an artist, but the encouragement she took from them probably did not equal what she had already received in childhood. Cather's will to make herself into the artist she aspired to become was unrelenting and steeped in her own remarkable determination. "The fact I was a girl," she once remarked, "never damaged my ambitions to be a pope or an emperor." [3]

Cather gave a version of this ambition to Thea Kronberg, and in *The Song of the Lark* she wrote what was perhaps the first birth of an artist story that imagined a woman fulfilling that role. The life of Cather's heroine was not defined by her sexual identity; nor was Thea punished for refusing the conventional sexual roles assigned to female heroines, whether written by women or men. Though she marries and her match is a good one for her, marriage is not a defining element of her story except in the paradoxical sense that it is secondary to her ambition to become an artist. She is not asexual – in fact she has sex before she is married with the man she will eventually marry. What defines her is not her relationship to men, but that her art will always come first.

Thea claims the same prerogative that a male character of Tolstoy or Joyce would, and thus her story is not limited to her role as a mother, a daughter, or a wife. The heroines of the Prairie Trilogy consistently subvert the gendered conventions established by the history of the novel before Cather. In *O Pioneers!*, Alexandra is set above her brothers to run the family farm, and her vision brings success to their enterprise. Antonia has a child out of wedlock but this act does not prevent her from becoming married and raising a family. Cather, an avid reader of Tolstoy, allows Alexandra and Antonia the ecstasy of raising food from the land that Levin enjoys among the peasants in *Anna Karenina* (1877) yet makes them responsible for the yield of their crops in a way that Levin never is. Moreover, they run their households from the kitchen to the fields and achieve a power unknown to male heroes. Although each character encounters social resistance, their lives are portrayed as perfectly ordinary. Cather's heroines are not revolutionaries, even if her novels are. They seize life as they find it and make of it what they can.

Cather's career as a writer followed a path similar to her heroines'. She refused to allow the expectations of what was proper for a woman writer to determine her choices as an artist. She also declined to assert that her literary choices constituted a revolution in what or how women could write. Unlike Virginia Woolf, who admired Cather's work, she did not construct a theory of women's writing that justified or "theorized" her efforts to create. She did as any other writer would do: she tried to write the best she could. She was a woman and she wrote.

Cather, like her famous heroines, quietly claimed for herself the same possibilities to create as men did. Nor did she restrict herself to writing only the stories of women. After the Prairie Trilogy, Cather began to write novels about men. The Pulitzer Prize–winning *One of Ours* (1922) focused on men at war. *Death Comes to the Archbishop* and *Shadows on the Rock* (1927) are unsentimental religious novels featuring celibate men living on the frontier. Because she wrote so powerfully about men and women, even employing a male persona to write about women, she meets the ideal of the androgynous artist that Virginia Woolf describes in *A Room of One's Own* (1929). All of these novels attracted wide readerships, but major male critics questioned their fitness as literary subjects and Cather's authority to write them. *One of Ours*, in particular, was attacked by H. L. Mencken, Edmund Wilson, and Ernest Hemingway, among others. Although recent feminist critics have reclaimed Cather as a lesbian author (a reading never endorsed by Cather), her career unfortunately remains a textbook case of how sexual politics can affect a writer's literary reputation and fundamentally obscure his or her literary importance.

Had Cather retired after *My Antonia*, or continued to write books in the vein of the Prairie Trilogy, she would not be such a complex and misunderstood figure in the American literary tradition. Her turn from writing female-centered books with *One of Ours* triggered a reevaluation of Cather that has not been resolved to this day. Instead of being perceived as a major new voice in American literature, as H. L. Mencken and Randolph Bourne had declared, she became the embodiment of the woman writer who could not stay in her place. No one questioned that Cather's prose was beautiful. Measured, precise, every word in its perfect place: her writing has the beauty of an ancient rock above a river, its stern features carved by centuries of wind. Instead of recognizing the uniqueness of her achievement, male critics from the 1920s to 1950s attacked her choice of subject matter and deemed it inappropriate for "a lady novelist." Robert Spiller's 1963 *Literary History of the United States* summed up decades of biased criticism when it declared Cather to be "preservative, almost antiquarian, content with much space in little room – feminine in this." [4]

Critics of her era wrongly labeled her as a minor writer principally concerned with small domestic spaces. In this context, Cather's work may be contrasted with that of the American author with whom she is most often associated, Henry James, a writer more often concerned with domestic spaces than Cather ever was. The reason why Cather has been so linked to James is not because their visions of America or American life are compatible. They are not. Cather's America does not begin or end in New England. Neither is it an inheritance from England or an escape to England. In fact, one of Cather's crucial contributions as an American novelist was to demonstrate that the foundations for an American literature and history are no more embedded in New England than they are in Nebraska, Colorado, New Mexico, or Arizona. New England is simply one of many places where Europeans landed.

In his biography of Hawthorne, James suggested that American culture was intellectually impoverished and socially backward. James pointed to the "absent things" in American life, by which he meant the kinds of social hierarchies and institutions that accrued in Europe after the Middle Ages and Renaissance. James's choice to make a career in Europe was justified by his brilliant works, but Cather proved that James's assumption that America did not have the materials for creating a great literature was simply wrong. Along with creating roles for female characters that broke with the tradition of the novel, Cather portrayed the scope of the European engagement with the natural landscape of North America, never forgetting that people were here before Europeans arrived. She refused to treat American literature as if it were but the expression of or revolt against the Puritan New England mind, and used her version of the American novel to imagine an America other than the one implied by Hawthorne and James.

The reason that Cather has been so often compared with Henry James, and not Mark Twain, who is often given the credit for "Westernizing" American literature when Cather arguably achieved this task more thoroughly than Twain, is because her novels are beautifully written and formally ingenious. Cather learned well from James's narrative experiments in point of view. As in James, Cather's novels often seem to stop just short of explaining some crucial moment in a character's development, revealing, in Cather's words, "the inexplicable presence of the thing not named" (*Stories* 837). The lives of the protagonists in *A Lost Lady* and *My Mortal Enemy* are conveyed through what the narrator does not know and cannot say. In neither of these novels is the full story of the narrative's protagonist told. Instead, the heroines' stories are framed through the limited perspectives of other characters. While Cather's heroines have suffered, one also senses that they have accepted their suffering as an inevitable part of having tried to live according to their own sense of beauty and even splendor. Cather's deft artistry creates a context in which the perspective and implied judgment of the narrator do not coincide with the heroine's implied view of herself and her story.

In 1931, Cather observed that when she began, the aspiring American writer looked to "Henry James and Mrs. Wharton … our most interesting novelists." Writers who "followed their manner" wrote about "smart people or clever people," and thus "the drawing room was considered the proper setting for a novel" (*Stories* 963–4). Ultimately, Cather overturned the tradition of Henry James in two important ways. First, Cather broke with James and the modernists by choosing not to locate her fiction within the complexity of a given character's consciousness. Though highly wrought, Cather's fiction does not make subjectivity, or consciousness, its focus. She is a brilliant storyteller and her stories concern characters who do not lead the kinds of lives that intellectuals typically experience or value. Yet, by leaving the drawing room and locating her dramas within the natural world that extends from Mexico to Canada, Cather portrayed a wider range of American possibility and doing than had any previous American author.

In Cather's world, by contrast to James's, characters are too busy doing things to be trapped by or within their thoughts. Only when they stop working, as St. Peter does in *The Professor's House* (1925), are they prey to the kind of stasis that afflicts Isabel Archer. Her characters may pursue an ideal – Cather said that the purpose of art is to connect with "some highest thing" – but it leads them into the world that is greater and more diverse than any drawing room (*Kingdom* 132; 12). Nor do they embody some preexisting trait of *Americanness*. Cather's characters are revealed through their actions and their heroism consists in their willingness to risk themselves in action to pursue an ideal. They are engaged in acts of history making. The heroines of *O Pioneers!* and *My Antonia* literally create lives out of the landscape. The characters in *Shadows on the Rock* sacrifice themselves for an ideal of civilization that the wilderness of Quebec only deepens. The priests of *Death Comes for the Archbishop* enact the collision between Europe and the New World and are part of the transformation of a continent that would make possible the career of Henry James. Although James insisted that it takes a great deal of history to produce a little literature, it was Cather, foremost among all American novelists, who portrayed how literature is made from the creation of history.

Critics of her era sometimes complained that Cather's fiction did not confront the present moment but in this she resembles Hawthorne, Twain, and Faulkner, who also situated their major works in the past. Cather was criticized for creating fictions that were riches in a little room, but few if any American novelists take in as much space or time as Cather did. For Cather, the American story had its precedent both in the Roman Empire (hence her love for Virgil) and in the remains of the Indian civilizations in the American Southwest. Thus, the founding of Quebec by the French in the seventeenth century or the Catholic efforts in the Mexican (formerly Spanish) territories to convert Indians to Christianity are as "American" as the pioneering efforts in *O Pioneers!* and *My Antonia* to create the farms that will sustain the towns of Colorado and Nebraska. Cather's fiction moves easily across the territory between Mexico and Canada; it goes from New York to California; it travels like a boomerang over the Atlantic Ocean as her characters repeatedly move between the two continents. In addition to the wide expanse of time and space, Cather's novels bring a wide world to the reader through the spectrum of peoples she includes within her works. Canadians, Mexicans, Indians, slaves, immigrants from virtually every European country; Catholics, Episcopalians, Baptists, Lutherans, Jews; pioneers, opera singers, professors, engineers, railroad magnates, millers, missionaries, soldiers, counts, bishops, priests, farmers, ranchers, music teachers, actresses, dressmakers, bakers, pharmacists, doctors, lawyers, married women, unmarried women, married men, unmarried men, and children of all ages are portrayed with great intelligence and sympathy in her novels. Cather is a quintessentially American novelist, yet there is no single typical or representative American in her fiction.

Because Cather refused to accept that American history begins with the Puritans or is simply an Anglo-American tradition, Cather's conception of America and American literature is broader than most intellectual histories of American culture have allowed. Cather's America has little to do with the conventional boundaries of the United States. *Shadows on the Rock,* drawn from the histories of Francis Parkman, concerns French characters living in Quebec nearly one hundred years before George Washington became president. Much of *Death Comes to the Archbishop*, perhaps her most enduring novel, takes place in Arizona and New Mexico before they became American territories. The two main characters, Father Latour and Father Joseph Vaillant, are French, not American, and struggle to speak Spanish, not English, to the Mexicans and Indians whom they try to convert to Catholicism. During the course of the novel, the U.S. war against Mexico occurs and the territory where they work changes governments. Yet, this seemingly decisive historical event is at best incidental to their work. The outcome of the war is not celebrated – it is barely noticed – and the priests continue their labors.

While Cather's fiction can be interpreted to celebrate the "conquest" of America by Europeans, it is not actually that interested in claiming this event as either an American achievement or even one that is exceptional. Likewise, Cather's characters are rarely identified as "American," and when they are, it is not usually a favorable description. Her novels identify the characters by country of origin and are almost always more sympathetic to immigrant characters living in exile than to the Americanized ones. One cannot say that characters in her fiction triumph since the work they perform is provisional and in a sense never-ending. At best her characters' actions are part of a larger ongoing action that will achieve greater significance after their deaths: Auclair and his daughter settling Quebec, the pioneers converting the land-scape so that towns and cities may be built, the priests bringing Catholicism to the unconverted.

Inspired by Virgil's *Aeneid*, Cather situated her characters' modest triumphs within the epic context of empire building. Her work does not imply that America is the New Rome, though, and it is not meant to triumphantly poeticize the founding of an empire. Implicit within her fiction is the sense that nothing endures except the commitment to an ideal. What is built in pursuit of this ideal, no matter how ingenious or substantial, will perish. Thus Cather's immigrant characters find inspiration not only in the customs they carry with them, but also in their recognition that peoples unknown to them have left previous marks in the sand.

Along with stressing the polyglot nature of American existence, Cather repeatedly looks to the example of peoples who preceded the European arrival on this continent. In *Song of the Lark*, Thea's birth as an artist begins when she is living among Indian ruins. The fragments of pottery Thea finds "were like fetters that bound one to one long chain of human endeavor" (*Early* 553). Her desire to create is sustained by the Ancients who had "lengthened her past" and revealed her to have "older and higher obligations" (*Early* 555). In *The Professor's House*, Professor St. Peter and Tom Outland likewise find inspiration in ruins of the Anasazi dwellings. In *Death Comes for the Archbishop*, Father Latour refuses to correct an Indian who says that the stars are gods and instead acknowledges that the Indian's gods are as living as his Catholic God.

In Cather's capacious vision, the American literary tradition is a mingling of peoples and an overlapping of historical epochs. Rather than restricting her work to a narrow view of her immediate present, Cather established a living continuity between the past civilizations, European and non-European, and her "American" one. In so doing, Cather gave American literature a perspective sufficiently broad that future Americans might situate their present within her fiction.

In the revisionist novel *Blood Meridian* (1985), set in the middle of the American nineteenth century, Cormac McCarthy works within Cather's tradition when his characters confront the ruins of the Anasazi. Confronting the remains of "the old ones" who "once lived here," the judge says of them that "the tools, the art, the building – stand in judgement on the later races." The spirit of this prior people is "entombed in stone" and the implication of the passage is that Americans "conquering" the West will not dislodge the presence of the "dead fathers" whose works they encounter.[5]

The judge's acknowledgment of the vanished Anasazi evokes the famous image in *My Ántonia* of a plough's long shadow being cast across the prairie by the setting sun. A Virgilian tribute to the civilization being created through the use of that plough, this image also conveys an almost divine balance between human will and nature's force that is present throughout Cather's fiction. Yet, the balance is fleeting since soon the sun sets and "the forgotten plough" must "sink back into its own littleness somewhere on the prairie" (*Early* 866). Written in prose so chiseled and pure that it seems only stone can contain it, Cather's work imagines the end in the American beginning. When American literature ceases to be written, Cather's fiction will endure, potsherds from which epochs may be pieced together.

## FURTHER READING

Acocella, Joan, *Willa Cather and the Politics of Criticism*, New York, Vintage Books, 2002.

Cather, Willa, *Not Under Forty*, Lincoln, University of Nebraska Press, 1988.

Hoover, Sharon (ed.), *Willa Cather Remembered*, Lincoln and London, University of Nebraska Press, 2002.

Lee, Hermione, *Willa Cather: Double Lives*, New York, Random House, 1989.

Lindemann, Marilee, *Willa Cather: Queering America*, New York, Columbia University Press, 1999.

Murphy, John J. (ed.), *Critical Essays on Willa Cather*, Boston, G. K. Hall, 1984.

O'Brien, Sharon, "Becoming Noncanonical: The Case against Willa Cather," *American Quarterly*, 40.1 (1988): 110–26.

Schroeter, James (ed.), *Willa Cather and Her Critics*, Ithaca, N.Y., Cornell University Press, 1967.

Woodress, James, *Willa Cather: A Literary Life*, Lincoln, University of Nebraska Press, 1987.

## NOTES

1 Willa Cather, *The Kingdom of Art: Willa Cather's First Principles and Critical Statements*, ed. Bernice Slote (Lincoln, University of Nebraska Press), p. 438. Hereafter cited as *Kingdom* in the text.

2 Cather, *Early Novels and Stories*, ed. Sharon O'Brien (New York, Library of America, 1987), p. 718. Hereafter cited as *Early* in the text.

3 Cather, *The World and the Parish: Willa Cather's Articles and Reviews, 1893–1902*, ed. William Curtin, 2 vols. (Lincoln, University of Nebraska Press), vol. I, p. 368.

4 Robert E. Spiller et al., eds, *Literary History of the United States: History*, 3rd ed. rev. (New York, Macmillan, 1963), p. 1216.

5 Cormac McCarthy, *Blood Meridian or the Evening Redness in the West* (New York, Random House, 1985), p. 148.

# 10

# F. Scott Fitzgerald

RUTH PRIGOZY

All he was was one of our best novelists, one of our best novella-ists, and one of our finest writers of short stories.

John O'Hara

In a new biography of J. D. Salinger, we learn that F. Scott Fitzgerald was one of the most important influences on the writer of the novel that was to become one of the most popular of the twentieth century – and beyond, *The Catcher in the Rye* (1951). Salinger had met Hemingway in 1945, shortly after the American troops of World War II entered Paris. He knew from Hemingway's writings that he could be found at the Ritz Hotel, so Salinger wrote to "Poppa" and asked whether he could meet him at the Ritz Bar. He knew of the conflict between Fitzgerald and Hemingway and was careful not to reveal his admiration for the writer who, for him, far exceeded the merits not only of Hemingway, but of William Faulkner and Sherwood Anderson as well. Indeed, for Salinger, Fitzgerald belonged with Hawthorne, Melville, Mark Twain, Henry James, and the other masters of fiction from the previous century.[1]

The importance of *The Great Gatsby* rests partly on its entrance into our vocabulary – as a word with specific connotations: "gatsbyesque" today is short for the desire to raise oneself out of a lower-class background, to achieve in life the dreams that the early settlers of the country pursued until they were able to rise on the social ladder, realizing the possibilities they had always believed awaited them. Although this classic sells more than 300,000 copies every year, it did not achieve the instant success that might have been expected. Fitzgerald's first novel, *This Side of Paradise* (1920), was the work that catapulted him into instant fame. Although it was rejected in its original form, titled *The Romantic Egotist*, the editor Maxwell Perkins, with whom Fitzgerald had been corresponding, urged him to revise it and to resubmit it to Scribner's.

Although Fitzgerald's first novel was not published until 1920, he had been writing from his early years when he attended, first, St. Paul Prep and, later, the Newman School in Hackensack, New Jersey. Those early publications suggest the close connections between his life and his fiction. It is also apparent that like many of our greatest novelists Fitzgerald felt intricately connected to the history of his country. Born in 1896, he experienced the changes that accompanied the turn of the century: World War I, the "boom" of the 1920s (which Fitzgerald named "the Jazz Age"), the Great Depression (or "the bust") of the 1930s, and the melancholia that identified that era.[2]

Because of his poor grades, he moved from St. Paul to the East, a move that was to provide the inspiration for much of his future work. It was close to New York City, which offered the excitement he craved and was crucial to his literary career: New York had everything he had missed, and it carried the promise of the success that would ultimately give him both happiness and tragedy.

Fitzgerald was accepted at Princeton conditionally but never graduated. It was there that he formed friendships with Edmund Wilson and John Peale Bishop, both of whom would stimulate the "Fitzgerald Revival" decades later. He would not tell classmates that he was from St. Paul, but rather that he was a Princeton man – for he found this appellation more appealing to the young women to whom he was attracted. Unfortunately, the Minnesota debutante with whom he fell in love, Ginevra King, although drawn to Fitzgerald, would not consider him seriously as a suitor. The comment by Daisy Buchanan, "Rich girls don't marry poor boys," so familiar today, was actually Ginevra's when she rejected Fitzgerald's proposal in 1917. It was a remark that almost certainly she wished him to hear. She was a femme fatale reflected in early stories as well as in Gloria in *The Beautiful and Damned* (1922) and later in Daisy Buchanan and Nicole Diver. Fitzgerald himself indicated the extent to which his portraits of women in his stories and novels were based upon his wife, Zelda, although there are many female characters drawn from other women he encountered over the years, including the actress Lois Moran, and his last lover, Sheilah Graham.[3]

Drinking was central to the social life at Princeton, and it was at this time that Fitzgerald took his first shot of whiskey. During the Prohibition years, both Scott and Zelda felt the new excitement, although she simply enjoyed getting high, while he was to become an alcoholic, probably a condition inherited from his father as well as his own need to release his inhibitions to impress others. When the couple moved to New York City, he was twenty-three and she was nineteen. They had met while he was stationed in Alabama during his brief stint in the army. She would become the model for most of the women in his fiction from 1917 to the end of his life.[4] After she rejected his marriage proposal because he lacked the income to support her, he soon returned to St. Paul and finished – and rewrote – the novel he had been working on while in the army, *This Side of Paradise*.

In a series of printings, it sold just less than fifty thousand copies; Sinclair Lewis's *Main Street* (1920) sold almost 300,000. The awareness of youth and the new world that awaited this generation are conveyed experimentally – conversations presented as short dramas, vivid and accurate accounts of young love and courtship, glimpses into the aspirations, failures, and successes of the young college student, Amory Blaine. Under its "original" title *The Romantic Egotist*, Scribner's found two problems with it: the hero, then named Stephen Palms, was not developed sufficiently to sustain interest in his life, and the novel seemed to be filled with irrelevant details. The most important aspect of the book that warranted revision was the degree to which Fitzgerald would convey the hopes and dreams of the young postwar generation. He won praise for the revised work, and the *New York Times* regarded it as almost perfect. Despite its obvious immaturity (Fitzgerald was twenty-three when it was published, the same age as Amory Blaine), the novel touched a wide audience. By the end of the novel, Amory has experienced disappointment in love and in his life as a student. He has learned the difference between, as Monsignor Darcy (based on his own mentor, Father Sigourney Fay) explained, a *personality* and a *personage* – the first, "a physical matter almost entirely," that lowers the people it acts on, and the latter, "who is never thought apart from what he has done."[5] The first gets by on charm, the second by what he has accomplished.

One major change in the social lives of his generation was the relationship between the sexes – so important to this novel. Indeed, Amory's development rests on his encounters with three young women. His contacts with them reach the most intense moment – conveyed with dialogue and stage directions – when Amory tries to persuade Rosalind to marry him. She understands her part in this war between the sexes, and her comprehension of the economic issues involved in dating and kissing reflects the clarity of her vision, and her awareness of the economics that underlie social and sexual decisions, even kissing. Amory falls deeply in love with her, but as in his personal life, she rejects him in favor of wealthy suitors. Her excuse is that she needs the wealth to preserve her beauty – saying much of what Zelda said in rejecting Scott. The impact of *This Side of Paradise* (hereafter *TSOP*) lies in the development of Amory Blaine, as he matures from a callow youth to the wiser, more mature, potential personage, ready for whatever the future might hold.

The novel did not make Fitzgerald wealthy, but it filled him with hope and made it possible for him to marry Zelda. Their life together as a major symbol of the Jazz Age was beginning, although his fondness for alcohol now became the recognizable addiction that would ultimately destroy him.

The royalty checks for *TSOP* began to pour in, astounding the young writer, who could now afford the exciting life that New York City offered, supporting the kind of life that the Fitzgeralds craved and that was sought by so many of his generation. Magazines that had initially turned down his work now were eager to publish anything he might write, and his short stories appeared with regularity in *The Saturday Evening Post (SEP)*. He started work on *The Beautiful and Damned* (serialized in the *Metropolitan Magazine* in September 1921 through March 1922). To many of the novel's readers, it bore a close similarity to his stories, which had been appearing with regularity. Many of them focused on the young, ambitious heroes who identified financial success with happiness, reflected in the lives of the upward aspiring young man who falls in love with the beautiful but unattainable woman of his dreams. That, of course, is Fitzgerald's own story, and the extent to which his work reflects his own life would be apparent throughout his career. His best stories of this period would emphasize the sadness that had engulfed him after Zelda's initial rejection of his marriage proposal.

The major subjects in *TSOP* are the sadness of the unfulfilled life and the unrecapturable moment of bliss, the romantic imagination and its power to transform reality, and finally love, courtship, and marriage and the problems they bring; the plight of the poor outsider seeking to enter the world of the very rich; the cruelty of beautiful and rich young women; the generation gap; the moral life; manners and mores of class society; heroism in ordinary life; emotional bankruptcy and the drift to death; the South and its legendary past; and, finally, the meaning of America for individuals and for modern history. To these subjects that had intrigued him from adolescence, he added Hollywood, where the American dream seemed to so many of his generation to have reached its apotheosis. Fitzgerald's prose was unlike that of any writer of his era – lyrical, poetic at times, dramatically intense, and absorbing – although until *The Great Gatsby* (1925) only a few of the stories hinted at the novel that would become one of the defining works of American literature.

Later, he would write "Crazy Sunday" (1932), based upon his own experience at a party at the home of Irving Thalberg, the head of Metro-Goldwyn-Mayer studios, who became the model for Monroe Stahr in his last, unfinished novel, *The Last Tycoon* (1941). In his late works, dating from 1936 to his death, Fitzgerald's style was markedly different from that of his early work. The tone becomes flat, almost essayistic; narrative is unemotional and economical, yet strangely haunting in its dry precision.

These short works ("An Author's House," "Afternoon of an Author," "An Author's Mother," "An Alcoholic Case" [all 1936]) and several others were all published in *Esquire*. His work for the studio was his major source of income, but after he had to leave MGM, he never attained the financial security he sought. To support Scottie and Zelda, whose condition was rapidly deteriorating, he would write short stories and essays, mostly for *Esquire*, for the rest of his life.

Fitzgerald's second novel, *The Beautiful and Damned*, was published in March 1922 in a first printing of 20,600, and the family (Zelda was now pregnant) left St. Paul, where he had been writing reviews for the St. Paul newspapers, literary magazines, and New York papers. However, his new novel did not achieve the reception or the monetary success of his first.

Unlike Amory Blaine of *TSOP*, Anthony Patch is older, perhaps not wiser, and follows a downward path as he attempts to realize his dreams of love and success. Amory could conclude on a hopeful note: despite many losses of love and friendship, he is able to look back upon his young life and face the future: "I know myself ... but that is all" (308). The fascination for the reader is in Gloria's and Anthony's reckless pursuit of what they believe will bring them happiness and fulfillment. Knowing as we do today how Zelda threw herself into the world of enchantment of New York, we perceive the close connection between this novel and the couple's sojourn in New York City as well. We can also understand the elegiac note that haunts his late essays. In this novel, narrative shifts in point of view between the author and the major characters may raise questions for the reader, whom Fitzgerald often seems to be addressing directly. As in his earlier works, some of the passages are lyrical, and the organization loose (as in *TSOP)*. We do know the time frame (1913–21) but learn surprisingly little about some of the broader historical significance of events occurring throughout the world in this tumultuous era. It is not until the end that Fitzgerald reveals the meaning of the novel: the often contradictory values reflected in the lives of the major figures, particularly Gloria's refusal to blame Anthony for being an "ineffectual idler" as long as he sincerely believes that "nothing much was worth doing."[6] It becomes clear that the main characters are as empty as the world they inhabit. Unlike *The Great Gatsby* and *Tender Is the Night* (1934), this novel does not extend beyond the limits set by the Patches and the social life of the period. Anthony's downward spiral reminds us of characters in naturalistic novels by Frank Norris, James T. Farrell, and Theodore Dreiser (in *An American Tragedy*, published in the same year as *Gatsby*). Despite the focus on Anthony and Gloria, Fitzgerald here captures the excitement of the time, the headiness of life in the city, with the crowds at Times Square, "beautiful and bright and intimate with carnival" (*Beautiful*

21). The story of Anthony Patch is that story, but it is also a story about the effect of alcohol on the lives of the new generation – the sense of drift that would characterize the era.[7] Above all, the novel questions the idea of work – a center of the American ethos made popular to a general public in the late nineteenth-century tales of Horatio Alger. Anthony Patch, emboldened by the new cynicism of the era, refuses to work until he finds his income severely diminished and he is forced to look for employment. The final pages trace his decline into a state of perpetual childishness, even as his court case for his grandfather's estate is settled in his favor. The irony here, and it is one of the finest moments in the novel, is that the money is irrelevant, for Anthony, still a young man, is infirm, in a wheelchair, relegated to the old age he had so defiantly fought throughout his life. By the time they have the money, Anthony and Gloria have lost everything that the inheritance might have bought and preserved. The ending of the novel is effectively descriptive and ironic. But the sense of tragedy that is conveyed in *The Great Gatsby* and *Tender Is the Night* is absent.

After his play *The Vegetable*, which he had been working on for some time, was published and failed at a tryout in 1923, the peripatetic family now sailed for France, settling in St. Raphael on the Riviera. But Fitzgerald kept working on *Gatsby*, writing to Perkins, "I'm thrown directly on purely creative work.... This book will be a consciously artistic achievement and must depend on that as the first books did not."[8]

*The Great Gatsby* was published on April 10, 1925, to mixed reviews. Because he had become so identified with the Jazz Age, critics, although praising his cleverness, generally concluded that it was a novel of limited scope, with a trivial subject. There were certainly those who recognized it as a masterpiece, but it was a small minority – William Rose Benet, Herbert S. Gorman, Lawrence Stallings. Mencken regarded it as "a glorified anecdote."[9] Fitzgerald was deeply disappointed in the response and in the poor sales. He received praise from T. S. Eliot ("It seems the first step that American fiction has taken since Henry James"), from Gertrude Stein, and from Edith Wharton that cheered him, but he was deeply disappointed in the response from Great Britain, where it was rejected by Collins (they believed that it would not appeal to British readers) and published later, in 1926, by Chatto and Windus. But Fitzgerald himself always regarded the novel as his greatest, "dragged ... out of the pit of my stomach in a time of misery."[10]

*The Great Gatsby* has generally been regarded as a postwar novel, but as Ronald Berman has suggested, most readers have the wrong war in mind. The changes that are reflected in the novel date to the nineteenth century, between the Civil War and World War I.[11] Great writers of that era –Mark Twain, William Dean Howells, Henry James – and others in such fields as science, education, and philosophy recalled a time that was lost to them, while a new world had yet to be found. Events seemed to be in flux, and, as noted, Fitzgerald's own lifetime coincided with the major changes that occurred before the Second World War, notably in the increasing numbers of immigrants, and, perhaps most important, in the rise of wealth. "From just a few millionaires before the war, the number reached to over 4000 by the 1890s."[12] The disaster of the war (more than 4,000,000 served, and more than 350,000 perished) and its aftermath resonated in the United States and abroad; the futility of the effort is reflected in novels by Hemingway, Erich Maria Remarque, and e. e. cummings. Throughout *Gatsby* the war is a persistent echo, and Fitzgerald's attitude toward it is complex. Indeed, Gatsby's participation in the two bloodiest battles of the war, the Marne and the Argonne, both in 1918, the latter resulting in more than 26,000 deaths and more than 97,000 wounded, supports the view of his heroism.

Prohibition saw a rise in crime along with bootlegging and encouraged the many lavish parties and the general relaxation of inhibitions in the speakeasies that provided jazz, liquor, and dancing. He saw from his friend Ring Lardner's lawn across the bay the parties at the mansion of the *New York World* publisher Herbert Bayard Swope, who printed the story of the minor underworld figure Herman Rosenthal, who refused to pay extortion money to a police officer, a confession that would lead to his murder. Wolfshiem, while at lunch with Jay Gatsby, refers to the case and the parties that often last until sunrise and become the central focus of the novel. By the last chapter, we realize that *The Great Gatsby* is constructed on the basis of parties: alternating large parties with small parties, both inevitably leading to violent conclusions. Throughout the novel, there are a series of mysteries, notably regarding Gatsby, whose background is not revealed until the end. Carefully placed flashbacks fill in the vague outlines of Gatsby's history. In the last pages we finally learn who he is and how far he had come to find his dream: his dream that resides in the unattainable woman, Daisy Buchanan, who symbolizes the beauty that wealth preserves and protects, a beauty that for Gatsby represents all of the possibilities of this life and of eternal life. His quest for Daisy is no less than his search for destiny, for the very meaning of human existence. He has embodied his spiritual journey in the material world where personal identity resides in the perceptions of others. The brooding eyes of Dr. Eckleburg and the differing impressions of Gatsby's house as it appears to Nick, to Daisy, and to Mr. Gatz suggest how dependent the sense of an outer world is on the way it is viewed by others. Fitzgerald touches on a theme that had haunted American writers: in a society without an established class structure, where the idea of a privileged class is based on British models, how does an individual compete with the descendants of "old money," who may in reality have invented a royal ancestry to fit into the class system that the past century expansion had created. Tom Buchanan is the defender of that system, while through the development of Nick Carraway, the novel becomes a search for moral order. His faithfulness to Gatsby's dream is itself a bulwark against the disorder that threatens our world. His final words express the meaning of life to which Gatsby has opened our eyes. The "green light" – the "orgastic future" – may be receding from our vision, but we "beat on, boats against the current, borne back ceaseless into the past."[13] Those last words have been the subject of many interpretations and speculations, and perhaps that was Fitzgerald's intent. For the mysteries in *Gatsby* and much of its power cannot be resolved. Despite the powerful image of loss, we share Gatsby's romantic hope, his vision that to this day is shared not only by Americans, but by the world.

In the increasingly difficult years following the publication of *Gatsby*, Fitzgerald produced fewer stories than he had in the past; it was clear that he could no longer write the kinds of stories that had appealed to readers of the *SEP* in the past and he could find no new subjects that might be acceptable to the readers, certainly not stories about young love. His last story earned only $2,500 and his earnings for 1932 were less than $16,000. His health was suffering, and he was treated at Johns Hopkins for typhoid fever and mild tuberculosis. Zelda's condition, too, had worsened, and she was admitted to Sheppard Pratt Hospital near Baltimore in a catatonic state. It was clear that she would never recover and that their marriage was over. He wrote in his Notebooks, "I left my capacity for hoping on the little roads that led to Zelda's sanitarium."[14]

*Tender Is the Night* was published on April 12, 1934, and the first printing (seventy-six hundred copies) sold out, as did two more totaling eight thousand. It reached the middle of the best-seller list but made him only $5,000. It is remarkable that with his ill health and his wife's tragic mental problems, he was able to continue writing the short pieces for *Esquire*. The reviews of the novel were mixed, many critics finding structural weaknesses in the narrative voice. The chronology was felt to be confusing, and some reviewers believed that there was not sufficient cause for Dick Diver's deterioration. As he had with *Gatsby*, Gilbert Seldes praised the new novel unreservedly and was joined by Burton Rascoe and Robert Benchley. Fitzgerald revised the book to make the chronology clearer (published posthumously), but many felt that the earlier version was superior. The power of the novel lay in the portrait of expatriate Americans and the wealth that ultimately corrupts, and in the examination of America and its history. It is a poignant tale of loss, particularly as it reflects the Fitzgeralds' own lives. Dick Diver's decline mirrored Fitzgerald's sense of his own lost hopes, as he would express in *Esquire* stories and articles in his last years.

Despite the adverse publicity that resulted from a sensational interview that the journalist Michael Mok wrote for the *New York Post,* he was asked, through the help of friends, to work at MGM for six months at a salary of $1,000 a week, increasing to $1,250 if the option were renewed. His debts at this point amounted to $40,000, and he drew up a careful plan that would allow him to pay them in full, support Scottie in school, and meet the costs of Zelda's treatment. Until his death, he would continue to support his family and try to meet his financial obligations. He wrote seventeen Pat Hobby stories, which *Esquire* continued to publish even after his death. He lived on the next block from Sheilah Graham until his health so deteriorated – he had recurrent dizzy spells – that after his first heart attack, she moved him into her apartment, where he continued to write on a specially constructed board that stretched across his bed. One night, after they had attended a preview of a film, he had to hold on to Sheilah for support. The doctor was scheduled to visit him the next day, and as he waited, eating a chocolate bar as Sheilah was reading and listening to Beethoven's *Eroica* (part of the education that he had designed for her), he rose from his chair, grabbed the mantelpiece, and fell to the floor. He died instantly, at 5:15 P.M., December 21, 1940. His funeral was held in Bethesda, Maryland, and he was buried in Rockville Union Cemetery. He was reburied there in 1975 at St. Mary's Cemetery alongside Zelda, and before Scottie died, in 1986, she asked to be buried with her parents.

At his death, Fitzgerald had paid off most of his debts, leaving only about $12,000, most of it to Highland Hospital and to Scribner's. His insurance policy covered his remaining debts and provided an annuity for Zelda and Scottie. After Edmund Wilson's edited version of *The Last Tycoon* was published in 1941, most of the critics were generous in their appraisal, incomplete as the novel was. Zelda was a victim of the fire that swept through Highland Hospital in March 1948, trapped in the attic.

Thus the tragic lives of Scott and Zelda Fitzgerald ended. Although he had said that there are no second acts in American lives, his own second act began just a few years after his death, and today, he is secure in the pantheon of American writers. Like *Gatsby*, he remained faithful to his dream, and we are the fortunate beneficiaries of his enduring legacy.

## FURTHER READING

Berman, Ronald, *The Great Gatsby and Fitzgerald's World of Ideas*, Tuscaloosa, University of Alabama Press, 1997.

*"The Great Gatsby" and Modern Times*, Urbana, University of Illinois Press, 1994.

Bruccoli, Matthew J., *The Composition of "Tender Is the Night": A Study of the Manuscripts*, Pittsburgh, University of Pittsburgh Press, 1963.

*Fitzgerald and Hemingway: A Dangerous Friendship*, New York, Carroll & Graf, 1994.

*F. Scott Fitzgerald: A Descriptive Bibliography*, rev. ed., Pittsburgh, University of Pittsburgh Press, 1987.

*"The Last of the Novelists"; F. Scott Fitzgerald and* The Last Tycoon, Carbondale, Southern Illinois University Press, 1977.

*Some Sort of Epic Grandeur: The Life of F. Scott Fitzgerald*, rev. ed., Columbia, University of South Carolina Press, 1994.

Bruccoli, Matthew J. with the assistance of Jennifer McCabe Atkinson, *"As Ever, Scott Fitz,"* letters between Fitzgerald and his literary agent, Harold Ober 1919–40, Philadelphia, J. B. Lippincott, 1972.

Bruccoli, Matthew J. and Margaret Duggan (eds.) with the assistance of Susan Walker, *Correspondence of F. Scott Fitzgerald*, New York, Random House, 1980.

Bruccoli, Matthew J., Scottie Fitzgerald Smith, and Joan P. Kerr (eds.), *A Pictorial Autobiography of F. Scott and Zelda Fitzgerald*, New York, Scribner's, 1974.

Bryer, Jackson R, *The Critical Reputation of F. Scott Fitzgerald*, Hamden, Conn., Archon, 1967 and supplement 1984.

*F. Scott Fitzgerald: The Critical Reception*, New York, Burt Franklin, 1978.

*New Essays on F. Scott Fitzgerald's Neglected Short Stories*, Columbia, University of Missouri Press, 1996.

Bryer, Jackson R, Alan Margolies, and Ruth Prigozy (eds.), *F. Scott Fitzgerald: New Perspectives*, Athens, University of Georgia Press, 2000.

Bryer, Jackson R, *The Short Stories of F. Scott Fitzgerald: New Approaches in Criticism*, Madison, University of Wisconsin Press, 1982.

Callahan, John, *The Illusions of a Nation: Myth and History in the Novels of F. Scott Fitzgerald*, Urbana, University of Illinois Press, 1972.

Cowley, Malcolm, *Exile's Return: A Literary Odyssey of the 1920s*, New York, Penguin, 1976.

Cowley, Malcolm, *A Second Flowering: Works and Days of the Lost Generation*, New York, Viking, 1973.

Curnutt, Kirk (ed.), *A Historical Guide to F. Scott Fitzgerald*, Oxford and New York, Oxford University Press, 2004.

Dickstein, Morris (ed.), *Critical Insights: The "Great Gatsby,"* Pasadena, Calif., and Hackensack, NJ., Salem Press, 2010.

Donaldson, Scott. *Fitzgerald and Hemingway: Works and Days*, New York, Columbia University Press, 2009.

Eble, Kenneth (ed.), *F. Scott Fitzgerald*, New York, Twayne, 1963, rev. 1977.

Graham, Sheilah, *College of One*, New York, Viking, 1967.

with Gerold Frank, *Beloved Infidel*, New York, Henry Holt, 1958.

Hemingway, Ernest, *A Moveable Feast*, New York, Scribner's, 1964.

Kazan, Alfred, *F. Scott Fitzgerald: The Man and His Work*, 1951, New York, Collier Books, 1967.

Kennedy, J. Gerald and Jackson R. Bryer (eds.), *French Connections: Hemingway and Fitzgerald Abroad*, New York, St. Martin's Press, 1998.

Kuehl, John, *F. Scott Fitzgerald: A Study of the Short Fiction*, Boston, Twayne, 1991.

Kuehl, John and Jackson R. Bryer (eds.), *Dear Scott, Dear Max: The Fitzgerald/ Perkins Correspondence*, New York, Scribner's, 1971.

Lanahan, Eleanor, *Scottie: The Daughter of ...*, New York, HarperCollins, 1995.

Latham, Aaron, *Crazy Sundays: F. Scott Fitzgerald in Hollywood*, New York, Viking, 1971.

Lehan, Richard D., *F. Scott Fitzgerald and the Craft of Fiction*, Carbondale, Southern Illinois University Press, 1966.

Le Vot, Andre, *F. Scott Fitzgerald: A Biography*, trans. William Byron, New York, Doubleday, 1983.

Mangum, Bryan, *A Fortune Yet: Money in the Art of F. Scott Fitzgerald's Short Stories*, New York, Garland, 1991.

Mizener, Arthur, *The Far Side of Paradise: A Biography of F. Scott Fitzgerald*, Boston, Houghton Mifflin, 1951, rev. 1959.

Prigozy, Ruth, *F. Scott Fitzgerald: An Illustrated Life*, London and New York, Penguin and Overlook Press, 2002.

Prigozy, Ruth (ed.), *The Cambridge Companion to F. Scott Fitzgerald*, London and New York, Cambridge University Press, 2002.

Ring, Frances Kroll, *Against the Current: As I Remember F. Scott Fitzgerald*, Berkeley, Calif., Creative Arts, 1985.

Sklar, Robert, *F. Scott Fitzgerald: The Last Laocoon*, Oxford, Oxford University Press, 1967.

Stern, Milton, *The Golden Moment: The Novels of F. Scott Fitzgerald*, Urbana, University of Illinois Press, 1970.

Turnbull, Andrew, *Scott Fitzgerald*, New York, Scribner's, 1962.

## NOTES

1 Kenneth Slawenski, *J. D. Salinger: A Life* (New York, Random House, 2010), pp. 136–7.

2 For background on this era, see Ronald Berman, *The Great Gatsby and Modern Times* (Urbana, University of Illinois Press, 1994), pointing out the importance of the new philosophy of the era.

3 For a detailed discussion of Fitzgerald's life from youth until his death, see Matthew J. Bruccoli, *Some Sort of Epic Grandeur: The Life of F. Scott Fitzgerald* (London, Cardinal, 1991).

4 The interest in Zelda Fitzgerald was great in the early years of the feminist movement; there are several biographies of her dating from the 1970s.

5 Scott Donaldson, *F. Scott Fitzgerald: Fool for Love* (New York, Congdon and Weed, 1983), p. xxiii.

6 F. Scott Fitzgerald, *The Beautiful and the Damned*, (New York, Signet, 2007), p. 172. Hereafter *Beautiful* and cited parenthetically.

7 See Berman, *Great Gatsby*, pp. 11–27.

8 Fitzgerald, *Letters*, ed. Andrew Turnbull (London, Head, 1963), p. 163.

9 See Jackson R. Bryer, ed., *The Critical Reputation of F. Scott Fitzgerald, a Bibliographical Study* (Hamden, Conn., Archon Books, 1984), pp. 59–70, for reviews of the novel.

10 Matthew J. Bruccoli, Margaret M. Duggan, and Susan Walker (eds.), *Correspondence of F. Scott Fitzgerald* (New York, Random House, 1980), p. 239.
11 Berman, *Great Gatsby and Modern,* p. 32.
12 Jay Martin, *Harvests of Change: American Literature,* 1865–1914 (Durham, N.C., Duke University Press, 1967), pp. 1–24.
13 Fitzgerald, *The Great Gatsby* (Oxford, Oxford University Press, 1998), p. 144.
14 Matthew J. Bruccoli (ed.), *The Notebooks of F. Scott Fitzgerald* (New York, Harcourt Brace Jovanovich, 1978), p. 104.

# 11

# Ernest Hemingway

EUGENE GOODHEART

Born in 1899 in Illinois, Ernest Hemingway (1899–1961) came of age during World War I. Rejected by the army because of his defective vision, he volunteered as a Red Cross ambulance driver in Italy and was seriously wounded. He returned home for a brief stay, married and sailed with his wife to France where he settled in Paris and became part of a loose fraternity of American expatriate writers, among them Gertrude Stein, F. Scott Fitzgerald and Ezra Pound, who in various ways influenced his art. As a journalist, he covered the Spanish civil war between the republican government and the fascist Falangists led by Franco. An outdoorsman, he hunted big game in Africa, fished in the waters of Key West and found the spectacle of the matador's artful encounter with the bull an analogue to his own art. All this activity found its way into his writing as journalist, short story writer, novelist and memoirist. Petrina Crockford vividly sums up the heroic legend that Hemingway fashioned for himself: "He lived a vigorous, adventurous life as brash and uncompromising as that of his greatest characters, inhabiting a male dominated, solitary, and stoic world."[1] The trouble with the legend, as I hope to show, is that by simplifying his achievement it fails to do it full justice.

Hemingway began his literary career as a short story writer and became one of its greatest masters. No one has better characterized his style than Hemingway himself. "The dignity of the movement of an iceberg is due to one-eighth of its being above water."[2] His sentences are characteristically crisp, understated (spare in their use of adjectives and adverbs) and resonant, requiring the reader to see and hear what is below the water. The protagonist of his first collection of stories, *In Our Time*, mostly set in the American Midwest, is the young Nick Adams. "Indian Camp" is exemplary of the iceberg effect. Nick accompanies his father, a doctor, to an Indian camp, where he is to perform without anesthesia a cesarean operation on an Indian squaw. Nick averts his eyes as his father accomplishes the task with admirable skill, but with a less appealing bravado. Nick cannot, however, escape a scene of horror: the husband of the squaw, also a witness, finding the operation unendurable, cuts his own throat. Nick questions his father about dying: "Is it hard?" His father blithely responds: "It's pretty easy" with the qualification "it all depends." As his father rows home, Nick, seated in the stern of the boat, observes, "a bass jump[ing], making a circle in the water" and, unexpectedly to the reader, feels "quite sure he would never die."³ The reader is left to puzzle out what Nick has learned from the experience. Is he in denial, too young to accept the reality of dying and death? Or is he showing resilience in the face of what he has witnessed? The answer, I think, is intimated in the image of the bass, alive and jumping from *below the water*. Nick with years ahead of him turns away from death to affirm life.

The doctor's skill is one of a number of skills exhibited by Hemingway's characters. In "Big Two-Hearted River," we observe Nick's expertness in baiting a hook, in making a fire and in using his confident knowledge of the wilderness. In "The End of Something," Nick instructs his girlfriend, Marjorie, in the art of catching perch. "Nick caught three of them with his hands and cut their heads off and skinned them while Marjorie chased with her hands in the bucket, finally cut its head off and skinned it.... Nick looked at her fish. 'You don't want to take the ventral fin out. It'll be alright for bait, but it's better with the ventral fin in'" (*SS*, 108). In his later work, Hemingway is precise and eloquent in describing a hunt, the sailing of a boat, the choreography of the matador's combat with a bull. Portions of Hemingway's fiction read like artistically heightened manuals of conduct. In a tribute to Hemingway, Ralph Ellison, author of *Invisible Man*, writes, "Because he wrote with such precision about the processes and techniques of daily living that I could keep my brother and myself alive during the 1937 Recession by following his descriptions of wing-shooting."⁴

There are stories in a much darker vein. "In a Clean Well-Lighted Place," a customer, an old man, has attempted suicide. The reason, a waiter tells a fellow waiter, was "nothing": existential despair. The word at the end of the story is translated into Spanish and becomes an incantation. "Our nada who art in nada, nada be thy name thy kingdom nada thy will be nada in nada as in nada" (*SS*, 383). In "Soldier's Home," Krebs returns home from war "after the greeting of heroes was over" and finds that in order to get himself listened to he must lie and exaggerate his exploits. "A distaste for everything that had happened to him in the war sets in because of the lies he had told" (*SS*, 145). As days pass, he seems to lose interest in everything. His girlfriend asks him whether he loves her and he responds with no more than "Uh huh." When his mother asks the same question, he is finally able to say the truth, "I don't love anybody" (*SS*, 152). He has been hollowed out by the war, which will become the subject of his major novels. In "In a Way You Will Never Be," Nick Adams, now grown up, has gone to war. Severely wounded, he has been ravaged psychologically as well as physically. Harry, the protagonist of "Snows of Kilimanjaro," meditates on his failed career as writer as he lies dying of gangrene. These disturbing stories do not square with the heroic legend.

Hemingway's great theme is courage, and it is powerfully dramatized in arguably the greatest of his stories, "The Short Happy Life of Francis Macomber." On a safari with his wife in Africa to hunt lions, Macomber hears their roaring at night and experiences fear. What he doesn't know is that he is not alone in his fear; nor does he know the Somali folk saying that "a brave man is always frightened three times by a lion; when he first sees his track, when he first hears him roar and when he first confronts him" (*SS*, 11). The following day, faced with a lion speeding toward him, Macomber turns tail and flees. Robert Wilson, the guide, stands his ground and kills the lion. He withholds comment about Macomber's turning tail, but what he can't abide is his constantly talking about it. Macomber's wife, already contemptuous of him, berates him for his cowardice. In the evening, she goes to Wilson's tent and spends the night. Macomber will redeem himself the following day by standing his ground this time in the face of an onrushing buffalo. The moral: you may act cowardly, you may disgrace yourself by wallowing in talk about your failure, but you can redeem yourself by learning from your cowardice. Courage, Hemingway seems to be saying, is not something instinctive, something you're born with. What is instinctive is fear. The fine Hemingway critic Philip Young is mistaken simply to characterize Macomber as a coward. His running from the lion is cowardly, but a single act does not define a person, since there is always the possibility of redemption. Hemingway's definition of courage as "grace under pressure," the most famous phrase in the Hemingway legacy, conceals the struggle that goes into achieving it. The religious connotation of grace makes it a matter of endowment (you simply have it or don't have it), in which case there is no story to tell. In Hemingway's godless world, temperament may play a part, but, as we find in all his work, courage is always a struggle to sustain.

Courage will take different forms in Hemingway's major novels, *The Sun Also Rises, A Farewell to Arms,* and *For Whom The Bell Tolls*, all of which have war as their background or foreground. *The Sun Also Rises* is the story of a circle of mainly American expatriates and an English woman set in Paris after World War I (then called the Great War). The war may have ended, but it has taken a permanent toll in the life of its narrator and protagonist, Jake Barnes. Wounded in the war, he is sexually impotent. But Jake is not alone in his suffering. The terrible ravages of war have marked the lives of everyone who survived it. A remark by Gertrude Stein in conversation serves as an epigraph to the novel, "You are all a lost generation." Jake and his cohort, writers and would-be writers among them, seem always to act from whim, drifting aimlessly from café to café and from city to city (Paris to Barcelona and back to Paris) in search of experience, with little hope of finding purpose in their lives. They eat, drink heavily and make love (Jake, of course, the exception), enjoy the spectacle of a bullfight in Barcelona, but seem always on the verge of despair. In the postwar setting, the test of courage is the capacity to possess oneself and resist despair. It has nothing to do with mere physical prowess. The moral coward is Robert Cohn, introduced in the first sentence of the novel as having once been "middleweight boxing champion at Princeton"; in a fit of jealous rage, he knocks down the matador Romero, his rival for the affections of Lady Brett. Out of control, he turns violent against Jake Barnes, only to find himself in the grip of remorse and self-pity. Hemingway's characterization of Cohn as a Jew reflects what was a feature of the time, a gratuitously fashionable anti-Semitism, shared by many modern writers. Cohn is a would-be writer, and his clear-seeing lover Frances tries to teach him a lesson that it is doubtful he will ever learn:

> "Listen, Robert dear. Let me tell you something. You won't mind, will you? Don't have scenes with your young ladies. Try not to. Because you can't have scenes without crying, and then you pity yourself so much you can't remember what the other person said. You will never be able to remember any conversations that way. Just try and be calm. I know it's awfully hard. But remember, it's for literature."[5]

This is a lesson both Jake, a writer, and his creator, Hemingway, learned.

The battlefield has always been the great testing ground for manly courage. In an extraordinary act of imagination, Hemingway creates a hero who *seems* to have lost his manhood in the war, *seems*, because, as the narrative will show, of all the circle of expatriates, Jake emerges as the most admirable of characters. Romero merits our admiration as well, not only because of the courage and skill with which he performs as matador in the arena, a simulacrum of the battlefield, but also because of the way he refuses to stay down as Cohn knocks him down again and again. Courage lies in the response to defeat. There is always the temptation of despair, to which Jake refuses to succumb. He can stand back from himself and view his condition dispassionately. "I was pretty well through with the subject. At one time or another I had probably considered it from most of its various angles, including the one that certain injuries or imperfections are a subject of merriment while remaining quite serious for the person possessing them" (*TSAR*, 27). No wonder he is the narrator, the writer's surrogate; he alone has the capacity to see from "various angles" and hear and remember what people say. Disabled in war and incapable of sexual love, he is nevertheless capable of imagining the sufferings and the losses experienced by others – as in the following meditation on his friendship with Lady Brett:

> Women made such swell friends. Awfully swell. In the first place, you had to be in love with a woman to have a basis for friendship. I have been having Brett for a friend. I had not been thinking of her side of it. I had been getting something for nothing. That only delayed the presentation of the bill. The bill always came. That was one of the swell things you could count on.

> I thought I had paid for everything. Not like the woman pays and pays and pays. No idea of retribution or punishment. Just an exchange of values. You gave up something and got something else. Or you worked for something. You paid some way for something that was good. (*TSAR*, 148)

Note the repetitiveness, another feature of Hemingway's style – in this instance, a kind of exercise of Jake's mind in coming to terms with his condition. The dissoluteness that pervades the novel is periodically held in check by acts of kindness and generosity such as Brett's decision to leave Romero for his own good.

*A Farewell to Arms* is a love story set on the Italian front during World War I, its protagonist and narrator, Frederic Henry, another one of Hemingway's wounded heroes. The main action of the novel is not the battlefield, but the hospital where Frederic is recovering and where he falls in love with his nurse, Catherine Barclay. The battlefield, once the occasion for courageous deeds, has become a scene of carnage and defeat. Frederic would prefer not to think of it. In an exchange with Catherine on their first meeting, Frederic says, "Let's drop the war." Catherine responds, "It's very hard. There is no place to drop it."[6] Language itself is a casualty of war. Listening to an Italian comrade who cannot bear the idea of losing the war vaunt his patriotism, Frederic silently reflects on words that inspire action on the battlefield: "sacred, glorious, and sacrifice. ... Abstract words such as glory, honor, courage, or hallow were obscene beside the concrete names of villages, the numbers of roads, the numbers of regiments and the dates" (*FA*, 184–5). (In the novel *To Have and Have Not*, even the word "love" comes under suspicion: Richard Gordon calls it "just another dirty lie."[7]) It is not that Frederic has given up on the idea of bravery or courage or honor on the battlefield; it is that he sees the actual brutality and fog of war, which the inflated rhetoric obfuscates. (He is partly responsible for the loss of three ambulances, and in despair about the war he deserts the battlefield and becomes the victim of circumstance.) At the heart of Hemingway's style is seeing things as they actually are.

In the epic tradition, the passions of love and war are irreconcilable. Love is a weakness and distraction for the warrior, who must be single-minded on the battlefield. The title of the novel is a phrase from *Othello*, the eponymous hero of Shakespeare's play, who, having been undone by love and jealousy, ceases to be the heroic warrior he once was. In a kind of ironic twist, the scene of bravery in *A Farewell to Arms* is the love affair of Frederic and Catherine. The true hero of the novel is Catherine, as Frederic himself acknowledges. She sacrifices herself, tending to the wounded and her wounded lover, and dies at the end in childbirth. In conversation with Catherine, Frederic praises her for bravery and goes on to distinguish it from cowardice, citing an unnamed source: "The coward dies a thousand deaths, the brave but one." Catherine's response is truer, closer, I think, to Hemingway's own view. "He was probably a coward.... He knew a great deal about cowards but nothing about the brave. The brave dies two thousand deaths, if he is intelligent. He simply doesn't mention them" (*FA*, 139–40). Frederic honors Catherine by calling her "brave" and is truthful in disclaiming bravery for himself.

Hemingway is notorious, though not alone among American male writers, in his hostile or dismissive portraits of women, for instance, Mrs. Macomber. In Catherine Barclay, however, he has created one of his most admirable characters: self-sacrificing, brave, generous, loving, perhaps more ideal than real. Critics have read Hemingway's own love life and several marriages into the relationships between his characters and the women in their lives. Rather than simply focusing on Frederic's failed manhood (some critics speak disparagingly of his feminine nature in his dependency on Catherine) and by extension on Hemingway's character, we might praise Hemingway as a writer for his implicit awareness of his own vulnerability.

The Hemingway hero finds himself again at war in *For Whom the Bell Tolls*. Civil war has broken out in Spain. The protagonist, Robert Jordan, has joined the republican side against the fascists led by Franco. Jordan and his Spanish comrades are behind enemy lines, their task the blowing up of a bridge held by the fascists. The republican cause enlisted volunteers (Jordan among them) from many countries; the civil war and the battle against fascism foreshadowed World War II. Unlike World War I, the war in Spain was a Cause in the eyes of those who fought for it. There is an epic elevation in the prose unlike that of the previous novels. We are prepared for it in the epigraph to the novel taken from John Donne: "No man is an *Island*.... any man's death diminishes *me*, because I am involved in *Mankind*. And therefore never send to know for whom the *bell* tolls; it tolls for *thee*." Hemingway introduces Jordan as someone who has heard the tolling of the bell:

The young man, whose name was Robert Jordan, was extremely hungry and worried. He was often hungry, but he was not usually worried because he did not give any importance to what happened to himself, and he knew from experience how simple it was to move behind enemy lines in all this country. It was only giving importance to what happened to you if you were caught that made it difficult; that and deciding whom to trust. You had to trust the people you worked with or not at all, and you had to make decisions about the trusting.[8]

The novel gives us a splendid gallery of characters (the strong-willed and profane woman Pilar, the morally scrupulous Anselmo, the enigmatic Pablo, the extremely intelligent Soviet emissary Karkov, among others), all seen through the eyes of Jordan, who has to decide at crucial moments whom to trust. Jordan's beautifully rendered love for Maria, who had been raped by the fascists, is a selfless love (of which Frederic Henry is incapable) without diminishing its erotic charge.

We are apparently past the postwar despair of *The Sun Also Rises* and the disillusionment with war in *A Farewell to Arms,* and yet something of the despair and disillusionment lingers in *For Whom the Bell Tolls.* What Jordan and other idealists discovered was that the moral divide in the conduct of war between the republicans and the fascists was not so great. War tends to be a moral equalizer. Both sides committed atrocities. The republicans fought in the name of democracy, but their side was compromised by the dominant position of the Spanish Communist Party and Soviet emissaries, vividly represented by Karkov, who played a major role in the prosecution of the war on the republican side. Hemingway was not a political thinker. In contrast to other writers about the war, for instance, George Orwell in *Homage to Catalonia,* he gives very little sense of the ideologies that informed the struggle. He is always a keen observer of "the facts on the ground," as the saying goes. And what we see in the Spanish war is what we see in all wars: brutality, killing, and betrayal. "What were [Robert Jordan's] politics then? He had none, he told himself. But don't ever admit that to others, he thought." Jordan has a sentimental devotion to democracy and a loathing of fascism. "If the Republic lost, it would be impossible for those who believed in it to live in Spain. But would it? Yes, he knew that it would be, from the things that had happened in the parts that the fascists had already taken." Pablo, a comrade, had gone over to the other side and Jordan judges him as a "swine." (Pablo will switch sides again and return to the republican fold.) He knows, however, that "the others are fine people" (*FWBT,* 163).

What was clear to Jordan was that Spain, the country he loved, had to be saved from the fascists and that though he had no affection for the

Communists, "they offered the best discipline and the soundest and the sanest for the prosecution of the war," a judgment with which Orwell would have disagreed. But that is not the whole story or rather the deepest motive in Jordan and in Hemingway. "I am going back," Jordan says to himself, "and I'm going to write a true book" (*FWBT*, 163). The subtext in most of Hemingway's work is the lonely act of writing. Jordan's unwillingness to tell others about his politics reflects a tension in the novel between his selfless devotion to the antifascist cause and his sense of apartness from others. Jordan behaves with courage and skill in the execution of the plan to destroy the bridge and gives his life for the cause, but we feel throughout that he is always holding himself in reserve, that his experience is finally material for the book he hopes to write but never will. It is, of course, the book that his creator has written.

The bullfight is a recurrent theme in Hemingway's work, and it makes an appearance in *For Whom the Bell Tolls*. Nothing fascinated Hemingway more than the spectacle of the bullfight in which the matador displayed his courage and skill in his encounter with the bull – in its most impressive manifestations an instance of "grace under pressure." To understand what fascinated Hemingway in the bullfight, we need to suspend whatever revulsion we feel in contemplating the killing of the innocent bull. Hemingway himself was revolted by the indiscriminate, chaotic violence of modern war, but he was in a sense a throwback to an earlier epic tradition and its aesthetic of heroic battle. In the *Iliad*, the greatest of epics, the Greek hero and the Trojan hero, facing each other on the battlefield, acknowledge the other's greatness before the mortal combat in which one of them will be killed. (Modern warfare has made the heroic encounter a thing of the past.) In the heroic tradition, the scene of violence, whether it is the hunt for a lion ("The Short Happy Life of Francis Macomber") or the encounter with the bull (*A Farewell to Arms, Death in the Afternoon*), requires adversaries worthy of each other – and, from the writer's perspective, worthy of representation. The aging fisherman Santiago in *The Old Man and the Sea* sounds like a singer in an opera absurdly addressing the giant marlin that he is trying to reel in: "Never have I seen a greater, or more beautiful, or a calmer or more noble thing than you, brother. Come on and kill me. I do not care who kills who" (92).[9] This is straining for heroic effect, and Santiago immediately knows that he is "confused in his head."

No American writer of the twentieth century has had so great an influence on our literature and culture as Hemingway. With Hemingway in mind, Norman Mailer fashioned a heroic self-image. At the other end of the spectrum, the quiet desperation of some of Hemingway's short stories has found its way into Raymond Carver's stories. We see the influence in the laconic, hard-boiled style of detective fiction (Hemingway's own *To Have and Have Not* qualifies), the verbal reserve and swagger of the western hero of the cinema confronting danger and in the understated style of so many lesser writers. What Hemingway's heirs mostly miss is the ferment that underlies the style. Drawn to the epic imagination, he is inescapably a modern writer. At his best, Hemingway takes us behind the scenes of courage and heroism, where we find psychic wounds, fear, anxiety, depression and the threat of nothingness, which he experienced in his personal life. He ended his life as a suicide in 1961. Courage has no guarantees; it requires thought, will and determination. There are enclaves of experience (the hunt, the fishing expedition, the bullfight) in which victories occur. But the most interesting characters struggle inwardly, valiantly, and not always successfully to come to terms with failure and defeat.

A character in Aleksandr I. Solzhenitsyn's *The Cancer Ward* recalls a saying attributed to Tolstoy about his brother: "He has all the gifts of a writer, but not the failings that make the writer."[10] Hemingway had the gifts and the failings.

## FURTHER READING

Astro, Richard and Benson, Jackson R. (eds.), *Hemingway in Our Time*, Corvallis, Oregon State University Press, 1974.

Baker, Carlos, *Ernest Hemingway: A Life Story*, New York, Charles Scribner's Sons, 1969.

    *Hemingway: The Writer as Artist*, Princeton, N.J., Princeton University Press, 1972.

Berman, Ronald, *Fitzgerald, Hemingway and the Twenties*, Tuscaloosa, University of Alabama Press, 2001.

Donaldson, Scott, *By Force of Will: The Life and Art of Ernest Hemingway*, New York, Viking Press, 1977.

Gadjusek, Robert E. (ed.), *Hemingway in His Own Country*, South Bend, Ind., University of Notre Dame Press, 2002.

Goodheart, Eugene (ed.), *Critical Insights: Ernest Hemingway*, Pasadena, Calif., Salem Press, 2010.

Kennedy, J. Gerald, *Imagining Paris: Exile, Writing and American Identity*, New Haven, Conn., Yale University Press, 1993.

Meyers, Jeffrey, *Hemingway: Life into Art*, New York, Cooper Square Press, 2000.

Nagel, James (ed.), *Hemingway: The Writer in Context*, Madison, University of Wisconsin Press, 1984.

Kert, Bernice, *The Hemingway Women*, New York, Norton, 1998.

Rovit, Earl and Arthur Waldhorn, *Hemingway and Faulkner in Their Time*, New York, Continuum, 2005.

Scafella, Frank, *Hemingway: Essays of Reassessment*, New York, Oxford University Press, 1990.

Smith, Paul (ed.), *New Essays on Hemingway's Short Fiction*, Cambridge, Cambridge University Press, 1998.

Young, Philip, *Ernest Hemingway: A Reconsideration*, University Park, Penn State University Press, 1966.

## NOTES

1 Petrina Crockford, *Paris Review*, 189 (2009): 17.
2 Ernest Hemingway, *Death in the Afternoon* (New York, Scribner, 1932), p. 192.
3 Hemingway, *The Short Stories: The First Forty-Nine Stories with a Brief Preface by the Author* (New York, Scribner, 1966), p. 95. Hereafter SS.
4 Ralph Ellison, *Shadow and Act* (New York, Random House, 1953), p. 145.
5 Hemingway, *The Sun Also Rises* (New York, Scribner, 1954), p. 50. Hereafter *TSAR*.
6 Hemingway, *A Farewell to Arms* (New York, Scribner, 1957), p. 26. Hereafter *FA*.
7 Hemingway, *To Have and Have Not* (New York, Scribner, 1953), p. 185.
8 Hemingway, *For Whom the Bell Tolls* (New York, Scribner, 1940), p. 4. Hereafter *FWBT*.
9 Hemingway, *The Old Man and the Sea* (New York, Scribner, 2003), p. 92.
10 Aleksandr I. Solzhenitsyn, *The Cancer Ward* (New York, Dell, 1968), p. 94.

# 12

# William Faulkner

PHILIP WEINSTEIN

Readers seduced by the power of William Faulkner's rendering of the South may think that he invented the region, but it was already – and had been for centuries – a heavily written-about place. To understand Faulkner's contribution to American fiction, we need to consider the background of southern attitudes that developed and took hold in the half-century following the Civil War.[1] During this period a number of southern writers transformed, retrospectively, the meaning of the Civil War – from a history of defeat to the myth of the Lost Cause. In the writings of Thomas Dixon (*The Clansman*, 1905) and Thomas Nelson Page (*The Old Dominion*, 1908), for example, the South "became" a place of aristocratic gallantry, a preserve of Old World culture. Joel Chandler Harris's Uncle Remus stories, published throughout the first two decades of the twentieth century, softened the portrait of race relations as well, giving it a picturesque, fit-for-children charm. The South's humiliation of 1861–5 was thus reconfigured to read as tragic despoliation, entailing the release of lawless black beasts upon the American scene. D. W. Griffith's immensely popular film version of Dixon's *The Clansman – Birth of a Nation* (1915) – crystallizes this reactionary vision of the South. That Faulkner's first-grade teacher would give him a copy of *The Clansman* to express her appreciation of the boy's promising talents suggests how far the myth had penetrated into the precincts of normative southern self-awareness (Blotner 1: 94)

Faulkner inherited such a notion of his region – his great-grandfather had been a flamboyant defender of the Old South during and after the Civil War – and vestiges of the myth recur as a sort of default dimension of his weaker writings. But his great work – the work that reveals Faulkner *as* Faulkner – sees strenuously through this myth. Indeed, the act of seeing through this myth enables Faulkner to become the most powerful white novelist of race relations this country has yet produced. No reader of his work before *Light in August* (1932), however, could have predicted such a turn in his career. For that reader, Faulkner was compelling for quite other reasons:

*The Sound and the Fury* (1929), *As I Lay Dying* (1930), and *Sanctuary* (1931) had dramatically changed the landscape of American fictional possibilities. With the publication of these three novels in less than seventeen months he seemed to appear out of nowhere, all of a sudden America's leading novelist. He too was amazed by his meteoric ascent; nothing in his earlier career had prepared him for it.[2]

A precocious loner whose studies never went past the tenth grade, Faulkner knew by his early teens that he would become a writer. He began writing poetry in his teens, eventually publishing *The Marble Faun* (1925) before reorienting himself as a writer of fiction. That reorientation can be pinpointed precisely: the first six months of 1925, during Faulkner's extended visit to the New Orleans world of Sherwood Anderson and his coterie of footloose writers and artists. Under Anderson's heady influence – literally and figuratively intoxicating, pitting New Orleans bohemianism against Mississippi's rural proprieties – the poet Faulkner became the novelist Faulkner. Anderson recognized the younger man's gifts and used his influence to persuade Horace Liveright (the leading publisher of American modernist literature in the 1920s) to accept Faulkner's first novel, *Soldiers' Pay* (1926), on condition, it is said, that Anderson would not have to read it first.[3]

Anderson was at the height of his fame during these years; *Winesburg Ohio* (1919) had established him as a major novelist of his generation. He not only opened up publishing possibilities for Faulkner; his work served as a conduit for the "modern" element in post–World War I American literature. The cast of misfits who grope their way unavailingly through *Winesburg* reveals the influence of Freud on American sensibilities. Rather than enact the normative drama of encountering obstacles, moving through maturation, and achieving progress, Anderson's stunted characters suffer from childhood trauma and unspeakable distress; their alienation is permanent. We may add to this narrative of incurable malaise three other widespread genres equally somber and equally compelling for the young Faulkner. First, there is the genre of "Lost Generation" novels emerging throughout the 1920s. John Dos Passos's *Three Soldiers* [1921] and e. e. cummings's *The Enormous Room* (1922) both appear before *Soldiers' Pay*; Ernest Hemingway's *The Sun Also Rises* comes out in the same year. Second, these years mark the acme of naturalist fiction in America. The troubled novels of Stephen Crane, Jack London, Theodore Dreiser, and Frank Norris – with their focus on natural and social forces disorienting and overpowering human will – dominate the first two decades of twentieth-century American fiction. Third, there lurks a regional genre virtually steeped in post–Civil War southern blood: the novel of the South's defeat by forces greater than its own. All of these darker themes and forms (childhood deformation, unspeakable distress, the incapacity of sensitive individuals to surmount an array of destructive social forces) reach and affect Faulkner's deep-seated penchant for melancholy sequences – for encounters not amenable to resolution. They will ignite into incandescent tragedy in *The Sound and the Fury* (1929).

Faulkner writes *Flags in the Dust* (revised and published as *Sartoris*) only a year before *The Sound and the Fury*. Yet to an attentive reader they may seem to have been written in different centuries. It is commonly claimed that with *The Sound and the Fury* Faulkner enters upon a world stage. To see what this claim means, we must broaden our focus and consider a European rather than an American culture of ideas and literary forms. The extraordinary outburst of Western modernist writing takes place in Europe decades before it migrates to America. Without that migration Faulkner might have written *Flags in the Dust*, but not *The Sound and the Fury*. To the name of Freud, mentioned earlier, we must add those of Conrad, Joyce, and Eliot. Conrad and Freud may be seen as "secret sharers" – Conrad's phrase and a fitting one for the uncanny (and unwanted) similarities between his work and Freud's. Both of them stress the occlusions that bedevil any attempt to lead a moral life; both trace the effects of earlier traumas on later behavior; both complicate beyond recognition any straightforward narrative structure in which an individual conceives, pursues, and achieves a project. Conrad's *Nostromo* (1907) remains unparalleled in its plot complexity – its sustaining of half a dozen narratives dizzyingly at odds with each other – until the appearance in 1936 of Faulkner's even more intricately plotted *Absalom, Absalom!*

Eliot's *The Waste Land* (1922) reprises in poetic form the alienation fueling the 1920s novels of the "Lost Generation"; indeed, that poem crystallized an entire generation's sense of what – spiritually and emotionally – World War I had actually *meant*. Meandering and recursive (like Freud's model for self-errance and like Conrad's nonlinear narrative structures), *The Waste Land* articulates – for many modernist sensibilities – the end of the dream of liberal progress. Freud, Conrad, and Eliot mark Faulkner's fiction abidingly, but his work is perhaps most startlingly indebted to Joyce's *Ulysses* (1922). There, in the representation of Stephen Dedalus's and Leopold Bloom's minds, Joyce perfects a technique for writing interiority – what is loosely referred to as "stream of consciousness" – whose influence on both *The Sound and the Fury* and *As I Lay Dying* is incalculable. These two masterpieces, however original and deserving of their reputation, may be conceivable without Joyce – but they are not *writable* without him. Not that either of them is derivative; Faulkner deploys stream of consciousness to dramatically different effects (poetic rather than commonplace) from

Joyce. But he retains Joyce's technique for writing the "quick" of individual consciousness – for narrating its ungrammatical twists and turns, for capturing its quirky unpredictability. The result is a capacity to write the pathos of moment-by-moment unpreparedness, the sense of being overwhelmed by unmanageable thoughts and feelings, that no prior novelistic models of syntax could enable.[4] To see what this claim might mean specifically, let us "eavesdrop" on *The Sound and the Fury*'s Quentin Compson:

> *I have committed incest I said Father it was I it was not Dalton Ames* And when he put Dalton Ames. Dalton Ames. Dalton Ames. When he put the pistol in my hand I didn't. That's why I didn't. He would be there and she would and I would. Dalton Ames. Dalton Ames. Dalton Ames. If we could have just done something so dreadful and Father said That's sad too people cannot do anything that dreadful they cannot do anything very dreadful at all they cannot even remember tomorrow what seemed dreadful today and I said, You can shirk all things and he said, Ah can you. And I will look down and see my murmuring bones and the deep water like wind, like a roof of wind, and after a long time they cannot distinguish even bones upon the lonely and inviolate sand. Until on the day when He says Rise only the flat-iron would come floating up. It's not when you realise that nothing can help you – religion, pride, anything – it's when you realise that you dont need any aid. Dalton Ames. Dalton Ames. Dalton Ames. If I could have been his mother lying with open body lifted laughing, holding his father with my hand refraining, seeing, watching him die before he lived. *One minute she was standing in the door.*
> (937–8)

To find his way thus into Quentin's distress, Faulkner had to break with an entire tradition's way of writing inner trouble. That tradition – as countless novels reveal, as *Sartoris* reveals as well – insisted on proper syntax and grammar. It bound its materials into the decorum of complete sentences: a subject, a verb, and a object. Such sentences – the bread and butter of fiction – represented the human being as a discrete doer performing his discrete deed. The bare bones of such sentences enacted a little parable of potency. They said by their very form, *I can do this.* All of which is absent here. Quentin's clauses either lack verbs or mix their tenses indiscriminately – present perfect, past, conditional, conditional perfect, present, future. The nineteenth-century tools that Faulkner inherited could represent a figure in distress only as someone seen from a certain distance and clothed in appropriate syntax. Such a figure appeared – proper syntax makes this happen – as something stable, gathered into presence, in black and white. By contrast, Faulkner knew that a figure in distress was someone moved and moving, penetrated by absent forces, his mind hurtling through multiple spaces and times—a figure of desire and lack—and in color.

To articulate the color of distress, Faulkner repositioned Quentin in space, time, and the field of others. More, Faulkner got his delegated narrator out of his sentences. He had to articulate – as though it were happening without anyone telling it – the drama of Quentin careening among multiple spaces and times, drowning in the emotional force field of absent others. Space in the quoted passage loses its coherence. The reader is swallowed up in Quentin's place-shifting interiority, as his frantic mind darts to the scene the previous summer with Caddy's first lover, Dalton Ames; then to his dark conversations with Father; then to his fantasy of looking down on himself as a suicide so deep in the waters of the Charles River that even Christ's call for resurrection will fail to make him stir; and then to the even stranger fantasy of being secretly present at Ames's conceiving, himself becoming Ames's mother, who removes Ames's father's penis just before ejaculation, thus killing Ames before he can be born. Faulkner's new way of representing time is equally deranged. The Dalton Ames moment, the Caddy at the door moment, and the moment with Father are in this new rhetoric pressed together while remaining apart – not fused but confused. The passage eclipses time's cleanly forward motion from A to B to C (perhaps the deepest assumption that our sanity requires and that conventional narrative happily respects). Finally, absent others lodged inside the self – Ames, Father, Caddy – speak in a deafening roar. Often silent in the presence of friends or acquaintances, Quentin is bedlam inside. His mind is a defective transformer through which human voices pass like so many incompatible electric charges. He is in pain and going down. Faulkner has learned how to make Quentin's hurt not only transparent but radioactive. In his demise we see the failure of once-aristocratic southern culture to pass on to its young the filters necessary for screening and negotiating experience, for surviving it.

*As I Lay Dying*, following hard on *The Sound and the Fury* and written in barely seven weeks, is even leaner and more jagged. The book seems to center on something one might think beyond fiction's capacity to say: "That pride, that furious desire to hide that abject nakedness which we bring here with us ... carry stubbornly with us into the earth again" (*AILD* 31). Pride and nakedness: *As I Lay Dying* probes the all but unrelinquishable barriers we require to conceal our psychic nakedness from others, the unmanageable distress that occurs when those barriers are breached. Many of the book's fifty-nine sections articulate the self's insistent yet imprisoning inwardness, even as this is silently experienced in the presence of vocal others. Addie Bundren, the dead mother, had felt her imprisonment inside selfhood the most keenly. Her awareness (earlier, as a teacher) of her students, "each with his and her secret and selfish thought," drove her wild. She would whip them with a switch, thinking with each blow, "Now you are aware of me!

Now I am something in your secret and selfish life, who have marked your blood with my own for ever and ever" (114). Mere words, Addie knew, were incapable of crossing this divide: "We had had to use one another by words like spiders dangling by their mouths from a beam, swinging and twisting and never touching, and that only through the blows of the switch could my blood and their blood flow as one stream.... I would think how words go straight up in a thin line, quick and harmless, and how terribly doing goes along the earth" (115–17).

Words that swing and twist and never touch – reminiscent of Faulkner's earlier poetry and first novels – are no good. They fail to penetrate the pride-installed boundaries that protect the self's exposure, its lifelong nakedness. What is needed are words that wound, words that break through the self's defenses. Addie's intact husband, Anse, will go to his grave unmarked and virginal (despite his having fathered four children), having remained cradled throughout his life, thanks to the cottony insulation of the words he lives within and takes to be real. *The Sound and the Fury* was Faulkner's first novel to hew its way into "wordless" territory, beyond convention. In it he twisted syntax and procedure with such violence that the familiar word parade ceases, the televisionlike sound subsides, and the released word image escapes its familiar boundaries. Released, it enacts, "terribly," not a saying but a doing that "goes along the earth." It seeks not to entertain, not even to deliver truths, but to penetrate the reader's heart. With these two novels behind him, and the even starker (and lurid) *Sanctuary* appearing in 1931, it is no surprise that Faulkner was suddenly recognized as America's leading novelist.

One further flowering lay in store for him, as unpredictable as the one in 1929 that produced *The Sound and the Fury*. Faulkner was to become the supreme white writer of race relations in his century.[5] The breakthrough novel is *Light in August* (1932). It is as though Faulkner sat up in bed one night after a nightmare and asked himself, What would I feel like if I suddenly found myself to be one of them? What would *I* feel like: there was no question of *them*. The novel did not ask who (as a community living in segregated "freedman's" districts of every town in the South) they might be: no empathic entry into southern blackness, virtually no blacks in the novel at all. No: what was required was that the one suffering from race relations be white – a man trapped in a weave of racial rumor about his identity at its core genetic level. He had to be unable to know what blood ran in his veins. This narrow optic brought to focus an extraordinary insight. Beneath the surface confidence of southern whites ran a racial insecurity bordering on hysteria. If a drop of black blood was thought to make a white man black, who might not unknowingly carry this toxic drop? No one could see the internal wreckage that drop would have wrought. Invisibly infected carriers might be anywhere. Such anxiety might be enough to make many a white man in the segregated South have trouble going back to sleep, once he had sat bolt upright at 3 a.m. and wondered, What if I were black and didn't know it?

One might ask how racial identity can be a serious question in *Light in August,* since the novel has virtually no black characters. Yet racial hysteria – like a bomb threat – can flare up, uncontrollably, with neither blacks nor bombs anywhere to be found. In an essay entitled "Stranger in the Village," James Baldwin explains the logic of this hysteria: "At the root of the American Negro problem," he writes, "is the necessity of the American white man to find a way of living with the Negro in order to live with himself.... 'The Negro-in-America is a form of insanity which overtakes white men'" (88). It is as though the American white man has been surreptitiously infected with Negroness. The insanity that ensues is white alone. My figure of speech invokes the blood, which is *Light in August*'s obsessive concern. Joe Christmas is incapable of finding a way of living with the Negro in order to live with himself, and this because he senses his dark twin living inejectably, blood-coiled, beneath his skin.

The brilliance of the novel inheres in Faulkner's ways of keeping everyone – which includes the reader and Christmas himself – in the dark about Christmas's racial identity. Southern white men cannot bear not to know who is white and who is not. Christmas must be hunted down and executed not because he is black – southern whites have learned over generations how to "handle" blacks – but because, not looking or "acting" black, he cannot be reliably quarantined *as* black. Like a contagion, he sparks white hysteria, since if he is black, who else might not be? By way of Christmas Faulkner finds his way to the unconscious nerve center of racist anxiety. What is most intolerable about "them" is the possibility – never quite repressed – that "they" may be no different from "us."

Miscegenation thus becomes the cardinal focus of Faulkner's imaginative entry into southern race relations, even as the need to keep racial identity a mystery controls the narrative procedure. In *Absalom, Absalom!* (1936) Faulkner makes both this focus and this narrative procedure yield their most prodigious insights. No reader knows until the end of the novel that the mysterious *what* – Charles Bon's unexplained murder – screens an even more mysterious *who*: Bon's racial identity. Thanks to such screening, Bon elicits a remarkable act of vicarious projection from characters in the novel and from the reader as well. He performs as a sort of blank slate on whom others project their desires. Faulkner thus yokes the mystery of Bon's identity to the capacity for love itself – the human propensity to project onto the other and see one's own dearest possibilities at stake there.

Such misrecognition cannot last; Bon must be "outed" as black. Once he is identified thus, he must submit to be "nigger" or die the death. Henry pleads with him – "You are my brother" – and Bon replies, "No I'm not. I'm the nigger that's going to sleep with your sister." He is both. No other novelist approaches Faulkner when it comes to loving what you hate, hating what you love. This unmanageable heart truth suffuses *Absalom* and makes it continue to live and breathe. "The human heart in conflict with itself": so Faulkner characterized his core concern when receiving the Nobel Prize in 1950. What is this but to center his great work on the plight of human beings who find themselves intolerably entrapped – not by being mistaken for someone else, but by being who they are?

For *Absalom* to "work," Bon must not look black. And this suggests that Faulkner could enter black identities most resonantly only if, within his own imaginary, they *were* white – yet tragically ensnared by being socially defined as black. Put otherwise, Faulkner envisages in *Absalom* a transcendence of racial difference itself. Thanks to the suasions and arabesques of the novel's form, we see – in action – not race but the entire deforming edifice of racial construction. Blacks and whites do not otherwise differ, and *Absalom* seems to whisper, deep down, that whites, unconsciously, do not want them to differ. How telling it is, finally, that this greatest of his race-obsessed novels can envisage a racial solution only by transcending the very terms of race. Utopian, yes, and necessarily so: anything less falls afoul of the unremovable racist blinkers of 1930s southern thinking and feeling. Faulkner's vision is shaped by these blinkers exactly as deeply as he might wish it were not. It takes *both* these optics to reveal, to a twenty-first-century liberal readership that fantasizes itself beyond race, how race has disfigured the emotional texture of American lives.

Faulkner was to write two more novels about race relations in the South – *Go Down, Moses* (1942) and *Intruder in the Dust* (1948) – and both of them pursue racial identity as "known" but abused. Their imaginative freight, correspondingly, lessens in intensity. This last claim may be made, unfortunately, for the remaining novels that Faulkner wrote until his death in 1962: the impressive Snopes trilogy (*The Hamlet* [1940], *The Town* [1957], and *The Mansion* [1959]), *Requiem for a Nun* (1951), the extraordinarily ambitious *A Fable* (1954), and the graceful swan song, *The Reivers* (1962). Impressive – and occasionally sublime – as these later novels are, Faulkner's reputation as a supreme American novelist rests on the earlier fiction examined in this essay.[6]

Although Faulkner was generous toward others' work, he remained abidingly resistant to the larger, more socialized role of "man of letters." Reclusive to the end, claiming to be just a "farmer," he nevertheless found himself committed to speaking out on civil rights during the 1950s – if only because he could not in conscience avoid it. This is not to say that his "go slow now," "man in the middle" stance earned him either support from blacks and northern liberals or understanding from southern conservatives and reactionaries.[7] He was at once too understanding of America's race problem and not understanding enough.

Faulkner did not seek cohorts, and he might have been bemused by the notion of a "Southern Renaissance." Yet Katherine Anne Porter, Flannery O'Connor, Eudora Welty, and Carson McCullers all developed their own writerly identities (during the 1930s through the 1950s) under the shadow of his fame. (Asked about Faulkner's impact on other southern writers, Flannery O'Connor famously quipped: "Nobody wants his mule and wagon stalled on the same track the Dixie Limited is roaring down.") Though Faulkner insisted on remaining a loner, his reputation did not magically follow from the sheer power of his work. It flourished in the 1950s and 1960s in good part because well-known southern intellectuals – Cleanth Brooks, Robert Penn Warren, Allen Tate, and John Crowe Ransom (leaders of what became known as the New Critics) – recognized and praised his work as an exemplary blend of formal intricacy and undogmatic moral seriousness. Malcolm Cowley's *Portable Faulkner* (1946) rescued Faulkner's work from oblivion (all of it but *Sanctuary* out of print then), and a scant three years later he was awarded the Nobel Prize in literature. During the two decades that followed, with New Critical tenets in the ascendancy in college English Departments throughout the country, his best novels became canonical. No English major could easily escape him.

Faulkner's impact on subsequent American novelists is likewise massive, and this essay may close by identifying two writers whom his work helped to find their own distinctive voices. William Styron's *Lie Down in Darkness* (1951) reads as a tragic love song to the doomed Caddy Compson in *The Sound and the Fury*. (Styron's later *The Confessions of Nat Turner* [1967] reveals, as well, a sort of Faulknerian courage in its engagement with explosive race relations; many black civil rights leaders were stung by Styron's bold attempt to speak Nat Turner "from inside.") Finally, perhaps our most distinguished contemporary novelist, Toni Morrison, wrote her master's thesis on Faulkner and Woolf, and he has demonstrably remained on her mind. It is hard not to read her most remarkable novel, *Beloved* (1987), as an attempt to grasp American history as a racial *haunting* in terms (this time, black rather than white) that recall the reach and depth of Faulkner's *Absalom, Absalom!*[8]

## FURTHER READING

Bleikasten, André, *The Ink of Melancholy: Faulkner's Novels from* The Sound and the Fury *to* Light in August, Bloomington, Indiana University Press, 1990.

Godden, Richard, *Fictions of Labor: William Faulkner and the South's Long Revolution*, New York, Cambridge University Press, 1997.

Hannon, Charles, *Faulkner and the Discourses of Culture*, Baton Rouge, Louisiana State University Press, 2005.

Irwin, John T., *Doubling and Incest, Repetition and Revenge: A Speculative Reading of Faulkner*, Baltimore, Johns Hopkins University Press, 1976.

Kartiganer, Donald, *The Meaning of Form in Faulkner's Novels*, Amherst, University of Massachusetts Press, 1979.

Morris, Wesley and Barbara Alverson Morris, *Reading Faulkner*, Madison, University of Wisconsin Press, 1989.

Polk, Noel, *Children of the Dark House: Text and Context in Faulkner*, Jackson, University Press of Mississippi, 1996.

Robinson, Owen, *Creating Yoknapatawpha: Readers and Writers in Faulkner's Fiction*, New York, Routledge, 2006.

Ross, Stephen, *Faulkner's Inexhaustible Voice: Speech and Writing in Faulkner*, Athens, University of Georgia Press, 1989.

Snead, James, *Figures of Division: William Faulkner's Major Novels*, New York, Methuen, 1986.

Sundquist, Eric, *Faulkner: The House Divided*, Baltimore, Johns Hopkins University Press, 1983.

Wadlington, Warwick, *Reading Faulknerian Tragedy*, Ithaca, N.Y., Cornell University Press, 1987.

Weinstein, Philip, *Faulkner's Subject: A Cosmos No One Owns*, New York, Cambridge University Press, 1992.

## NOTES

1 Commentary on the Old South is legion. Two good discussions of the differences between the realities of the region's history and mythic transformations of that history are Joel Williamson, *William Faulkner and Southern History* (New York, Oxford University Press, 1991), and John Matthews, *The Sound and the Fury: Faulkner and the Lost Cause* (Boston, Twayne, 1991).

2 For further commentary on Faulkner's unpreparedness for sudden fame, see my *Becoming Faulkner* (New York, Oxford University Press, 2010), chapter 2.

3 See John Matthews's *William Faulkner: Seeing through the South* (Malden, Mass., Wiley Blackwell, 2009), pp. 25–30, for Liveright's importance as publisher of modernist literature.

4 For a more detailed argument about the contribution of these four modernists to Faulkner's developing writerly identity, see my "Make It New: Faulkner and Modernism," in *A Companion to William Faulkner,* ed. Richard C. Moreland (Malden, Mass., Blackwell, 2007), pp. 342–7.

5 This argument about Faulkner's significance as a writer of race relations draws on chapter 3 of my *Becoming Faulkner*.

6 Not all of Faulkner's commentators agree, of course, that the bulk of the work after *Go Down Moses* (1942) is of lesser quality. For a spirited defense of the later work, see both Theresa Towner, *Faulkner on the Color Line: The Later Novels* (Jackson, University Press of Mississippi, 2001), and John Matthews, *William Faulkner: Seeing through the South* (Oxford, Blackwell, 2008).

7 Both quoted phrases articulate Faulkner's deeply troubled response in the 1950s to civil rights turmoil. For more commentary on Faulkner and civil rights, see Charles Peavy, *Go Slow, Now: Faulkner and the Race Question* (Eugene, University of Oregon Press, 1961), and Grace Hale and Robert Jackson, "We're Trying Hard as Hell to Free Ourselves," in *A Companion to William Faulkner*, ed. Richard C. Moreland (Malden, Mass., Blackwell, 2007), 28–45. See as well my *Becoming Faulkner*, chapter 3.

8 For extensive analysis of Faulkner's work in relation to Morrison's, see my *What Else but Love? The Ordeal of Race in Faulkner and Morrison* (New York, Columbia University Press, 1996), as well as Carol Kolmerten, Stephen Ross, and Judith Wittenberg, eds., *Unflinching Gaze: Faulkner and Morrison Re-envisioned* (Jackson, University of Mississippi Press, 1997).

# 13
# Henry Roth

HANA WIRTH-NESHER

"I – I'm losted," sobs six-year-old David Shearl in Henry Roth's (1906–95) novel *Call It Sleep* (1934), as a passerby on New York's Lower East Side tries to help the quivering child, who cannot find his way back home. Although he can answer her question, "Don't you know where you live?"[1] with a specific address, this information is useless because neither she nor the policeman at the local precinct can discern the name of the street from his heavily accented English. David knows that he lives at "A hunner 'n' twenny six Boddeh Stritt" (99), which could be anything from Potter to Bahrdee, or as the Irish cop tells his mother when she arrives at the station, "I'm thinkin' ye'd best put a tag on him, fer he sure had us up a tree with his Pother an' Body an' Powther!" (106). On the margins of the manuscript of *Call It Sleep*, Roth scribbled various ways of transcribing the sound of this unnamed street as voiced by a sobbing child, ending with "Body Street," the mother's body as the ultimate home that a six-year-old lost on the streets of New York would be seeking. Yet when his mother arrives at the station, we understand along with David that his mother is also lost, for this immigrant, whose conversations with her son prior to this scene convey her intelligence, sensitivity, and eloquence, can barely utter, "T'anks so viel!" (106). We suddenly grasp that up to this moment her speech has been rendered to us in a nuanced and lyrical English that has actually been a translation from an absent Yiddish original, in her mother tongue. Infantilized as an immigrant, Genya Shearl can no longer fully protect her own child in a world in which she herself cannot find her way.

Published in 1934, Henry Roth's brilliant novel *Call It Sleep* captures being "losted" in diverse ways that are intertwined: geographical, social, psychological, cultural, and linguistic. According to Ruth Wisse, "the author was born into a Babel of cultures, none of them comfortably his own."[2] Henry Roth was two years old when his parents immigrated to the United States in 1907 from the Austro-Hungarian province of Galicia to join masses of Eastern European Jewish immigrants on New York's Lower East

Side, who, along with other Eastern and Southern European newcomers, struggled to eke out a living in one of the most congested urban areas in the world. Roth's family subsequently moved uptown to Harlem, and Henry, who spoke Yiddish at home, eventually studied English literature at the City University of New York. With Yiddish as his mother tongue, Hebrew as the language of the religious practice that he had learned as a child and later abandoned, and English as the language of the literature that he read with passion and ambition, Roth did indeed inhabit a Babel of languages, which was not unusual for immigrant children in this period of mass upheaval, migration, and deracination. In fact, deracination became a mark of modernity for millions of people during this period whether they left home or not, and among creative artists, deracination in the form of purposeful rejection of tradition became an inherent feature of modernism.

*Call It Sleep* dramatizes immigrant experience in the extreme, as David's parents, Genya and Albert Shearl, go to the United States from Eastern Europe, where America was known among Jews as "Die Goldine Medina," the Golden Land. They soon discover that life in New York is far from golden; that it is hard, particularly for a woman as sheltered and refined as Genya and for a man as paranoid as Albert, who suspects that everyone is mocking him. To preserve his manhood, he exerts authority at home, abusing his son, whose paternity he questions. The Shearls have immigrated to the New World for a fresh start after each of them has violated a tenet of the traditional society in the Old World. Since the story unfolds through the perspective of the child, we piece together the history of this family through fragments of conversations often beyond the boy's comprehension, but not the reader's. The bright light in an otherwise dark world is the curious, poetic, and sensitive mind of the child David, the creative prism through whom we experience fear, loss, and disorientation, as well as wonder

Like all great modernist novels, *Call It Sleep* can be read on several levels. In terms of social history, it portrays immigrant life in New York City at the beginning of the twentieth century with its pushcart peddlers, crowded cold water flats and outdoor toilets, polyglot streets, dark stairwells and gaping cellar doors, beckoning rooftops, and each day's struggle to procure food. It portrays the plight of workers at the mercy of their bosses, the necessity to take boarders into cramped quarters, and the ability of children to find magic and to carve out play spaces even in the most dire surroundings devoid of a blade of grass. It also draws attention to the pain of severing ties with the land, customs, languages, and familiarity of the Old Country, and how the memories of the parent generations, based on their actual experiences, are transmitted to their American-born children, who "remember" what they have only heard. David's surname "Shearl" is an apt indicator of the pain of severance, as it means scissors in Yiddish, his family's mother tongue. Moreover, cutting ties also describes the story of David in this novel, a boy of six undergoing the Freudian family drama. When the book opens, David and Genya are depicted as harmonious and loving mother and son; David feels secure in the knowledge that when the street becomes treacherous he can ascend to his mother's glowing kitchen and warm lap. He is also portrayed staring at his father's biceps, jealous and fearful of his father's masculine strength. Before long he will learn that his mother's protection has its limits. She cannot always shelter him from his punitive father, or from the brutal forces of the city. What he picks up from the speech and behavior of the street makes him see Genya not only as his mother, but also as a woman and object of the male gaze, a realization that distances her from him. He finally seeks protection from a power greater than his mother's, from the power unleashed between the car tracks that he ascribes to the divine light in the Hebrew prophetic text of Isaiah. True to his name, the child David Shearl will need to cut the bond to his parents, just as they, infantilized by being immigrants, also cut their bond to their parent culture.

The power of *Call It Sleep* as a modernist masterpiece does not lie in the naturalistic details of the hardships of immigrant life, although it does vividly document the congestion, noise, and overstimulation of Lower Manhattan's streets at the peak period of immigration to the United States. Its power lies in its articulation of loss conveyed through wordplay that negotiates a web of accents, dialects, and languages. As we have seen in the slipperiness of David's address when uttered with a Yiddish accent, heard by an Irish ear, and placed on the page by an author acutely aware of the discrepancy between writing and speech, social and linguistic diversity goes beyond mimesis to a self-consciousness about language characteristic of modernist literature, from Lewis Carroll to James Joyce. The feeling of loss that pervades this novel results from a series of inadequate translations in the broadest sense of that word. We have already seen how the inability to reproduce sounds in a newly acquired language, such as "thanks" for a Yiddish speaker who has never encountered "th" before, dwarfs the stature of Genya Shearl, eloquent speaker in her mother tongue. The adult immigrant's very body, her mouth and lips, resists forming the sounds of the language into which she translates her words, with the irony that in this instance the word beyond her articulation that causes her son to be lost is in fact "Body Street."[3] Such pronunciation hurdles represented on the printed page, however, also enable bilingual wordplay that draws attention to translation. When David hears the English word "alter" for the first time, he assumes that it is the Yiddish word for an old man, yet its English meaning signals the Christian Church and in the context of the plot is a code for his mother's secret, her affair with a gentile in the Old World, a man who abandoned her to face shame and humiliation in her community. In another example of many woven throughout this work, an immigrant child will tell another at the Christmas season, "Id ain' no Sendy Klaws, didja know?" (141). Roth will rely on his reader to recognize the sign of what is off limits to Judaism in the "claws" that mark nonkosher or unfit food.

As readers of *Call It Sleep*, we find ourselves translating these sounds into standard English as we read, just as we observe characters engaged in translating not only between languages, but also from ideas into words for experiences that portray loss beyond particular language or ethnicity. One of the most moving acts of translation between mother and child in this novel is Genya's inability to translate the concept of death to her six-year-old David, who wants to know what she means by "eternal years," her answer to his question as to how long a dead person sleeps. Attempting to convey the limited comprehension of human beings, she tries to explain "eternal" by analogy. Reaching for the sugar bowl, Genya lifts out a pair of tongs with which she carefully pinches a cube of sugar. "This is how wide my brain can stretch," she says, "No wider. Would you ask me to pick up a frozen sea with these narrow things?... The sea to this...." (69). David impatiently interrupts, insisting that the dead must wake up sometime, an observation that leads to her naturalistic admission that "there is nothing left to waken" (69). Her skepticism about the existence of an eternal soul does not stop her from performing religious rituals, such as the benediction over the Sabbath candles. Genya finds herself lost between declining faith and familiar ritual practice. As twilight gives way to darkness, she ushers in the Sabbath with her blessing over the candles, appearing disoriented in her new home, while David's awe at "the hour of tawny beatitude" adds to this sense of disorientation with its echo of the beatitudes in the Sermon on the Mount (71).

The most striking example of cross-cultural (mis)translation in the novel is David's rendering of a passage from the Book of Isaiah into the language of his everyday urban reality. His religious school instruction follows traditional Jewish pedagogy, namely, translation of Hebrew verses into Yiddish. When David takes this one step further and translates the sacred light of Isaiah's coal into the American cityscape, he nearly pays with his life. Captivated by the image of an angel cleansing the prophet's mouth with a burning coal, David knows from his own tenement that "in a cellar is coal," a dark place that strikes fear into him whenever he passes its trapdoor. "Where is god's cellar?" he wonders. "How light it must be there" (231). This observation reminds him of the day that he was bullied by other boys on the street who tricked him into dropping a zinc rod into the space between the car tracks, which released dazzling light. Convinced that this must be God's light, and therefore a power greater than any other in his world, he seeks out the tracks again the next time his father is about to punish him, confident that God's light will protect him from paternal wrath. But David learns that New York is not a sacred landscape, and God is not to be found between the train tracks unless the electrical charge that unleashes the light signifies the omnipotence of America's mechanical and industrial power.

By inscribing the book of Isaiah into his novel, Henry Roth makes a space for the drama of Jewish American literature and culture in the making. Since Isaiah prophesies the coming of the Messiah, it accentuates the critical difference between Judaism and Christianity. While both subscribe to Isaiah's Messiah as a descendant of the House of David, Judaism does not recognize Jesus as the fulfillment of that prophecy. To explore the vexed relationship between these religions further, Roth has the children in David's class recite passages in preparation for the festival of Passover, which appears in the Gospels as the Last Supper, and which serves Jews as the foundational story of the Children of Israel, freed from bondage in Egypt and destined for nationhood in the Promised Land. The Passover season, therefore, dramatically enacts the severing of Christianity from Judaism, while historically it has been fraught for Jews in Europe, where violence against them was intensified by Christians taking revenge on those they regarded as Christ killers. Roth depicts how this anti-Semitism crossed the shores to America when Gentile boys taunt and bully David as soon as they recognize him as a Jew. The Passover story plays a major role in the envisioning of America in its earliest stage. Insofar as the Puritan founding fathers were Christians, they read the story of the Hebrews' flight from slavery in Egypt as a prefiguring of the narrative of Christ that superseded the Old Testament. For them, the story of bondage to liberation serves as an allegory of the journey of the Christian soul. However, the Puritans also read the Passover story as scriptural history in which *they* were the genuine Children of Israel, the new Chosen People, and America was the new Promised Land. This reading posed a problem for Jews entering America's account of its own origins, a problem that Roth dramatizes.

Puritan rhetoric has had a profound effect on all subsequent generations of Americans who readily embrace the notion that America fulfills biblical prophecy by relocating the Promised Land to the West rather than to the East, displacing the Old Testament story that Jews continued to believe. Every Christian could adopt this vision of America, whereas Jews would have to find a way to merge radically different views, as their own foundational narrative of the Exodus from Egypt also became a foundational narrative for America, one that called theirs into question. On the one hand, America's conception of itself to the extent that it is based on its Puritan origins has been a response to the story of the Hebrews in the Bible. On the other hand, the Jews' entry into this conception of America would pose a threat of erasure of their own collective identity. This tension is brilliantly staged in *Call It Sleep* when David, having seen an image of Christ for the first time on the crucifix in his Polish Catholic friend's home, dreams that he speaks verses from the Passover ceremony while on the cross, verses that would identify Jesus as an observant Jew. Through David's imagination, therefore, Roth stages the re-Judaizing of Christ and the reappropriation of the story of Exodus by Jews in the land that had adopted this same story as a statement of its own divine mission. Roth's novel enacts the dialectical nature of Jewish and American culture by demonstrating how each of these terms is partially a product of its interaction with the other. In other words, Roth's artistry in this book highlights how "Jewish" and "American" in the United States of America are concepts that are mutually constituted.

I have been referring *to Call It Sleep* as a modernist masterpiece, and by now a modernist classic. I have refrained from calling it ethnic literature, not because that category would be inaccurate, but because it too often leads to false conclusions about its artistic achievement. American literary history has tended to keep the terms "modernist" and "ethnic" apart, retaining the first term for experimental works of literature that self-consciously resisted traditional plots with fully resolved closure and omniscient narration, and that sought new forms to convey concepts of character that stressed subjectivity and consciousness, from James to Faulkner. The term "ethnic" has tended to signal literature that depicted "reality" in terms of material and social forces, with ethnic characters perceived as outsiders. In other words, subjectivity was a matter of privilege, and sociology was a matter of disadvantage. In Werner Sollors's *Ethnic Modernism*, he has shown how America's gradual sense of itself as a multiethnic country has made it possible to read works such as Roth's *Call It Sleep* as models of how ethnicity and modernism are not mutually exclusive terms. On the contrary, he traces how European modernism often made its way to America precisely through these "outsider" groups that were perceived as ethnic.

Roth's novel is exemplary as a work of ethnic modernism, if we define the ethnic writer as one who is perceived, or perceives himself, as a member of a group that is a minority or an outsider by virtue of descent. Yet modernist writers like Henry Roth or James Joyce challenge the either-or paradigm of outsider or insider, minority or majority: either Henry Roth is an American writer (designated as a universal term), or he is a Jewish writer (designated as an ethnic particular term). If we assume that writers have multiple identities that coexist, we will gain a greater understanding of what the universal and the particular meant in the worlds they created in their novels. Roth acknowledged his profound debt to Joyce, who both documented the details of Dublin as a discriminated minority in the British Empire and transformed Dublin into a palimpsest of Western civilization with a modern-day *Ulysses* (1922). Leopold Bloom reenacts the Odyssey as an Irishman and cosmopolitan, as Jew and Greek, as the embodiment of Hebraism and Hellenism.

In precisely the same way, Henry Roth depicts David Shearl as both a Jewish immigrant child in New York City in the first decades of the twentieth century and an archetypal figure who, by sustaining an injury causing him temporarily to lose consciousness, descends into an underworld and ultimately returns to the world of living. This makes David a mock epic hero in myth, and a mock Christ figure, as he "dies" and is reborn. The section of the book when this occurs is a tour de force of modernist writing. In his coma as he lies prostrate on the cobblestones, David's unconscious is rendered as a series of images, voices, and fragments of texts in a stream of consciousness we have come to associate with modernist prose. The chapter is composed of a collage of voices and multiple perspectives. The huddled masses on the city streets, like a polyglot Greek chorus, bewail David's fate in dialects, accented English, revolutionary slogans, bitter plaints, and pleas for help, from the technical cause of the accident, "Shawt soicit, Mack" (420), to the medical cure of smelling salts, "He's mecking him t'breed!" (423). The Irish cops part the sea of onlookers – "Back up youz!" – lumping the Jews among them by their generic tag, "'Didja hea' me Moses?" (423). Onlookers drawn into the spectacle of an accident also scrutinize David's face for signs of his ethnicity. "Looks Jewish t' me," says one. "Yeah," replies the other. "Map o' Jerusalem, all right" (427). To others he is simply a "poor bastard" (427). From this chorus of new American voices, we learn that he has sustained a burn on his foot, whose swelling identifies him as another figure from Greek myth, Oedipus, the inspiration for Freud's Oedipal family drama that the child David is also experiencing along with the drama of immigration and acculturation.

The sights and sounds coursing through his mind after his injury appear in modernism's trademark style, stream of consciousness. His hallucinating mind becomes an arena for the cultures, myths, and religions that this Jewish child attempts to navigate as he searches for his place in America. Swimming into view are the tongs that his mother invoked in her attempt to explain death and eternity, the crucifix on Leo's wall where one sacrifice, that of God's son to redeem mankind in Christianity, morphs into the sacrifice of the paschal lamb recalled at Passover by Jews, which in turn morphs into images from modernist literature such as "heart of darkness" (429). When David awakens from his failed quest for the sacred, he finds his father chastened and mindful of his responsibility for the son he recognizes as his own and his mother tenderly offering him food. He awakens with myriad images and words that he can recall by closing his eyes and retreating into his imagination. Through David's reveries, *Call It Sleep* charts the exacting price of immigration and of modernity, without nostalgia for the traditional world left behind except perhaps for its languages. Caught between Old World restrictions and prejudices, on the one hand, and unrestricted ruthless American capitalism, on the other, the child immigrant finds comfort in one undisputed ray of light, his own artistic mind, which sees magic and wonder even in the grimmest circumstances. Just as light is released from the black coal in the prophetic Book of Isaiah, so David on the closing page of the novel can strike sparks into the dark by winking his eyelids shut and giving names to the endless items of the cityscape that floated into his mind that day. The artist's daunting ambition to call things by their names, to "call it sleep," and to do so with the words and texts that each specific culture makes available, marks the end of this extraordinary novel (441).

The reception of *Call It Sleep* is also a story of near-death and rebirth. Published in 1934 during the Great Depression to almost unanimous positive reviews (with the exception of criticism on the Left for inadequate exposure of the plight of the proletariat), the novel was out of print and nearly forgotten for decades before its legendary comeback. Named twice by the literary critics Leslie Fielder and Alfred Kazin as one of the most neglected books of the previous twenty-five years in a symposium conducted by the *American Scholar*, *Call It Sleep* was reissued in 1960, was acclaimed as a landmark of American literature, and sold more than a million copies. It has been translated into numerous languages and has never been out of print since its well-deserved revival. Subsequent to the publication of *Call It Sleep*, Henry Roth suffered from an extended writer's block. With the exception of a collection of his short works edited by Mario Materasi entitled *Shifting Landscape* (1987), Roth did not publish another novel until 1994, a half-century from the printing of *Call It Sleep*. Entitled *Mercy of a Rude Stream*, it was the first of a projected five-volume work of this title, four of which have appeared (two posthumously). The first volume was subtitled *A Star Shines over Mount Morris Park* (1994), and the other three are *A Diving Rock on the Hudson* (1995), *From Bondage* (1996), and *Requiem for Harlem* (1998). Although the characters' names are not the same as those in *Call It Sleep*, Ira Stigman's story could be read as a sequel to that of David Shearl, beginning at the outbreak of the First World War, when Ira was still a teenager. With italicized interludes in the present as the writer reflects upon his life and work addressed to his computer, Ecclesias,

*Mercy* has many autobiographical elements woven into it. However, Roth insisted that "this is a fiction" on the frontispiece. The books chronicle the moral, emotional, and creative development of Ira Stigman, a portrait of the artist as a young man making his way from his immigrant family in Harlem to the literary world of Greenwich Village. In *Mercy of a Rude Stream,* Roth continues to explore the claustrophobic Jewish family, the multiethnic and multiracial cityscape of New York, and the social and psychological perils of the life of the writer in the making. Raw, gritty, erudite, and often lyrical, *Mercy* testifies to the creativity of the author in his later years, but *Call It Sleep* remains his triumph and one of the pinnacles of the American novel.

## FURTHER READING

Baumgarten, Murray, *City Scriptures: Modern Jewish Writing*, Cambridge, Mass., Harvard University Press, 1982.

Bercovitch, Sacvan, 1975, *The Puritan Origins of the American Self*, New Haven, Conn., Yale University Press, 2011.

Cappell, Ezra, *American Talmud: The Cultural Work of Jewish American Fiction*, Albany, State University of New York Press, 2007.

Ferraro, Thomas, *Ethnic Passages: Literary Immigrants in Twentieth-Century America*, Chicago, University of Chicago Press, 1993.

Howe, Irving, *World of Our Fathers*, New York, Simon & Schuster, 1976.

Kellman, Steven G., *Redemption: The Life of Henry Roth*, New York, Norton, 2005.

Miller, Joshua, *Accented America: The Cultural Politics of Multilingual Modernism*, Oxford, Oxford University Press, 2011.

Roth, Henry, *Call It Sleep* (1934), New York, Farrar, Straus & Giroux, 1991.

    *Shifting Landscape*, ed. Mario Materasi, Philadelphia, Jewish Publication Society, 1987.

    *Mercy of a Rude Stream: A Star Shines over Mt. Morris Park*, New York, St. Martin's Press, 1994.

    *A Diving Rock on the Hudson*, New York, St. Martin's Press, 1995.

    *From Bondage*, New York, St. Martin's Press, 1996.

    *Requiem for Harlem*, New York, St. Martin's Press, 1998.

Rubinstein, Rachel, *Members of the Tribe: Native America in the Jewish Imagination*, Detroit, Wayne State University Press, 2010.

Sollors, Werner, *Ethnic Modernism*, Cambridge, Mass., Harvard University Press, 2008.

    "'A World Somewhere, Somewhere Else': Language, Nostalgic Mournfulness, and Urban Immigrant Family Romance in *Call It Sleep*." *New Essays on Call It Sleep*, ed. Hana Wirth-Nesher, Cambridge, Cambridge University Press, 1996.

Wirth-Nesher, Hana, *Call It English: The Languages of Jewish American Literature*, Princeton, N.J.: Princeton University Press, 2006.

Wisse, Ruth, "The Classic of Disinheritance." *New Essays on* Call It Sleep, ed. Hana Wirth-Nesher, Cambridge, Cambridge University Press, 1996.

## NOTES

1  Henry Roth, *Call It Sleep* (New York, Farrar, Straus & Giroux, 1991), p. 99. Hereafter CIS.
2  Ruth Wisse, "The Classic of Disinheritance," in *New Essays on* Call It Sleep, ed. Hana Wirth-Nesher (Cambridge, Cambridge University Press, 1996), p. 73.
3  Along the top margin of one of the examination booklets that served as Roth's manuscript, he experimented with the names of David's street in nine different versions: Baraday, Bar, Bah, Bod, and Boday Streets. The name "Body Street" appears four times. The manuscript is at the Henry W. and Albert A. Berg Collection of English and American Literature, New York Public Library. For further discussion of Roth's wordplay in the manuscripts and for a reproduction of his interlingual marginalia, see Wirth-Nesher, "Jewish Writing and Modernism: Henry Roth," in *Call It English: The Languages of Jewish American Literature* (Princeton, N.J., Princeton University Press, 2006), pp. 76–100.

# 14

# Djuna Barnes

ALEX GOODY

"There is not a person in the literary world who has not heard of, read and some stolen from NIGHTWOOD. The paradox ... is ... I am the 'most famous unknown of the century!'"[1] Writing to Natalie Clifford Barney in the 1960s Djuna Barnes (1892–1982) makes a hyperbolic claim about both her 1936 novel *Nightwood* and her oxymoronic obscurity, but in neither case is she wholly misguided. *Nightwood*, described on publication as a book that "does not belong to any easily definable class,"[2] is a defining work of the twentieth century but woefully absent on roll calls of the American novel. Barnes has been a marginal figure in the literary canon, a repeated anecdote of expatriate American modernism rather than a writer of influence. Barnes is difficult, what Daniela Caselli describes as an "improper modernist" not easily suiting labels such as "queer," "feminist," or "avant-garde," and her fictional style can still disconcert the most diligent of readers. But Barnes's major fiction shows that she is much more than a literary anecdote. Exploring Barnes's career as a writer and novelist it becomes clear that she offers a particular response to the cultural and literary tumult of the early twentieth century and is a unique voice in the history of the American novel.

## New York Journalism

Barnes began her writing career as a journalist in New York at the age of twenty-one, employed as a writer and illustrator for the *Brookyln Daily Eagle* in spring 1913. She was soon writing and interviewing for a range of New York publications including the *New York World Magazine*, *New York Tribune*, and *New York Morning Telegraph Sunday Magazine*. Established as a successful freelancer, Barnes went on to write for *Vanity Fair* after her move to Paris in 1919 and for the *Theatre Guild Magazine* in the early 1930s. Her early journalism, often accompanied by her distinctive illustrations, explores spectacularity and performance, the cultural diversity of the city, the construction of celebrity, and the politics of the body: she covers prize fights, Coney Island freak shows, and Greenwich Village bohemia; interviews a female gorilla, Flo Ziegfeld, and James Joyce; and reports on the experience of force feeding and ways of dying stylishly. Barnes's writing also takes part in radically new genres of journalism – urban travel writing, stunt journalism, creative nonfiction journalism – and consistently undermines the stability and neutrality of the investigative gaze. The epigrammatic, self-reflexive, and deliberately obtuse style of her journalism also characterizes the short stories Barnes was writing and publishing at the time. Her first story, "The Terrible Peacock" (1914), involves a young newspaperman's pursuit of a beautiful, elusive woman, "a slinky female with electrifying green eyes and red hair, dressed in clinging green-and-blue silk," a "Somebody," who turns out to be a publicity stunt for her husband's tearoom.[3] Barnes's 1920s stories, sometimes published under the pseudonym "Lydia Steptoe," explore a variety of experiences of relationships, remembrance, and death and show a particular interest in the interface of innocence and experience, using the character of the "precocious child" to undermine "nostalgic fantasies of wholeness and belonging."[4] The absence of psychological depth and eschewal of the objective verisimilitude of realism in Barnes's short fiction, along with a heightened language and narrative self-consciousness, foreshadow the techniques of her later writing.

Barnes's newspaper and magazine writing was a financial necessity; she had received little formal education and had had an unconventional upbringing in Cornwall-on-Hudson, New Jersey, as the daughter of the polygamist Wald Barnes and his first wife, Elizabeth Chappell. Elizabeth was forced out of the family home when, faced with legal questions, Wald chose his second wife and children over her, and she moved to Brooklyn with Barnes and her brothers in 1912. Supporting herself with her writing, Barnes rented her own flat in Greenwich Village in 1915–19, lived mostly in Paris in the 1920s and 1930s, and returned to New York for the last forty-two years of her life; she was consistently reliant on patronage and the financial support of friends and fellow writers. Barnes's movements put her in contact with much of the modernist literary avant-garde of America and Europe, and these were crucial influences on her writing. Nevertheless Barnes never affiliated herself with any modernist movement, and her fiction remains resolutely obdurate to co-optation to any specific literary school.

## Ryder

By 1928 Barnes had published two books, *The Book of Repulsive Women* (1915), a volume of eight poems and five illustrations of spectacular, decadent femininity and sexuality, and *A Book* (1923), a collection of short stories, poems, dramas, and drawings. But in this year Barnes simultaneously published her first novel, *Ryder*, and the pseudonymous *Ladies Almanack*. *Ryder* was published in New York by Boni and Liveright; a novel that mixes genres, structures, and registers, it was a surprising success, reaching the best-seller list in September 1928. But there were some issues over the more bawdy references, and *Ryder* was subject to censorship, what Barnes's playfully outspoken "foreword" describes as "a vogue in America as indiscriminate as all such enforcements of law must be." Barnes chose to indicate expurgations in her text with a row of suggestive asterisks to show "plainly where the war, so blindly waged on the written word, has left its mark." As a result, in chapters such as "Sophia's Last Will and Testament," we read of her wish to be buried with her husband with her "left hand ... placed palm in and about that part of him which \*\*\*\*\*\*\*\*\*\*\*, as the evening star rests upon the finger of the dawn."[5] Some of Barnes's chapter illustrations for the book were also censored, including a farting angel and a gigantic Kate Careless urinating in the street (from chapters 12 and 15, respectively). These expurgations indicate quite clearly aspects of the tone of, and influences on, *Ryder*; the Rabelaisian carnivalesque is prominent, as is the eighteenth-century novel tradition of Henry Fielding and Lawrence Sterne, along with Joyce's modernist epic *Ulysses* (1922). Barnes also offers a whole chapter in parodic Chaucerian rhythm and language, echoes the King James Bible, and takes Whitman's American vision to task. The result of this polyphony and irreverent use of literary predecessors is a novel that rejects the authority of literary history, embodies a ludic linguistic energy, and mocks myths of origin and originality.

*Ryder* has often been read, as has Barnes's late play *The Antiphon* (1958), as a heavily autobiographical text with its polygamous protagonist, Wendell; his manipulative mother, Sophia; his first wife, Amelia, and second wife, Kate Careless; and Amelia's daughter, Julia, closely modeled on Barnes and her own family upbringing. Though it may have close parallels, *Ryder* cannot be taken as a confessional or autobiographical text simply because its tone, form, and mixing of genres frustrate expectations and reject the possibility of a simple truth: as in Barnes's short stories, innocence, simplicity, and truth are always under question. *Ryder* opens with a frontispiece illustration, "The Tree of Ryder," which implies the novel will be a family chronicle, charting the fortunes of the hero, Wendell, and his kin making their way in the New World. But this illustration mocks such a pretension, mixing animals, mistresses, illegitimate offspring, and the tombstone of a woman dead in childbirth at the foot of the tree. As the text of *Ryder* deconstructs the family, so does it also disassemble the novel, the genre that was founded structurally and thematically on nineteenth-century structures of family and legacy, challenging the paternal authority, reproductive sex, and female self-repression that serve it. The family and the novel are similarly undermined by the polyphony of *Ryder* and by specific characters such as Molly Dance, the unmarried mother of many children, and the queer Catholic, Dr. Matthew O'Connor.

*Ryder* begins by introducing Wendell as "Jesus Mundane" in a parody of the Bible that offers Wendell as an embodied savior celebrating a doctrine of abundant procreation, a "harvest" of "a going and a coming, a coming and a going" (5) He professes his desire to be "Father of All Things" and bequeaths this philosophy to his son, Timothy, near the end of the novel (210). Wendell proffers a Whitmanesque rebellion against the restrictive moral and religious doctrine of provincial American Puritanism, a rebellion that *Ryder* simultaneously celebrates, for its rejection of repression and bodily denial, and mocks for its arrogantly masculinist claims. Wendell's list of nicknames in "The Occupations of Wendell" play on his supposedly phallic prowess, but the text disrupts, in different ways, the authority of the phallus and the male progenitor. Thus, the ancestries of both Wendell and his wives are shown in the narrative, but not in strict sequential order, which would mean a capitulation to ideas of lineage and linearity that *Ryder* explicitly disrupts. *Ryder* also offers a counter to conventional creation narratives with alternative tales ("Sophia Tells Wendell How He Was Conceived," "Kate and Amelia Go A-Dunging," "The Beast Thingumbob," "Fine Bitches All, and Molly Dance") that bear some comparison to Elizabeth Cady Stanton's undertaking in *The Woman's Bible* (part I, 1895; part II, 1898).[6] These alternate tales, particularly Molly Dance's, stress the role of women in creation, countering myths of phallic primacy and highlighting the exploitation and degradation of women in such myths.

In the stories of Thingumbob's strange female mate, Wendell's grandmother, Cynthia, and elsewhere, *Ryder* illustrates the terrible price paid by women in the reproductive, heterosexual family, what chapter 13 terms the "Midwives Lament." Exhaustion, madness, and death await the fertile woman in Wendell's saga of abundant procreation. In a similar vein *Ryder* presents a culture in which women are deemed culpable in their own sexual exploitation ("Rape and Repining!" chapter 5) and who enforce their own subordination through subsequent generations. But this is not a novel that rejects the physical; the bawdy language of the text and the persistent celebration of the body, both verbally and in illustrations, make for a novel marked by female bodily power and the disruptive potential of the grotesque. It also celebrates, however ambivalently, the ability of Sophia, Wendell's mother and Julia's grandmother, to manipulate and command respect of both men and women, and to develop her own voice and subjectivity.

In one of the stories of conception in the novel, Amelia dreams of a great black ox (chapter 20), and this illustrates how the animal and bestial feature in Barnes's blurring of categories and disruption of hierarchies. In *Ryder* and in other writings, Barnes points to vestiges of the bestial in human memory and to the connection and communion between the human and the non-human natural world. Wendell's sense of his own empathy with animals and nature does evince the influence of Thoreau and Emerson, but Barnes's human-animal proximities also have their sources in European folk culture. The woodcut-style illustrations in *Ryder* draw directly on the images collected in Pierre Louis Ducharte's and René Saulnier's 1925 *L'imagerie populaire*, fifteenth-century human-animal hybrids who enact a carnivalesque overturning of categorization and order. *L'imagerie populaire* also informed the style of illustration in the quite different fictional text Barnes published in the same year as *Ryder*.

Barnes's *Ladies Almanack* was published privately and pseudonymously in Paris in 1928, with some of the 1,050 copies hand-colored by Barnes and her friends. It is a fully illustrated mock-almanac tracking the months of the year, with the narrative of Dame Musset and her coterie of allegorically named characters at the center of its disquisition on lesbian sexuality, textuality, and women's bodies. Very light on plot and mingling obsolescent archaisms, neologisms, indeterminate maxims, and rhetorical questions, this text is something of a roman à clef, with Dame Musset and her followers corresponding to Natalie Clifford Barney and her associates at her Paris salon: Barney's salon was the center of Parisian sapphic modernism, a group that Barnes knew well but with whom she did not affiliate herself. The tone of *Ladies Almanack* is its most ambivalent aspect. The skeptical voice of Patience Scalpel (corresponding to Barnes's friend Mina Loy) questions Dame Musset's religion of lesbianism but is herself subject to the satire of the authorial voice. *Ladies Almanack* is thus neither a straightforward celebration of lesbian pleasure nor a cynical parody but a further example of Barnes's questioning attitude to truth, (literary) representation and her own participation in the texts she writes.

## Nightwood

The representation of lesbian desire and Barnes's personal relationship to the subject material of her fiction writing are issues often brought to bear on her best-known work, *Nightwood*. The royalties for *Ryder* had dwindled by the October 1929 crash, and the subsequent years were ones of financial uncertainty for Barnes. She began writing *Nightwood* between 1927 and 1931, when her intimate relationship with the artist Thelma Wood foundered and came to an end: the tragic female lovers in *Nightwood* are based on this relationship. In the summers of 1932 and 1933 Barnes wrote and rewrote the novel at Peggy Guggenheim's summer residence in England, Hayford Hall, but it was rejected by American publishers despite Barnes's redraftings in 1934 and 1935. Emily Coleman, whom Barnes had first met in Paris in 1929 as part of Guggenheim's circle, was a crucial friend for Barnes during the writing of *Nightwood* as she advised on the editing and organizing of the narrative and petitioned T. S. Eliot at Faber to accept the book. Eliot was quite enthusiastic but had opinions about chapter arrangement and deletions, mostly agreeing with Coleman, and he also blue-penciled phrases relating to sexuality, particularly homosexuality, and insalubrious references to religion. *Nightwood* was published in Britain in 1936 and in America in 1937 with an influential introduction by Eliot.

*Nightwood* tells the story of the American Robin Vote; her European Jewish husband, Felix Volkbein; Nora Flood, also American, who has an intense relationship with Robin; Dr. Matthew O'Connor, who offers a form of consolation to many of the characters; and the various inhabitants of the European subcultural world the characters pass through. Eliot's introduction asserts that, in contrast to "most contemporary novels [which] are not really 'written,'" *Nightwood* "demands something of the reader that the ordinary novel-reader is not prepared to give,"[7] a summation of *Nightwood* that was echoed by Graham Greene, who asserted that "it is no more for the general and indiscriminate reading than is Mr Joyce's *Ulysses*."[8] Barnes's language and style in *Nightwood*, as in *Ryder*, do (deliberately) resonate with Joyce's modernist novel; *Nightwood* in particular displays an affinity with Joyce's Circean "Night Town." But the imagery, tone, and language are also a clear development from the very earliest of Barnes's short stories and journalism; part surreal and part decadent, a complex pattern of allusion, metaphorical substitution, and linguistic transformation, it marks out the distinctiveness of Barnes's novelistic voice.

During the composition of *Nightwood* Barnes considered other titles for her novel, "Bow Down," "Anatomy of Night," "The Beggars' Comedy,"[9] but the title she eventually chose, approved but not, as the Barnes biographer Andrew Field claims, suggested by Eliot, encapsulates effectively the novel's night world of early twentieth-century Europe (Vienna, Berlin, Paris) and the dark ambit of Nora's love for Robin. *Nightwood* is a text that epitomizes the urban modernist imagination of the dispossessed and marginal, and it opens with figures who embody and bodily inscribe this marginality and dispossession, beginning with the story of Baron Felix Volkbein, displaced orphan Jew. Like Proust and Joyce, Barnes takes the Jew to figure as and for the alienated subject of twentieth-century urban culture. But through the opening chapter, which explores Jewish alienation both historically and philosophically, Barnes also questions the radical Othering of Jewishness. From his wanderings across a Europe in decline, Felix eventually finds himself in 1920s Paris among circus people, where he also meets Dr. Matthew O'Connor, a character carried over from *Ryder*. After a chance encounter, Felix meets and marries the expatriate Robin Vote, who bears him a mentally and physically disabled son, before she embarks again on her incessant nighttime wanderings.

In these opening chapters Barnes reworks some of the concerns of her journalism, spectacularity, marginality, performance, and urban subcultures, and, in addition to exploring the alterity of the Jew, gives a vivid depiction of the abjected, objectified, and disruptive bodies of circus performers. These performers include "Nikka the nigger" "tattooed from head to heel" with a polyphony of cultural and literary texts (14), and the aerialiste the "Duchess of Broadback," who appears to "have a skin that was the pattern of her costume": body and costume merge for the Duchess and "the span of the tightly stitched crotch was so much her flesh that she was as unsexed as a doll" (12). The spectacularity of popular culture and the way that it constitutes subjectivity and sexuality is also explored in the character of Robin, introduced in the second chapter passed out in a hotel room in a scene echoing the cinematic framing of stars such as Marlene Dietrich and referencing the representation of women in Western art. In presenting the character of Robin, Barnes also draws on gothic tropes of femininity, with Robin imagined as a somnambulist or *détraqué* in her intoxicated wanderings through streets, bars, and cafes, figurations that again have their markers in cinema. Robin exists only through such framing devices and surfaces, and the text makes no attempt to offer any interiority or psychological depth to her character: she exists only in and through the eyes of others, "monstrously alone, monstrously vain" (131).

The disruptive energies of the circus are reworked in the lesbian relationship of Nora and Robin, who meet at the Denckman circus in New York and who decorate their apartment with the detritus of European culture: "circus chairs, wooden horses bought from a ring of an old merry-go-round, Venetian chandeliers from the Flea Fair, stage-drops from Munich, cherubim from Vienna, ecclesiastical hangings from Rome, a spinet ... music boxes" (50). Their relationship is not a carnivalesque overturning of cultural hierarchies, however, but a mournful mirroring – Nora cries out at one point, "A woman is yourself, caught as you turn in panic; on her mouth you kiss your own" (129) and describing Robin as "incest," "my love and my child"

(141). Elsewhere Dr. O'Connor describes the "love we have for an invert" as a degenerate fairy tale; for him "we were impaled in our childhood upon them as they rode through our primers, the sweetest lie of all, now come to be in boy or girl, for in the girl it is the prince, and in the boy it is the girl that makes a prince a prince" (123). O'Connor, the queer, cross-dressing would-be gynecologist, the "greatest liar this side of the moon" (122), masturbates in a church, subordinates time and history to his own narrative, and offers a sacrilegious mysticism of the outcast peoples of the Night: prostitutes, freaks, queers, Jews, performers, black peoples. Irrupting into the text as grotesque abundance of physicality and language, O'Connor castigates Nora for her proprietary and Puritan love for Robin, saying, "You were sitting up high and fine, with a rose-bush up your arse," and juxtaposes the "dishevelled and wise" European to the American Anglo-Saxon, who has "washed him too clean for identification" (151).

Little space is devoted in *Nightwood* to the years of intimacy between Nora and Robin, for the novel is less a narrative than a symbolic treatise on loss, obsession, and alienation; it is the end of the relationship, the intervention of Jenny Petherbridge, the "Squatter," who takes Robin from Nora, and Nora and Felix's attempts to understand Robin and their relationship to her that compose the majority of the text. Structurally *Nightwood* turns around the two central figures of Robin and Dr. O'Connor: estranged misfits both, they mirror and contradict each other. Robin the slim, boyish American is first seen in flannel trousers and pumps, while O'Connor, Irish-American lapsed Catholic, sleeps in a woman's nightgown with a blonde wig, rouge, and mascara. Robin remains elusive and silent, spoken of (she speaks only twice in the novel) but nevertheless the object of Felix, Nora, and Jenny's desire and the actant around whom the narrative revolves. In contrast, O'Connor's loquacious monologues dominate sections of the novel, advising and philosophizing on Felix, Nora, and Jenny's desire and on their (and his own) perversions, but O'Connor remains a Tiresian observer of the lives around him, not a participant. Both are nevertheless versions of the "beast turning human" (33), Robin with the iris of "wild beasts" (33) and a strange affinity with the circus lions that Nora witnesses and O'Connor "like Red Riding Hood and the wolf in bed" (71), forms of the disturbing human/nonhuman proximities that repeatedly occur in Barnes's writing. Robin and O'Connor body forth the liminalities, transitions, and becomings that characterize both the narrative and the style of *Nightwood* and exemplify the antitheses that permeate the novel and that are never resolved.

In an earlier draft of *Nightwood* the narrative closes at the end of chapter 7, "Go Down, Matthew," with Dr. O'Connor's drunken collapse in the Café de la Marie du VIᵉ and his ominous final words "the end – – mark my words – – now *nothing, but wrath and weeping*!" (149). In the published novel, however, Barnes shifts the focus back onto Nora and Robin and away from O'Connor's disintegration and the cafes and bars of Europe. *Nightwood* ends in America, a return to the New World that does not signify an Edenic new beginning nor the fulfillment of a destiny. Nora follows Robin, gone to New York with Jenny, where Robin has resumed her nighttime wanderings, finally making her way to Nora's family home in the woods upstate. When Nora comes upon her, Robin is in the weather-beaten chapel, crouching, barking, and weeping in an "obscene and touching" communion with Nora's dog, the two creatures finally lying on the floor before the altar at the conclusion of the novel (153). This ending has confused critics and readers alike with its suggestion of a regression to the primitive, a redemptive deevolution, or a profane bestiality. Barnes was adamant that the ending had no sexual connotations, and it is perhaps better to read it as a deliberate moment of confusion and darkness, a definitive rejection of the order of the realist novel and the stability of a hierarchical world.

*Nightwood* did not become a best seller; it was actually out of print in the United States by 1945, and after completing it Barnes turned to focus on other forms of writing. Devoting her subsequent years to the three-act verse tragedy *The Antiphon* and to poetry, much of which remained unpublished, Barnes lived a reclusive old age at Patchin Place, New York City, and died in relative obscurity in 1982. Nevertheless, her work had received some attention on the European continent, more so than in English-speaking countries, with translations into French, German, Italian, Spanish, and Swedish. Barnes's influence and reputation continue to grow, benefiting from feminist revisionist histories of modernism, and *Nightwood* has been influential on a range of other writers. Dylan Thomas professed a deep admiration for the novel, though his praise was couched in problematically gendered terms, and the title of his own *Under Milk Wood* (1954) was indebted to Barnes's novel.[10] The Irish writer Aidan Higgins has noted his own interest in Barnes, William Burroughs described her style as "entirely unique" and dubbed *Nightwood* "one of the great books of the twentieth-century,"[11] and her legacy can be seen in British women novelists such as Angela Carter and Jeanette Winterson, who wrote the preface for the 2007 Faber edition of *Nightwood*. Jane Marcus suggests affinities between Barnes and a host of writers including Gabriel Garcia Marquez, Günter Grass, Sylvia Townsend Warner, Rebecca West, and Joanna Russ,[12] and Barnes has elsewhere been compared to Marguerite Duras, Gertrude Stein, and even Ernest Hemingway. But she remains unassimilable, a writer who made a profoundly singular but nonetheless profound contribution to the history of the novel. What Aidan

Higgins writes of *Nightwood* is true also of Barnes herself: "If there is such a thing as a modern classic this must be it."[13]

## FURTHER READING

Caselli, Daniela, *Improper Modernism: Djuna Barnes's Bewildering Corpus*, Burlington, Vt., Ashgate, 2009.

DeLauretis, Teresa, "Nightwood and the 'Terror of Uncertain Signs,'" *Critical Inquiry*, 34, Winter 2008, 117–29.

Edmunds, Susan, "Narratives of a Virgin's Violation: The Critique of Middle-Class Reformism in Djuna Barnes's Ryder," *Novel: A Forum for Fiction*, 30.2, Winter 1997: 218–36.

Goody, Alex, *Modernist Articulations: A Cultural Study of Djuna Barnes, Mina Loy and Gertrude Stein*, Basingstoke, Palgrave Macmillan, 2007.

Horner, Avril and SueZlosnik, "Strolling in the Dark: Gothic Flânerie in Djuna Barnes's *Nightwood*." *Gothic Modernisms*, ed., Andrew Smith and Jeff Wallace, Basingstoke, Palgrave, 2001, 78–94.

Kaup, Monika, "The Neobaroque in Djuna Barnes," *Modernism/modernity*, 12.1, 2005, 85–110.

Marcus, Jane, "Laughing at Leviticus: *Nightwood* as Woman's Circus Epic." *Silence and Power, a Reevaluation of Djuna Barnes*, ed. Mary Lynn Broe, Carbondale and Edwardsville, Southern Illinois University Press, 1991, 221–50.

Parsons, Deborah, *Djuna Barnes*, Horndon, England, Northcote House, 2003.

Ponsot, Marie, "A Reader's *Ryder*." *Silence and Power, a Reevaluation of Djuna Barnes*, ed. Mary Lynn Broe, Carbondale and Edwardsville, Southern Illinois University Press, 1991, 94–135.

Taylor, Julie. *Djuna Barnes and Affective Modernism*, Edinburgh, Edinburgh University Press, 2012.

Warren, Diane, *Djuna Barnes's Consuming Fictions*, Burlington, Vt., Ashgate, 2008.

## NOTES

1 Djuna Barnes to Natalie Clifford Barney, 31 May 1963. Djuna Barnes Papers, Special Collections, University of Maryland Libraries, Series II, Box 1, Folder 45.

2 Edwin Muir, "New Novels," *Listener*, 28 October 1936.

3 Djuna Barnes, "The Terrible Peacock," in *Smoke and Other Early Stories* (Los Angeles, Sun & Moon Press, 1993), p. 25.

4 Daniela Caselli, *Improper Modernism: Djuna Barnes's Bewildering Corpus* (Burlington Vt., Ashgate, 2009), p.124.

5 Djuna Barnes, *Ryder* (Normal, Ill., Dalkey Archive Press, 1990), p.79; subsequent references are to this edition.

6 See Dianne Warren, *Djuna Barnes' Consuming Fictions* (Burlington Vt., Ashgate, 2008), pp. 59–61.

7 Djuna Barnes, *Nightwood* (London, Faber & Faber, 2007), p. 2; subsequent references are to this edition.

8 Graham Greene, "Fiction Chronicle," *Tablet*, 14 November 1936.

9   Cheryl J. Plumb considers the titles considered for *Nightwood* in *Djuna Barnes, Nightwood: The Original Version and Related Drafts* (Normal Ill., Dalkey Archive Press, 1995), p. viii; Barnes lists possible titles (including the suggestion "The Beggars' Comedy") in a 1930s address book in the Papers of Frances McCollough, Special Collections, University of Maryland Libraries, Box 2.

10  See John Goodby, "Djuna Barnes as a Source for Dylan Thomas," *Notes and Queries* 58.1 (2011): 127–30.

11  William Burroughs letter to Mary Lynn Broe, January 1985; printed in *Silence and Power: A Reevaluation of Djuna Barnes,* ed. Mary Lynn Broe (Carbondale, Southern Illinois University Press, 1991), p. 206.

12  Jane Marcus, "Laughing at Leviticus: *Nightwood* as Woman's Circus Epic," in *Silence and Power: A Reevaluation of Djuna Barnes,* ed. Mary Lynn Broe (Carbondale, Southern Illinois University Press, 1991), pp. 221–50.

13  Aidan Higgins, "*Liebestod,*" *Hibernia,* 15 October 1979; reprinted in Aidan Higgins, *Windy Arbours: Collected Criticism* (Normal Ill., Dalkey Archive Press, 2005), p. 14.

# 15

# Zora Neale Hurston

LOVALERIE KING

Zora Neale Hurston (1891–1960) was a natural born storyteller, whose capacity for the southern rural black vernacular can be compared to Mark Twain's for the southern rural white vernacular. In her best-known work, *Their Eyes Were Watching God* (1937), she provides an intimate portrait of early twentieth-century black southern rural life via the personal story of a young woman whose quest for love leads her instead to self-knowledge. Hurston's protagonist, Janie Crawford, has become one of the best-known heroines in American literature, whose internal quest can be compared to that of Kate Chopin's Edna Pontellier of *The Awakening* (1899). Certainly, the central black woman's quest narrative in *Their Eyes* served as inspiration for Gwendolyn Brooks's title character in *Maud Martha* (1953), the women in Ntozake Shange's *for coloured girls who have considered suicide when the rainbow is enuf* (1975), Alice Walker's Celie in *The Color Purple* (1985), and indeed a variety of subsequent characters in the works of authors from Toni Morrison to Alice Randall and Sister Souljah. *Their Eyes* was bold and audacious for its time. Hurston broke with black literary establishment prescription and told a story about working-class southern rural black folk living their everyday lives (warts and all), about a woman for whom sexual pleasure was an important aspect of marriage, and finally about a woman whose self-identity was ultimately not tied to marriage. Time and again in her work, Hurston explores (with a rare honesty) the complexities of gender role expectations in heterosexual relationships. Though her attention to women's lives makes her part of feminist literary history, Hurston was a staunch individualist who was politically conservative. She faced harsh criticism from black critics as well as from leftist critics – regardless of race. She responded to critics by becoming even more conservative, an orientation that increasingly marginalized her in black literary circles. Richard Wright, Ralph Ellison, and W. E. B. DuBois all expressed public disapproval of her and her work for a variety of reasons. In 1948, Hurston published *Seraph on the Sewanee* (1948), which centered on a family of white southerners, a fact that signaled for some a complete selling out by Hurston. The novel was on its way to commercial success when Hurston was falsely accused of sexually abusing a retarded adolescent and arrested on a morals charge. Though she was eventually cleared of the charge, Hurston seems to have never fully recovered from what she saw as a total betrayal. A steady decline in her career followed the incident, which, according to her biographer Robert Hemenway, made her contemplate suicide. Though she died in poverty and relative obscurity, Hurston is today considered one of the preeminent writers of the twentieth century for her mastery of the southern rural vernacular, her focus on gender matters in heterosexual relationships, her pioneering work in folklore, and her ability to produce more volumes of work than any other black woman of that time while confronting the many obstacles placed in her path.

Hurston published seven books during her lifetime: *Jonah's Gourd Vine* (1934); *Mules and Men* (1935); *Their Eyes Were Watching God* (1937); *Tell My Horse* (1938); *Moses, Man of the Mountain* (1939); *Dust Tracks on a Road* (an autobiography; 1942); and *Seraph on the Suwanee* (1948). Hurston's first novel, *Jonah's Gourd Vine*, is autobiographical in that it revisits the relationship between Hurston's own mother and father. The title *Jonah's Gourd Vine* refers to the biblical story of Jonah, specifically Jonah 4:6–10, a parable about a gourd vine that grows to huge proportions overnight only to be destroyed by a worm. The story offers a warning about the destruction that can result from lack of self-knowledge and awareness, with the central character John Buddy Pearson's lack of awareness being manifest most obviously in his philandering and his lack of appreciation for his sheltering family. The folktales collected in Hurston's *Mules and Men* are like much of African-American folklore in terms of form and function. What makes the volume unique is Hurston's patented participatory form of mediation, during which she becomes part of the communities under study. *Their Eyes Were Watching God* begins with the female protagonist Janie's return to Eatonville, Florida, in the 1920s. Though her reflections about part of her mother's and grandmother's lives extend the story's period back to the beginning of the Civil War and other locales, most of the tale unfolds during the early twentieth century in Eatonville, an actual town located some ten miles northeast of Orlando, Florida. We follow the teenage Janie from the West Florida home of her grandmother to her first marital home in the same general area, on to Eatonville with her second husband, and farther south to the Everglades – specifically Belle Glade – and marriage to her third husband. Though the most dramatic aspects of Janie's journey toward self-discovery and awareness take place in Belle Glade, Janie returns home alone to Eatonville in the end. In 2005, Oprah Winfrey released a made-for-television movie based on *Their Eyes*, which is Hurston's most widely read and taught novel.

In *Tell My Horse*, Hurston's second collection of folktales and traditions, her presence as narrator/observer/participant/researcher in Haiti and Jamaica is as apparent as it was during her time in the American South collecting material for *Mules and Men*. "Tell my horse," or "parlay cheval ou" in Creole, is a phrase Hurston heard often during her time in Haiti. According to lore, they are words uttered by Guede (pronounced geeday), a Voodoo god/loa/deity characterized as powerful and boisterous. Guede makes himself known by mounting or possessing someone and speaking through the person. According to Hurston, peasants in Haiti used the phrase as a disclaimer, invoking Guede as the force behind their caustic or frank comments. Thus, the phrase and the loa are identified with the common folk, who do not *bite their tongues* or *pull punches*. In *Moses, Man of the Mountain*, Hurston uses the mythic story of Moses, best recognized in Western culture as the biblical Hebrew hero of the book of Exodus who led his people out of Egyptian bondage into Canaan/Israel/the Promised Land, to create an allegory of African-American life from slavery to freedom. She uses the Moses story to present a timeless and universal tale of the individual's quest for self-determination and the full meaning of freedom.

Hurston's 1942 autobiography, *Dust Tracks on a Road*, was originally shaped by the publisher J. P. Lippincott to target a largely white readership. A somewhat different version that includes Hurston's notes is available in the James Weldon Johnson Collection at Yale's Beneicke Library. Hurston noted that "parts of this manuscript were not used in the final composition of the book for publisher's reasons." New releases of *Dust Tracks on a Road* in the late twentieth century appended or restored the excised and/ or dispersed material. Draft manuscripts reveal that Hurston was forced time and again to change her own words and perspectives on topics from race and politics in general, to the American military presence in developing nations and global imperialism. Hurston never produced a contracted second volume of her autobiography. Her final published volume, *Seraph on the Suwanee,* is presented as a love story about a psychologically repressed and emotionally underdeveloped white woman and her chauvinist but loving and prosperous husband. While the surface narrative reflects Hurston's desire to show that, regardless of skin color, human beings essentially want the same things out of life, a deeper understanding of the story reveals a narrative that reveals the implications of being white, male, and economically privileged.

In addition to her seven books, Hurston produced scores of shorter works, including short stories, plays, and essays. Posthumously published and edited volumes of her work include *I Love Myself When I Am Laughing ... & Then Again When I Am Looking Mean and Impressive: A Zora Neale Hurston Reader* (1979); *The Sanctified Church* (1981); *Spunk: The Selected Short Stories of Zora Neale Hurston* (1985); *Mule Bone: A Comedy of Negro Life* (1991); *The Complete Stories* (1995); *Folklore, Memoirs, & Other Writings* (1995); *Novels and Stories* (1995); *Go Gator and Muddy the Water: Writings by Zora Neale Hurston from the Federal Writers' Project* (1999); and *Every Tongue Got to Confess: Negro Folk-Tales from the Gulf States* (2001).

Hurston's work received mixed and often negative reviews during her life. Early critics almost always missed both the nuance and the complexity of her work. Her unwillingness to engage primarily in social protest (what she referred to in "How It Feels to Be Colored Me" as the "sobbing school of Negrohood") earned her mixed reviews in literary circles. Richard Wright's scathing October 1937 review of *Their Eyes Were Watching God* in "Between Laughter and Tears" is one example. Indeed, among the black literary establishment, Hurston's work was often trivialized as entertainment and minstrelsy, rather than as serious literary achievement. Her insistence upon celebrating the oral rural southern vernacular and organic southern rural culture had the effect of charming some white critics while making some black critics nervous. Robert Hemenway's *Zora Neale Hurston: A Literary Biography* (1977), Valerie Boyd's *Wrapped in Rainbows: The Life of Zora Neale Hurston* (2003), and particularly M. Genevieve West's *Zora Neale Hurston and American Literary Culture* (2005) all allocate substantial space to further examination of the contexts for contemporaneous criticism of Hurston's work. Author Alice Walker has been largely credited with a 1970s era resurrection of Hurston as literary foremother, though Darwin Turner offered a review of Hurston's literary career in *In a Minor Chord* (1971), and Robert Hemenway followed up with his well-received 1977 literary biography. Walker recounts her search for literary foremothers, including Hurston, in 1975 and 1979 essays collected in *In Search of Our Mother's Gardens* (1983). Her work proved essential to directing attention to Hurston for womanist and feminist scholars. Contemporary criticism of Hurston's work focuses on her artistry in combination with her philosophy and how her body of work has continuing relevance for literary studies, African-American studies, gender studies, anthropology, and history.

Though she was actually born in Notasulga, Alabama, Hurston always called Eatonville, Florida, home and even named it as her birthplace in her autobiography, *Dust Tracks on a Road*. Eatonville has become famous for its long association with Hurston; since 1991, it has been the site of the annual multidisciplinary Zora Neale Hurston Festival of the Arts and Humanities

(ZORA! Festival), which lasts for several days. The festival's primary aim is to celebrate Hurston's life and work along with Eatonville's unique cultural history. Its broader aim is to call attention to contributions that people of the black African diaspora have made to world culture.

As a child young Zora excelled in the language arts and clearly benefited from her mother, Lucy Potts Hurston's, encouragement of her creativity and individuality. Lucy Potts Hurston urged all her children to "jump at the sun." Strong-willed and exuberant Zora always seemed to be at odds with her father, John Hurston, however. Nevertheless, she had much in common with him, including her capacity for hard work combined with a wanderlust and desire to seek out the horizon. Hurston's life took a turn for the difficult and chaotic after her mother died in 1904 and her father remarried; unable to live with the stepmother, Zora moved from relative to relative, home to home, and job to job for much of her adolescence. A job with a traveling actors' group led her eventually to Baltimore, Maryland, in 1918; there she changed her date of birth in order to take advantage of free public education. After attending Morgan Academy, she took classes that qualified her for the historically black Howard University in Washington, D.C.

As a student at Howard in the early 1920s, Hurston wrote bad poetry, joined the Zeta Phi Beta sorority, and met her fellow student Herbert Sheen, the man who became her first husband some years later. She joined the staff of Howard's literary club journal, the *Stylus*, where her first published short story, the somewhat autobiographical "John Redding Goes to Sea," appeared in May 1921. Hurston's affiliation with *Stylus* permitted her to attend poet Georgia Douglas Johnson's famous literary salons and rub elbows with poets, playwrights, novelists, and critics who would become Harlem Renaissance standouts. Hurston never completed the four-year degree program at Howard, because her literary talent caught the eye of philosophy professor Alain Locke, who would edit the collection that became synonymous with the Harlem Renaissance: *The New Negro* (1925).

Locke put Hurston in touch with Charles S. Johnson, editor of *Opportunity Magazine*, where she submitted the short story, "Drenched in Light"; the story appeared in the December 1924 issue. She moved to New York City the next month as she was turning thirty-four. On May 1, 1925, she won two cash prizes and two honorable mentions at the *Opportunity* literary contest awards dinner, where she also met three influential white Americans: Annie Nathan Meyer (1867–1951), a prolific author and a founder of Barnard College; Fanny Hurst (1889–1968), a prolific novelist and short-story writer, whose list of publications ultimately spanned five full decades; and the journalist, photographer, author, and patron Carl Van Vechten (1880–1964).

Two months after the *Opportunity* awards dinner, the *Spokesman* published Hurston's short story "Magnolia Flower," and in September the *Messenger* published her essay "The Hue and Cry about Howard University." Hurston's *coming out* year culminated in the November release of Alain Locke's *The New Negro*, which included her short story "Spunk" along with works by Richard Bruce Nugent, Claude McKay, Countee Cullen, Langston Hughes, Georgia Douglas Johnson, Anne Spencer, Angelina Grimke, and other authors associated with the Harlem Renaissance. Hurston had indeed arrived. Finally, in December, she published "Under the Bridge" – a short story whose themes she would repeat in "Sweat" (1926) – in *The X-Ray: The Official Publication of Zeta Phi Beta Sorority*. While she attended classes at Barnard, she joined Hughes, Thurman, and several other younger artists in the publication of the short-lived *FIRE!!*, a literary journal that saw only one issue, in November 1926, and to which Hurston contributed a revised version of her play *Color Struck* and the short story, "Sweat."

Hurston continued to publish in a variety of venues and to cement her status as a member of the black literary world. Between 1930 and 1932, she worked at organizing her research notes for *Mules and Men*. In 1930, she tried to collaborate on *Mule Bone* (a play) with Langston Hughes; the attempted collaboration would drive a wedge between the two friends. In 1931, she wrote skits for a doomed theatrical review called *Fast and Furious*. In January of 1932, she wrote and staged another theatrical review, *The Great Day*, which premiered on Broadway at the John Golden Theatre on January 10. She also worked to produce a concert program under the auspices of the Creative Literature Department at Rollins College in Winter Park, Florida, and she staged *From Sun to Sun* (a version of *The Great Day*) there in 1933. In 1931 and 1933, respectively, she published "Hoodoo in America" in the *Journal of American Folklore* and "The Gilded Six-Bits" in *Story*. Her busy teaching, research, production, and publishing schedule continued through the decade of the Great Depression. She had a stellar year in 1934, contributing six essays to Nancy Cunard's anthology *Negro* and publishing both *Jonah's Gourd Vine* and "The Fire and the Cloud" (the seed story for *Moses, Man of the Mountain*) in *Challenge*.

Hurston had her first formal theater experiences in 1934, when she traveled to Bethune-Cookman College in Florida to establish a school of dramatic arts; she also saw the production of *Singing Steel* (another version of *The Great Day*) in Chicago. In 1935, she joined the Works Progress Administration's Federal Theatre Project as a drama coach. Guggenheim fellowships sponsored her travels to Jamaica and Haiti during 1936 and 1937 to collect folk materials that would appear in *Tell My Horse*. During her first trip to Haiti in 1936, she wrote *Their Eyes Were Watching God* over a seven-week period. By April of 1938, she had joined a Federal Writers Project in Florida to work on *The Florida Negro*. In 1939, she published "Now Take Noses" in *Cordially Yours*, received an honorary doctor of letters degree from Morgan State College, and published her third novel, *Moses, Man of the Mountain*. Hurston's formal studies suffered as a result of all her other activities, and she failed to fulfill the requirements for the Ph.D. in anthropology at Columbia. She simply did not have time to attend classes. She traveled to North Carolina in 1939 to work as a drama instructor at North Carolina College for Negroes (now North Carolina Central) at Durham. During this time, Hurston met the famed University of North Carolina professor of drama Paul Green.

Original scripts for ten Hurston plays deposited in the United States Copyright Office between 1925 and 1944 – all but one previously unproduced and unpublished before they appeared in *The Copyright Drama Deposit Collection* (1977) – are housed at the Library of Congress's Manuscript, Music, and Rare Books and Special Collections Division. Titles include "Cold Keener: A Review," "De Turkey and de Law: A Comedy in Three Acts," "Forty Yards," "Lawing and Jawing," "Meet the Mamma: A Musical Play in Three Acts," "The Mule-Bone: A Comedy of Negro Life in Three Acts," "Poker!" "Polk County: A Comedy of Negro Life on a Sawmill Camp with Authentic Negro Music in Three Acts," "Spunk" (also the title of the short story she published in *The New Negro*), and "Woofing." Thus, we have abundant evidence of Hurston's strong, but perhaps unfulfilled, interest in drama.

Hurston traveled to South Carolina in the summer of 1940 to collect folklore; the following year she worked on her manuscript for *Dust Tracks on a Road*, published "Cock Robin, Beale Street" in *Southern Literary Messenger*, and began a fifteen-month (October 1941–January 1943) stint as a story consultant for Paramount Pictures. Her 1942 publications include *Dust Tracks on a Road*, "Story in Harlem Slang" in the *American Mercury*, and a profile of Lawrence Silas in the *Saturday Evening Post*. The following year *American Mercury* included "The 'Pet Negro' Syndrome" in its May issue, and *Negro Digest* published "My Most Humiliating Jim Crow Experience" in its June 1944 issue. She wrote another novel, *Mrs. Doctor*, which dealt with upper-class blacks; however, her publisher, Bertram Lippincott, rejected it. She nevertheless continued to have success with smaller pieces, including "The Rise of the Begging Joints" in the March 1945 issue of *American Mercury*, "Crazy for This Democracy" in the December 1945 issue of *Negro Digest*, and a 1947 review of Robert Tallant's *Voodoo in New Orleans* in the *Journal of American Folklore*. October 1948 brought publication of her fourth novel, *Seraph on the Suwanee*.

September 1948 began a devastating period for Hurston when she was arrested after being falsely accused of molesting a ten-year-old boy; the case was dismissed six months later, but the damage had been done. Though Hurston had endured numerous forms of prejudice for much of her life, the charge of molestation and the arrest surrounding it took its toll. Notwithstanding the biographer Robert Hemenway's assessment that she returned to her usual exuberant and enthusiastic self after a brief period, Hurston's professional life clearly suffered after 1949. She published "Conscience of the Court" in the *Saturday Evening Post* in March 1950 while working as a maid in Rivo Island, Florida; she followed with "What White Publishers Won't Print" in the *Saturday Evening Post*'s April issue, and "I Saw Negro Votes Peddled" in *American Legion* magazine's November 1950 issue. Both periodicals again published her work in 1951: *American Legion* published "Why the Negro Won't Buy Communism" in June, and the *Saturday Evening Post* published "A Negro Voter Sizes up Taft" on December 8. In 1952, the *Pittsburgh Courier* hired Hurston to cover the Ruby McCollum matter, a highly publicized 1952 case in which an affluent black woman was charged with the murder of a white man. As the decade wore on, Hurston's politics became increasingly conservative, her rugged individualism never more evident than in her August 11, 1955, piece in the *Orlando Sentinel* criticizing the Supreme Court's decision in *Brown v. Board of Education of Topeka Kansas* (1954).

Hurston devoted substantial effort to a work on the life of Herod the Great but was unable to find a publisher for the manuscript. Between 1951 and 1956, she lived in Eau Gallie, Florida, on very little money. Her biographer Robert Hemenway writes that despite her poverty, Hurston was essentially at peace during this time – though he acknowledges that the morals indictment had earlier driven her to near-suicide. In her final years, Hurston earned a small income from substitute teaching and other jobs; she also received welfare and unemployment benefits. In 1956, she began a job as a librarian at the Patrick Air Force Base in Florida, but she was fired in 1957. Between 1957 and 1959, she wrote "Hoodoo and Black Magic," a column for the *Fort Pierce Chronicle*. She also worked as a substitute teacher at Lincoln Park Academy in Fort Pierce, Florida, in 1958. Proud, alone, and without funds, the author simply worked until she no longer could work. A stroke in 1959 forced her into the St. Lucie County (Florida) welfare home, where she died on January 28, 1960, of hypertensive heart disease. The woman who had appeared on the cover of the *Saturday Review* and who had during her lifetime been the recipient of numerous honors and awards, including a Rosenwald Foundation Fellowship, two Guggenheims, an honorary doctor of letters degree from Morgan State College, an Anisfeld-Wolf Book Award in Race Relations, the Howard University Distinguished Alumni Award, and Bethune-Cookman College's award for education and human relations, was buried in an unmarked grave at Fort Pierce's segregated cemetery, the Garden of Heavenly Rest.

Alice Walker led the way to Hurston's resurrection as a literary fore-mother just in time for the flowering of black women's literature during the final decades of the twentieth century. Hurston's outstanding work in the woman-centered narrative is an important link between African-American women's literary production in the second half of the twentieth century and beyond to African-American women's literary production in the nineteenth century. The topic of African-American identity and black female subjectivity so deftly explored in *Their Eyes Were Watching God* not only evokes such works as Harriet Jacobs's *Incidents in the Life of a Slave Girl* (1861) and Harriet Wilson's *Our Nig* (1859) but also looks ahead to Ann Petry's *The Street* (1946), Gwendolyn Brooks's *Maud Martha* (1953), Toni Morrison's *The Bluest Eye* (1970) and *Sula* (1974), Alice Walker's *The Color Purple* (1982), and Alice Randall's *The Wind Done Gone* (2001). Hurston's literary resurrection became a central element in the second and third waves of black feminist thought, even as the literary world geared up to make her one of the most notable figures in American literary history and one of the five or six most recognized African-American writers in the world. Against gender and racial bias, she managed to publish more than any other woman associated with the Harlem Renaissance era. Today, Zora Neale Hurston is as important to the canons of African-American literature and American literature as is the internationally celebrated Nobel laureate Toni Morrison.

## FURTHER READING

Boyd, Valerie, *Wrapped in Rainbows: The Life of Zora Neale Hurston*, New York, Scribner's, 2003.

Glassman, Steve and Kathryn Lee Seidel (eds.), *Zora in Florida*, Orlando, University of Central Florida Press, 1991.

Harris, Trudier, *The Power of the Porch: The Storyteller's Craft in Zora Neale Hurston, Gloria Naylor, and Randall Kenan,* Athens, University of Georgia Press, 1996.

Hemenway, Robert, *Zora Neale Hurston: A Literary Biography*, Urbana-Champaign, University of Illinois Press, 1980.

Holloway, Karla, *The Character of the Word: The Texts of Zora Neale Hurston*, New York, Greenwood Press, 1987.

Hurston, Zora Neale, *Dust Tracks on a Road* (1942), New York, HarperCollins, 1996.

*Jonah's Gourd Vine* (1934), New York, HarperPerennial, 1990.

*Moses, Man of the Mountain* (1939), Urbana and Chicago, University of Illinois Press, 1984.

*Seraph on the Suwanee*, New York, Charles Scribner's Sons, 1948.

*Their Eyes Were Watching God* (1937), Urbana and Chicago, University of Illinois Press, 1978.

King, Lovalerie, *The Cambridge Introduction to Zora Neale Hurston*, Cambridge, Cambridge University Press, 2008.

Lowe, John, *Jump at the Sun: Zora Neale Hurston's Cosmic Comedy*, Chicago and Urbana, University of Illinois Press, 1994.

Meisenhelder, Susan Edwards, *Hitting a Straight Lick with a Crooked Stick: Race and Gender in the Work of Zora Neale Hurston*, Tuscaloosa, University of Alabama Press, 1999.

Plant, Deborah G., *Every Tub Must Sit on Its Own Bottom: The Philosophy and Politics of Zora Neale Hurston*, Urbana and Chicago, University of Illinois Press, 1995.

Walker, Alice, *In Search of Our Mothers' Gardens: Womanist Prose*, New York, Harcourt Brace, 1983.

Wall, Cheryl, *Women of the Harlem Renaissance*, Bloomington, Indiana University Press, 1995.

Wall, Cheryl A. (ed.), *Zora Neale Hurston: Folklore, Memoirs, and Other Writings*, New York, Library of America, 1995.

West, M. Genevieve, *Zora Neale Hurston and American Literary Culture*, Gainesville, University Press of Florida, 2005.

Zora Neale Hurston annual festival site: http://www.zoranealehurstonfestival.com/.

# 16

# Richard Wright

WILLIAM DOW

The argument for Richard Wright (1908–60) as one of the most influential American novelists of the twentieth century rests on his essayistic and naturalistic novel *Native Son* (1940) and his fictionalized autobiography, *Black Boy* (1945). Wright's trademarks as an urban naturalist and modernist tracing chronic hunger, racial conflict, social disempowerment, family dysfunction, and educational disadvantage pervade these two works. His quest throughout is to understand "the framework of contemporary living ... for theories to light up the shadows of conduct."[1] Charting a new and disturbing trajectory of race relations in America, Wright created both an autobiographical self and a male African-American subjectivity in *Black Boy* and *Native Son*. These works provide for the first time in American fiction, as Sterling Brown argues in his 1940 review of *Native Son*, a racially based "psychological probing of the consciousness of the outcast, the disinherited, the generation lost in the slum jungles of American civilization."[2] *Black Boy* and *Native Son* would establish the form for Wright's most effective kind of writing – autobiographical prose – that would not only underlie his most successful literary productions but dominate his later travel writings and literary journalism: the observer-participant *Black Power* (1954), *The Color Curtain* (1956), *White Man Listen*! (1957), and *Pagan Spain* (1957). All are written in this particular prose, which would confirm Wright's status as an enduring talent and "global man of letters."[3]

Richard Wright had one of the most inauspicious starts of any major American novelist and, paradoxically, was one of first African Americans to gain a major reputation in twentieth-century American literature. Born on September 4, 1908, near Roxie, Mississippi, to Ellen and Nathan Wright and raised in the American South during the Jim Crow era of racial segregation, Wright felt from an early age "cast out of the world" and "made to live outside the normal processes of life" (*BB*, 204). As he relates in one of the bleakest moments in *Black Boy*, "I seemed rather condemned, ringed by walls" (*BB*, 251). Faced with seemingly impossible obstacles to literary achievement – intense poverty, family disorganization, a deeply entrenched racist environment – Wright, nevertheless, became a seminal writer who changed the course of American literature.

Wright's early manifesto, the Marxist-inflected "Blueprint for Negro Writing" (1937), can be considered as *the* blueprint of literary composition that he himself applied throughout his career. It outlines what Wright considered to be African-American literature's lack of independence and verve: "Negro writing in the past had been confined to humble novels, poems, and plays, prim and decorous ambassadors who went a begging to white America ... dressed in the knee pants of servility."[4] A result of his acute intellectual and social vision based on the racism and poverty that he experienced in the American South, it calls for "[an] emphasis upon tendency and experiment, a view of society as something becoming rather than as something fixed" (*Blueprint*, 1404). Attempting to strike a balance between representing in fictional forms "a theory about the meaning, structure and direction of modern society" (*Blueprint*, 1408) and preserving an artistic sense untainted by didacticism, Wright forecasts the kind of "global perspective" that will pervade his entire canon: "Perspective for Negro writers will come when they have looked and brooded so hard and long upon the harsh lot of their race and compared it with the hopes and struggles of minority peoples everywhere that the cold facts have begun to tell them something" (*Blueprint*, 1408).

Struggling with his own conflicted American identity, Wright offered his experiences as a template for contemporary history but had to go far beyond America to do so. He was able to move himself into the "sphere of conscious history,"[5] but only by positioning himself alongside the twenty-seven nations meeting together at the 1955 Bandung conference in Jakarta, Indonesia. As he writes in *The Color Curtain*: "I feel that my life has given me some keys to what they would say or do. I'm an American Negro. I've had the burden of race consciousness. So have these people. I've worked in my youth as a common labourer and I've a class consciousness. So have these people. I grew up in the Methodist and Seventh Day Adventist churches and I saw and observed religion in my childhood; and these people are religious."[6] Wright had to journey outside himself and his American environments (Jackson, Mississippi; Memphis, Chicago, New York) in order to maintain a connection with his racial and cultural roots. Wright, as Keneth Kinnamon has argued, "is a phenomenon not easy to explain."[7]

And yet so much of Wright's fiction makes use of a clarifying narrator, a persona of Wright, or a protagonist feeling obliged to explain or justify himself/herself to others, be those others readers or other characters or some imagined or real community. "If I become polemic," Wright stated in a 1960 interview, "it is because I am trying to tell the reader something and I am afraid he does not understand."[8] In such works as *Black Boy, Lawd Today!* (written in 1934–5 but not published until 1963), *Savage Holiday* (1954), *The Long Dream* (1958), and *Twelve Million Black Voices* (1941), there seems to be the assumption that this other will not be able to understand without such explanations – or, in one of Wright's favorite terms, without "revelation." Wright, in his words, insisted that "fiction and writing in general" was always "a means of revealing the truth of life and experience," and thus "literature ought to be a sharp instrument to reveal something important about mankind, about living, about life whether among whites or blacks."[9] By creating a social consciousness that would elucidate a collective sense of black life in America, Wright's autobiographical prose attempted to depart boldly from all previous forms of African-American writing. Through this prose, Wright not only portrayed "his liberal-radicalness, his blackness, his maleness, his Americanness"[10] but a new global perspective, which invariably included a look backward at the injustices, hunger, and despair of his earlier life.

Wright's first literary publication was not a novel but a collection of four short stories entitled *Uncle Tom's Children* (1938), for which he was awarded the Federal Writers' Project Story Magazine Prize for best work. By the time *Uncle Tom's Children* (1938) appeared, Wright had been a member of the Communist Party for four years, had developed friendships with many of the proletarian writers and socially engaged intellectuals of the time – among them, Nelson Algren, Jack Conroy, Arna Bontemps, and James T. Farrell – and between 1934 and 1937 had widely published stories, poems, reviews, and journalism in *Left Front, Anvil,* and *New Masses.*[11]

The 1938 edition of *Uncle Tom's Children* contained only four stories: "Big Boy Leaves Home," "Down by the Riverside," "Long Black Song," and "Fire and Cloud." When it was reissued by Harper in 1940, the autobiographical preface, "The Ethics of Living Jim Crow," and another story, "Bright and Morning Star," were added. Wright wrote all six pieces in Chicago, where he was an active member of the Communist Party and a leader in the new South Side Writers' Group. As if executing the tenets of "Blueprint," *Uncle Tom's Children*, as its title suggests, responds to Harriet Beecher Stowe's sentimentalist abolitionist novel *Uncle Tom's Cabin* (1852), and in particular to "Uncle Tom" stereotypes (presenting blacks as ignorant, docile, or devilish) and Stowe's racial theories. As the children of Uncle Tom, each of the characters in the collection reacts against the brutalization of whites – not ideologically but instinctively and intuitively – in striving for a more dignified life.

Collectively the stories illustrate Wright's Marxist positions in "Blueprint" by reflecting the need for a black working-class consciousness ("Bright and Morning Star"), interracial solidarity ("Down by the Riverside"), and the social realities of inevitable violence engendered by a system dependent on economic inequity and racial inequality ("Long Black Song"). Following the general pattern of proletarian fiction, Wright organized the stories in a sequence in which the black characters are first victimized but – as brought out in the last stories, "Fire and Cloud" and "Bright Morning Star" – eventually oppose the "white world" with potentially revolutionary action. And yet, as Robert Shulman has noted, the central character in "Fire and Cloud," the Reverend Taylor, interprets the social conflict of the community (the black community is hungry; the white relief officers are refusing to help) not as a contest "between owners and workers, as in the communist, Popular Front tradition, but between white owners and oppressed black people."[12] By foregrounding race and illustrating the importance of "the Negro church" to African-American culture, Wright fuses Christianity and Marxist ideology with democratic process to create another kind of liberation theology. In the process, he holds to a principal conviction in "Blueprint": "If the sensory vehicle of imaginative writing is required to carry too great a load of didactic material, the artistic sense is submerged" (*Blueprint*, 1409). Nevertheless, as Nicole Waligra-Davis has observed, "Communism and interracial cooperation emerge in this collection as partial solutions to poverty and racial discrimination."[13] Congruently, the stories in *Uncle Tom's Children* not only recreate the setting and atmosphere of Wright's childhood but are filled with the kinds of racial protest, literary naturalism, and some of Wright's problematic portrayals of women that prefigure *Native Son* and *Black Boy*. Like these latter works, *Uncle Tom's Children* "function[s] as a composite of American race relations, relations whose boundaries and racial codes are so absolute that by Wright's accounting any single misstep by a black American will likely produce lethal consequences."[14]

Reactions to the collection were varied. Leftist publications such as *Partisan Review*, *Daily Worker*, and *New Masses* gave it favorable to ambivalent reviews.[15] Leading critics and writers of the time, including Alain Locke, Malcolm Cowley, James T. Farrell, Countee Cullen, and Sterling Brown, saw it as a major literary achievement that realistically described the sufferings and demands of southern blacks and how Jim Crow had assailed black dignity. One of the most enduring and negative reviews of *Uncle Tom's Children* was that of the African-American writer Zora Neale Hurston (*Saturday, Review of Literature*, 1938), who criticized Wright's use of dialect, his male-dominated subject matter, his Marxism, and his failing to account for the "sympathy and understanding" of black culture.[16] Perhaps the harshest critic of the collection, though, was Wright himself, who wrote in 1940 that he "had written a book which even bankers' daughters could read and weep over and feel good about." Wright "swore" to learn from this "naive mistake" and promised himself that if he "ever wrote another book, no one would weep over it; that it would be so hard and deep that they would have to face it without the consolation of tears."[17]

*Native Son* was that book.[18] It was a Book-of-the Month selection, sold more than 200,000 copies within a month of publication, and in 1940 became the number one best seller in America. It earned Wright instant fame and revealed that he, after all, was perhaps his own best critic, at least in explaining his greatest novel, as he did in "How 'Bigger' Was Born" (1940) – an essay added to "the author's edition" of the novel in May 1940.[19] "It is an accusation against the society of the United States," Wright claimed in 1940, "and a defense of the Negro people, who still live in conditions very similar to slavery" (*Conversations*, 32). Composed of three parts – Fear, Flight, and Fate – the novel shows the influence of communism, a major intellectual and political force for Wright between 1933 and 1940; protest fiction, which extends the themes of racial fear and entrapment in *Uncle Tom's Children* (and anticipates them in *Black Boy*); and urban realism, naturalistic determinism, sociological theory, racial violence, and existentialism. As James A. Miller has argued, Bigger Thomas, the novel's protagonist and Wright's most "enduring character," has emerged as Wright predicted he would in "How 'Bigger' Was Born," as one of the most powerful symbolic figures in American life, "the heritage of us all" (*Bigger*, 451).[20]

The novel tells the story of Bigger Thomas, an impoverished twenty-year-old African American, who is living with his mother, brother, and sister on Chicago's South Side in the 1930s. Hired as a chauffeur, Bigger accidentally kills Mary Dalton, the daughter of wealthy (and "liberal"-minded) parents who are actually slum landlords and owners of the Thomases' kitchenette. Bigger burns Mary's body in a furnace then develops a plan to extort money from her parents. The first part is filled with socially realistic descriptions and symbolic scenes of black slum life. Images of curtains, blindness, walls, and "whiteness" – as an irrepressible naturalistic force – show the subsumed existence of blacks in white society. Part two traces how Bigger runs from the police; rapes and kills his girlfriend, Bessie; and is then caught and tried. Part three – more discursive, essayistic, and allegorical than the first two parts – outlines Bigger's trial, conviction, and death sentence. Ultimately, although struggling to "see himself in relation to other men,"[21] Bigger is part of the black race, which "constitute[s] a separate nation, stunted, stripped, and held captive within this nation, devoid of political, social, economic, and property rights" (*Native*, 397), an idea that gives fictional life to W. E.

B. Dubois's and Alain Locke's thesis that African Americans were trapped in a racially excluded subnation within a nation.[22]

Flawed though *Native Son* may be,[23] the critical consensus is that it became the novel that defined and influenced the entire spectrum of African-American literature of the post–World War II period.[24] The landmark themes and techniques of *Native Son* were instrumental in performing this task: Wright was the first to portray a distinctively black psychology, the first to depict black ghetto life intricately from the point of view of an undereducated and poor black man, the first to interrogate sexual fears as the base of racial segregation, and the first to calibrate an urban naturalism and modernism to what he called "the main burden of all serious fiction [which] consists almost wholly of character destiny and the items, social, political, and personal, of that character destiny" (*Bigger,* 459). Rejecting the ethic of racial celebration espoused by the Harlem Renaissance writers, Wright argued instead that African-American writers should strive to produce realistic accounts of the black masses' social and economic situations – and represent them through such destinies.

Wright did just this – marking equations between race and class – in his next work, the photo-essay *12 Million Black Voices* (1941). By tracing a collective African-American destiny, namely, "a complex movement of a debased feudal folk toward a twentieth-century urbanization," *Black Voices* presents how Wright – although he "quietly" left the Communist Party, probably around 1942 – remained faithful to a Marxist vision of social change.[25] In *Black Voices*, Wright is a "sociological informant"[26] and, as demonstrated in *Black Boy* and *Native Son*, a believer in viewing the individual as representative of a group. As he explains in *Black Boy*, "[my] reading in sociology had enabled me to discern many strange types of Negro characters to identify many modes of Negro behaviour" (*BB*, 284). But in focusing on "those materials of Negro life identified with the countless black millions" (*Preface*, xxi), *Black Voices* also asks its readers to engage with its fictionalization, its attempt to give voice, as Wright puts it in "Blueprint," to "unwritten and unrecognized" black folklore (*Blueprint*, 1405). At the same time the literary influences inherent in *Black Voices* reflect Wright's consideration that "Eliot, Stein, Joyce, Proust, Hemingway; and Anderson; Gorky, Barbusse, Nexo, and Jack London no less than the folklore of the Negro himself should form the heritage of the Negro Writer" (*Blueprint*, 1407). Congruently, it was *Black Voices* that, with "its investments in the Chicago School of Urban Sociology and the deterministic slant of its theories,"[27] would prove to be a starting point for Wright's later forays into what most critics have called his travel writings of the 1950s: *Black Power* (1954), *White Man Listen!* (1957), and

*The Color Curtain* (1956). *Black Voices* signals Wright's trials to develop a stylistics that would mark his purchase on the social data he wanted to transform into fiction.

The lyrical power that makes *Black Voice*'s structure impressionistic rather than logical carried over into the fictionalized autobiography, *Black Boy* (1940).[28] Returning to the more pessimistic, deterministic manner of *Native Son*, while extending the sociological critique he presents in *Black Voices*, *Black Boy* renders Wright's life from early childhood to his arrival in Chicago. Generally acclaimed as one of the finest autobiographies ever written by an American writer, *Black Boy* follows the long-standing tradition of African-American autobiographies – with its focus on "authenticity and sincerity."[29] Other examples include Frederick Douglass's *Narrative of the Life of Frederick Douglass*, 1845; James Weldon Johnson's *Along the Way*, 1933; Claude McKay's *A Long Way from Home*, 1937; Mary Church Terrel's *A Colored Woman in a White World*, 1940; and Malcolm X's *The Autobiography of Malcolm X*, 1965. But in so doing Wright provides a new definition of blackness – a blackness no longer based on a set of racial stereotypes but defined as a metaphysical condition of alienation and separation, a disturbing, complicated creation of contemporary culture. "Whenever I thought of the essential bleakness of black life in America," Wright laments in *Black Boy*, "I knew that Negroes had never been allowed to catch the full spirit of Western Civilization, that they had lived somehow in it but not of it" (*BB*, 37). In its racial resignification, *Black Boy* anticipates a conception of race that is unstable, transcultural, and international.

While changing the perception and reception of African-American and American literature, *Black Boy* elucidates perhaps the most severe economic hardships ever experienced by a major American writer and provides explanations for – and personal resistances to – those hardships. "I wanted to render a judgement on my environment," Wright said of *Black Boy;* "[t]hat judgement was this: the environment the South creates is too small to nourish human beings, especially Negro human beings" (*Conversations*, 64–5). Above all, *Black Boy* is a systematic unfolding of the processes of an *artistic* development in a disruptive and brutal environment, a development that comes to full fruition in the second part of the autobiography, *American Hunger*, published in 1977.

Wright would spend the rest of his life responding to the foreign environments he traveled or lived in – including England, France, Spain, Western Africa, Indonesia – in relation to his ongoing thinking about the racially imploding United States. He moved to Paris two years after *Black Boy* was published and would stay there until his death in 1960. His next work, *The*

*Outsider* (1953), represented a certain separation from his former writing and the political and social beliefs he held in America. In Paris Wright commented that "the break from the U.S. was more than a geographical change," but "a break with my former attitudes as a Negro and a Communist.... I was trying to grapple with the big problem – the problem and meaning of western civilization as a whole and the relation of Negroes and other minority groups to it."[30]

While living in France in the 1950s, Wright became associated with the French existentialists Jean-Paul Sartre, Simone de Beauvoir, Albert Camus and other writers involved with the journal *Les Temps Modernes*. Wright's concern with the situation of black intellectual in the West and his increasing engagement (and disengagement) with existentialism are represented by Cross Damon, the central character of *The Outsider*, and his rejection of essentialist forms of identity.

In the context of his own modern consciousness – and outside the confines of conventional racial ideologies – Wright, like Cross Damon, wished to understand race not as biological necessity but as a social category. Thus Cross, early in the novel, tells us in a flat existential declaration, "[a] man creates himself,"[31] though the novel both affirms and denies this claim: social forces, beyond Cross's control, eventually destroy him. At the same time, Wright, despite clinging to an independent (and racially conflicted) "outsider" status (as the narrators do in *Black Boy*, *Black Power*, and *The Color Curtain*), "never disavows his own experience of Black oppression and resistance" and the challenges that his environments posed.[32] On an aesthetic level, *The Outsider* is representative in demonstrating Wright' lifelong fascination for crime novels, pulp fiction, and the gothic – beginning with *Lawd Today!* but permeating such works as *Eight Men* (1961) and *Native Son* – along with his ability to combine such genres.

*The Outsider* received mostly mixed to negative reviews, as did Wright's next work, *Savage Holiday* (1954), a new orientation for Wright bearing witness to his fascination with Freudian psychology and his shift to exploring nonracial issues. Wright's last published novel in his lifetime, *The Long Dream* (1958), was somewhat of a return to the themes of *Black Boy* and the subject matter of *Uncle Tom's Children*: a black rural folk culture's imbrications with dominant white communities.

Influenced by his association with the writers of the Negritude movement, including Leopold Senghor and Aimé Cesaire, Wright became increasingly interested in Indonesian and African liberation movements. Between 1953 and 1957 he traveled to Spain, Indonesia, and Africa and completed work on four sociopolitical travel narratives and essays – *Black Power* (1954), *The Color Curtain* (1956), *Pagan Spain* (1957), and *White*

*Man Listen!* (1957). While many critics thought that Wright's best creative years were behind him because he became "cut off" from his native roots, his exile years, it can be argued, allowed him to write from a richer and more complex historical and psychological perspective. Rather than impoverishing Wright's work, his postwar years – as argued variously by the Wright critics Michel Fabre, Paul Gilroy, and Jerry W. Ward Jr. – can be seen as the most vital record for understanding his objectives and aspirations as a writer.

Most essentially, Wright's fiction and nonfiction demand to be taken beyond borders and boundaries, to be interpreted in relation to what it means to write the African-American literary text into a world literary history. Wright's crossover strategies between distinct literary genres, between "modernist" and "naturalist" and "high" cultures, on the one hand, and "popular" and "pulp" and "low" cultures, on the other; between writing about feeling at home (racially, culturally, socially) neither in one's native land (America) nor in one's land of exile (France) are only beginning to be recognized by Wright critics. His best work asks crucial questions with regard to national alienation and international belonging and to race as a superimposed category, rather than a biological reality. His fiction, and almost all his nonfiction, easily lifts beyond the center of African-American culture to explore the potentialities and limits of a black transnationalism, a transnative status, and Wright's perpetual "outsidedness" mixed with the "essential humanness"[33] of his activist and literary efforts.

Wright's *Black Boy* and *Native Son* make an irrefutable case for including his work and influence in the discursive histories of American literary history, but so too do his undervalued exile writings. With respect to his promotion of interethnic exchanges and his attempt to deal honesty with the ravages of racism and colonialism, his disorientation and distress – as related in *Black Power*, the *Color Curtain*, and *White Man Listen!* – provide alternative legacies to those of his preexile work. Like W.E.B. Dubois and Alain Locke, Wright perceived "African Americans as constituting a class within the larger American polity that would not achieve its goals without both common purposes and dedication to depicting those purposes through art."[34] That Wright believed in the socially transformative power of language is clear, but he also came to believe – running from *Uncle Tom's Children* and *Black Boy* to "A Man Who Lived Underground" (1945) and *A Father's Law* (2008) – in the importance of locating notions of race within larger hemispheric and colonial genealogies. He derived new meanings of black folk traditions and his own Jim Crow ethics by interpreting them through the lens of a transnational heritage. In effect, Wright ultimately became – or perhaps always was – a nonnative American son.

## FURTHER READING

Baker, Houston a. Jr., *Turning South Again*, Durham, N.C., Duke University Press, 2001.

Butler, Robert and Jerry Ward (eds.), *The Richard Wright Encyclopedia*, Westport, Conn., Greenwood, 2008.

Craven, Alice Mikal and William E. Dow (eds.), *Richard Wright: New Readings in the 21st Century*, New York and London, Palgrave Macmillan, 2011.

Edwards, Brent Hayes, *The Practice of Diaspora: Literature, Translation, and the Rise of Black Nationalism*, Cambridge, Mass., Harvard University Press, 2003.

Entin, Joseph B, *Sensational Modernism: Experimental Fiction and Photography in Thirties America*, Chapel Hill, University of North Carolina Press, 2007.

Ernest, John *Chaotic Justice: Rethinking African American Literary History*, Chapel Hill, North Carolina Press, 2009.

Graham, Maryemma (ed.), *The Cambridge Companion to the African American Novel*, Cambridge, Cambridge University Press, 2004.

Hakutani, Yoshinobu, *Cross-Cultural Visions in African American Modernism*, Columbus, Ohio State University Press, 2006.

Janmohamed, Abdul R., *The Death Bound Subject: Richard Wright's Archaeology of Death*, Durham, N.C., Duke University Press, 2005.

Jones, Gavin, *American Hungers: The Problem of Poverty in U.S. Literature, 1840–1945*, Princeton, N.J., and Oxford, Princeton University Press, 2008.

Mullen, Bill V. and James Smethurst, *Left of the Color Line: Race, Radicalism, and Twentieth-Century Literature of the United States*, Chapel Hill and London, University of North Carolina Press, 2003.

Robinson, Cedric J., *Black Modernism: A Critical Study of Twentieth Century Negro American Authors*, Chapel Hill, University of North Carolina Press, 2000.

Rowley, Hazel, *Richard Wright: The Life and Times*, New York, Holt, 2001.

## NOTES

1  Richard Wright, *Black Boy*, introduction by Jerry W. Ward Jr. (New York, Harper Perennial, 1998), p. 284. Hereafter *BB*.

2  Robert Butler, "Introduction," in *The Critical Response to Richard Wright*, ed. Robert Butler (Westport, Conn., and London, Greenwood Press, 1995), p. xxvii.

3  Cornell West, "Introduction," in *Black Power, Three Books from Exile: Black Power; The Color Curtain; and White Man, Listen!* by Richard Wright (New York, Harper Perennial, 2008), p. vii.

4  Wright, "Blueprint for Negro Writing," in *The Norton Anthology of African American Literature*, ed. Henry Louis Gates and Nellie McKay, 2nd ed. (New York, Norton, 2004), p. 1403. Hereafter "Blueprint."

5  Wright, *12 Million Black Voices*, foreword by Noel Ignatiev, introduction by David Bradley (New York, Basic Books, 2008), p. 147. Hereafter *Voices*.

6  Wright, "The Color Curtain," in *Black Power, Three Books from Exile: Black Power; The Color Curtain; and White Man, Listen!* (New York, Harper Perennial, 2008), pp. 440–1.

7  Keneth Kinnamon, *The Emergence of Richard Wright: A Study in Literature and Society* (Urbana, Chicago, and London, University of Illinois Press, 1972), p. 3.

8   Kinnamon and Michel Fabre, eds., *Conversations with Richard Wright* (Jackson, University Press of Mississippi, 1993), p. 240. Hereafter, *Conversations*.

9   Yoshinobu Hakutani, *Richard Wright and Racial Discourse* (Columbia, University of Missouri Press, 1996), p. 117.

10  Jack B. Moore, "A Personal Appreciation of Richard Wright's Universality," *Mississippi Quarterly* 50.2 (Spring 1997), 365–374.

11  James W. Tuttleton, "The Problematic Texts of Richard Wright," *Hudson Review* 5.2 (Summer 1992): 263.

12  Robert Shulman, "The Political Art of Wright's 'Fire and Cloud,'" in *Richard Wright: New Readings in the 21st Century*, ed. Alice Mikal Craven and William E. Dow (New York and London, Palgrave Macmillan, 2011), p. 236.

13  Nicole Waligora-Davis, "Weaving Jagged Words: The Black Left, 1930s–1940s," in *The Cambridge History of African American Literature*, ed. Maryemma Graham and Jerry W. Ward Jr. (Cambridge, Cambridge University Press, 2011), p. 320.

14  Ibid., p. 319.

15  Joyce Ann Joyce, "Richard (Nathaniel) Wright," in *African American Writers*, ed. Valerie Smith, Lea Baechler, and A. Walton Litz (New York, Charles Scribner's Sons, 1991). URL: http://go.galefroup.com/ps/i.do?&id=GALE, October 25, 2011.

16  Zora Neale Hurston, "Stories of Conflict," *Saturday Review of Literature* 17 (April 2, 1938): p. 32.

17  Wright, "How 'Bigger' Was Born," in *Native Son* by Richard Wright, introduction by Arnold Rampersad (New York, Harper Perennial, 1998), p. 454. Hereafter "Bigger."

18  It must be noted that because Harper required Wright to tone down the novel's sexual and political implications, the *Native Son* that he intended for publication in 1939 was never made available until 1991, when it was published in its entirety by the Library of America.

19  Kinnamon, "How Native Son Was Born," in *Writing the American Classics*, ed. James Barbour and Tom Quirk (Chapel Hill and London, University of North Carolina Press, 1990), p. 210.

20  James A. Miller, "Introduction," in *Approaches to Teaching Wright's Native Son*, ed. James A. Miller (New York, Modern Language Association of America, 1997), p. 11.

21  Wright, *Native Son*, introduction by Arnold Rampersad (New York, Harper Perennial, 1998), p. 361. Hereafter *Native*.

22  See Alain Locke, "The New Negro," in Locke, *The New Negro. 1925.* (New York, Atheneum, 1992), pp. 3–16; and W. E. B. Dubois, "Criteria of Negro Art" in *Crisis,* October 1926, pp. 290–7.

23  Although Irving Howe famously wrote in 1963 that "the day *Native Son* appeared, American culture was changed forever" (*Dissent*, Autumn 1963, p. 354), there were detractors as well, critics who claimed that the novel was "dull propaganda" (Howard Mumford Jones, *Boston Evening Transcript*, March 2, 1940) and flawed with "paper-thin characters" (Clifton Fadiman, *New Yorker*, March 16, 1940).

24  Henry Louis Gates and Nellie Y. McKay, eds., *The Norton Anthology of African American Literature.* 2nd ed. (New York, Norton, 2004), p. 1400.

25 Wright, "Preface" (1941), in *12 Million Black Voices* by Richard Wright, foreword by Noel Ignatiev, introduction by David Bradley (New York, Basic Books, 1941), p. xx. Hereafter *Preface*.

26 Carla Cappetti, *Writing Chicago: Modernism, Ethnography, and the Novel* (New York, Columbia University Press, 1993), p. 182.

27 Gates and McKay, eds., *Norton Anthology of African American Literature*, p. 1401.

28 The unexpurgated edition of Wright's autobiography would not appear until the Library of America printed the original manuscript as *Black Boy (American Hunger)* in 1991.

29 William L. Andrews, "Richard Wright and the African-American Autobiography Tradition," *Style* 27.2 (Summer 1993): 272.

30 Michel Fabre, *The Unfinished Quest of Richard Wright* (New York, William Morrow, 1973), p. 366.

31 Wright, *The Outsider* (1953), introduction by Maryemma Graham (New York, Harper Perennial, 2008), p. 65.

32 West, "Introduction," in *Black Power, Three Books from Exile: Black Power; The Color Curtain; and White Man, Listen!* by Richard Wright (New York: Harper Perennial, 2008), p. ix.

33 Wright, *Black Power*, p. 704.

34 Darryl Dickson-Carr. "African American Literature and the Great Depression," in *The Cambridge History of African American Literature*, ed. Maryemma Graham and Jerry W. Ward Jr. (Cambridge, Cambridge University Press, 2011), p. 300.

# 17

# Raymond Chandler

LEONARD CASSUTO

Frank MacShane prefaces the first full-length biography of Raymond Chandler (1888–1959) with a warning that he is "treating Raymond Chandler as a novelist and not simply as a detective-story writer."[1] If only it were that easy. The tension between genre fiction and self-consciously literary writing animated – and irritated – Chandler for his entire writing career. Though he did not publish his first novel until he was past fifty, that career spanned the possibilities for an American writer at midcentury, from literary fiction to mass market paperbacks, with the wild card of the movies thrown in.

At his peak, Chandler transcended the crime genre within which he honed and practiced his craft. He was praised by the literati, imitated widely by his crime writer peers, and avidly read by the general public – all before his most ambitious book, *The Long Goodbye* (1953), even appeared.

No one would have predicted such success for Raymond Chandler in the early years of his career. Though he was once a hot prospect, the sales of Chandler's early books discouraged him and his publisher. His reversal of fortune says something about the enduring qualities of his writing, especially his great creation, the private investigator Philip Marlowe. But it also tells us a lot about the workings of the American literary marketplace at a dynamic historical moment, and about the genre with which Raymond Chandler will, for better and worse, always be identified. Chandler's ups and downs are a story with its own sense of mystery. You could call it "the alchemy of a best seller."

Part of Raymond Chandler's legacy is that today's crime stories often seek, and sometimes attain, high seriousness. Crime stories started selling in great numbers as low literature. "Penny dreadfuls" and other lurid pamphlet literature of past centuries (which were based on true crimes) evolved into the genre fiction category that we now recognize. Sherlock Holmes gave a tonier sheen to the detective story in the late nineteenth century, but the reputation of the genre remained coarse for generations – and in the case of pulp fiction, literally so. Pulp magazines, which entered the scene in the 1920s, paid authors in the range of a nickel a word for detective stories, westerns, and other formula fiction (in contrast to the higher-priced, so-called slicks, which paid as much as a dollar a word). Pulp fiction got its name because the inexpensive paper on which it was printed had a high wood pulp content and felt grainy and rough to the touch.

Pulp magazines formed the crucible for some of the most important developments in American crime writing. The hard-boiled style – featuring tough, laconic, detached protagonists and a generally bleak worldview – evolved through the 1920s in the pages of the pulp magazines, most notably *Black Mask*, which was edited by the legendary Joseph Shaw.

The intervention of Alfred A. Knopf in the development of hard-boiled fiction in the late 1920s is an event whose signal importance can hardly be overstated. One of the most famous book publishers of the twentieth century, Knopf started his own publishing house in 1915 while still in his twenties. By 1925, writes the book historian John Tebbel, Knopf was "regarded with overwhelming respect, even awe, both in and out of the trade," and his eponymous imprint had become synonymous with intellectual quality and prestige.[2] (It remains so today, more than forty years after being acquired by Random House.) Knopf published "only the books he liked," says Tebbel, "with no particular regard for anyone's taste but his own – and [his wife] Blanche's."[3] When he read hard-boiled crime fiction, Knopf saw the best of it as something more than a dime novel in clean clothes.

Knopf first signed Dashiell Hammett, who honed his skills writing for *Black Mask*. Hammett wrote in 1928 that he wanted to take the detective story and "make literature of it."[4] The four novels that he produced in a burst beginning in the late 1920s – *Red Harvest* (1929), *The Dain Curse* (1929), *The Maltese Falcon* (1930), and *The Glass Key* (1931) – virtually reinvented crime literature in the United States.[5] Knopf also published James M. Cain, whose first novel, *The Postman Always Rings Twice*, fomented a minor controversy over its sexual frankness when Knopf brought it out in 1934.

Like Hammett, Chandler started out writing short stories for *Black Mask*, but he started a decade later than Hammett. When Knopf discovered Chandler in 1938 and decided to publish him, hard-boiled writing had already gained some cachet, though it hardly counted as highbrow literature. Knopf believed that Chandler would continue the march of hard-boiled crime fiction to literary respectability. The publisher believed that he had "found the next 'hard-boiled star,'" says Chandler biographer Tom Hiney, and that Chandler's appeal, like Hammett's, would extend beyond the fans of mystery writing.[6]

Knopf sought to take the Chandler show right to Broadway when he trumpeted the coming publication of Chandler's debut novel, *The Big Sleep* (1939), with a full-page, front-cover advertisement in *Publisher's Weekly*. The text of the ad was short. It read simply,

In 1929 Dashiell Hammett.

In 1934 James M. Cain.

In 1939 Raymond Chandler.[7]

Chandler, for his part, hoped that "the day will come when I won't have to ride around on Hammett and James Cain, like an organ grinder's monkey." He longed from the beginning to be taken seriously as something more than a mystery writer. Even early in his career he grasped gratefully the approbation of "a critic who confessedly does not like mystery stories." Bolstered by his later success, he would enlarge these sentiments. Nearly a decade later he would declare to the writer and editor Frederick Lewis Allen that he did not "care a button about the detective story as a form." Instead, he said he was "looking for an excuse for certain experiments in dramatic dialogue. To justify them I have to have plot and situation; but fundamentally I care almost nothing about either." The "richness of texture" of his "experiments" Chandler simply called "style." But as a serious writer who had chosen the mystery story as his métier, Chandler also resented those who would deprecate it. "People are always suggesting to writers of my sort, 'You write so well why don't you attempt a serious novel?'" he wrote to his British publisher, Hamish Hamilton. "They would probably be insulted if one suggested that the aesthetic gap, if any, between a good mystery and the best serious novel of the last ten years is hardly measurable." This vein of truculent contradiction runs through Chandler – and it glows brightly within his richest and most memorable creation, the detective Philip Marlowe.[8]

*The Big Sleep* introduces Marlowe, a character Chandler had been honing in the pulps, and who would take center stage in all of his novels. Marlowe takes an opening bow that is every bit as self-conscious as Knopf's *Publisher's Weekly* advertisement was. The first paragraph of Chandler's first novel has Marlowe dressing up to meet the wealthy General Sternwood. Resplendently attired in his best "powder-blue suit, with dark blue shirt, tie and display handkerchief," Marlowe strides confidently to "call [] on four million dollars." Once he enters the Sternwood mansion, the contradictions begin to pile up. He sees a stained glass panel depicting a "knight in dark armor rescuing a lady who was tied to a tree" and admits to himself the desire to help the knight. (Later, fondling pieces on a chessboard in his apartment, he muses that "knights had no meaning in this game. It wasn't a game for knights.") But for all of Marlowe's chivalrous desire, he warns

Sternwood, his prospective employer, "I test very high for insubordination." And for all of the sartorial respect that he shows for Sternwood's money at the outset, he later deflects his anger at Sternwood's daughter Carmen onto the Sternwood fortune when he declares, "To hell with the rich. They made me sick."[9]

The opening of *The Big Sleep* illustrates the tension that fuels Marlowe, and which makes him one of the great leading men that crime literature has ever produced. Marlowe loves nobility but hates pretension – and as a "shop-soiled Galahad," he is sorely vexed because modern-day chivalry encompasses nobility and pretension at the same time.[10] In holding conflicting responses in uneasy suspension Marlowe follows the lead of his creator. A few months after *The Big Sleep* was published, Chandler wrote tellingly to his fellow *Black Mask* writer George Harmon Coxe:

> I like a conservative atmosphere, a sense of the past. I like everything that Americans of past generations used to go and look for in Europe, but at the same time I don't want to be bound by the rules.[11]

Marlowe is cultured in much the way that Chandler is. He tells Sternwood with understated pride that he "went to college once and can still speak English if there's any demand for it,"[12] but at the same time he dislikes many of the sources of culturedness.

Marlowe works for Sternwood not because Sternwood is rich, but because Marlowe likes him. The detective story in *The Big Sleep* ends twice, in effect, restarting in the middle because of Marlowe's affection for the old, sad father who hired him. The first ending occurs when Marlowe defuses the blackmail threat that Sternwood originally hired him to investigate. "The smart thing to do," Marlowe concedes at that point, would be to leave things alone and "forget the whole mess." But he keeps searching for Sternwood's missing son-in-law, Rusty Regan. He does so without the old man's knowledge at first, because, Marlowe later tells him, "It's that you're still too proud to be played for a sucker – and you really liked Regan." Marlowe respects Sternwood, but not his oil money, which he renders as a field of "rusted metal and old wood and silent wells and greasy scummy sumps" that Chandler sees with the eye of the oilman that he once had been himself.[13]

Marlowe is drawn into the circle by human need, but he's repelled by human flaws, especially vanity. One of the few reviewers who noticed *The Big Sleep* described it as depraved. The description hurt Chandler, who saw what he was doing very differently. *The Big Sleep* is a grimy story involving pornography, drugs, and a particularly nasty hired killer in the employ of organized crime, but it's also a parable of loyalty and friendship. Chandler's best books turn similarly on Marlowe's capacity for emotional connection with men he doesn't even know very well. Sean McCann, one of Chandler's most acute readers, says that against the disconnectedness of the modern world, Chandler reposes his wobbly faith in a Deweyan "vision of male fellowship" that is repeatedly undermined.[14] Even so, Marlowe keeps coming back for more, and his conflicted humanism, rather than a burning need to find out whodunit, is what drives Chandler's stories forward.

*The Big Sleep* sold more than 10,000 copies when it was released as a Knopf front list title at a cover price of $2.00, equivalent to about $30.00 today. English sales, proportionately higher due to there being more libraries per capita, raised the total to 18,000. (Chandler's royalty rate was 20 percent of the wholesale price for the first 5,000 units sold, and 25 percent thereafter. Grosset and Dunlap also brought out a discount one-dollar edition of *The Big Sleep*, which sold another 3,500 copies, for which Chandler received a 5 percent royalty.) Altogether, Chandler earned about $2,000 in royalties for his first novel, not enough to alter his pen-to-mouth existence.[15]

The sales figures for *The Big Sleep* were very respectable for a mystery novel, but they did not represent the kind of crossover appeal that author and publisher both hoped for. A particular problem was a lack of reviews: the book received only four that Chandler saw, and only one of those was favorable.

Knopf, who was known for his patience and loyalty in his dealings with his authors, still believed in Chandler. One notable form that his belief took was his refusal to sell Chandler's novels to the cheap paperback industry that was emerging. These editions were called "pulp books," and they paid royalties of $750 per 100,000 copies sold at 25 cents per copy, a 3 percent rate. More important, being sold to the paperbacks amounted to a one-way ticket to a genre ghetto: an author who published pulp books had no hope of being taken seriously, no hope of being reviewed. It consigned him to a lower-tier career path, with no alternative but to continue writing paperbacks forever after.[16] For Chandler, who worked too slowly to make a good living pumping out pulp fiction and who wanted badly to be taken seriously, this was no viable path at all.

Chandler published his second novel, *Farewell, My Lovely*, in 1940. One of his finest works, it describes Marlowe's pursuit of a missing woman and a missing jade necklace. The two searches converge, and in the process of conducting them Marlowe becomes sentimentally attached to Moose Malloy, a huge, short-tempered ex-con searching for the girlfriend he left behind when he went to prison. Malloy becomes Chandler's unlikely Great Gatsby, and Velma, Malloy's missing sweetheart, becomes his Daisy. Like Gatsby, Malloy dresses well but is hardly genteel; he casually and brutally murders a man in the opening pages of the book. Velma, it turns out, is no virtuous lady in white either – the name she assumes, Grayle, suggests that she is a false (because misspelled) object of purity. But the passion that Moose bears for his "little Velma," and the simple faith he reposes in her, transcends its decidedly soiled object – as Gatsby's mistaken but still towering faith in Daisy does in F. Scott Fitzgerald's novel. Marlowe begins his acquaintance with Moose Malloy violently ("A hand I could have sat in ... took hold of my shoulder and squashed it to a pulp"), but Marlowe admires Malloy because "the big sap loved her," and he stays with Malloy to the end. In *Farewell, My Lovely*, as in *The Big Sleep* and all of Chandler's best books, Marlowe leaves his heart in the mean streets, where men carry it away as often as women do.[17]

*Farewell, My Lovely* sold fewer copies than *The Big Sleep* did, 11,000 in the United States and another 4,000 in Great Britain. Crime literature was doing hugely well during the 1940s. The average hardback crime novel sold about 3,000 copies domestically, so Chandler was doing better than average, but not better enough. The main problem was that his novels were not being reviewed, and without reviews he couldn't make the leap to the wider readership that he and Knopf both sought. He was also making very little money, not enough for him to live on comfortably, and Knopf was not making enough money off his books.

Knopf spent heavily to promote Chandler's third novel, *The High Window* (1942), an undistinguished effort by the author's standards. The publisher got little back for his money, as Chandler's American sales figures continued to drop (to 10,000 copies, though the novel did sell another 8,500 in Great Britain). This disappointment apparently exhausted Knopf's desire to hold off the pulp market. In 1943, shortly before Chandler's fourth novel, *The Lady in the Lake*, was set to appear, Knopf licensed *The Big Sleep* to come out as a cheap paperback.

Then something unexpected happened: the Avon paperback edition of *The Big Sleep* sold 300,000 copies almost right away. An Armed Services paperback edition of the novel, published the same year and given away to American soldiers in World War II, sold an additional 150,000 copies. Chandler had suddenly become visible.

This visibility quickly translated into further success. *The Lady in the Lake* (1943) garnered more critical reviews than any previous Chandler novel. These notices were generally favorable even though the novel, like its immediate predecessor, was not up to the level of Chandler's first two. Chandler's sales totals also experienced a significant uptick: *The Lady in the Lake* sold 14,000 copies in the United States, plus another 13,000 in Great Britain.

These dividends earned Chandler entry into a new market, as he was now invited to collaborate with Billy Wilder on the screen adaptation of James M. Cain's *Double Indemnity* (1936). A novel of illicit passion and murder for profit, *Double Indemnity* had resisted efforts at adaptation for years because its uncompromising sexual directness ran head-on into the movie censorship restrictions imposed on Hollywood by the Hays Code. Chandler and Wilder translated the book's steamy urgency into wit, with Chandler supplying some of the most memorable dialogue in the history of film noir. The screenwriters also displaced the doomed lovers' relationship from the center of the story, replacing it with one of the bonded male pairs so common in Chandler's best fiction. The "real love story" of the 1944 movie, Wilder often said, is between the murderer and the insurance investigator who exposes him. The screenplay of *Double Indemnity* was nominated for an Oscar, and Wilder's film was nominated for Best Picture. Chandler, meanwhile, made more money than he had ever seen before, with the promise of more to come. He worked on and off as a screenwriter for the rest of the decade, alternately seduced by the wages and repelled by Hollywood's pervasive failure "to exploit the writer as an artist of meaning to the picture-buying public."[18]

The success of the *Double Indemnity* movie was extended by additional film adaptations of Chandler's own novels. *Murder, My Sweet* (1944; a version of *Farewell, My Lovely*) was a critical and popular success, and *The Big Sleep* (1946) cast Humphrey Bogart as Philip Marlowe, a choice that Chandler advocated long before it became reality. Bogart, wrote Chandler to Hamilton, is "the genuine article," someone who "can be tough without a gun." Bogart's *Big Sleep*, another classic noir, was further enlivened, said Chandler, by "a director [Howard Hawks] with the gift of atmosphere and the requisite touch of hidden sadism."[19]

These movies in turn stimulated more reviews of Chandler's books, more paperback sales of his earlier titles, and more film adaptations. This feedback loop enriched Chandler in all kinds of ways. By the late 1940s his wallet had become fat, and his star had risen aloft. From a writer who just a decade earlier was trying to avoid being seen as a hack, Chandler had attained the first rank of literary artistry. The poet and critic W. H. Auden, for example, exempted Chandler's books from the mystery category entirely. Chandler's "powerful but extremely depressing books," wrote Auden in 1948, "should be read and judged, not as escape literature, but as works of art."[20] Chandler joked about Auden's taxonomy, but it's hard to imagine that he wasn't warmed by that description. When Chandler's fifth novel, *The Little Sister*, appeared in 1949, Evelyn Waugh called him "the best writer in America."[21]

That first paperback edition of *The Big Sleep* stands out as the key link in this upward-leading causal chain. Chandler may have been building up loyal reader support before 1943, but the success of that "two-bit edition" (as Chandler called it) catalyzed his career.[22] Why did *The Big Sleep* succeed so dramatically as a paperback after its hardback sales had been disappointing? My technical answer, grounded in years of study of crime novels and book history, is this: who knows? That's the alchemy of the book business. Why Chandler, and why then? We can only speculate.

My own speculation is that Chandler's overt sentimentality not only separated him from many of his peers but also took the hard-boiled style in a direction that it was straining to go in, a direction that Hammett and Cain had already pointed toward. *The Big Sleep*, for example, has many of the qualities of a sentimental novel: a broken family, a wayward daughter (two of them in this case), and a parent whose rectitude stands as a beacon rooted in the virtuous past. Essentially, it celebrates the "life in relation" that characterizes the sentimental genre.[23] In *The High Window*, to name another example, Marlowe breaks asunder one diseased family (it's afflicted by a murderous mother, among other problems) and mends a more wholesome one. The story ends with a cross-country drive to Kansas, where Marlowe deposits a damaged young female victim back home with her parents and leaves her "wearing a bungalow apron and rolling pie crust" in her mother's kitchen.[24] Chandler's method of writing the qualities of the sentimental into the tough-guy detective story – starting with the hard-boiled sentimental detective Marlowe – provided a template for hard-boiled writers by the score, a fact of which Chandler was well aware.[25]

*The Long Goodbye* stands as Chandler's crowning achievement. It's a different kind of hard-boiled novel, one that departs furthest from formula and comes closest to realizing Chandler's vision of using genre fiction as a platform for unique artistic achievement. In particular, *The Long Goodbye* is paced more slowly than Chandler's other books, fueled not so much by plot as by Marlowe's emotions as he is exposed to a set of mostly depressed and dissatisfied characters in a postwar California whose surface glitz spreads a thin veneer over pervasive hollowness within. Chandler's prose is more restrained in *The Long Goodbye* than in his earlier work, but his main character is less restrained, and less wittily sardonic. The change in Marlowe is on display from the beginning, when he befriends the hapless Terry Lennox, husband of a casually amoral rich woman, and takes a beating to help Lennox escape the police, who seek him for a murder. Lennox didn't commit the crime, but he betrays Marlowe in a different way.

Chandler exposes Marlowe more in *The Long Goodbye*. The detective loves more openly (he even goes to bed with one of the women he meets while investigating the case), but he also hurts a lot more, and *The Long Goodbye* conveys a more elegiac tone than Chandler's other novels. Even before Marlowe learns that Lennox used him, the depth of his own loneliness becomes clear in his dealings with other characters, including a commercially successful but frustrated writer, Roger Wade, whom some critics have seen as a projection of Chandler himself. Marlowe tells Wade that his work is "just a job," but when Wade dies, the distance between them collapses and Marlowe connects with him as a fellow "human being with blood and a brain and emotions." Lennox, on the other hand, he derides with the bitter passion of a lover scorned, as a "moral defeatist" who is "as elegant as a fifty-dollar whore."[26]

Chandler came unmoored after the death of his wife in 1954 and died in 1959. A final novel, *Playback* (1958), adapted from one of his own screenplays, shows the effects of his alcoholic grief, and is best left unremarked upon. But notwithstanding that desultory final effort, Chandler left behind a body of work distinguished for literary artistry within a set of generic conventions. As important, his novels extend the range of possibility of those conventions. In this respect, Chandler's work looks beyond later disciples like Robert B. Parker to writers like James Ellroy and Dennis Lehane. Their voices don't sound like Chandler's as Parker's does, but they draw on Chandler's ambitious example when they use the motifs of the crime novel on wide and varied canvasses, so that their writing spills out of genre categories in the same way that Chandler's novels – especially *The Long Goodbye* – did. Raymond Chandler's influence was considerable on the writers that followed him in his own time and ours. It is therefore appropriate that his work remains in print in both the Vintage Black Lizard crime series (which reprints old genre fiction) and the high-toned Library of America, the unofficial canon of American literature. This dual exposure shows the range of possibilities for a crime writer in America, a range that Chandler both sought and chafed under, and both defined and exemplified.

## FURTHER READING

Abbott, Megan, *The Street Was Mine: White Masculinity in Hardboiled Fiction and Film Noir*, New York, Palgrave Macmillan, 2002.

Gardiner, Dorothy and Kathrine Sorley Walker (eds.), *Raymond Chandler Speaking*, Boston, Houghton Mifflin, 1977.

Horsley, Lee, *Twentieth-Century Crime Fiction*, Oxford and New York, Oxford University Press, 2005.

Marling, William H., *Raymond Chandler*, Boston, Twayne, 1986.

Moss, Robert F. (ed.), *Raymond Chandler: A Literary Reference*, New York, Carroll & Graf, 2003.

O'Brien, Geoffrey, *Hard-Boiled America: Lurid Paperbacks and the Masters of Noir*, 1st ed., 1981, rpt. New York, Da Capo Press, 1997.

Panek, Leroy Ladd, "Raymond Chandler (1888–1959)," in *A Companion to Crime Fiction*, ed. Charles J. Rzepka and Lee Horsley, West Sussex, England, Wiley-Blackwell, 2010, 403–14.

Phillips, Gene D., *Creatures of Darkness: Raymond Chandler, Detective Fiction, and Film Noir*, Lexington, University Press of Kentucky, 2000.

## NOTES

1 Frank MacShane, *The Life of Raymond Chandler* (New York, E. P. Dutton, 1976), p. ix.

2 John Tebbel, *Between Covers: The Rise and Transformation of American Book Publishing* (New York, Oxford University Press, 1987), p. 228.

3 Tebbel, *Between Covers*, p. 233.

4 Dashiell Hammett to Blanche Knopf, March 20, 1928, in Dashiell Hammett, *Selected Letters of Dashiell Hammett: 1921–1960*, ed. Richard Layman with Julie M. Rivett (Washington, D.C., Counterpoint Press, 2001), p. 47.

5 Each of Hammett's first four novels was serialized in multiple issues of *Black Mask*; the dates given mark the novels' appearance as books.

6 Tom Hiney, *Raymond Chandler: A Biography* (New York, Atlantic Monthly Press, 1997), p. 105.

7 The advertisement appeared on Christmas Eve 1938. Cited in Hiney, *Raymond Chandler*, 105.

8 Raymond Chandler to Blanche Knopf, October 22, 1942; Chandler to Blanche Knopf, October 9, 1940; Chandler to Frederick Lewis Allen, May 7, 1948; Chandler to Mrs. Robert Hogan, March 8, 1947; Chandler to Hamish Hamilton, June 17, 1949. Raymond Chandler, *Selected Letters of Raymond Chandler*, ed. Frank MacShane (New York, Columbia University Press, 1981), pp. 22–3, 18, 114, 87–8, 181.

9 Chandler, *The Big Sleep* (1939; rpt. *Raymond Chandler, Stories and Early Novels* [New York, Library of America, 1995], pp. 587–764), pp. 589, 707, 594. 636.

10 Chandler, *The High Window* (1942; rpt. *Raymond Chandler, Stories and Early Novels* [New York, Library of America, 1995], pp. 985–1177), p. 1136.

11 Chandler to George Harmon Coxe, October 17, 1939. Chandler, *Selected Letters*, p. 11.

12 Chandler, *Big Sleep*, p. 594.

13 Chandler, *Big Sleep*, pp. 686, 751, 757.

14 Sean McCann, *Gumshoe America: Hard-Boiled Crime Fiction and the Rise and Fall of New Deal Liberalism* (Durham, N.C., and London, Duke University Press, 2000), p. 140.

15 See MacShane, *Life of Raymond Chandler*, 73; and Hiney, *Raymond Chandler*, pp. 108, 111–12.

16 Hiney, *Raymond Chandler*, p. 112.

17 Chandler, *Farewell, My Lovely* (1940; rpt. *Raymond Chandler, Stories and Early Novels*, 765–984), pp. 768, 976. It is worth noting that Chandler coined the phrase "mean streets" in his 1944 essay, "The Simple Art of Murder."

18  Chandler, "Writers in Hollywood" (1945; rpt. *Raymond Chandler, Later Novels and Other Writings* [New York, Library of America, 1995], pp. 993–1003), p. 999.

19  Chandler to Hamish Hamilton, May 30, 1946 (Chandler, *Selected Letters*, p. 75). As far back as 1939, Chandler had agreed with a suggestion made in the *Los Angeles Times* that Bogart should play the part (Chandler to Alfred A. Knopf, February 19, 1939, in *Selected Letters*, p. 4).

20  W. H. Auden, "The Guilty Vicarage" (1948; rpt. in *The Dyer's Hand and Other Essays* [New York, Random House, 1962], pp. 146–58), p. 151.

21  Quoted in Hiney, *Raymond Chandler*, p. 190.

22  Chandler to Alfred A. Knopf, February 8, 1943, in Chandler, *Selected Letters*, p. 23.

23  See Joanne Dobson, "Reclaiming Sentimental Literature," *American Literature* 69.2 (1997): 263–88.

24  Chandler, *High Window*, p. 1174.

25  This paragraph draws on ideas that I advanced in *Hard-Boiled Sentimentality: The Secret History of American Crime Stories* (New York: Columbia University Press, 2009), esp. pp. 80–100.

26  Chandler, *The Long Goodbye* (1953; rpt. *Raymond Chandler, Later Novels and Other Writings* [New York, Library of America, 1995], pp. 417–734), pp. 540, 732, 733, 734.

# 18

# Ralph Ellison

DAVID YAFFE

"In the dim beginnings, before I ever thought consciously of writing, there was my own name," wrote Ralph Waldo Ellison (1913–94), "and there was, doubtless, a certain magic in it." The words were delivered at a 1964 lecture to the Library of Congress, where Ellison's copious volumes of papers would eventually find a posthumous home. The title of the lecture, "Hidden Name and Complex Fate," refers to his near-namesake Ralph Waldo Emerson and to Henry James's proposition that it "is a complex fate, being an American." [1] A dozen years after the publication of *Invisible Man* (1952), his only completed novel, Ellison could already riff on the sage of Concord and what he called the "super subtle fish fry" [2] of James's House of Fiction, knowing that he had already been canonized.

The instant classic that seemed only to expand over time – it still expands today – documents a nameless hero who, in his junior year at a black college, unwittingly seals his fate when he drives a white trustee named Mr. Norton (as in the publishing house) to a bar called the Golden Day (as in the book by the American Renaissance scholar Lewis Mumford). Through a series of misadventures that include a black sharecropper's routine about father-daughter incest, the hero is kicked out of college and sent, with a batch of poison letters of recommendation, to a man called Mr. Emerson. (The hero only gets as far as meeting Mr. Emerson's son, a bundle of neuroses.) The self-destruction is devastating, but the satire is palpable in every detail, and the hero's dialogue with Mr. Norton demonstrates the palpable irony of Ellison's hidden name and complex fate:

"You've studied Emerson, haven't you?"

"Emerson, sir?"

I was embarrassed because I hadn't. "No, sir. We haven't come to him yet." [3]

The hero would have a lot to learn, and in this novel that Ellison would later describe as "self-generating," [4] so would his readers. His reputation, it would later be said, seemed to grow with every book he did not write.

Indeed, *Invisible Man* would continue to proliferate, looking ahead to civil rights, black power, diversity, and beyond. In many ways, we are still living in a country imagined by Ralph Ellison.

All this prophecy was a product of Ralph Waldo Ellison's self-reliance. He had risen from poverty in Oklahoma City (where he was born in 1913, not 1914, as had been assumed until Lawrence Jackson's 2002 Ellison biography), one of two sons of Ida and Lewis Ellison (who named his son Ralph Waldo in the hope that he would become a poet). While on the job, Lewis Ellison was fatally pierced by a shard of ice; Ralph was only three. His mother scrambled for work, and her children were plunged into poverty and uncertainty. Nevertheless, Ida would take literary classics and copies of *Vanity Fair* home for her son, encouraging him to be a Renaissance man.

Ellison's trumpet playing earned him a scholarship to the all-black Tuskegee Institute, and, with no ride, he had to hop a freight train, where he got into enough trouble to have a bandage covering much of his forehead when he had his student picture taken. Tuskegee's founder, Booker T. Washington, had already been attacked by W.E.B. Du Bois in *The Souls of Black Folk* (1903), and Ellison would find much to skewer about Tuskegee and about Washington in particular. He entered Tuskegee with the ambition to write a great symphony by the age of twenty-six, the age of Wagner when wrote his first major work.

Although classical music kept his discipline, it was the jazz of Count Basie, Charlie Christian, Hot Lips Page, and Jimmy Rushing (all of whom either grew up in or passed through Oklahoma City) along with Louis Armstrong and Duke Ellington that reached his soul and fed his muse. He thought he could resolve these sensibilities – a version of Nietzsche's Apollo and Dionysus – as a composer, until, during his sophomore year, he perused a reserved copy of T. S. Eliot's *The Waste Land* (1922). References to Wagner's *Tristan und Isolde* (1865) permeated the text along with allusions to Shakespeare, Dante, Tennyson, and much more. His breakthrough occurred even before he could identify all the allusions, when he found the affinities between *The Waste Land* and Louis Armstrong. Just as Eliot's fragments shored him against his ruins, Louis Armstrong's full-throated references to Gershwin and Verdi while soloing on Fats Waller's "Ain't Misbehavin'" made all the archival work seem like a game. Armstrong was a modernist, too. "Somehow [*The Waste Land*'s] rhythms were often closer to those of jazz than were those of the Negro poets," he wrote, "and even though I could not understand then, its rage of allusion was as mixed and varied as that of Louis Armstrong."[5] *Invisible Man* riffs on *The Waste Land* early on. Eliot used a popular ragtime song to illustrate his modernist take on Shakespeare: "O O O O that Shakespeherian Rag." In an early description of the college, Ellison riffed on Eliot: "And oh, oh, oh, oh those multimillionaires!"[6] Although he did not realize it right away, Eliot's poem sealed his fate. Ellison did not need to write a symphony. He needed to write a novel.

And he did not need to complete his degree, either. Although he moved to New York City to earn enough money to return to school, he never left. One day after he checked into the Harlem YMCA, he noticed the poet and Harlem Renaissance lion Langston Hughes in the lobby. Ellison was only twenty-one, already brimming with literary and musical sophistication. Hughes responded by giving him two books by Andre Malraux: *Man's Fate* (1933) and *Days of Wrath* (1936). Hughes, who did not have time to read Malraux's books, instructed Ellison to read and return them with whatever commentary Ellison thought was appropriate. Malraux became central to Ellison's literary vision – much more so than the work of Hughes himself. Ellison's self-possession was unstoppable.

Even though Ellison grew up in poverty, he also grew up in Oklahoma, incorporated in 1907, the only southern state with no history of slavery. It was never like the abolitionist North, but there was a brief moment when the state was filled with freedmen, who landed there by choice. It was a cultural experiment in diversity that lasted for a little more than a dozen years – Ellison's formative years. Although the Tulsa race riots in 1921 ravaged the state and effectively turned it into part of the Jim Crow South, Ellison's confidence, even at the age of eight, had already set in. As a territory child, he had white friends and even Jewish friends, and if there were any barriers, he did what he could to eviscerate them. He certainly knew how to impress Langston Hughes and many more important writers and intellectuals along the way. If this was climbing, it was almost balletic.

Ellison ceased to ingratiate himself to Hughes as soon as he no longer needed him (and as soon as Hughes provided a blurb for *Invisible Man* without reading most of it), but before he made it that far, it was Hughes who introduced him to Richard Wright. Ellison went to New York to become a sculptor but changed his plans when he met Wright. Wright was the darling of the literary Left; his short stories in *Uncle Tom's Children* (1938) defined how African Americans were going to be key players in the class struggle, and they made him famous. But Wright's later work would make those stories seem sentimental by comparison; *Native Son* (1940) would reach a large audience – it was accepted by the Book-of-the-Month Club, with revisions – "too hard for tears," claimed Wright. It was Wright who would solicit Ellison's first publications, starting with criticism at the *New Masses* and other proletarian little magazines, and eventually fiction. Working on the musician's model of practice and mimesis – first imitating his favorites, Hemingway and Faulkner – he eventually produced his first truly original work of fiction: a short story called "King of the Bingo Game" (1944), a brutal tale of a black man who wins bingo but is beaten and deprived of his prize. What could have been a crude racial allegory is saved by his savoring the moment of his win: like Camus's Sysiphus, the protagonist has freedom for just a moment, but it is a long moment.

Ellison began *Invisible Man* in 1945, and he was already on to something beyond Wright's influence. After Wright's death, Ellison criticized *Native Son's* Bigger Thomas. "Richard Wright could imagine Bigger, but Bigger could not possibly imagine Richard Wright,"[7] wrote Ellison in 1963. While Wright's *Black Boy (American Hunger)* (1945) was a stunning memoir of how Wright became Wright, Ellison, unlike Wright, considered Negro culture as rich as any in depth, beauty, and nuance. Wright had no such optimism. In contrast to Ellison's Oklahoma, Wright was born on a plantation in Mississippi. His bitterness was hard to argue with. He had no ear for music and thought that imitating Dostoevsky and Dreiser was the most a black writer could do; his image of black America was compelling, but also hopeless, even hostile. Ellison loved the prewar jazz of his youth, and once he was diverted from music to literature, his musical obsessions remained; he just transferred them to the page. Ellison chose to fuse memoir, satire, music, allusion, and much more in *Invisible Man,* which he began as a merchant marine stationed in Vermont – as white a state as there could be – perhaps recalling a comedian at the Apollo: *My family was so black, they were invisible!* Of course, Ellison did not see racism as a laughing matter. And yet satire and humor would guide this Kunstlerroman, not editing out the tragic, but, in the spirit of Voltaire's *Candide* (1759), using the horrible as an occasion for satire, exile, and cunning. Hence one of the great opening lines in American literature: "I am an invisible man."

Nothing could prepare the literary world for the novel, which took nearly seven years to write and was published in 1952. Between the ages of thirty-one and thirty-eight, he was still callow enough to need authority figures. (The book's dedication, "To Ida," may have seemed to be a nod to his doting mother, who died in 1937. In fact, *Invisible Man* was dedicated to the socialist philanthropist Ida Guggenheimer, who gave Ellison financial support while he was writing the book but took umbrage at its unflattering portrayal of Communists.) He found guidance from the critic Stanley Edgar Hyman – who took a giant chisel to early drafts – and his Random House editor Albert Erskine, who insisted on, among other things, the famous epilogue. The prologue and epilogue give the impression of closure, even though we do not know what the hero's next move will be. Ellison was already not only a promising writer but a great one; these bookends helped him contain the wild and untamed. The year 1952 was still modernism with a hangover. *Invisible Man* riffed Louis Armstrong's recording of "(What Did I Do to Be So) Black and Blue," Jimmy Rushing's "Harvard Blues" (with its reference to Rinehart, a pimp alter ego in *Invisible Man* and another identity in later fiction), Duke Ellington's "Jack the Bear," and so on. Ellison picked up the theme of the underground from Dostoevsky and the use of italics from Faulkner, but it was the "jazz, gin, and dreams" that buzzed around his head and gave readers a Jazz Age beyond anything Fitzgerald could have imagined.

The novel begins with the narrator's telling us that his invisibility is no mere metaphor; that people see him merely for *what* he is, not *who* he is. Perhaps still remembering Wright's contention that "the Negro is America's metaphor," Ellison plays out racism on an even grander scale: invisibility is, finally, a human phenomenon. For a book published when existentialism's influence was at its peak, Ellison's seven-year climb could not have been better timed. Ellison also anticipated – two years before *Brown v. Board of Education*, before Rosa Parks and Martin Luther King Jr. were household names – that a black man's hope for power, and perhaps for the disappointment to follow, would occur through public speaking. While Ellison himself was a tentative, if elegant speaker, his nameless hero spoke like a preacher, like a musician, like an artist. In the novel's prologue, the hero lives in a basement that resembled the one in which Ellison himself typed the novel's final pages when he was working as a super in his Washington Heights apartment. As the summer heat sweltered in that un-air-conditioned cellar, the hero wishes he could hear five recordings of Louis Armstrong singing Fats Waller and Andy Razaf's "(What Did I Do to Be So) Black and Blue." He had rejected other people, but the idea and the pleasure of Armstrong's music loomed larger; perhaps he yearned for five recordings because he was already an audiophile, and he imagined a basement surround sound.

Faulknerian italics take us to reveries, to the past, to nostalgia and humiliation. Two crucial moments that follow are the early scene when he is degraded by sinister white men while giving his high school graduation speech and the way he is rewarded much later when he gives a speech while seeing an elderly couple in Harlem evicted on a winter's day. This is the moment when he would finally be heard, when he has a black crowd to back him up and a member of a Communist-like group called the Brotherhood immediately offering an apartment and an income as a professional speech maker. It seemed an injustice to be kicked out of college by the Booker T.–like Dr. Bledsoe for introducing the white trustee Mr. Norton to the black farmer Jim Trueblood and his tales of incest. Finally, he thinks, he has learned the lesson.

Except, of course, he has not. After spending the early part of the book playing by the rules and being betrayed for it, the hero finally stands up and preaches as if he had been preparing for it his whole life. When the hero notices the details of what is being thrown out – the blues records, the breast pump – he calls attention to their humanity. As he stands as a buffer between a ready to riot mob and some policemen who see the hero as someone averting a crisis, for that moment, Ellison's hero can step into the public sphere as an ad hoc community organizer. In this emotive speech, the hero uses repetition, cadence, and a rising action to keep his crowd with him. Responding to an angry "heavyweight" from the crowd just waiting to start a riot, the hero riffs the man's word, "dispossessed": "Dispossessed?.... That's a good word. 'Dispossessed'! 'Dispossessed,' eighty-seven years old and dispossessed of what? They ain't *got* nothing, they caint *get* nothing, they never *had* nothing. So who was dispossessed?"[8]

This eviction speech was the most hopeful part of a novel where the hero would quickly become co-opted. In this troubled masterpiece of identity, there is no way out. Politics enter into the picture, and his best friend in the Brotherhood is gunned down. Even when he thinks he has finally shown himself, he is invisible once more. Being mistaken for a pimp named Rinehart is a fleeting lark, but he is eventually chased into his hole by a Garvey-like thug called Ras the Destroyer. Louis Armstrong and ice cream with sloe gin along with solitude and anonymity seem preferable. And yet while the narrator famously tells us that he, on the lower frequencies, speaks for us, he also tells us that he will be coming out soon. We never have any idea what he will do.

In 1953, Ellison became the first black writer to win the National Book Award (beating Hemingway and Steinbeck), and *Invisible Man* was immediately canonized. Some reviewers in the black press were critical, and even the *Atlantic Monthly* harrumphed that Ellison was not worthy of the award against such august company. But many reviewers in the mainstream press wrote love letters. One of the early hymns of praise was from the leftist intellectual Irving Howe in the pages of the *Nation*, who characterized the novel as a "soaring and exalted record of a Negro's journey through contemporary America," proclaiming it "one of the few remarkable first novels we have had in some years."[9] Howe was on the committee that bestowed Ellison's National Book Award and so must have felt free to wage a critique against Ellison later: not for his beautiful prose, but for his alleged lack of anger. In the essay "Black Boys and Native Sons," published in *Dissent* in 1963, Howe, still enamored of *Invisible Man*'s powers, thought that he and James Baldwin were lacking in what he saw as necessary "plight and protest."

Ellison's response, "The World and the Jug," first published in the *New Leader* and later collected in *Shadow and Act* (1964), insists that it is not up to Howe or anyone else to measure his pulse; he was, in this essay, the angriest black man who ever wrote a great novel, just not angry in the way Howe had in mind. But why should it be up to Howe to tell Ellison how to feel – especially about his blackness? "One unfamiliar with what Howe stands for would get the impression that when he looks at a Negro, he sees not a human being but an abstract embodiment of living hell."[10] No one, not even a New York intellectual, could tell Ellison who he should be, and how he should represent his pain or his pleasures.

This was a battle that, for most onlookers, Ellison would win. He would, in other venues, often be thrown off stride by the increasing amount of hostility he would encounter among radicalized black students in the 1960s; being called an Uncle Tom was painful. By then, he had been working on a second novel since around 1954, and it is a great loss that Ellison did not publish a second novel in the 1960s, when his voice was most desperately needed. He wrote reams of material and eventually published eight excerpts in literary journals between 1960 and 1977. Ellison was at no loss for honors. He was a fellow at the American Academy in Rome from 1955 to 1957. He shared a house with Saul Bellow and taught at Bard and was also the Alexander White Visiting Professor at the University of Chicago; taught at Rutgers, Brown, SUNY Stony Brook, and Yale; and was, between 1970 and 1979, the Albert Schweitzer Professor of Humanities at NYU, where he mostly taught Russian novels.

He was also awarded the Presidential Medal of Freedom in 1969 was named a Chevalier de l'Ordes des Arts et Lettres by Andre Malraux in 1970. He was one of the founders of Public Broadcasting Service (PBS) and cohosted two television shows on jazz featuring Charles Mingus and Cecil Taylor. *Going to the Territory*, a second essay collection, was published in 1986. The wait for the second novel assumed epic proportions, but as the waiting game continued, *Invisible Man* stayed relevant before and after Martin Luther King and Malcolm X, Stokely Carmichael, Rodney King, and beyond. Ellison insisted that anyone who read his work knew that he was enlisted in the freedom struggle. He simply had his own way of protesting, even if it was against a world he anticipated. And although he did occasionally lecture and read from his work in progress, he spent a good part of forty years sitting in his Riverside Drive apartment, first typing manually, then electrically, then, starting in 1982, on an Osborne pc, switching to an IBM in 1988. David Remnick covered Ellison's eightieth birthday for the *New Yorker* (it was actually his eighty-first), and, when the inevitable question of his second novel came up, Ellison assured him, "There will be something very soon."[11] Within a few months, Ellison had died of a cancer that was diagnosed only weeks before his death. He left no instructions for what to do with his work in progress.

Ellison's widow, Fanny, named John Callahan as literary executor. For a work that was to have three volumes, only volume two seemed salvageable. The result, with much editorial intervention, was named *Juneteenth,* after a published excerpt, referring to a holiday when blacks in Texas, after the end of the Civil War, were informed of their freedom – nearly three years after Lincoln's Emancipation Proclamation. The heart of the novel is about a boy of indeterminate race named Bliss, who is raised by a black man, a jazz musician turned preacher named Alonzo Hickman. Bliss grows up, passes for white (his actual ethnicity is never determined, possibly because Ellison had not decided on it), and becomes a race-baiting New England senator who is shot on the Senate floor. His reunion with Hickman at his hospital bed sparks a sequence of many reveries, many of which are so gorgeously rendered that they could stand alone as prose poetry. Reviews were mixed, but this one, by John Leonard in the *Nation,* would predict the manuscript's future: "Personally, I wish Random House had published all 2,000 pages, if not on a CD-ROM, then loose in a box for readers to assemble on our own, according to our solitary need, like a Matteo Ricci Memory Palace. Structure, about which he was so finicky, be damned."[12]

This is a lovely flourish for a review, but not something that could actually exist. Ellison did not leave behind two thousand pages of linear prose. He edited obsessively, rewriting, sometimes subtly and sometimes dramatically, material originally written in the mid-1950s as late as December 1993. Ellison never had writer's block. He just could not let his manuscript go, leaving gaping holes regarding structure and content. The longest possible version of what Random House was now calling "the unfinished second novel" contained a book i and a book II, the latter more or less containing a version of *Juneteenth.* The rest of the large book contains stand-alone pieces, all of the previously published excerpts, notes, and a glimpse of a radically rewritten episode from the end of book I that he reconceived as the last piece of writing he did, months before his death. The book, published in 2010, was *Three Days before the Shooting...* (the first words of the first book), and it was now coedited by Adam Bradley, author of *Ralph Ellison in Progress,* the definitive book about Ralph Ellison's literary activities after *Invisible Man.* When the Ellison confidant Albert Murray and the *New York Times* book critic Anatole Broyard (a black man who passed for white, who named his daughter Bliss) were critical of portions they read of the work in progress, Ellison responded: "Incompletion of form allows the reader to impose his own imagination upon the material with too little control from the author. Thus I don't like to show my work until it is near completion."[13]

That completion never occurred. Yet *Three Days before the Shooting...* is the fullest post–*Invisible Man* Ellison there will ever be. Bradley's book and the editorial commentary by Callahan and Bradley explain their efforts in deciding which version, among the variora they faced, would make it into the book. Historical continuity mattered more to the editors than it did to Ellison. They followed the book from early typescripts to the computer files. For many chapters, the prose dances across the page, crackling with satire, making a reader wish that this writing could have seen print as soon as possible, especially in the 1960s, when Ellison's voice was most needed. McIntyre, a white reporter, narrates book I, and his memory of his affair with Laura, a black woman, is heartbreaking; after she becomes pregnant, he ventures to Harlem to ask her family's approval of their union, and he is sternly shown the door. Ellison's point, whether as a novelist or as a reluctant polemicist, is that we are all racially mixed, dancing with our diversity. When read aloud, there are sections of dazzling beauty, hypnotic power that at times matches prose poetry. In the twenty-first century, readers want more than just a seamless text. If an author is as phenomenal as Ellison, we want the outtakes, even if he was still weighing his options. And, of course, *Invisible Man,* for all of its stature as a Great American Novel, still ends with a famous question mark: "Who knows but that, on the lower frequencies, I speak for you?" Ellison will continue to speak for us, and those who follow and beyond. If his career leaves a circle unclosed, one should remember his namesake, who knew something about circles. Closure, said the first Ralph Waldo, is an illusion: "There are no fixtures in nature. The universe is fluid and volatile. Permanence is but a word of degrees."[14]

### FURTHER READING

Bradley, Adam, *Ralph Ellison in Progress*, New Haven, Conn., Yale University Press, 2010.

Callahan, John F. (ed.), *Ralph Ellison's Invisible Man: A Casebook*, New York, Oxford University Press, 2004.

Callahan, John F. *Trading Twelves: The Letters of Ralph Ellison and Albert Murray*, New York, Modern Library, 2000.

Ellison, Ralph, *The Collected Essays of Ralph Ellison*, ed. John Callahan, New York, Modern Library, 2003.

*Invisible Man*, New York, Random House, 1952.

*Three Days before the Shooting... The Unfinished Second Novel*, ed. John Callahan and Adam Bradley, New York, Modern Library, 2010.

Jackson, Lawrence P., *Ralph Ellison: Emergence of a Genius*, New York, John Wiley & Sons, 2002.

O'Meally, Robert G, *The Craft of Ralph Ellison*, Cambridge, Mass., Harvard University Press, 1980.

Parrish, Timothy L. *Ralph Ellison and the Genius of America*, Amherst, Mass., University of Massachussetts Press, 2012.

Posnock, Ross, *The Cambridge Companion to Ralph Ellison*, Cambridge, Cambridge University Press, 2005.

Rampersad, Arnold, *Ralph Ellison: A Biography*, New York, Alfred A. Knopf, 2007.

Sundquist, Eric J., *Cultural Contexts for Ralph Ellison's "Invisible Man,"* Boston, Bedford/St. Martin's, 1995.

## NOTES

1 Henry James, letter to Charles Eliot Norton, February 4, 1872, in *Henry James: The Imagination of Genius, A Biography*, ed. Fred Kaplan (New York, William & Morrow, 1992), p. 132.

2 Ralph Ellison, "Introduction," in *Invisible Man* (New York, Random House, 1995). Hereafter IM.

3 Ibid, p. 41.

4 Ibid, p. *xxiii*.

5 Ellison, *The Collected Essays of Ralph Ellison,* ed. John Callahan (New York, Modern Library, 1995). Hereafter CE.

6 IM, p. 37.

7 CE, p. 37.

8 IM, pp. 277–8.

9 Irving Howe, "*Invisible Man*," *Nation*, May 10, 1952.

10 CE, p. 159.

11 David Remnick, "Seeing Ralph Ellison," *New Yorker,* May 2, 1994, p. 41.

12 John Leonard, "Emancipation Proclamation," *Nation*, May 27, 1999.

13 Michael Rogin, "On the Secret Joke at the Centre of American Identity," *London Review of Books* 22.5 (March 2, 2000): pp. 12–15.

14 Ellison. "Circles," *The Literature Page*, http://www.literaturepage.com/read/emersonessays1–149.html

# 19

# J. D. Salinger

SARAH GRAHAM

Jerome David Salinger (1919–2010) is almost as famous for not publishing as he is for writing *The Catcher in the Rye* (1951), the best-known coming of age novel in American literature. His twenty-five-year career as a published author came to an end in June 1965 with the appearance of "Hapworth 16, 1924" in the *New Yorker*. From that date until his death, Salinger published nothing and went to significant lengths to ensure not only that his existing work was printed only to his exact specifications, but also that none of the stories he deemed unfit to reprint – many of those published in magazines between 1940 and 1948 – appeared in anthologies. He took legal action against the independent publishers of a collection of his early stories in 1974 and later against John David California to block the U.S. publication of *Sixty Years Later: Coming through the Rye* (2009), an unauthorized sequel to *Catcher*. These occasional acts of litigation constitute the bulk of Salinger's public appearances after 1965, even though he continued to write, telling the *New York Times* in a rare interview, "Publishing is a terrible invasion of my privacy. ... I write just for myself."[1] This comment has led to intense speculation about the fiction that might become available posthumously and has, along with the popularity of Salinger's existing work, served to keep this very private writer in the public eye.

Salinger's determined withdrawal did not spare him the attentions of the media and admirers principally because of the enduring reputation of *The Catcher in the Rye*, his only full-length novel, which has sold more than 60 million copies and been translated into many languages. Consistently attracting critical acclaim, *Catcher* features in lists of the one hundred best novels of the twentieth century compiled by the Modern Library, *Time* magazine, and National Public Radio. Its first-person narrative is utterly distinctive and rich in its evocation of the troubled teenager Holden Caulfield. Holden's informal, intimate testimony creates a strong sense of connection between him and the reader, who is addressed as "you" throughout. *Catcher* also vividly presents what was a relatively new kind of character in the years following the Second World War: the discontented adolescent rebelling against society, now an American archetype.

*Catcher* has become an iconic text, but Holden's colloquial voice and the novel's central concept – that the young can both expose and suffer from the flaws and restrictions of the adult world – have precedents in canonical American literature. Holden's account of his days on the run from school, parents, and his own impending adulthood echoes Mark Twain's *The Adventures of Huckleberry Finn* (1884/5), whose eponymous narrator resists the "sivilizing" effects of the Widow Douglas as much as Holden fears the loss of innocence that maturity brings. Just as Twain deploys Huck's naive viewpoint to critique the racial inequalities of his era, so Salinger undercuts the optimism of postwar America through a protagonist who is weary and cynical before he even comes of age. Sensing that the ease and gloss of the revitalized nation are a façade, and that the price of success is conformity to dominant norms and anxious insularity, the narrative represents a challenge to the idealization of material success that remains central to American ideology. As this suggests, another of Salinger's literary antecedents is F. Scott Fitzgerald, not only because *The Great Gatsby* (1925) similarly exposes the fault lines of wealth and the "American Dream," but also because Amory Blaine, the disaffected young hero of *This Side of Paradise* (1920), undergoes a similar fall into disillusion.

Although somewhat perturbed by *Catcher*'s success, Salinger went on to publish significant novellas and "long short stories" during the 1950s, all of them in the *New Yorker*: *Franny* (1955), *Raise High the Roof Beam, Carpenters* (1955), *Zooey* (1957), and *Seymour – an Introduction* (1959). While the short stories that Salinger published in the 1940s are preoccupied with the effects of the Second World War and consistently focus on death, the longer work considers how to live in postwar America. *Catcher*, which is deeply concerned with both literal death and the loss of self in a conformist, repressive era, thus marks a turning point in Salinger's oeuvre, as Holden is a traumatized survivor, reflecting on the events that propelled him to crisis. Repeatedly, Salinger's longer fiction suggests that American society is mired in self-serving superficiality – which Holden terms "phoniness" – and is hostile to anyone in search of greater meaning than that promised by a new house, two cars, and a job for life.

Unlike many white Americans, who were willing to settle for the consolations of postwar prosperity, Salinger's characters search for an alternative, and this quest shapes the novellas. Repeatedly, the fiction attests to the influence of childhood on adult life, the instability of identity, and the loneliness that results from feeling at odds with one's society, developing for some into an existential crisis. In the short stories and *Catcher*, children are exemplars of clear-sightedness to which adults should aspire, but they feature less often in the novellas. However, the desire for childlike purity and potential remains: the Glass stories, although typically told by and concerning the members of the family in adulthood, regularly allude to their childhood, and adults at their best are without the cynicism and guile that accompany age. The Glass family exemplifies openness to experience and a commitment to finding enlightenment that can be read as an adult, informed adaptation of a child's response to life.

The thematic coherence provided by the Glass family's shared experiences and aims is matched by consistent literary strategies across Salinger's fiction. Although renowned for its accessibility and realistic dialogue, his writing style is deceptively simple: everyday events and sympathetic characters are conveyed through intense focus on the material world, showing how the specific ways in which a protagonist dresses, smokes, or emphasizes a word reveal his or her personality and unexpressed desires. Equally, Salinger's varied use of narrative point of view – including unreliable first-person, omniscient first-person, and limited third-person – underscores the central premise of the fiction: the difficulty of locating or achieving authenticity in an increasing superficial society.

It is ironic that the popularity of *Catcher* stems in large part from the honesty with which its protagonist describes his emotions, as he is not a reliable narrator. This is not because, as Holden freely admits, he is a "terrific liar" (14) or even that he tells his story from a mental health facility, but because he cannot see how unconvincing his pseudoadult persona is to those he encounters, causing him to misread many situations.[2] While this humorously communicates his in-between position as an adolescent, it also complicates Holden's rage at the "phony" quality he sees in almost everyone around him. What makes him distinctive is not his honesty, which is in doubt, but his sincerity. The pain that Holden feels over his brother Allie's death is genuinely debilitating, and his desire to protect other children from the same fate – from either literal death, like Allie's, or a fall from innocence, like his own – is a result of grief that cannot be fully expressed. Despite the apparent fullness of Holden's narrative, this lacuna at its heart creates a compelling poignancy. For all his disclosure, Holden's crippling sense of loss and the damage it has done to him are implied by his actions and responses, and the reader's attachment to him is based as much on what he cannot reveal as what he does. "Don't ever tell anybody anything," he cautions in the novel's final lines. "If you do, you start missing everybody" (192), underscoring that his revelations have a psychological cost.

*Catcher* is not an especially long novel and Salinger's previous experience as a writer of short stories is evident throughout, as characters in each scene rarely reappear, creating a story-sequence effect. Salinger struggled with the extended form of the novel, as evidenced in his assertion that he saw himself as a "dash man, not a miler," and, although given cohesion by Holden's distinctive voice, *Catcher* has a disjointed, episodic quality that reflects his unstable perspective.[3] *Catcher* was the last of Salinger's works to feature the Caulfield family. His novellas all focus on the Glass family, principally the older brothers Seymour and Buddy, both writers and teachers, and their youngest siblings, Franny and Zooey, both actors.[4] The number of locations and characters in *Catcher* is akin to that in *Raise High the Roof Beam, Carpenters*, Buddy's account of Seymour's wedding day. Like the novel, it is a first-person narrative with comic elements, structured on a journey around New York that brings together a range of disparate figures. By contrast, *Franny*, which depicts the eponymous protagonist's emotional crisis while on a date with her boyfriend, and *Zooey*, in which Franny's brother attempts to help her recover from that crisis, together sustain an extended narrative with far fewer scenes and personalities, lending them an intensity and unity that belie the time lag between their publication dates.[5] In *Seymour – an Introduction*, Buddy attempts to capture his beloved late brother in words; as in *Catcher* and *Carpenters*, the wandering first-person narrative draws in many varied times and locations, but through the narrator's memories rather than a physical journey. The novellas, like the Glass family members, are all obviously related – sharing themes, characters, and similar techniques – yet they range from humor that borders on farce to philosophical debates and eulogy.

Salinger's writing is distinguished by narrative voices that evoke speaking rather than the written word; the rhythms of speech are evoked through patterned repetition of phrases such as "I mean" and "I don't know" and emphasized by italic: "You didn't *get* it? I mailed it on *Wednesday*."[6] The fiction is typically heavy with dialogue and light on plot exposition, offering familiar, everyday situations; extensive detail of the material world; and characters who speak idiomatically. However, the fiction also engages with complex subject matter and subtly offers access to the interiority of its characters. Even though Salinger's omniscient third-person narratives rarely comment directly on characters' thoughts, he allows insight into them through detailed descriptions of how they perform everyday acts, such as Zooey shaving without using a mirror to discourage narcissism.[7] Through unwittingly unreliable first-person narrators and the limited omniscience of third-person narrators, Salinger creates what his alter ego Buddy Glass describes as "prose home movies," suggesting texts that depict intimate scenes of family life, unsophisticated in presentation, but with the capacity to be moving and profound.[8]

*Franny* is the shortest of Salinger's late works, but it exemplifies his preoccupations and strategies. It stands alone but is most effective read as the first part of a novella, of which *Zooey* is the second. Salinger rarely allows his female characters much depth unless they are children, but Franny is an exception. Like many of Salinger's male protagonists, Franny is disillusioned with contemporary American society, a feeling that comes to a head on a date with her boyfriend, Lane. Franny's unhappiness stems in part from her dissatisfaction with Lane: "I've missed you," she tells him, and immediately realizes that "she didn't mean [it] at all" (7). More importantly, she is also discontented with her own life, which she considers as banal as that of her peers; she rejects "all the *ego*" and the craving for success ("everybody ... wants to *get* somewhere") she sees in herself and others (19–20). Franny's commitment to personal growth is evidenced through her comments on poetry, while Lane's responses exemplify his intellectual, unemotional perspective, placing him in opposition to her. Franny argues that there is a difference between poets, who "do something beautiful," and people who "write poems that get published"; Lane's exasperation with this distinction reveals that he is unmoved by the concept of art for its own sake, preferring to be a critic, a "tearer downer" (12). Thus the two characters represent opposed ways of responding to art and to experience, one aspiring to enlightenment and renewal, the other to pleasure and surface.

Since Franny constantly reiterates how "off" and "funny" she is feeling (11–13), it is easy for Lane to dismiss the implication of her comments, which is that her sense of a spiritual void has led to a religious awakening. Several of Salinger's characters are interested in alternatives to the sociable Christianity that dominated postwar America; Franny's focus is on a demanding Russian Christian text titled *The Way of a Pilgrim*, which promises "an absolutely new conception of what everything's about" through constant recitation of the "Jesus Prayer" (25). At the story's close, Franny faints. The final image of her lying still, with only her lips moving, suggests that she has taken up the prayer and is leaving Lane's world behind, fulfilling her desire to replace the corporeal and material with the metaphysical. This new way of being has a cost, however, and *Zooey* describes what happens when a distraught Franny then returns to the Glass family home and takes up permanent residence on the living-room couch with the cat.

*Zooey* maintains the theme of a quest for meaning through a depiction of an intimate relationship that recurs in Salinger's work, that between siblings. Zooey blames the intense home schooling that older brothers Seymour and Buddy provided for him and Franny as the source of the younger Glass children's maladaptation as adults to the conventional demands of postwar America: "We're *freaks*, the two of us, Franny and I," Zooey tells their mother, "and both those bastards are responsible" (68). However, the idiosyncratic Glass family that has fostered Franny's unhappy withdrawal from society now provides the answers she needs to progress. Inked on the back of the older brothers' bedroom door are extracts from texts such as the *Bhagavad Gita* and *The Gospel of Sri Ramakrishna* and quotations from writers like Epictetus, Kafka, and Tolstoy. These works challenge the ethos of the era: their foreignness counters American isolationism, and their belief systems offer alternatives to the dominant Protestantism of the time.

Taken together, *Franny* and *Zooey* raise, debate, and resolve a question central to Salinger's work: is it possible to live honorably as an artist in a spiritually impoverished society? Although claiming that Buddy and Seymour have made their siblings' lives difficult by opening them up to innumerable ways of thinking about existence, Zooey's resolution for Franny is drawn from Seymour's own teaching, emphasizing his role as both the family's spiritual leader and a symbol for wider society of new ways of thinking. When all the Glass children were appearing on the radio quiz series "It's a Wise Child," Seymour advised Zooey to shine his shoes "for the Fat Lady"; Franny remembers being told to "be funny for the Fat Lady" (130). Although the children imagined an overweight woman listening to the radio, which was enough to inculcate in them a sense of duty, Zooey now realizes that "*there isn't anyone out there who isn't Seymour's Fat Lady ... don't you know who that Fat Lady really is? ...* It's Christ himself" (131). This revelation fills Franny with "joy" and frees her from the restrictions that the Jesus Prayer imposes (131). Rather than detach herself from everything she knows in favor of a reclusive life, she can pursue her career in theater in a meaningful way by being "*God's* actress" (129). Zooey suggests that there is no need to withdraw from the world and miss the "*nice* things" to achieve spiritual depth (99), because work itself can be a sacred endeavor, especially if it is not driven by financial gain. In fact, "goddam religious action" can be found in the everyday life of the home (127). These novellas thus exemplify how Salinger explores the possibility of experiencing the extraordinary within the ordinary by engaging with the world rather than withdrawing from it.

Like *Franny* and *Zooey*, *Raise High the Roof Beam, Carpenters* (1955) focuses on the "enormous" Glass family and alludes to events described in earlier short stories that feature them, such as "A Perfect Day for Bananafish" (1948).[9] Narrated by Buddy, *Carpenters* is an account of the day that Seymour is meant to marry Muriel Fedder: when his brother fails to appear for the wedding ceremony, Buddy finds himself trapped in a limousine with some of Muriel's friends and family, all of whom, bar one very elderly man, are enraged with Seymour. After Buddy, in desperation, takes the group to the apartment he shares with his brother, it emerges that Seymour has asked

Muriel to elope, and the anger that has been directed at Buddy in Seymour's absence dissipates. *Carpenters* is one of Salinger's most humorous works, and it displays the naturalistic dialogue and deft, concise descriptions that characterize his fiction. However, the comic narrative is not *Carpenters'* only element: it also engages with Salinger's recurring theme of how best to live, which it presents through the inclusion of different types of "communication via the written word" (41), including a Taoist tale; a quotation from Sappho; a letter from the eldest Glass daughter, Boo Boo; and Seymour's diary. This mixture of texts blurs the boundary between comic and serious, connecting the spiritual and the quotidian.

Seymour's diary does more than offer an alternative perspective on him: it implicitly contends that any way of understanding experience that does not rely on modern American social conventions and Christianity risks being pathologized by others. In common with all of Salinger's later work, the difficulty and necessity of being nonconformist in a society deeply invested in normalcy are the central themes of this story. Seymour confounds conventional expectations by claiming that he is "too *happy* to get married" (25), an attitude that the commentators in the limousine take as evidence that he is "crazy" (25). In Glass family terms, however, to be happy is to be problematically agitated, since they believe that calm acceptance of existence based on spiritual enlightenment is the ideal way to live. This strongly counters the idea that happiness is achieved through the acquisition of wealth, plainly the position of those in the limousine. However, their perspective is challenged by an alternative in their midst, underscoring the theme that there is more than one way to live in fifties America. The serene "tiny elderly man" (20), who shares the limousine and never speaks, is exemplary of the kind of calm contentment to which Seymour aspires, so Buddy feels drawn to him. When it emerges that the man's tranquil acceptance of circumstance is due to his being a deaf-mute, the implication is that only by being protected from the "noise" of modernity – the resentful wedding party, materialistic boasting, the brash parade that stops the car – can transcendence be achieved. To Buddy, the man is, in a positive sense, a "blank sheet of paper" (57), a symbol of purity. Capable of communication without words, his presence helps Buddy reach a new level of understanding, as Franny did when Zooey helped her reconsider the "Fat Lady."

Like *Carpenters*, *Seymour – an Introduction* is narrated in the first person by Buddy, but the novella is complicated by the blurred boundary between Buddy and Salinger himself. Whereas in *Carpenters*, Buddy alludes to events in the Glass family that readers will recognize from other Salinger stories, in *Seymour* he lays claim to actually being their author: "I've written and published two short stories that were supposed to be directly about

Seymour," notes Buddy before summarizing *Carpenters* and "A Perfect Day for Bananafish."[10] Paradoxically, this strategy both distances Salinger from his work – by implying that someone else wrote it – and moves him overtly into the foreground of the narrative. This device highlights that *Seymour* is concerned with the difficulties of writing itself: while Buddy struggles to "introduce" Seymour (some ten years after his first appearance in print), so Salinger refers self-reflexively to the demands of creating both Buddy's voice and, through it, Seymour's life. This preoccupation with crafting fiction is confirmed by a number of aspects of the narrative, not least Buddy's parenthetical criticisms of his writing technique, "(All right, *cut that out.*)" (103) and "(the quotes are *unnecessary*)" (115), which lend the narrative a postmodern self-consciousness about its own fictionality.

In this novella, Salinger implicitly becomes a member of the Glass family, an autodidactic and self-protective unit that he celebrates for its idiosyncrasies and self-belief. Salinger makes clear the centrality of Seymour to his writing project by having Buddy focus on his brother, retrieving him from the past and from death because he has shaped the family that has survived him, itself a model of how to respond to contemporary society. *Seymour* is suffused with nostalgia: not only a longing for the past, when Buddy and Seymour were children, but also for home, a sense of belonging that is made harder to attain with the loss of Seymour and the encroachment of adulthood, a slipping away of innocence and the possibility of transcendence that reflects the spiritual depletion of the nation. The fragmentation that this causes the individual, family, and state is echoed in the novella's achronological, ruminative narrative style, which Buddy describes as a "thesaurus of undetached prefatory remarks about [Seymour]" that pay as much attention to his brother's facial features and love of sports as his wisdom and poetry (68). Buddy also condemns modern spiritually informed writers, such as those of the Beat Generation, as "the Beat and the Sloppy and the Petulant ... and Zen-killers" (62), distancing himself from a counterculture he considers inauthentic. Yet, as in *Carpenters* and *Zooey*, Buddy's story ends on a note of understanding: the struggle to represent Seymour leads him to realize that everyone is important and deserves his attention, compassion, and wisdom. Buddy's female students, whom he cannot face teaching, are, he realizes, as much his family as Franny or Boo Boo. Rather than being isolated with only memories of his brother, Buddy – like Franny, Zooey, and Holden – can learn to engage with the world and be happy after all, following the example of Seymour, who was "wild about everyone in the family and most people outside it" (114).

Salinger's final publication appeared six years after *Seymour*. "Hapworth 16, 1924" is a novella that filled an entire issue of the *New Yorker* in 1965.

It consists of a letter written home from summer camp by seven-year-old Seymour, presenting an impossibly erudite and gifted child. It combines familiar elements of Salinger's work: the focus on the Glass family, especially their childhood; the use of nonliterary narrative forms, in this instance, the letter; the evocation of a by-now-recognizable ethos that prioritizes spiritual exploration over conventional religion and materialism. "Hapworth" was not warmly received by critics, who had already responded negatively to *Seymour*, and its publication was followed by a forty-five-year silence, filled with speculation about the author, academic scrutiny of his fiction, and imitations of Salinger's style and concerns in innumerable novels and films. These traces of influence attest to Salinger's importance to American culture. While *The Catcher in the Rye* dominates his legacy, his novellas are equally rich in their literary technique and themes. As well as his ability to integrate philosophical debates into accessible fiction, the comedy he finds in interactions between people and his skill in evoking the spoken word are matchless. His preoccupation with new forms of spirituality and the challenges of living in the modern world, which echoes Emerson's desire that each generation should "enjoy an original relation to the universe" rather than rely on the beliefs of forebears, continues to resonate with readers in the twenty-first century.[11] Emerson's impassioned response to the conformity of mid-nineteenth-century America is evident in Salinger's postwar novellas in their avowals that life should be meaningful and society's edicts never passively accepted. In turn, these beliefs thread through the work of other seriously playful writers as diverse as Jack Kerouac, Thomas Pynchon, and Margaret Atwood. Despite producing a relatively small body of work, Salinger remains significant because although his work details the preoccupations of mid-twentieth-century, middle-class white America, it evokes a desire to connect with the world beyond its purview, to embrace rather than fear other ways of being.

## FURTHER READING

French, Warren, *J. D. Salinger Revisited*, Boston, G. K. Hall, 1988.

Graham, Sarah (ed.), *J. D. Salinger's* The Catcher in the Rye, Abingdon, N.Y., Routledge, 2007.

Grunwald, Henry Anatole (ed.), *Salinger: A Critical and Personal Portrait*, New York, Harper Colophon, 1962.

Hamilton, Ian, *In Search of J. D. Salinger*, London, Bloomsbury, 1998.

Laser, Marvin and Norman Fruman (eds.), *Studies in J. D. Salinger: Reviews, Essays, and Critiques of* The Catcher in the Rye *and Other Fiction*, New York, Odyssey Press, 1963.

Lundquist, James, *J. D. Salinger*, New York, Frederick Ungar, Continuum, 1979.

Salinger, Margaret, *Dream Catcher: A Memoir*, New York, Simon & Schuster, 2000.

# 20

# Patricia Highsmith

## JOAN SCHENKAR

There may be the girl waiting, the kiss in the dark, the whispered word
of promise, the sun in the park or the swans on the lake. The job for me
and the job for him and for him, the flag waving bold and free forever,
and over and over again the handsome boy meeting lovely girl and all
the lovely love pursued and captured. It might all be for the best ... but
I don't see it that way. I never will. I just don't see it that way.
Patricia Highsmith, *Cahier* 6, May 7, 1942

Let's not waste a moment. Miss Highsmith has been waiting a long time.

Patricia Highsmith (1921–95), who spent half her life outside the United
States and saw her best works corralled into categories that couldn't begin
to account for their depth, their dazzle, and their direct attack on her readers, wrote six or seven of the darkest, most delinquent novels of the last half
of the twentieth century.[1]

At least two of them, *Strangers on a Train* (1950) and *The Talented Mr.
Ripley* (1955), are masterpieces of midcentury American fiction – and in the
old-fashioned sense, too. They shed light and throw shade on the modali-
ties, manners, *moeurs*, and psyches of profoundly transgressive, specifically
American characters[2] in ways that should have staked Highsmith's claim
to a corner of literature's best back lot (strewn, now, with crumpled car-
bon paper, point-less fountain pens, and discarded typewriters) – the Great
American Novel.

Great novels about America were just what the young Pat Highsmith had
in mind when she began her ferociously productive career. In 1942, a senior
at Barnard College (where she edited the college literary magazine, acquired
a sound classical education, and developed the strength to overcome it), she
was already halfway through her sixth writer's journal: electrified with ambition, determined to explain her country to itself, certain of her success.

Leviathan![3] I should like to call my first book. It should be long and deep and
wide and high. Thick and rich, too, like America....

I should have that peculiar early twentieth century spirit.... I should answer the question why America chooses to dwell on the surface [and] leave[s] the depths unexplored and vacant.[4]

It didn't exactly work out that way. Highsmith's booby-trapped plots, double-gated psychologies, and reflective "realities" (as in Jean Genet's definition of "reality": two mirrors facing each other) channeled the American Zeitgeist through her own characteristic ambivalence and divided nature. ("Deep in my heart stands a silver sword with two edges.")[5] And they ended by bringing her acclaim as a serious novelist in every country *but* the United States. Until the beginning of this century, her place in America's consciousness was chiefly sustained by film adaptations of her first and fourth published novels, *Strangers on A Train* (Alfred Hitchcock, 1951) and *The Talented Mr. Ripley* (Anthony Minghella, 1999); her reputation was that of a cult purveyor of perverse and noirish works of "crime" and "suspense."[6]

Perverse, she certainly is – her imagination, greatly exhilarated by transgression, is a dangerous instrument – and the toxic trail of her work has added some resplendent shades of black to the palette of American Noir. (In just the sense that D. H. Lawrence meant when he assessed the Pilgrim fathers as "black, masterful men" who came over the "black sea" in a "black mood" and in a "black spirit" of revulsion).[7] But "crime" and "suspense" in their conventional meanings were never the strangest attractors in Patricia Highsmith's slow, insidious pull on the gravitational field of modern fiction. Her ability to claw comes from her explorations of the ravaged psychologies, triturated egos, and fractured identities of her murderers – not from the dull mechanics of their deeds.

An outsider artist of savage talents and obsessional interests, Highsmith invested her creative capital in the dark side of the American Dream: a shadow world of homicidal alter egos, criminal desires, subverted successes, and narratives of such shimmering negativity that they are like nothing else in their immediate literary landscapes. In the extremity of her methods (murder was always on her mind, and her fictional killings brought her a kind of relief) and in the radicalness of her effects (a close experience of her work leaves readers in considerable moral and psychological disarray), she is as unsettling a novelist as America has ever produced.

Highsmith did what the best American writers have always done: she "made it new." In the acid bath of her detail-saturated prose she developed her own image of an alternate earth, Highsmith Country: a territory where good intentions corrupt naturally and automatically, guilt often afflicts the innocent and not the culpable, hunter and prey reverse roles at a moment's notice, and life is a suffocating trap from which even her most accomplished escape artists cannot find a graceful exit.

> Guy had a horrible, an utterly horrible thought all at once, that he might ensnare Owen in the same trap that Bruno had used for him, that Owen in turn would capture another stranger who would capture another, and so on in infinite progression of the trapped and the hunted.[8]

In her afterword to the 1989 republication of her other midcentury masterpiece, *The Price of Salt* (1952) – a lesbian love story written in the richly figured language of pursuit, betrayal, and murder – Highsmith, always anxious to escape stereotype and as deft as her "hero-criminal" Tom Ripley in deflecting it, wrote: "I like to avoid labels. It is American publishers who love them."[9]

If Patricia Highsmith is anything at all, she's a *punishment* novelist, not a crime novelist; as cruel to her characters as Henry James and as relentless in their entrapments as Marcel Proust.[10]

Born on Edgar Allan Poe's birthday in 1921 in Fort Worth, Texas, Patricia Highsmith's birth (nine days after her artist mother divorced her illustrator father) was the first of many paradoxes that shadowed her intensely creative, highly destructive life. She was "legitimate" *and* "born out of wedlock," and the simultaneous occupation of both sides of every question became her modus operandi as well as the line of beauty running through much of her work.[11]

A wrenching love-hate relationship with her stylish, erratic mother, Mary Coates Plangman Highsmith, sundered Highsmith's character, haunted her life, and became the model for all the Noir bitches in her work and all the heartbreaking blondes in her life. Her feelings for her mild-mannered stepfather, Stanley Highsmith, were simpler: she wanted to kill him and said so. Guilt and shame were her default emotions; ambivalence, her organizing principle. The Patricia Highsmith who did the writing and the Pat Highsmith who lived the life, like terrible twins arising from the vapors of her youthful obsession with doubling, stalked each other for more than fifty years, forging out of their deep and necessary doubling a very profitable partnership.

At ten, she began her self-instruction in abnormal psychology (Menninger's *The Human Mind* [1930] and Krafft-Ebing's *Psychopathia Sexualis* [1886]); at twelve, she saw herself plain: "I am a walking perpetual example of my contention: as I said brilliantly at the age of twelve, a boy in a girl's body."[12] At sixteen, instead of stealing a book, she wrote a short story about a girl who steals a book. "Every artist," she said, "is in business for his health."[13] Fiction would always be for what she *wished* would happen.

At nineteen, she summed up the "ever-present subject" of her sexuality in a couplet: "I am married to my mother," / "I will never wed another."[14] And at twenty-one, her focus was fixed: "Obsessions are the only things that matter. Perversion interests me most and is my guiding darkness."[15]

Highsmith's roots in Alabama and her Texas heritage marked her prides and prejudices as deeply as her adolescent life in Greenwich Village; her early, note-taking travels across the United States and Mexico; her countless affairs with the beautiful, intelligent women who were her lovers and Muses (and with the few good men who were not); her incessant drinking; her secret seven-year career as a scriptwriter for superhero comics;[16] and her restless self-exile in Europe. She lived for love but could not live *with* it – and she killed for it, over and over again in her novels. "Murder," she wrote, "is a kind of making love, a kind of possessing."[17] A Freudian in spite of herself, she murdered her fictional victims in locations where she had made love in life. Her emotions – artistic and otherwise – followed the great divide in her psychology: they ran in opposing pairs.

Did anyone work harder than the talented Miss Highsmith? Her little train of daily accomplishments – freighted with book themes, articles, short story beginnings, observations, notebook and diary entries, and five to eight neatly typed pages of fiction – chugged steadily between the twin terminals of her self-regard and her depressions, and kept her very busy filling up its cars. And still she was afraid of not doing enough.

Along with her published works, she left 250 unpublished manuscripts of varying length, as well as 38 writer's notebooks (or *cahiers*, as she rather grandly called them) and 18 diaries in five languages – four of which she didn't actually speak. She drew, she sketched, she made sculptures.[18] She handcrafted furniture out of wood and carved out little statues. She pasted up her own Christmas and birthday cards and decorated the covers of all fourteen of her fat press books with cutouts and designs of her own devising.

Thousands of personal letters (in her peculiarly impersonal style) rolled from the platen of her favorite 1956 coffee-colored Olympia Deluxe portable typewriter – the machine on which she committed most of her fictional murders and unpicked the psychologies of her perpetrators. The Olympia got the same unsparing treatment she gave to herself.

Her pitiless self-exposures in the witness stand and judge's chair (she occupied both positions, always) of her eight thousand pages of private notebooks – slightly compromised by the ice-cold glances she darted toward posterity while making them – have preserved what is probably the longest "perp walk" in American literary history. Written in a far more direct and forthcoming voice than the low, flat, compellingly psychotic murmur she increasingly used for her fictions, the notations in these journals[19] are like tissue cultures excised from the skin of her unruly instincts and unholy feelings.

"We live on the thin ice of unexplained phenomena. Suppose our food suddenly did not digest in our stomachs. Suppose it lay like a lump of dough inside us and poisoned us."[20]

"I am four people: the Jewish intellectual, the success, the failure, and the Fascist-snob. These shall be my novel characters."[21]

"I am not interested in people, knowing them. But I am intensely interested in a woman in the dark doorway on Eleventh Street, reading with difficulty the name plates by the light of a match."[22]

"God knows love, in this room with us now, is not kisses or embraces or touches. Not even a glance or a feeling. Love is a monster between us, each of us caught in a fist."[23]

"One situation – maybe one alone – could drive me to murder: family life, togetherness."[24]

"I shall have the best, in the long run. Not a house with children, not even a permanent thing (what is permanent in life or art? ...) but the best will always be attracted to me. For this, I do, most sincerely, thank God."[25]

All the signs of her fictional style (her coroner's eye for detail; her hyper-consciousness of the way human abnormalities can be enumerated; the high optical refractions she scanned into her increasingly plain prose) and every one of its signifiers (the lists, maps, and charts that obsessed her; her adept's feel for stalking and sadomasochism; her obsessive attention to dress; her psychological difficulties with women; her preference for forged art and faked signatures; her nonnutritive relationship with food; her passion for everything doubled and for the best of everything) were rehearsed and refined in the closely written pages of these secret, concurrently kept notebooks – long before they appeared in her fictions. No American writer has more successfully concealed the ways in which her art and her life transfused each other's material than Pat Highsmith did.

Moving from country to country, drink to drink, and woman to woman in Europe (the worse her relationships went, the better she wrote, was the general rule), Highsmith aged and iced inside her cone of watchful darkness, became a literary best seller on the Continent, kept a lover's quarrel with America on the boil (but died an American citizen in Switzerland), and continued to curate her private museum of American maladies. It proved to be a rich resource for the bleakly original novels and crankishly perceptive short stories that poured out of her long, strange self-exile.

Her novels and stories splay across genres, interrogate gender, disrupt the idea of character (especially in long fictions like *Strangers on a Train*, *The Talented Mr. Ripley*, *The Blunderer* [1954], *Ripley Underground* [1970],

*Edith's Diary* [1977], *This Sweet Sickness* [1960], *Those Who Walk Away* [1967], *The Tremor of Forgery* [1969], *The Cry of the Owl* [1962] and in short ones like "The Great Cardhouse" [2002], "The Trouble with Mrs. Blynn, the Trouble with the World" [2002], "Mrs. Afton, among Thy Green Braes" [1970], "The Terrors of Basket-Weaving" [1981]), and provide as thorough an anatomy of guilt as can be found in modern literature.

The news Highsmith brought back from the ends of her nerves is never more apparent than in her first two published novels, *Strangers on a Train* (1950) and *The Price of Salt* (1952). Written from opposing sides of her psychological divide, they are the bookends to the feverishly creative period of her late twenties.

The celebrated "germ" of *Strangers on a Train* — two strangers, Guy and Bruno, who agree to exchange murders and "get away with it" – was the inspired result of a winter's walk with her mother and stepfather: the two people on earth most likely to provoke her to thoughts of homicide. Highsmith transformed her double-indemnifying nugget into what would become the essential Highsmith Situation: two men bound together by the stalker-like fixation of one upon the other, a fixation that always involves a murderous, implicitly homoerotic fantasy.

Guy Haines's moody purity and perfect relationship with his girlfriend, Anne (the first of the thinly drawn, fictional blonde beauties Highsmith would approach with a bouquet in one hand and a headsman's ax in the other), invite corruption by Charles Bruno, the subliterate, psychopathic master-mind and "unseen part" of Guy, who "waits in ambush" for him. In their tranced and mutual psychological seduction, these Terrible Twins vacate their characters at the drop of a threat, destabilize their gender as casually as they trade hats, and mingle their identities and misdirect their pursuer. The bulk of their narrative is conveyed in a writing voice cloaked (but not necessarily concealed) by another (but not exactly opposite) gender.

*The Price of Salt* takes some of the elements of *Strangers* and subdues them to the subject of requited lesbian love – the "crime" Highsmith mostly left out of her other fictions. This was a new idea for midcentury American literature. But requited love in Highsmith Country is unlike other loves in Novel Land: *Salt* glows with a luminous halo of maternal incest and a little light pedophilia; its lovemaking metaphors are weaponized (it's the only Highsmith novel without a murder in it); and its sexual consummations are spied upon, recorded, and employed as threats.

Carol Aird, *The Price of Salt*'s alluring blonde beauty – as steely-minded as any executive – keeps a gun in her glove box, turns a divorce detective's pursuit of her on its head, and has the courage and cruelty to give up her child for Therese Belivet, her jailbait-aged, artistic, and equally steely lover.

Highsmith said – who can doubt her? – that the novel came right up out of her bones. Published pseudonymously, *The Price of Salt* sold hundreds of thousands of copies and made its author uneasy all her life.

In *The Talented Mr. Ripley*,[26] Highsmith created an iconic character: the charming, deadly, murderer/forger/identity impersonator Tom Ripley, whose confusion of love with murder and whose passion for "the best" in life were Highsmith's own.

"I often had the feeling Ripley was writing it and I was merely typing,"[27] she wrote, disconcertingly, about the alter ego aspects of their first novel together – and went on to furnish Ripley's houses of fiction with the large and small irritants of her daily life.

When Highsmith gave Ripley a superhero's charmed and parentless existence, a wealthy, socially poised alter ego (Dickie Greenleaf), and a conscience-free modus operandi, she released herself from her usual subject – guilt – and launched her "hero-criminal" into his elaborate European career of identity impersonation, serious fraud, and serial killing.[28] His rewards for hard work (Highsmith was a Calvinist) were considerable: health, wealth, his own Fortress of Solitude, and the harpsichord lessons his author had always wanted for herself.

When Highsmith made impersonation, forgery, and the instability of identity the foundation of Ripley's character – and then infused her favorite sociopath with her own ruthless interpretation of the American Dream – she exposed the dark side of her country's Zeitgeist and came close to answering her youthful question about "why America chooses to dwell on the surface [and] leave[s] the depths unexplored and vacant."[29]

Like most of Highsmith's male characters – the copycat lawyer in *The Blunderer* (1954), the monied maniac in *Deep Water* (1957),[30] the spurned lover who gives a name and another life to the hidden side of his psychological split in *This Sweet Sickness* (1960), the inadvertent stalker of *The Cry of the Owl* (1962) – Tom Ripley is barely interested in sex with women. His marriage to a French heiress (her golden hair reminds him of money) includes his preference for separate bedrooms and her taste for ocean cruises with a woman friend. Highsmith is as unconscious a "gay male novelist" as Ernest Hemingway, and as gifted an anatomist of male sexual anxiety as Norman Mailer.

The deep psychological divisions Highsmith's protagonists suffer as they slip into crime and finely graduated degrees of madness – for Edith, the disintegrating wife of *Edith's Diary* (1977), it is the false journal she keeps that permits her to overlook the murder her worthless son commits; for Howard Ingam, the displaced writer in *The Tremor of Forgery* (1969), it is his destabilizing collision with another culture that allows him to kill an

Arab intruder and ignore the crime — arose from a relentless examination of her own wayward tastes: "I can't think of anything more apt to set the imagination stirring, drifting, creating, than the idea – the fact – that anyone you walk past on the pavement anywhere may be a sadist, a compulsive thief, or even a murderer."[31]

In all Highsmith's novels, and in her most accomplished short stories, there is always something wounding, something disorienting, something deeply damaging to the reader. Few authors have been so willing to bite the hand that buys them. Her slow, literary crawl over the surface of things – as indelible as a tattoo and as American as rattlesnake venom – produced hundreds of raspingly acute portraits of quietly transgressive acts. Anyone who has read even one of her works with close attention takes out citizenship papers in the country she created – and is provided with a passport that can never be revoked.

The last word should be Miss Highsmith's. Here she is in the fall of 1954, finishing *The Talented Mr. Ripley* and having her own, very special, kind of fun.

> What I predicted I would once do, I am already doing in this very book…, that is, showing the unequivocal triumph of evil over good, and rejoicing in it. I shall make my readers rejoice in it, too.[32]

## FURTHER READING

The Patricia Highsmith Papers at the Swiss Literary Archives in Berne, Switzerland. Available online. URL: http://ead.nb.admin.ch/html/highsmith.html.

Schenkar, Joan, *The Talented Miss Highsmith: The Secret Life and Serious Art of Patricia Highsmith*, New York, St. Martin's Press, 2009; New York, Picador, 2011.

All other works consulted are cited in the Endnotes. Patricia Highsmith's quotations are printed with the kind permission of Diogenes Verlag.

## NOTES

1 Highsmith's published works include twenty-two novels, nine short story collections, a children's book (illustrator), and a writer's manual.

2 Many of her protagonists are psychopathic lone killers and/or obsessional stalkers – America's *specialité de la maison*.

3 Highsmith, afraid of drowning, loved Melville's *Moby-Dick* (1851) — in which the great white whale is apostrophized as "Leviathan."

4 Cahier 6, 2/23, 1942.

5 Cahier 12, 4/6, 1945.

6 Patricia Highsmith didn't, in her own words, "take herself seriously as a suspense writer as to category." She wrote as a non-genre novelist; Dostoyevsky was her preferred comparison. Not that she eschewed the delights of crime: she never

produced a work without a crime in it; she repeatedly returned to the suggestively crooked streets of Greenwich Village for locations at which crimes could be committed in her fictions; she scoured newspapers for crimes and their per-petrators all her life and found in one journal the sneering photograph of a murderer who enriched her characterization of Charles Bruno, the psychopath of *Strangers on a Train*. Nor did she ever refuse the pleasures of suspense: it was *Ellery Queen's Mystery Magazine* that published most of her short sto-ries – although she always hoped for the *New Yorker*. In 1965, Highsmith wrote *Plotting and Writing Suspense Fiction*, a short manual for writers. It is notable for its back-of-the-matchbook prose, its insistence on the economical use of leftover scraps of emotional memory, its careful consultation of "germs" of inspiration, its focus on "formidable losses" (because "one can learn a lot from failure"), its loose definition of suspense as a story "in which the possibility of violent action, even death, is close all the time." True to form, she repudiated her definition of suspense quickly: "much of what I have said applies to writ-ing in general[;] the suspense label ... is only a handicap to the imaginations of young writers" – and added that "most of Dostoyevsky's books ... [would be considered] suspense books" by publishers today." Highsmith's writing was so linked to the facts and feelings of her life – and in this book she considers the craft of writing in such a carpenter-like way – that *Plotting* slips the bonds of its form and reassembles itself as a covert autobiography whose own suspense depends upon just which hitherto-unpublished secrets of her life the reclusive Miss Highsmith is going to reveal next.

7   D. H. Lawrence, *Studies in Classic American Literature* (New York, Viking Press, 1966), p. 5.

8   Highsmith, *Strangers on a Train* (New York, W. W. Norton, 2001), p. 270.

9   Highsmith, "Afterword," in *The Price of Salt* (Tallahassee, Fla., Naiad Press, 1993), unpaginated and dated May 24, 1989.

10   Highsmith turned Henry James's central premise for *The Ambassadors* (1903) upside down (the only way she could imagine it) and smuggled it into *The Talented Mr. Ripley*. And Marcel Proust's *The Captive & The Fugitive* (1923; 1925) provides a perfect expression of the central situation in many Highsmith fictions: "It is terrible to have the life of another person attached to one's own like a bomb which one holds in one's hands, unable to get rid of it without com-mitting a crime."

11   Highsmith attributed her lifelong ambivalence to "a very simple combination of love & hate in myself in regard to my parents [which] will finally drive me mad" (Cahier 19, 7/ 22/50).

12   Cahier 19, 7/22/50.

13   Cahier 28, 8/31/66.

14   Cahier 2, July 9, 1940.

15   Highsmith, Diary 3, Sept. 17, 1942.

16   Beginning in December of 1942 until at least 1950 – long before she was a pub-lished novelist – Patricia Highsmith wrote scripts and scenarios for America's most successful publishing industry: the comics. She created dialogue and story lines for hundreds of desperate alter egos trailing their superior selves and/ or secret identities through violently threatening terrains and luridly colored fantasies. The threatening terrain, the lurid fantasy, the desperate pursuit of alter

egos by each other is the central obsession of practically every novel Patricia Highsmith ever wrote, from *Strangers on a Train* to *The Boy Who Followed Ripley* (1980). But she worked the alter ego theme in the comics long before she worked it into her fictions, never admitting to the length of her employment or to the characters she wrote for: second-class superheroes like Black Terror, Flying Yank, The Whizzer, Pyroman, The Destroyer, Golden Arrow, etc. Virtually the only woman writing for comics during the The Golden Age of American Comics, Highsmith – like everyone else who worked in this (at the time) lowly regarded form – was ashamed of her association with comics and regarded it as "hack" work.

17 Cahier 19, 7/1/50.

18 Born left-handed, Highsmith wrote with her right hand and drew with her left hand.

19 Although the *cahiers,* begun in her midteens, were for ideas about her art, and the diaries, started at nineteen, were for narratives about her life, they tracked each other as obsessively as the alter egos in her novels.

20 Diary 2, 4/27/41.

21 Cahier 5. 9/16/41.

22 Cahier 6, 1/15/42.

23 Cahier 6, 12/17/41.

24 Cahier 31, 8/15/72.

25 Cahier 18, /27/49.

26 There were eventually five Ripley novels: Highsmith and Ripley couldn't leave each other alone.

27 Highsmith, *Plotting and Writing Suspense Fiction* (New York, St. Martin's Griffin, 1990), p. 76.

28 After he batters his *semblable*, Dickie, to death for love and a better bank account, Tom murders only when necessary.

29 Cahier 6, 2/23/42.

30 A special case, Vic Van Allen of *Deep Water,* moves out of his wife's bedroom in sexual disgust, dons an apron, cooks and vacuums, makes himself responsible for the care of his child, and – he is a completist – murders his spouse *and* two of her lovers.

31 Janet Watts, "Love and Highsmith," *Observer Magazine*, September 9, 1990.

32 Cahier 23, 10/1/54.

# 21

# Vladimir Nabokov

JULIAN W. CONNOLLY

"I am as American as April in Arizona."[1] With this affirmation in 1966, Vladimir Nabokov (1899–1977) both declared his firm allegiance to the country to which he had emigrated in May 1940 and displayed a salient feature of his verbal art: his creative approach to language and his fondness for rejuvenating dead clichés ("American as apple pie"). Yet he also declared in 1966 that "the writer's art is his real passport" (*SO*, 63), and one senses that as he matured as a writer of English-language fiction, Nabokov sought to promote a synthesis of the best of Russian, European, and Anglo-American literary traditions. Indeed, in answering a question about national identity in 1964, Nabokov touched upon the many places he had lived (and the many cultures he had experienced): "I am an American writer, born in Russia and educated in England where I studied French literature, before spending fifteen years in Germany" (*SO*, 26). In his best work he combines vividly observed details about personalities and settings with allusive references to a range of literary material, from medieval Russian epics to French symbolism to the latest manifestations of popular culture.

Nabokov had been a leading figure in the Russian émigré literary community (having published eight novels, more than forty short stories, and dozens of poems) when he arrived in the United States. Now he was faced both with the daunting prospect of reinventing himself as a writer in English and the more immediate task of trying to support himself, his wife, and his young son in a new country. Initially, he had to rely on charity and on private language instruction. Over time, he began publishing book reviews in the *New Republic* and short stories and poems in the *Atlantic Monthly*. He taught summer courses at Stanford in 1941 and obtained a part-time position as a lecturer at Wellesley College that eventually became a full-time position, with courses on literature and on the Russian language. He also worked at the Museum of Comparative Zoology at Harvard University, researching and cataloging butterflies.

The early 1940s were a time of firsts for Nabokov: his first poem to be published in the *New Yorker* ("A Literary Dinner," April 6, 1942); his first short story written in English, "The Assistant Producer" (*Atlantic Monthly*, May 1943); and most significantly, his first English-language novel, *The Real Life of Sebastian Knight* (1941). Already aware in the late 1930s that prospects for maintaining a viable career as a Russian-language writer were waning, Nabokov had decided to try writing fiction in English. He composed the novel in late 1938 and early 1939 while still living in France, but the book awaited Nabokov's arrival in America to find a publisher. Nabokov had learned English as a child and had become proficient in the language while at Cambridge, but the task of composing an original novel in English was nonetheless challenging. He chose as his topic favorite themes: the creative life of a writer and the problem of composing a biography uncontaminated with the biographer's own projections. V, the narrator of the novel, seeks to retrace the life of his half brother, the writer Sebastian Knight, who had an English mother and a Russian father. This quest leads him into experiences that surprisingly overlap and interlace with his brother's prior experiences. Eventually V believes that Sebastian's spirit is guiding his quest and that he has come to know Sebastian's soul so well that he seems to merge with Sebastian: "I am Sebastian, or Sebastian is I, or perhaps we both are someone whom neither of us knows."[2] Nabokov's first effort at an English-language novel shows remarkable complexity and subtlety, and it hints at the prominence of certain elements in his later work, including the plight of the gifted individual adrift in an alien environment and the magic of multilingual virtuosity.

Nabokov's second English-language novel, and his first to be composed in America, conveys a very different mood. *Bend Sinister*, published in 1947, reflects the oppressive strains of twentieth-century totalitarianism. Set in an imaginary country with features reminiscent of Nazi Germany and Stalinist Russia, the novel centers on the perceptions of a philosopher named Adam Krug, who is overwhelmed by the recent death of his beloved wife, Olga. Blinded by his grief, Krug fails to comprehend the tide of tyranny rising around him as the Party of the Average Man, led by Krug's old schoolmate Paduk, tightens its grip on the land. It is only when Paduk, in an effort to secure Krug's endorsement for his policies, seizes Krug's son, David, that Krug begins to acknowledge what is truly transpiring. Now ready to sign any document to save his son, Krug is horrified to learn that his son has been killed in an experiment the regime conducted with violent criminals. Krug goes numb with shock, and the narrator-creator of the novel spares Krug from further pain by sliding toward him in his prison cell along a beam of pale light, "causing instantaneous madness" but saving him "from the senseless agony of his senseless fate."[3] The narrator subsequently rescues Krug from imminent death by getting up from his writing desk to investigate the sound of a moth hitting a window screen. With this metafictional twist, Nabokov advocates for the power of the individual creative consciousness and the importance of pity in the face of blunt tyranny. Still, the very style of *Bend Sinister* reflects Krug's predicament as it evinces a sense of exhaustion, almost as if its narrative consciousness is too tired or distraught to provide complete descriptions or maintain a consistent tone.

Unable to secure a permanent position at Wellesley, Nabokov moved to Ithaca, New York, in July 1948, to begin a teaching career at Cornell University. In the same year, the *New Yorker* published "Symbols and Signs," one of the best short stories Nabokov wrote in English (and better known under its original title, "Signs and Symbols"). The story provides a haunting depiction of an elderly émigré couple's anxiety over the fate of their son, a young man institutionalized in a mental hospital because of "referential mania," the belief that everything in his environment contains "a veiled reference to his personality and existence."[4] The story itself is replete with images that lead the reader to imagine the boy's destiny: will he succeed in his attempts at suicide, or will his parents save him? This story, along with "The Vane Sisters" (written in 1951 and published in 1958), stands as one of the finest examples of Nabokov's short American fiction. The latter tale is also richly allusive, and its ending contains a message that is often missed by the first-time reader: the first letters of the words in the final paragraph form an acrostic transmitting a communication from one of the dead sisters to the self-centered and uncomprehending narrator.

In 1951, Nabokov published the first version of his autobiographical memoir. Originally entitled *Conclusive Evidence*, the work was translated into Russian, expanded, and published in 1954 under the title *Drugie berega* [Other Shores]. Nabokov then revised the memoir once again and published it anew as *Speak, Memory* in January 1967. Focusing on his childhood and youth, and to a lesser degree on his experiences in Western Europe, the memoir offers a highly lyrical treatment of Nabokov's growing enchantment with the surrounding world. Treating his life somewhat as a literary work, the writer identifies and traces "themes" in his past, and the reader senses the author's desire to overcome the limitations of linear time with its inevitable losses.

While teaching at Cornell, Nabokov also began working on what would turn out to be his most famous novel – *Lolita* (1955). Originally entitled *The Kingdom by the Sea*, this account of a thirty-seven-year-old man's obsession with a twelve-year-old girl forms one of the most compelling novels of the twentieth century. In many respects, this is Nabokov's most "American" novel, and he conducted extensive research in preparation for its creation. As he was to write in his essay "On a Book Entitled *Lolita*," it had taken him forty years to "invent" Russia and Western Europe, and now he was "faced with the task of inventing America."[5] He studied such things as the physical development and speech patterns of pubescent girls, the workings of American handguns, and the titles of popular music recordings, and he added to this his own vivid observations of the realia of American life gathered while on his summertime trips across the United States in search of rare butterflies and invigorating landscapes. At times he felt the task to be so daunting that he despaired of its success, and his wife, Véra, had to intervene to prevent him from burning the manuscript in their backyard incinerator.

Finally, however, the work was complete, and Nabokov tried to find a publisher who would take it on. Rebuffed by five American publishers, Nabokov turned to a French agent to see whether the work could be published abroad. The agent found Maurice Girodias, the owner of Olympia Press, who gladly accepted the assignment. Unbeknown to Nabokov, among the works Girodias published were pornographic novels for English-speaking travelers. Girodias saw no problem with *Lolita*, and the novel appeared in two volumes in 1955. It might well have languished in obscurity were it not for the fact that Graham Greene proclaimed it one of the best books of the year in the Christmas edition of the London *Sunday Times*. This in turn provoked a harsh rebuttal in the London press by one John Gordon, and a spirited controversy soon erupted. Publishers in the United States grew interested, and *Lolita* was finally published in New York in August 1958. Within a month, it had reached the top of the best-seller list, and it remained there for seven weeks.

*Lolita* presents an extraordinary blend of lyricism, humor, and pulsing pathos. The narrator, who calls himself "Humbert Humbert," is an urbane, witty European, whose breezy chatter has often seduced readers into finding him a sympathetic and even "touching" figure (*SO*, 94). Humbert is profuse and eloquent in his profession of love for Dolly (as in the famous opening phrase: "Lolita, light of my life" [*Lo*, 9]), and he is scathing in his criticism of those he regards as standing between him and the girl, including her mother, Charlotte. Yet those readers who may find themselves momentarily charmed by a clever turn of phrase or sharp observation then become dismayed when they realize they have been sympathizing with a man who has subjected a defenseless girl to a relentless regime of physical and mental abuse. This realization arises in moments of penetrating lucidity (for Humbert and the reader alike), such as when Humbert summarizes the tenor of his first cross-country trip with Dolly: "And I catch myself thinking today that our long journey had only defiled with a sinuous trail of slime the lovely, trustful, dreamy, enormous country that by then ... was no more to us than a collection of dog-eared maps, ruined tour books ... and her sobs in the night – every night, every night – the moment I feigned sleep" (*Lo*, 176).

The critical reaction to the novel has been extensive and varied. Many early critics sided with Humbert and took a dim view of Dolly Haze (Dorothy Parker, for one, called Dolly "a dreadful little creature, selfish, hard, vulgar, and foul-tempered").[6] Indeed, the very term "nymphet" that Humbert uses to describe girls he is attracted to has come to mean in popular usage a sexually precocious and provocative girl. Yet later critics challenged this view and began to see in Dolly a plucky child striving mightily to establish a semblance of normalcy in a life that has been anything but normal. Critics have also debated the moral tenor of Nabokov's novel. Citing Nabokov's assertion in "On a Book Entitled *Lolita*" that *Lolita* "has no moral in tow" (*Lo*, 314), some have readily concluded that the novel is amoral, if not downright immoral. Yet in the same passage Nabokov writes that for him, a work of fiction exists only insofar as it affords him what he calls "aesthetic bliss, that is a sense of being somehow, somewhere connected with other states of being where art (curiosity, tenderness, kindness, ecstasy) is the norm" (*Lo*, 314–15). One should note that two of the qualities associated with "art" are tenderness and kindness, and these qualities have, in Nabokov's creative world, a definite ethical and moral content. Nabokov does not deny the importance of morality in art; he simply rejects works that preach to their readership, proffering an easily detachable moral message. In fact, *Lolita* is a highly moral piece of fiction in that every page confronts the reader with moral and ethical issues that the reader, as well as Humbert, may ponder.

In addition to debating the issue of morality in *Lolita*, some critics perceived that Humbert's acerbic depiction of American mores implied that his creator held a condescending view of his adopted country as well. Nabokov strenuously objected to this conclusion. Addressing the question of whether *Lolita* is "un-American," Nabokov lamented: "This is something that pains me considerably more than the idiotic accusation of immorality.... Humbert is a foreigner and an anarchist, and there are many things, besides nymphets, in which I disagree with him" (*Lo*, 315).

The significant disparity between the narrator's and the author's perspectives in *Lolita* also plays an important role in Nabokov's next novel, *Pnin*. Several chapters of *Pnin* were published in the *New Yorker* from 1953 to 1955, but the full version of the novel only appeared in 1957. *Pnin* may well be Nabokov's most "accessible" English-language novel, and it focuses on the travails of a Russian émigré trying to secure a permanent position as an instructor at "Waindell College." One of Nabokov's most endearing creations, Pnin appears to be comically inept in his efforts at coping with his environment. Although the narrator of the novel (who remains in the background for most of the tale) seems to be trying to depict Pnin as a figure of fun, the sensitive reader recognizes that Pnin possesses an enormous capacity for tenderness and compassion – for a stray dog, a thirsty squirrel, and other peoples' suffering. Pnin's own attempts to find security in the present are highlighted by the reader's awareness of the losses he has suffered in the past, including the gruesome death of an early love, Mira Belochkin, in a Nazi extermination camp. Yet Nabokov's treatment of the character suggests that Pnin's life has been touched by something akin to magic, particularly after the visit of Victor Wind, the son of Pnin's ex-wife, Liza. In the final chapter of the novel, the narrator suddenly emerges in the foreground, arriving at Waindell to take up a teaching position that Pnin can never attain. It turns out that the narrator was Liza's lover before she married Pnin, and although the narrator wishes to make contact with Pnin, the latter escapes the narrator's reach, and at the end of the novel, Pnin is shown driving off along a shiny road "where there was simply no saying what miracle might happen."[7]

Pnin resurfaces as a minor (and less attractive) character in Nabokov's next novel, *Pale Fire* (1962). With this novel, Nabokov moves further into multinational or transnational literary terrain. The novel ostensibly focuses on a long narrative poem by an American poet, John Shade, and it includes a commentary written by Shade's neighbor, Charles Kinbote. Kinbote's commentary, however, comes to dominate the novel. Over the course of the commentary, Kinbote transforms Shade's poem, with its delicate meditations on death and on the loss of his daughter, Hazel, to suicide, into a coded depiction of the fabulous kingdom of Zembla (whose language combines Slavic and Germanic elements), the deposed king of which, the reader soon surmises, is none other than Kinbote himself.

The situation in which a voluble commentator appropriates for his own purposes the narrative poem for which he is supposed to be providing scholarly commentary surely reflects a parodic version of Nabokov's own experience providing a translation of and multivolume commentary on one of Russian literature's greatest achievements – Alexander Pushkin's novel in verse *Eugene Onegin* (the four-volume Nabokov edition appeared in 1964). Yet the novel also touches upon some of Nabokov's most cherished themes, such as the question of whether the life of an individual comes to an end with death, or whether something of the individual spirit survives, perhaps to overcome time and space and the loss of life, loved ones, and homeland.

At first glance, Kinbote's odd ramblings seem to have little relation to Shade's carefully constructed poem, but as one reads the poem and commentary more closely, numerous interconnections and points of contact swim into view. These links have led some commentators to identify one or the other of the two main figures as the creator of the other, and indeed, standing behind the figure of Charles Kinbote seems to be another character, a professor named V. Botkin. (Behind them all, of course, stands Vladimir Nabokov.) The involuted, self-referential nature of the work would seem to make it a prime example of literary postmodernism: at first glance it would appear that all signs point not to some "reality" we can comprehend outside the text, but only to the text itself, or perhaps to the consciousness that generates the text. Yet this is not a sterile exercise in idle pattern making. Shade's quest to probe the mystery of death has an impressive depth and urgency, and Brian Boyd has argued that evidence planted in the novel suggests that the spirit of Hazel Shade lives on after her death, helping inspire Shade's poem and Kinbote's Zemblan fantasies.[8]

The tremendous commercial success of *Lolita* and the ensuing rediscovery and republication of Nabokov's earlier work, now in English translation, meant that Nabokov could resign his teaching position and devote himself to literary activities full time. He and Véra moved to Europe to be closer to their son, who was pursuing a career as an opera singer, as well as to other family members. Though he fully intended to return to the United States, Nabokov eventually took up residence in the Montreux Palace Hotel in Montreux, Switzerland, where he continued to write, check translations and galley proofs, and receive a steady stream of interviewers and admirers. While still in Ithaca Nabokov had begun work on what would ultimately become his longest novel, *Ada or Ardor: A Family Chronicle* (1969), but the novel only sprang into life after he had moved to Montreux.

*Ada* combines a philosophical treatise on the nature of time with an elaborate story of an obsessive love between two precocious children, Van and Ada Veen, who discover that they are not cousins, but brother and sister. The form of the novel is a memoir written primarily by Van with assistance from Ada in their declining years. The memoir evokes an Edenic summer of first infatuation with the pains of jealousy and separation that followed in later years. Reunited in middle age, Van and Ada revel in their recovery of the enchanted past. Yet they are also aware that their bliss has come at a heavy cost. Their half sister Lucette, who witnessed their early love and then become infatuated with Van herself, was overstimulated by their romance but continually rebuffed in her efforts to partake of its charm by becoming Van's lover too. Eventually, her frustration led her to suicide. Thus, Van's joyful memoir is at the same time permeated with a sense of Lucette's loss.

The novel is set in a strange world called Demonia or Antiterra, which has affinities with our world but which displays an odd mixture of Russian and North American history and topography. Some inhabitants of this world believe in an alternate world called "Terra the Fair," which seems more like the world inhabited by the novel's readers, and some readers have questioned whether Antiterra is actually Van's own creation. *Ada* reflects the increasing transnationalism of Nabokov's art, and the demands it makes on a trilingual reader who can cope with allusions to at least three literatures, English, French, and Russian (it opens with a parodic distortion of Tolstoy's *Anna Karenina* [1877]) have both intrigued and tantalized Nabokov's readers.

As Nabokov's life neared its end he went on to complete two more novels, *Transparent Things* (1972) and *Look at the Harlequins!* (1974), and he began work on an unfinished novel entitled *The Original of Laura*. *Transparent Things* again spans continents and countries. An awkward American literary editor named Hugh Person visits a writer in Switzerland and falls in love with a shallow woman named Armande. Although he succeeds in marrying her, his quest for happiness comes to naught when he strangles her during a nightmare in a misguided attempt to rescue her from an imagined fire. Years later, his own life flickers out when he tries to retrace the steps of his early relationship with Armande and dies in a real hotel fire. In the novel's final lines, however, Hugh is helped over the threshold of death by the ghost of the writer Mr. R, who turns out to be the narrator of the entire text, and Nabokov again indicates that not all ends with corporeal life. In that otherworld, humans have the opportunity to transcend the limitations of time and space and to roam unfettered across countries and consciousnesses alike.

In *Look at the Harlequins!* Nabokov provides an odd reworking of *Speak, Memory*. He creates a parodic alter ego named Vadim Vadimych N, who is the author of such works as *Tamara* (cf. *Mary*), *Camera Lucida* (translated as *Slaughter in the Sun*; cf. *Kamera obskura*, translated as *Laughter in the Dark*), and *Kingdom by the Sea* (*Lolita*). This VV is desperately unlucky in love and marriage (as the novel begins, he cannot recall whether he had three or four wives in succession), but by the end of his narrative, he has found a woman who provides him true love and support. He addresses her simply as "you," just as Nabokov had addressed Véra in *Speak, Memory*. Nabokov's final, unfinished work, *The Original of Laura*, offers only hints of what it might have become, but once more it features an unhappy marriage and a self-absorbed philosopher who tries to transcend the humiliation of his corporeal existence by erasing himself through a mental exercise. One card on which Nabokov's notes for the novel were written simply lists appropriate synonyms: "efface," "expunge," "erase," "delete," "rub out," "wipe out," "obliterate."[9]

By the time of his death in 1977, Nabokov was already recognized as one of the major American writers of the twentieth century, and his reputation has only grown since then. A master stylist, an exquisite observer of human behavior, and a suggestive thinker about the joys, sorrows, and possibilities of human existence, Nabokov earned the praise of numerous modern writers, from John Updike to Joyce Carol Oates and Zadie Smith. What is more, his work has had a palpable impact on subsequent generations of American and international authors, including Thomas Pynchon, W. G. Sebald, Michael Chabon, and Orhan Pamuk. This remarkable Russian-born writer has earned a distinctive place in the pantheon of American literature.

## FURTHER READING

Alexandrov, Vladimir E. (ed.), *The Garland Companion to Vladimir Nabokov*, Garland Reference Library of the Humanities 1474, New York, Garland, 1995.

Barabtarlo, Gennadi, *Phantom of Fact: A Guide to Nabokov's* Pnin, Ann Arbor, Mich., Ardis, 1989.

Boyd, Brian, *Nabokov's Ada: The Place of Consciousness*, 2nd ed., Christchurch, Cybereditions, 2001.

*Vladimir Nabokov: The American Years*, Princeton, N.J., Princeton University Press, 1991.

*Vladimir Nabokov: The Russian Years*, Princeton, N.J., Princeton University Press, 1990.

Connolly, Julian W., *A Reader's Guide to Nabokov's "Lolita,"* Boston, Academic Studies Press, 2009.

Connolly, Julian W. (ed.), *The Cambridge Companion to Nabokov*, Cambridge, Cambridge University Press, 2005.

De La Durantaye, Leland, *Style Is Matter: The Moral Art of Vladimir Nabokov*, Ithaca, N.Y., Cornell University Press, 2007.

Kuzmanovich, Zoran and Galya Diment (eds.), *Approaches to Teaching* Lolita, New York, Modern Language Association, 2008.

Nabokov, Vladimir, *Lectures on Literature*, ed. Fredson Bowers, New York, Harcourt Brace Jovanovich/Bruccoli Clark, 1980.

Pifer, Ellen, *Nabokov and the Novel*, Cambridge, Mass., Harvard University Press, 1980.

*Vladimir Nabokov's* Lolita: *A Casebook*, Oxford, Oxford University Press, 2003.

Wood, Michael, *The Magician's Doubts: Nabokov and the Risks of Fiction*, Princeton, N.J., Princeton University Press, 1995.

## NOTES

1 Vladimir Nabokov, *Strong Opinions* (New York, Vintage International, 1990), p. 98. Hereafter *SO*.
2 Nabokov, *The Real Life of Sebastian Knight* (New York, Vintage International, 1992), p. 203.

Kerouac's journal entry would prove prescient. Despite receiving a favorable review by Gilbert Millstein in the *New York Times*, *On the Road* and Kerouac himself were quickly recontextualized as advocates of a wide range of subversive countercultural practices and un-American activities because of the novel's thematic content. As reasons to exclude *On the Road* (and his subsequent novels) from consideration as a serious work of literary fiction, critics cited Kerouac's frank depictions of nonnormative sexuality and drug use; his characters' seeming disillusionment with the workaday world and its catalyst, the American Dream; and also the author's affiliation with Allen Ginsberg, whose collection *Howl and Other Poems* (1956) was embroiled in an obscenity trial that would not conclude until October 1957. Although Kerouac would later publish several essays attempting to redefine the Beat Generation – the name of the literary movement that included Kerouac, Ginsberg, William S. Burroughs, Gregory Corso, and others – the media-dubbed "King of the Beats" could not convince a skeptical public that the term implied "no hoodlumism" but instead signified a particular postwar historical moment that had already passed by the time the term was popularized in John Clellon Holmes's article for the *New York Times Magazine*, "This Is the Beat Generation," on November 16, 1952 (*GB*, 48–51).[2]

Pilloried by the mainstream press, Kerouac correctly anticipated an attack from within the literary community as well. When asked for his opinion of *On the Road*, Truman Capote famously said, "That isn't writing at all. It's typing."[3] A guest with Norman Mailer on David Susskind's television program *Open End* in 1959, Capote was responding both to the myth of Kerouac's method of composition and to the narrative style of the novel: it was believed that Kerouac had conceived and written *On the Road* over three weeks in April 1951 and published it without making any significant corrections, a myth Kerouac himself helped perpetuate in various print and television interviews (*GB*, 62).[4] Allowing that Kerouac did begin and complete the first full draft of the novel during that time – a single-spaced, single-paragraphed text typewritten on a handmade "scroll" of semitranslucent paper measuring 120 feet – scholars such as Howard Cunnell and Matt Theado convincingly argue that the received wisdom is patently false, drawing their conclusions from various archival notes and prose experiments that show him working on the road novel long before and after drafting the scroll manuscript.[5] Further, a skeptical reader need only compare the novel as published and the text of *On the Road: The Original Scroll* (2007) to understand *On the Road* as the product of sustained artistic endeavor. Kerouac entered mainstream literary culture at a particularly inauspicious era of literary criticism for his emerging narratological style, a time that situated the literary work as a self-contained, self-referential aesthetic object that could be understood primarily through the practice of close reading. Believing that the new postwar subjectivity, understood as fragmented and indeterminate, could not be effectively narrated through formal conventions codified before World War II, the spread of totalitarianism, and the technological threat to embodied subjectivity inherent in the atomic bomb, Kerouac was one of many artists who believed that literary form and the historicopolitical moment were mutually constituting. He claimed that his art could help shape the development of his historical moment and that as a writer his "mission [was] to present Beauty to the Collectivists, and in turn, introduce the men of Beauty to Collectivism."[6] While he does not identify specific "men of Beauty" by name, one might presume that he means the entrenched class of literary critics who Kerouac claims to "loathe" (*LVI*, 42).

Kerouac's reputation as a novelist has always contended with his characterization as a subversive, the persistence of *On the Road*'s creation myth and its implications concerning his seriousness, and critical neglect, lingering inflections that have rendered Kerouac not a famous literary artist, but an infamous celebrity, a middle-aged *enfant terrible* whose personal shortcomings are often cited as grounds to foreclose discussion of his contribution to the American novel. Now, as in Kerouac's time, corrective interpretations of his work are often discounted by detractors as subjective misreadings that speak more forcefully about their authors' inability to step outside their own positionalities than about the novels themselves.[7] Because of the nature of his exclusion from the critical conversation, Kerouac's early supporters had to pitch his novels in a mode akin to boosterism, hybridizing analysis with public relations, inadvertently affirming the primacy of his personality even as they reposition his texts as objects for critical scrutiny. Such divergent perceptions limn the aesthetic field in which Kerouac's work continues to be contested.

Kerouac imagined his collected novels as a cohesive whole he called the Duluoz Legend, "one enormous comedy" narrated by Jack Duluoz, whose surname nods gratefully toward James Joyce's Stephen Dedalus (*VoC*, foreword).[8] The legend is capacious: if *The Town and the City* demonstrates Kerouac's homage to romantic autobiographical fiction in the mode of Thomas Wolfe, Kerouac's sixteen subsequent novels reveal his appropriation and reimagining of modernist stream-of-consciousness narratology across a variety of generic categories. One might read the Duluoz Legend as a chronological series of romans à clef beginning with *Visions of Gerard* (written 1956, published 1963), Kerouac's appropriation of the sentimental novel in which five-year-old Jackie Duluoz narrates the death of his nine-year-old brother Gerard, and concluding with *Satori in Paris* (1965), the travelogue of an adult Duluoz who journeys to France and Brittany in search of genealogical records of lost familial roots. As such, the legend might be understood as a collective bildungsroman in which thematic pre-occupations emerge and develop diachronically as the first-person narrator grows from childhood to middle age.

The most significant thematic continuity in Kerouac's Duluoz Legend novels is, perhaps, the deeply divided protagonist's attempt to forge a coher-ent, legible self from seemingly heterogeneous beliefs and practices within a disaggregating society.[9] Kerouac's protagonists are invariably dashed against the rocks of an unknowable internal coast, a liminal space where the multiplicity of possibilities for one's personality refuses to adhere into a unified identity knowable to either the reader or the protagonist. One sees such a pattern emerge when Dean Moriarty and Carlo Marx evenly divide Paradise's photo-booth picture in *On the Road;* when Japhy Ryder triumphantly summits Matterhorn, Henry Morley triumphantly lounges below, and Ray Smith dejectedly clings to the mountain face in terror in *The Dharma Bums* (written 1957–8, published 1958); and when "chimerical" Leo Percepied of *The Subterraneans*(written 1953, published 1958) fails to reconcile his writerly life at home with his mother and his erotic life with his partner, Mardou: semiautobiographical protagonists find themselves caught between paradigms of their own devising, whether Duluoz calls it "guts against brains" (*DA*, 114) or Paradise designates it "a war with social overtones" between his middle-class friends and the "new beat generation that [he] was slowly joining" (*OTR*, 54).[10] Significantly, the Duluoz Legend concludes (chronologically) with *Satori in Paris*, a novella in which Kerouac travels first to Paris and then to Brittany with the intent to know himself through genealogical records, yet he ultimately realizes that any attempt to render himself legible through library research is itself "worthless unless you can find the actual family monuments in fields" (*SP*, 34).[11] One must, he suggests, incorporate both guts and brains to know one's self, an embodied subjectivity his protagonists cannot maintain for long amid the centrifugal tug and pull of multiple cultural institutions.

In his first two published novels, Kerouac uses his fictional character-izations – the ambiguously ethnic Martins and Paradises, respectively – to sublimate his own cultural uncertainties, and in each representation of Americanness, the discontinuities suggest the difficulty of performing another self as authentic. In his representations of identity formations, Kerouac pri-marily draws upon his own subject positionality as a subordinated ethnic French Canadian in New England, yet critics often describe his protago-nists as engaging in the institutionalized privileges afforded white men in the United States.[12] Born to the first-generation French-Canadian immigrants

Leo and Gabrielle on March 12, 1922, in the Massachusetts mill town of Lowell, Jean-Louis "Jack" Kerouac – the youngest of three children – attended French-Canadian schools and worshipped in French-Canadian Catholic churches. Until he was six years old he exclusively spoke *joual*, a Québécois dialect of French considered a marker of lower-class identity because of its difference from formal, Parisian French.[13] Derogatorily dubbed "Canucks" or referred to as *les blancnègres*, "white niggers," or "dumb Frenchmen" by Anglos in New England, Kerouac's white-ethnic community was routinely subjected to discrimination and bias.[14] In a letter to a French-Canadian reviewer of *The Town and the City*, Kerouac admits that he "has no native home any more, and [is] amazed by that horrible homelessness all French-Canadians abroad in America have" (*LVI*, 228). Such psychic homelessness, he further explains, led him toward "'Englishizing [himself]'" in high school, his term for attempting to pass ethnically and socioeconomically with his affluent peers: he sold term papers to fellow Horace Mann School for Boys students in order to finance trips downtown with them (*LVI*, 229). Continuing to inhabit a liminal, third space between two identities in which he never feels truly at home, Kerouac contends that it is "true that French-Canadians hide their real sources. They can do it because they look Anglo-Saxon," a type of masquerade Kerouac dramatizes in his early fiction (*LVI*, 229). While Kerouac's experiences as a marginalized, white ethnic subject neither excuse nor justify racist and sexist representations in his texts – Leo Percepied's exoticization of Mardou's genitalia bespeaking a troubling racist essentialism in *The Subterraneans*, for example – his phenomenological awareness of performative identity foregrounds a more nuanced understanding of systemic oppression than the traditional, default binary by which his work is often judged. In *On the Road*, for example, an Okie family of cotton pickers beats a Mexican male in the migrant workers camp, and the narrator, Sal Paradise, claims, "From then on I carried a big stick with me in the tent in case they got the idea we Mexicans were fouling their trailer camp. They thought I was a Mexican, of course; and in a way I am" (*OTR*, 98).[15] While it is possible to dismiss Sal's self-identification with Mexican culture as based upon romantic, essentialist assumptions about race and ethnicity, representation of ethnic identity in this case may offer a different perspective when triangulated with Kerouac's own positionality and contemporary theoretical lenses such as Richard Rodriguez's browning of America or José Esteban Muñoz's disidentification. In subsequent novels, however, Kerouac grants some protagonists a French-Canadian heritage, and he even begins to compose some drafts in French, attempting to parlay formally experimental narratology into the successful articulation of a coherent identity.

Framing Kerouac's work in the context of the Duluoz Legend, however, reveals several limitations. How does one account for novels with different points of view, such as *The Town and the City*, or for Pictorial Review Jackson, the ten-year-old black, southern protagonist of *Pic* (written 1951 and 1969, published 1971), whose subject position does not easily fit among the other, more homogeneous narrators within the legend? Even as these qualities mark disruptions, they coalesce around questions of form and genre, developments that can be mapped onto the order of composition. In his earliest work, Kerouac uses genre as a ready-made formula to be filled with content, while in his middle period (approximately 1951–7) he understands form and generic content as dialectically constructed and mutually constituting, and finally in his later work he systematizes his narratology into its own conventional genre.[16] Often incorrectly described as apolitical or reactionary, Kerouac's earliest writing draws from postwar historicopolitical contexts even as its sympathies align with prewar liberalism. For his early literary models he looked back at radical writers "so well typified by a Sinclair Lewis or an Arthur Koestler or a [early] John Dos Passos" who used writing to level powerful critiques of American consumer culture, the hegemony of social elites and the subordination of the working class, and totalitarianism (*LVI*, 18). Following this tradition, Kerouac's early short fiction, such as "The Birth of a Socialist" (1941), *The Sea Is My Brother* (written 1942, published 2011), and *The Town and the City* engage thematic conventions of a third-person social realism in order to portray the decaying material conditions of working-class protagonists due to the erosion of the entrepreneurial middle class and the proliferation of unskilled wage labor.

As he considered projects after *The Town and the City*, Kerouac still believed that he had a responsibility to create fiction that reconciled two separate Americas, one built upon universal assumptions of nationhood and citizenship (which he associated with Thomas Wolfe) and another articulated in his own postwar moment (*LVI*, 36). As Kerouac reflects in *Vanity of Duluoz*, the effects of World War II left "us eviscerated of 1930's innocent ambition" (*VoD*, 16), and his sense of the writer's responsibility in annealing these contradictory images of America bespeaks the anxiety of a decade characterized by the displacement of utopic ambition in favor of skepticism.[17] Kerouac intended to modify the tradition of earlier writers such as Dos Passos and Joyce, developing a modern realism that he hoped would reproduce with more mimetic fullness the phenomenological experiences of cold war subjectivity. While he valued the formal experiments of modernist authors, he held that even American modernists maintained roots in European narrative and were motivated by a cynical negation of American culture, whereas his "new style for American culture" affirmed what was worth keeping and developing (*GB*, 47, 52, 56). Believing that "Joyce abused the stream of consciousness by making it too intensely personal, in the sense that it had to be more uncommunicative," Kerouac felt that his new narratological method would "exercise creative selectivity upon the stream of consciousness," therefore creating a distinctly American narrative "that lumps the multiverse trivialities in one universal pattern, puts it in its proper place, and explores in turn more exhaustively the creatively interpretive introspective mind, the trained subconscious."[18] He called this new style "spontaneous prose" or "bop prosody," and for his method he would "write excitedly, swiftly" (*GB*, 70–1).

Kerouac broke through to his new form by drafting the scroll manuscript in April of 1951, an achievement marking the unification of his aesthetic project with his material praxis that he would polish into a finished novel six years later.[19] The narratological model for the novel originates in his concept of the "circle of despair," his name for the sense of lived experience as a "regular series of deflections" that perpetually diverts one from his or her intended goal even as it circumscribes an unknowable object that is "central to our existence" and "what's left after everything else has collapsed" (*WW*, 250–1).[20] As such, Sal Paradise performs continuous movement, believing that the act of searching – even in the absence of a coherent destination – rids him of "confusion and nonsense," a belief repaid when Sal accidentally meets "the girl with the pure and innocent dear eyes that I had always searched for and for so long" in the novel's final chapter, Kerouac's revision of a traditional comedic ending (*OTR*, 134). Kerouac trains his reader for this discursive narrative by foregrounding Sal's efforts at planning his first trip west and his frustration at the material obstacles he encounters on his journey. He realizes "it was my dream that screwed up, the stupid hearthside idea that it would be wonderful to follow one great red line across America instead of trying various roads and routes" (*OTR*, 11). Dissatisfied with the scroll manuscript, however, Kerouac immediately began a new draft of the novel that opens with a series of sketches that emphasize the subtlety of his attention and the capacity for description to generate narrative, but continues by incorporating transcriptions of recorded conversations between Cassady and him as well as prose experiments modeled on the discursive quality of those conversations. Published posthumously as *Visions of Cody* (1972), the novel characterizes the full flowering of Kerouac's narrative development. As Ginsberg remarks, at the time of the novel's composition "the author K.'s obviously given up entirely on American Lit., on Town & City, on On the Road, on Himself & his history, and let his mind loose. The resulting book is full of charming sounds and jokes & jokes, he didn't think he was Finnegan's [*sic*] wake; but some American Mouther Fucker" (*VoC*, 414).

After the success of *On the Road*, publishers capitalized on Kerouac's fame by rushing into print the more experimental novels he had written during the mid-1950s like *Dr. Sax* and *The Subterraneans*. The publication of seven new novels within the next three years seemed to emphasize the myth of Kerouac's practice as slapdash, the proximal dates of publication used as grounds to interpret the generic discontinuities within his work as haphazard accidents and lack of talent, not as aesthetically motivated features used for expressive purpose. In part because of the poor critical reception of these novels, Kerouac relied upon a conventionalized form of spontaneous prose in his final novels. While these novels are well formed, they lack the narratological urgency of his mid-1950s work. In November of 1957, two months after the publication of *On the Road*, Kerouac himself capitalized on his fame by writing *The Dharma Bums*; attempting to capture lightning in a bottle, Kerouac composed *The Dharma Bums* on a scroll, his first use of the technique in seven years. While the use of a scroll for composition marked a radical break in Kerouac's writerly practice in 1951, his use of scrolls in the late 1950s and 1960s functions as a method by which he could ventriloquize his own narrative voice. Although Ray Smith's narrative voice echoes the earlier Paradise, *The Dharma Bums*' chronological narrative features fewer digressions and discursive asides than *On the Road*, resulting in a more easily digestible novel that satisfied his editor, Malcolm Cowley, at Viking Press. *Desolation Angels* (written 1956 and 1961, published 1965) continues the narrative that ends *The Dharma Bums*, the first section of the novel (written 1956) capturing Kerouac's experimental form by interweaving prose narrative sketches with "dharma pops," Kerouac's name for his form of American haiku, while the second section, "Passing Through" (1965), uses the conventional *Road*esque narratology to dramatize his experiences of early 1957. A thoroughly disillusioned Kerouac writes his last novel, *Vanity of Duluoz* (written 1967, published 1968), on a scroll while grieving over the death of his sister, Caroline. In the first paragraph a seemingly defeated Duluoz professes that his "very 'success' [as a writer], far from being a happy triumph as of old, was the sign of doom" and vows in this novel to "use regular punctuation for the new illiterate generation" for "nobody loves my dashes anyway" (*VoD*, 9).

The Duluoz Legend concludes with *Satori in Paris*, a work of nonfiction recounting his 1965 trip to "search for this [family] name in France" (*SP*, 8). Kerouac is unable to locate the necessary records, the attendant informing him that the National Archives kept no records of "'*les affaires Colonielles*' (colonial matters)," a designation that causes him to erupt in a "real rage" (*SP*,

50). Unhomed in the United States and Canada, Kerouac attempts to render himself legible in his ancestral homeland only to be reduced to a "cowardly Breton ... watered down by two centuries in Canada and America" (*SP*, 77). The legend has played out, finally. The prose proceeds in a tidy, linear narrative, suggesting that Kerouac has exhausted his experiment to capture postwar subjectivity through form, and the themes that have attended each novel remain, it would seem, unresolved. Reminding the reader of the circle of despair, he writes what might ultimately be the central tenet of the legend: "This book is to prove that no matter how you travel, how 'successful' your tour, or foreshortened, you always learn something and learn to change your thoughts" (*SP*, 43). As the legend draws to a close, Kerouac and the reader learn that one can no longer hope to know oneself solely through an ethnicity or the abstraction of the nation-state, that perhaps no structure can be devised to narrate a distributed self into a coherent whole. No country will claim him, so Kerouac declares, "I'll use my real name here, full name in this case, Jean-Louis Lebris de Kérouac" (*SP*, 8), for the first time and at the last claiming himself.

## FURTHER READING

Belgrad, Daniel, *The Culture of Spontaneity: Improvisation and the Arts in Postwar America*, Chicago, University of Chicago Press, 1999.

Begnal, Michael H, "'I Dig Joyce': Jack Kerouac and *Finnegans Wake*," *Philological Quarterly*77.2 (1998): 209–19.

Charters, Ann, *Kerouac: A Biography*, New York, St. Martin's Press, 1994.

Edington, Stephen, *Kerouac's Nashua Connection*, Nashua, N.H., Transition, 1999.

Gussow, Adam, "Bohemia Revisited: Malcolm Cowley, Jack Kerouac, and *On the Road*," *Georgia Review*, 28.2, 1984, 291–311.

Holladay, Hilary, and Robert Holton (eds.) *What's Your Road, Man? Critical Essays on Jack Kerouac's* On the Road, Carbondale, Southern Illinois University Press, 2009.

Hrebeniak, Michael, *Action Writing: Jack Kerouac's Wild Form*, Carbondale, Southern Illinois University Press, 2006.

Hunt, Tim, "The Misreading of Kerouac," *Review of Contemporary Fiction*3.2, 1983, 29–33.

*Kerouac's Crooked Road: The Development of a Fiction*, Carbondale, Southern Illinois University Press, 2010.

Johnson, Joyce, *Minor Characters: A Young Woman's Coming-of-Age in the Beat Orbit of Jack Kerouac*, New York, Penguin, 1999.

Johnson, Ronna C., "'You're Putting Me On': Jack Kerouac and the Postmodern Emergence," *College Literature*27.1 (2000): 22–38.

Johnson, Ronna C., and Nancy Grace (eds.), *Girls Who Wore Black : Women Writing the Beat Generation*, New Brunswick, N.J., Rutgers University Press, 2002.

Kerouac, Jack, *Jack Kerouac: Selected Letters*. Vol. 1, 1940–1956, ed. Ann Charters, New York, Penguin, 1996.

*Jack Kerouac: Selected Letters.* Vol. 2, *1957–1969*, ed. Ann Charters, New York, Penguin, 1999.

*Empty Phantoms: Interviews and Encounters with Jack Kerouac*, ed. Paul Maher Jr., New York, Thunder's Mouth Press, 2005.

*Windblown World: The Journals of Jack Kerouac, 1947–1954*, ed. Douglas Brinkley, New York, Viking, 2006.

Kerouac, Jack and Allen Ginsberg, *Jack Kerouac and Allen Ginsberg: The Letters*, ed. Bill Morgan and David Stanford, New York, Viking, 2010.

Kupetz, Joshua, Introduction, "'The Straight Line Will Lead You Only to Death': The Scroll Manuscript and Contemporary Literary Theory," in *On the Road: The Original Scroll*, by Jack Kerouac, ed. Howard Cunnell, New York, Viking, 2007, 83–96.

Maher Jr., Paul, *Kerouac: The Definitive Biography*, New York, Taylor, 2004.

*Jack Kerouac's American Journey: The Real-life Odyssey of* On the Road, New York, Thunder's Mouth Press, 2007.

Mouratidis, George, Introduction, "'Into the Heart of Things': Neal Cassady and the Search for the Authentic," in *On the Road: The Original Scroll*, by Jack Kerouac, ed. Howard Cunnell, New York, Viking, 2007, 69–82.

Myrsiades, Kostas, *The Beat Generation: Critical Essays*, New York, Peter Lang, 2002.

Nicosia, Gerald, *Memory Babe: A Critical Biography of Jack Kerouac*, Berkeley, University of California Press, 1994.

Skerl, Jennie, *Reconstructing the Beats*, New York, Palgrave Macmillan, 2004.

Theado, Matt, *Understanding Jack Kerouac*, Columbia, University of South Carolina Press, 2000.

Vlagopoulos, Penny, Introduction, "Rewriting America: Kerouac's Nation of 'Underground Monsters,'" in *On the Road: The Original Scroll*, by Jack Kerouac, ed. Howard Cunnell, New York, Viking, 2007, 53–68.

Weinreich, Regina, "The Brothers Martin or the Decline of America," *Review of Contemporary Fiction* 3.2 (1983): 75–82.

*Kerouac's Spontaneous Poetics: A Study of the Fiction*, New York, Thunder's Mouth Press, 2001.

## NOTES

1 Howard Mumford Jones (1892–1980) was a U.S. writer, literary critic, and professor of English at Harvard University, as well as the book editor for the daily afternoon newspaper the *Boston Evening Transcript*. Jack Kerouac, *Windblown World: The Journals of Jack Kerouac, 1947–1954*, ed. Douglas Brinkley (New York Viking, 2006), p. 276. Hereafter *WW*. No set of critical editions yet exists for Jack Kerouac's collected works, although the Library of America volume *Road Novels 1957–1960*, edited by Douglas Brinkley, collects *On the Road*, *The Dharma Bums*, *Tristessa*, *The Subterraneans*, and *Lonesome Traveler*.

2 Jack Kerouac, *Good Blonde and Others* (San Francisco, Grey Fox Press, 1993), p. 48–51. Hereafter *GB*.

3 Gerald Clarke, *Capote: A Biography* (New York, Simon & Schuster, 1988), p. 314.

4 Ibid.

5   For information on Kerouac's drafting of *On the Road*, see Howard Cunnell, "Fast This Time" in Jack Kerouac, *On the Road: The Original Scroll*, ed. Howard Cunnell (New York, Viking, 2007), pp. 1–52, and Matthew Theado, "Revisions of Kerouac: The Long, Strange Trip of the *On the Road* Typescripts," in *What's Your Road, Man? Critical Essays on Jack Kerouac's* On the Road, ed. Hilary Holladay and Robert Holton (Carbondale, Southern Illinois University Press, 2009).

6   Jack Kerouac, *Jack Kerouac: Selected Letters: Volume 1, 1940–1956* (New York, Penguin, 1996), p. 40. Hereafter *LVI*.

7   David Brooks argues as much in "Sal Paradise at 50," claiming these readings amount to mere "Boomer Narcissism," apparently unaware that George Mouratidis, the first critic he cites, is an Australian in his thirties. David Brooks, "Sal Paradise at 50," *New York Times*, October 2 2007: A25(L). September 29, 2011. URL: http://www.nytimes.com/2007/10/02/opinion/02brooks.html.

8   Jack Kerouac, *Visions of Cody* (New York, New Directions, 1973). Hereafter *VoC*.

9   Such a process, argues Regina Weinreich, is the "major obsession of the post-war literary period." See Regina Weinreich, "The Brothers Martin or the Decline of America," *Review of Contemporary Fiction* 3.2 (1983): 75–82.

10  Jack Kerouac, *Desolation Angels* (New York, Coward-McCann, 1965), p. 144, hereafter *DA*; Jack Kerouac, *On the Road* (New York: Viking Press, 1957), pp. 37, 54. Hereafter *OTR*.

11  Jack Kerouac, *Satori in Paris* (New York, Grove Press, 1966), Hereafter *SP*.

12  For example, see Nancy Grace's paradigmatic "A White Man in Love: A Study of Race, Gender, Class, and Ethnicity in Jack Kerouac's *Maggie Cassidy, The Subterraneans*, and *Tristessa*," *College Literature* 27.1 (2000): 39–62.

13  Stephen Edington, *Kerouac's Nashua Connection* (Nashua, N.H., Transition, 1999), p. 37.

14  Gerald Nicosia, *Memory Babe: A Critical Biography of Jack Kerouac* (Berkeley, University of California Press, 1994), p. 15.

15  Jack Kerouac, *On the Road* (New York, Viking Press, 1957). Hereafter *OTR*.

16  See Paul Maher Jr., *Kerouac: The Definitive Biography* (New York, Taylor, 2004) for the context of each novel's composition.

17  Jack Kerouac, *Vanity of Duluoz* (New York, Coward-McCann, 1968). Hereafter *VoD*.

18  Jack Kerouac, "Notes on 'Galloway' Style" (leaf), folder 43.17. *Jack Kerouac Papers: 1922–1977*, Berg Collection, NYPL.

19  See Cunnell, "Fast This Time," pp. 1–52.

20  See Joshua Kupetz, "The Straight Line Will Lead You Only to Death" in Jack Kerouac, *On the Road: The Original Scroll*, ed. Howard Cunnell (New York, Viking Press, 2007), pp. 83–96.

# 23

# Saul Bellow

VICTORIA AARONS

When Saul Bellow's (1915–2005) Artur Sammler, Holocaust survivor, transplanted "refugee in Manhattan," wonders, "Is our species crazy?" he can only reply, with the absolute conviction born of experience and observation: "Plenty of evidence."[1] Artur Sammler, the protagonist of Bellow's novel *Mr. Sammler's Planet*, published serially in 1969 in the *Atlantic Monthly* and in book form in 1970, is a man betrayed by history. He is a Jew who barely escaped the Holocaust with only one good eye, the other "struck ... by a gun butt and blinded" (*SP* 137). He is a man who, condemned to die, "clawed his way out" of the mass grave that he was forced to dig, emerging while his wife and others "had been buried alive" (*SP* 273). Having dug his way, "inside death," Sammler inexplicably resurfaces, literally scrambling from the grave that was not yet to be his (*SP* 273). And then, with the eventuality of inexorable oddity, by way of a displaced persons (DP) camp in Salzburg, the bewildered Sammler, resurrected from the grave, finds himself reassigned to America, "advertised throughout the universe as the most desirable, most exemplary of all nations" (*SP* 14). It is here in America that, far from the European nightmare of Sammler's ever-receding past, the unimaginable might finally be imagined. Having thus survived, Sammler finds himself in America in the midst of a century that has seen, in Bellow's own words, "a crime so vast that it brings all Being into Judgment."[2] And Sammler, "separated from the rest of his species, if not in some fashion severed," must come to grips with his reconstructed life, must attempt to reinvent himself by negotiating "the charm, the ebullient glamour, the almost unbearable agitation that came from being able to describe oneself as a twentieth-century American" (*SP* 43, 73).

Having fortuitously left behind the terrifying madness of Europe, Sammler unpredictably confronts a different kind of madness, thrust amid a people haphazardly "casting themselves into chaos" (*SP* 124). It is here in America that Sammler finds himself against a landscape of contradictions, an uneven topography of paradoxes, "a glorious planet. But wasn't everything being done to make it intolerable to abide here?" (*SP* 135). For the planet that Sammler now inhabits is as conflicted as Sammler himself, a universe "at grips with historical problems, struggling with certain impossibilities" (*SP* 146). Bellow's America is a site of absurd incongruities, at once a land of unabashed possibility, of freedom and mobility, of the promise of self-discovery and self-reinvention, but also a place of unrestrained excess, upon which is enacted an immoderate surfeit of emotion, desire, stealth, debasement, and deceit. Although Sammler has left behind the intolerable madness of a Europe in ruins, he finds himself against a deafening confusion, a "Sodom and Gomorrah ... things ... falling apart," a landscape given into the "excuse of madness," symptomatically defining and motivating (*SP* 304, 89). Here in New York, "the soul of America," Sammler finds himself among a people reacting to the leadenness of "bourgeois solidity" by discarding structures of decency and propriety, instead "justifying idleness, silliness, shallowness, distemper, lust – turning former respectability inside out," disposing of the "civil margin" (*SP* 146, 9, 48). To be sure, Sammler's planet is Saul Bellow's America, one we encounter in all his fiction, the landscape upon which his characters graft their most elegant desires and their worst fears.

It is here in America that Sammler, once buried under a pile of bodies and left for dead, finds madness of a different order. For in America, civility turns into something sinister, treacherous even, and Sammler discovers a universe both unimpeded and unhinged by the past, by the brutalities and monstrous inventions of the twentieth century. Bellow's New York in the late 1960s and early 1970s is a place of debauchery, depravity, criminality, profligacy, self-indulgence, and grasping excess, "an unconscious collaboration of all souls spreading madness and poison" (*SP* 135). Here the bewildered Sammler discovers that the desired "liberation into individuality has not been a great success" (*SP* 228–9). A place of inexhaustible possibility and disproportionate appetite, America, epitomized by the overflowing ebullience of New York City, is glaringly immoderate. But Bellow's America, epitomized by the richly hewed cosmopolitan corruption of New York City, reveals, as Artur Sammler discovers, "the magic of extremes" (*SP* 135). America is a burlesque version of itself, a theater of the absurd, where, as Sammler realizes, "certain forms of success required an element of parody, self-mockery, a satire on the-thing-itself" (*SP* 70). But it is behind the "jeweled door" of American chance and cunning that one finds almost impossible contradictions: privilege and proscription, luxury and coarseness, civility and barbarity, sophistication and raw primitivism, artful ingenuity and vulgar ineptitude (*SP* 7). Bellow constructs in *Mr. Sammler's Planet*, as he does elsewhere, an extraordinarily tactile experience achieved through the simulacra of the sounds and sensations of living in New York in the midst of the tortuous and exhilarating tumult of the latter half of the twentieth century.

It is against this volatile landscape that Sammler must negotiate the unstable terrain of the past, attempting to reconcile his persistently and insistently felt past with a post-Holocaust universe upon which "the sun shone as if there were no death" (*SP* 44). Sammler's difficulty in reconciling his past experiences – the very collapse of European civilization as he witnessed it – to life in New York is made largely impossible because he has reemerged into a universe from which history has been elided. To reinvent life in America necessitates a kind of historical amnesia, the slate wiped clean. Sammler, the flotsam of his experiences trailing him, emerges into the light of American prosperity and privilege with a deep mistrust of the permanence of all things animate and inanimate. Sammler, in his New York apartment, "leaning on a soft, leatherlike ... sofa, feet on an umber Finnish rug," recognizes the utter futility in attempting to put to rights his past life with his present circumstances:

> When [his wife] Antonina was murdered.... When he and sixty or seventy others, all stripped naked and having dug their own grave, were fired upon and fell in.... Struggling out much later from the weight of corpses, crawling out of the loose soil.... Nearly thirty years after which, in April days, sunshine springtime, another season, the rush and intensity of New York City about to be designated as spring. (*SP* 91)

The New York sun shines on a different planet than the one on which Sammler previously resided. And the denial of the collapse of the civilized world, the intentional turning from the realities of death, hatred, and inhumanity, suggests a kind of temporary stasis. Here he lives among a people caught in limbo, a people arrested in time because, for them, there is nothing to hold them accountable, living, falsely in Bellow's perspective, with "a kind of impunity, because no one cared what happened" (*SP* 144).

In *Mr. Sammler's Planet*, as elsewhere in his fiction, Bellow creates a portrait of postwar existence that acutely exposes the consequences of living in the decades following, in Bellow's words, "the most atrocious [war] in history."[3] Bellow, an intellectual whose critical commentary on the transgressions and pathologies of twentieth-century life and thought has defined him throughout his literary career, creates in his fiction the conditions under which we might come to acknowledge the near if not certain "collapse of civilization" (*SP* 304). Bellow was writing at an important time in history, both in terms of world and of Anglo-American literary history. Work on his first novel, *Dangling Man*, published in 1944, was begun in 1942, a year that marked the implementation by the Nazis of the Final Solution. Those novels written in the aftermath of the war, *The Victim* (1947) and *The Adventures of Augie March* (1953), show Bellow's attempts to come to grips with a world emerging from the ruins of war and the devastation of European Jewry. Writing as a Jew and as an American (though Canadian born), Bellow writes about what it means to live in postwar America, "the mental life of the century having been disfigured" by the unconscionable actions and pathological motives that engineered the Holocaust (*Letters* 439). What is left for us to do, Bellow seems to ask, after such recognition? Can civilization – reason, judgment, ethical conduct, and human decency – be redeemed or reclaimed?

All of Bellow's novels, published over a span of half a century, from *Dangling Man* in 1944 to *Ravelstein* in 2000, pose the question of the requirements for living in a world that acknowledges the baseness of human motives, the countless atrocities of human invention, and the necessity for accountability. Bellow directly addresses in novels such as *Mr. Sammler's Planet* and *The Bellarosa Connection* (1989), and indirectly in novels such as *The Victim* (1947), *Herzog* (1964), and *Humboldt's Gift* (1975), the ways in which the defining moment of the Holocaust shaped and refashioned our experience of what it means to be human. In fact, *Mr. Sammler's Planet* may well be read as a meditation on the Holocaust and on the human condition left in its wake. Significantly, Bellow's novels take place in America, a landscape on which one might start anew, where a survivor such as Artur Sammler might reconstruct his life within the knowledge of the limitations and tenuous circumstances that all of Bellow's characters suffer. Like Sammler, Bellow "was not against civilization, nor against politics, institutions, nor against order," but rather against the manipulations of such agencies of design that would crush the individual conscience (*SP* 277). Like Sammler, Bellow, too, is in favor of "eliminating the superfluous. Identifying the necessary" (*SP* 278). And finding the means and the courage to do so becomes the central challenge that Bellow's characters must confront.

Artur Sammler, a man remaindered by the past, "one of the doomed who had lasted it all out," though at times he imagines it "scarcely worth so much effort ... to stretch the human material too far," is shown to be both observer and judge of ethical life in America (*SP* 140). Once a witness to the atrocities of the Holocaust, he is now witness to the theatrical expanse of American opportunism and display. The excess of intellect, of explanations, rationalizations, and oddly self-defeating justifications that Sammler observes around him, as well as the many cryptic ambiguities that, for Bellow, constitute American culture, point to the ironic position in which he finds himself. A witness once again, "like many people who had seen the world collapse once, Mr. Sammler entertained the possibility it might collapse twice....You could see the suicidal impulses of civilization pushing strongly.... Enlightenment? Marvelous! But out of hand, wasn't it?" (*SP* 33–4). And Sammler, decades after surviving conditions that would speak to the end of the civilized world, finds himself once again a judge, "no judge but himself," to the pathologies of the age in which he, unpredictably, against all the odds, lives.

Sammler is a man who has experienced the worst of his times, who lived through, as Bellow elsewhere puts it, the "forces of deformity that produced the Final Solution," a man taken out of the immediate present by a history that defrauded him (*Letters* 438). Ironically, Sammler finds himself repositioned in America, in a culture that seems to deny the past and ignore the future – all forsaken for the ever-present now. Sammler, on the other hand, exudes history: the diasporic history of the Jews, whose collective narrative of anti-Semitism, of suffering, of expulsion, and of annihilation becomes the defining signifier of personhood. Sammler is a man who has experienced the combination of atrocities that have come to define him, a legacy that if not willingly at least obligatorily he bears. Sammler is thus constructed by Bellow as the embodiment of history against which all things American are measured. His critical assessment of himself and the psychic and material landscape around him locate him directly in the teetering and teeming immediacy of this world. The noises of Bellow's city streets mimic and are mimicked by the constant clamor of desire to be heard, an insistence on selfhood, the deceptive belief that the fulfillment of longing will bring about some kind of relief. To this end, Bellow's protagonists are pursued by the ever-constant and despairing voice of yearning, as is Bellow's wealthy American protagonist, Eugene Henderson, on a quest for meaning that will make him run from America to the African veldts in the novel *Henderson the Rain King* (1959), cheered on by the reverberating clatter of "I want, I want, I want."[4] But Bellow's characters are never certain about *what* they want, only *that* they want. And so they stumble over one another in an elaborate kind of dance searching for the stuff of fulfillment. Bellow's protagonists either are forever in pursuit of what they cannot have, such as Asa Leventhal in *The Victim*, or Tommy Wilhelm in *Seize the Day* (1956); or, like Moses Herzog in Bellow's novel *Herzog*, they are buttressed by an ironic view of the world in which they live. What else is there, Bellow seems to ask, but to thrust oneself into the world, into the very fraught, chaotic, folly of planet earth.

Sammler is an inveterate Bellovian protagonist, one who inhabits all his novels: self-conscious, hyperaware of himself and the world around him, both plagued and unshackled by his candid, judicious, and analytic comportment – in all ways, a creature of his own making in Bellow's America: a watcher in the observed world. And Sammler, like Bellow, is a most keen observer. Indeed, Sammler's divided vision suggests the inherent contradictions and juxtapositions that hold this novel in tight control. His disjunctive vision is an ironic reflection on the world he inhabits and an opening into the interstices of that world: "He had only one good eye. The left distinguished only light and shade. But the good eye was dark-bright, full of observation" (*SP* 4). The one eye makes up for the other; acting in concert, they reveal at once what is hidden, but also what is unswervingly illuminated. As Sammler ironically puts it, "Our weak species fought its fear, our crazy species fought its criminality. We are an animal of genius" (*SP* 305). The double nature of things, as viewed both indistinctly and distinctly by Sammler, exposes the contradictory and thus, in a strange way, alluring nature of human existence. And Sammler is in the perfect position to expose this phenomenon, as one who can speak "from personal experience, from the grave" (*SP* 305). What Sammler knows of life and death – and *can* only know from experience – is the truth of Bellow's worldview: "In their peculiar transformation… man is a killer. Man has a moral nature" (*SP* 198). The two different perspectives from which Sammler views the world – the one hazy, clouded, and the other keenly lucid with sharp perspicuity – mirror the ironic duality of human existence as Bellow sees it: the working in tandem of the shadowy motives of human behavior amid the glaring realities that shape twentieth-century American life and thought.

Sammler thus calls into question what it means to be in this world. And his alienation, his disenfranchisement, and the dire circumstances that have placed him on the margins ironically heighten his sensitivities, making him a deft observer of Bellow's universe. The jostling noises of the streets of New York join in a kind of dialogue with Sammler's internal imaginings. New York here is the center of America, a place where failure is so much more evident exactly because of its opposing other: the possibility of genius, of educated, cultured knowledge and the capacity, if not to amend the wrongs of the past, then to emerge from under them with a recognition of historical significance and the wherewithal not to fall into the old ways, and thereby to avoid the predatory impulses of humankind. In disturbing ways, however, New York is shown here to be a living graveyard of war-torn Poland, where "buses were bearable, subways were killing" (*SP* 5). The claustrophobia that Sammler feels, in fact, the sense of suffocation that Bellow's protagonists generally experience, creates a disjunctive discord amid the airy spaciousness of American buoyancy. In fact, the ethos of the American city in Bellow's fiction reveals a discord between the guise of openness and the cramped, shuttered spaces that define urban life in America. This love-hate relationship with America persists for all Bellow's characters. The utter fascination, ebullience, and exhilarating headiness of being a part of the adventure that is America allow Bellow's impassioned protagonist Augie March, for example, to introduce himself in animated celebration: "I am an American, Chicago born."[5] America, its life force overflowing in Bellow's New York and Chicago cityscapes, is the place of imagined self-fashioning. But America is both antagonist and collaborator, adversary and coconspirator, although the real nemesis, that which stands in the way of Bellow's characters' most fervent desires, is their own fraught sense of incompleteness, their apprehensive assurance that their fear will make them vulnerable to the unwelcome imposition of others.

It is significant that Bellow makes the urban setting – largely the streets and sights of New York and Chicago – home to his characters, rather than the vast, rural open spaces of America. The city is, indeed, the dramatic force in Bellow's novels; it is on the streets of Bellow's urban landscapes that his characters, in close and often stifling proximity, must confront themselves in themselves and in others. Oppressive heat is generated by the passions and fevers of the inhabitants of Bellow's cities – the pickpockets, the money launderers, the gangsters, the intellectuals, the marginalized, the displaced – who all join together in creating a heightened sense of the world careening out of control. All the disparate characters inhabiting Bellow's urban settings are playing out their lives together, vying for autonomous self-invention. These are the same city streets upon which Asa Leventhal, the protagonist of Bellow's *The Victim*, gingerly navigates the confusion of "people thronging the streets, barbaric fellahin," linked to one another in a kind of collective anxiety.[6] The very ethos of the city prevents the kind of free will that Bellow's characters believe they desire. The packed-in, airless conditions of the urban landscape preclude the freedom to move beyond the confines of that psychic and material life. Sammler's nightmarish experience, for example, traveling by bus in Manhattan – surely reminiscent of murderous modes of deportation from another life – reflects the stifling lack of momentum that characterizes Bellow's narrow city spaces, as Sammler hanging onto the bus strap finds himself "sealed in by bodies, receiving their weight and laying his own on them" (*SP* 6). We are, Bellow suggests, in this together.

Such claustrophobic anxiety is a symptom of a fraught sense of vulnerability for many of Bellow's characters. In, for example, *The Victim*, Asa Leventhal, hounded by his double and adversary, the anti-Semitic Kirbee Allbee, finds the city's claustrophobic environs threateningly menacing. The world that he inhabits aggressively insinuates itself upon him. In fact, the very atmosphere presses upon him: the sun's "glare was overpowering...."

The heat of the pavement penetrated his soles" (*Victim* 160). The reiterative references throughout this novel to the oppressive heat of the day and the heavy, sun-soaked landscape – "the street ... deadened with heat and light," "clouds ... heavily suspended and slow," "brackish air"– create the suffocating conditions of Leventhal's relentless claustrophobia, symptomatically making all the more emphatic his ubiquitous fear and ill-defined anxiety (*Victim* 40, 158). Such descriptions of the suffocating heat and crowded airways become a rhythmic patterning in the novel, creating a kind of background noise against which Leventhal's escalating apprehension and dread become real. As we follow the increasingly unbalanced Leventhal hastening to the novel's disturbing close, the nightmarish quality of existence increases; the already oppressively overbearing heat takes on a fiery hue. It is an ominous landscape that Bellow creates amid the cosmopolitan mobility and openness of New York, and it is upon this unstable and fearful terrain that the unhinged Leventhal is forced to negotiate his life.

Bellow's novels show experience refined to its essence – stark, honest, candid, unsparingly exposed – human life laid bare. To this end, what Bellow's characters do best is talk – reason, deliberate, explain, and negotiate – against a world that would otherwise confound and silence them. And more often than not, they hold elaborately contrived colloquies with themselves, as does Moses Herzog, who, in a series of internally composed, unmailed letters to friends, family, and celebrated figures both dead and alive, expresses his deep disappointment in the state of humankind. In fact, all of Bellow's fiction might be thought of as a meditation on the human condition, an exposition of the weary yet insistently performative "theater of the soul" (*SP* 234). Bellow will begin his novel *Herzog* with the protagonist Moses Herzog's famously memorable lines "If I am out of my mind, it's all right with me."[7] And Herzog's ironic certainty of his own insanity, both self-protective and comically self-admonishing, is articulated in a variety of utterances throughout Bellow's novels. Bellow would have us applaud the ironic good humor of a character who, in acknowledging his insanity, proves himself to be sanely aware of his own foibles and self-delusions.

For Bellow, like his central characters, is a scrupulous observer, casting a shrewdly judicious moral gaze upon the projects and endeavors of his world. Ever vigilant, Bellow demands that we account for what it means to be human. To be sure, what Bellow himself does best is talk, offering unimpeded, extended expositions on human behavior and motives. Bellow persistently asks us to consider the hard questions, not only how to live in this world, but how to live in the world among others. From what deep wells might one find the resources to continue, especially in the face of the litany of miseries, incredulities, and insanities that, largely of its own making, befall humankind? Bellow, in recreating and then assessing the impossibly conceived and articulated life of the Job-like Mr. Sammler, will himself wonder at the cost of it all: "This too great demand upon human consciousness and human capacities has overtaxed human endurance" (*SP* 232). Indeed, Sammler's question is the central question that all of Bellow's fiction asks: "What is the true stature of a human being?" (*SP* 232). To put it another way: What is the measure of humankind?

In Bellow's fictive universe, the ancient Hebraic covenant is rescripted and revised. No longer do we begin with Eden before the fall. Rather, the covenant is rewritten for enlightened modernity. Here America is the new point of origin with the fall already well under way and with the certain knowledge that we are a corrupted, shameful species; a "crazy" species, even; "a strange species ... which had organized its planet to such an extent" (*SP* 254). To be sure, Bellow presents in his fictional universe the Edenic fall in reverse order: from the depths, expulsion, and worse, to the fertility, fecundity, and promise of America, the new world. This rebirth, of sorts, is not without its Bellovian pitfalls; its ironic, misguided, and fanatical transgressions; its failures and darkly comical catastrophes; and the innumerable assaults on human endurance. Might one get to the point, as Sammler entertains, of begging, as does Job, one's "release from being human ... petitioning for a release from God's attention?" (*SP* 251). Just when it seems that human beings might have come to the end of the line, played themselves out, Bellow offers us another chance. The tendency to surrender, we are cautioned, to the unhappy verdict that "reality was a terrible thing, and that the final truth about mankind was overwhelming and crushing," is, finally, a "vulgar, cowardly conclusion, rejected by Sammler with all his heart"; and, so too, by Bellow (*SP* 280). Under the ever-watchful gaze of Bellow, his characters, not entirely unhappy in their fate, will, with untold, unhampered enthusiasms, proceed, if haphazardly, on course. They will join in life's embrace.

On both Bellow's and Sammler's planet, basic human decency defines responsible, ethical living. For Bellow there is a kind of courageous resolve in navigating this life time and time again, in returning to the "end of the line" to begin anew, to get it right (*SP* 274). As Bellow makes very clear, one must have guts to face contemporary life. Bellow's characters show a kind of nerve in managing the basic requirements of arising each day, of honest assessment, of meeting one's obligations to self and to others, and then, exhausted, often disappointed, but altogether resolved, to wake up and do it again. And again. And again. Until death's final call, the "phone ringing.... 'Hello? Ah, you at last'" (*SP* 138). But until then, one continues as one must, constantly vigilant, fulfilling one's obligations, keeping things together as one

should; it is a necessary cycle, as Sammler ironically but not unhappily concludes: "The waking, like a crew, worked the world's machines, and all went
up and down and round about with calculations accurate to the billionth of
a degree.... The sleeping, brutes, fantasists, dreaming. Then they woke, and
the other half went to bed.... And that is how this brilliant human race runs
this wheeling globe" (*SP* 254). For Bellow, there is something, if not heroic,
then good-humoredly courageous in proceeding through life with history as
our legacy and with our imperfect conscience as our guide.

Saul Bellow's distinctive literary career – novels, short stories, memoirs,
and essays spanning more than half a century – responds with elegance and
sagacity to the turbulent and muddled history of our times. With considerable insight, Bellow's fiction confronts the most spectacular accomplishments and most ruinous failures of the twentieth century. His portrait of
American life and thought and the social, political, and cultural movements
that have formed America in the postwar period are brought into sharp
perspicuity in Bellow's searing novels, which depict both the corruption and
the decency that weigh with anxious reckoning on his protagonists. One of
the major writers of the post–World War II period, Bellow has fashioned a
generation of writers, shaping and defining the rich possibilities not only for
Jewish expression but for American letters.

## FURTHER READING

Aarons, Victoria. "Saul Bellow." *Critical Insights*, ed. Allan Chavkin, Pasadena,
    Calif., Salem Press, 2011.
"A Half Life: An Autobiography of Ideas," *Bostonia/1990*, November/December
    1990, 37–47.
Atlas, James, *Saul Bellow: A Biography*, New York, Random House, 2000.
Bach, Gerhard (ed.), *Saul Bellow at Seventy-Five: A Collection of Critical Essays*,
    Tubingen, Gunter Narr, 1991.
Bellow, Saul, "Interview with Myself," *New Review* 2.18 (1975): 53–6.
    *To Jerusalem and Back: A Personal Account*, New York, Viking, 1976.
Bloom, Harold (ed.), *Saul Bellow*, Modern Critical Views, New York, Chelsea,
    1986.
Cronin, Gloria L. and Ben Siegel (eds.), *Conversations with Saul Bellow: Selected
    Interviews*, Jackson, University Press of Mississippi, 1994.
Cronin, Gloria L. and L. H. Goldman (eds.), *Saul Bellow in the 1980s: A Collection
    of Critical Essays*, East Lansing, Michigan State University Press, 1989.
Goldman, L. H., Gloria L. Cronin, and Ada Aharoni (eds.), *Saul Bellow: A Mosaic*,
    Twentieth-Century American Jewish Writers 3, ed. Daniel Walden, New York,
    Peter Lang, 1992.
"Introduction." *Great Jewish Short Stories*, ed. Saul Bellow, New York, Dell, 1963.
Kremer, S. Lillian, "Saul Bellow." *Holocaust Literature: An Encyclopedia of Writers
    and Their Work*, Vol. 1, ed. S. Lillian Kremer, New York, Routledge, 2003, pp.
    124–34.

"Saul Bellow and the Holocaust," special issue, *Saul Bellow Journal*, ed. Alan L. Berger, 23.1–2 (Fall 2007/Winter 2008).

Trachtenberg, Stanley (ed.), *Critical Essays on Saul Bellow*, Critical Essays on American Literature, Boston, G. K. Hall, 1979.

## NOTES

1 Saul Bellow, *Mr. Sammler's Planet* (1970; rpt., New York, Penguin, 1984), pp. 6, 92. Hereafter *SP*.

2 *Saul Bellow: Letters*, ed. Benjamin Taylor (New York, Viking, 2010), pp. 438–9.

3 Saul Bellow, *It All Adds Up: From the Dim Past to the Uncertain Future* (New York, Viking Press, 1994), p. 41.

4 Saul Bellow, *Henderson the Rain King* (New York, Viking Press, 1959), p. 233.

5 Saul Bellow, *The Adventures of Augie March* (New York, Viking Press, 1953), p. 3.

6 Saul Bellow, *The Victim* (1947; rpt., New York, Signet, 1965), p. 11.

7 Saul Bellow, *Herzog* (New York, Viking Press, 1964), p. 1.

# 24

# Kurt Vonnegut

TODD DAVIS

At the heart of Kurt Vonnegut's (1922–2007) career as a novelist rests an idealism dressed up in the playful trappings of a rebellious teenager who thumbs his nose at the establishment for supremely moral reasons. A countercultural figure who gained literary celebrity in the late 1960s and early 1970s, Vonnegut is best characterized as an American trickster whose values are an ad hoc mixture of the public school education he received in the Midwest during the Great Depression, his own family's religious skepticism, and his experiences as a prisoner of war who survived the firebombing of Dresden, Germany.

His ascendancy as a novelist parallels the rise of postmodern fiction in America as practiced by such luminaries as Thomas Pynchon, Donald Barthelme, Richard Brautigan, and John Barth. But Vonnegut's own work, while highlighting its constructed nature through a range of metafictional techniques and its adamant assertion that there is no essential center of reference, nonetheless argues for a consistent morality that might best be called postmodern humanism. Vonnegut's fiction should be seen as an antecedent for the work of such contemporary novelists as David Foster Wallace, Sherman Alexie, and Dave Eggers, and his legacy continues to influence both public and literary spheres.

Vonnegut fell into his writing career in a haphazard fashion. After attending public school in Indianapolis, Indiana, he matriculated at Cornell University in 1940 to begin his studies in chemistry. While his father and grandfather were architects, his older brother, Bernard, was a graduate of the chemistry department at M.I.T. and would go on to an illustrious career in that field. As Vonnegut explains, "Chemistry was everything then. It was a magic word in the thirties. The Germans, of course, had chemistry, and they were going to take apart the universe and put it together again."[1]

Following in his brother's footsteps, Vonnegut began his scientific studies in Ithaca, New York, but his academic career was mediocre at best. His love for writing continued to interrupt his scholarly work and led him, as it did in high school, to serve as an editor for the student newspaper. It is in these early journalistic and editorial forays that we first see the playful and irreverent humor that would later serve him well as the satiric harlequin of American fiction, or what some have described as a hippie Mark Twain.

With the escalation of World War II, in 1943, before finishing his degree at Cornell, Vonnegut enlisted in the United States Army, and on December 22, 1944, he was captured by German troops at the Battle of the Bulge and interned as a prisoner of war in Dresden. On February 13, 1945, he survived the Allied firebombing of Dresden, in which more than 130,000 civilians died. This singular event would haunt Vonnegut for nearly a quarter of a century as he struggled to write about it. As he confesses in the first chapter of *Slaughterhouse-Five* (1969), "When I got home from the Second World War twenty-three years ago, I thought it would be easy for me to write about the destruction of Dresden, since all I would have to do would be to report what I had seen. ... But not many words about Dresden came from my mind then – not enough of them to make a book, anyway."[2]

Upon his return to the United States, he married and headed to Chicago, where he worked for the Chicago City News Bureau and studied anthropology at the University of Chicago. Again, before attaining his degree, he left the university in order to work as a publicist for the General Electric Corporation, where his brother served as a research scientist. Vonnegut was later awarded a master's degree in anthropology from the University of Chicago for *Cat's Cradle* (1963), and he often spoke in interviews and in lectures about cultural relativity, a noted theme of that early novel: "I didn't learn until I was in college about all the other cultures, and I should have learned that in the first grade. A first grader should understand that his culture isn't a rational invention; that there are thousands of other cultures and they all work pretty well; that all cultures function on faith rather than truth; that there are lots of alternatives to our own society."[3]

It was during the late 1940s that Vonnegut began to write fiction regularly, and in 1950 he published his first short story in *Collier's*. Over the next fifteen years, Vonnegut's fiction would appear consistently in such magazines as *Saturday Evening Post*, *Cosmopolitan*, *Argosy*, *Redbook*, and others that flourished during this period. These stories functioned as Vonnegut's true apprenticeship in the craft of storytelling and helped keep his family financially solvent.

Vonnegut's first novel, *Player Piano*, was published in 1952 by Scribner's, a distinguished New York City publishing house that championed the work of such important modernists as Ernest Hemingway and F. Scott Fitzgerald. This dystopian novel set in the not too distant future proffered Vonnegut's vision of corporate manufacturing and industrialization and was based upon his experiences at General Electric. His dark vision of where such practices might lead included two of the enduring questions that he would continue to revisit over the course of his career: What are people here for, and how can they find meaning and purpose for their lives? In an interview, Vonnegut suggests such themes are why many young people like his work: "Maybe it's because I deal with sophomoric questions that full adults regard as settled. I talk about what is God like, what could He want, is there a heaven, and if there is, what would it be like?"[4]

*Player Piano* (1952) was not a commercial or critical success, receiving little publicity from Scribner's and virtually no reviews. As a result, Vonnegut, who had quit his job at General Electric to pursue his career as a writer, was forced to find work of all kinds, including teaching at the Hopefield School on Cape Cod, working for an advertising agency, and opening the second Saab auto dealership in the United States.

From 1952 until 1969, Vonnegut continued to write short fiction, which was collected in several books, including *Canary in a Cat House* (1961) and *Welcome to the Monkey House* (1968). In addition, he produced four novels, all of which were published as paperback originals. Being relegated to the paperback stand, where many of his books were hawked as straight science fiction or spy novels, seems an unlikely path for one of America's most influential novelists, and the irony of seeing his work ensconced between salacious covers of scantily clad women was not lost on him.

Ultimately, Vonnegut's penance as a paperback writer led to the creation of Kilgore Trout, a recurring character and thinly veiled alter ego in Vonnegut's fictional world. A science fiction writer whose work is consigned to publication as filler in pornographic magazines, Trout creates story lines that are consistently used as parables of sorts, offering Vonnegut the chance to propose thematic and moralistic anecdotes as asides or as punch lines to jokes that interrupt the dominant plotline of Vonnegut's own stories. Vonnegut's use of Trout suggests a complex and tenuous relationship, culminating in 1973 in *Breakfast of Champions*, in which Trout is offered a literary award at an arts festival in Midland, Ohio. There Vonnegut confronts his own creation in a moving scene and sets Trout free, supposedly never to be consigned to fictional servitude again. As with many characters in Vonnegut novels, however, Trout and his offspring do appear in subsequent books.

Fortunately, Vonnegut himself escaped Trout's publishing fate. In 1965, with the release of *God Bless You, Mr. Rosewater,* Vonnegut was offered a two-year residency as a professor at the University of Iowa Writers' Workshop. As a teacher, he influenced many future writers, including another important American novelist, John Irving, who has written favorably about Vonnegut's fiction and friendship. In 1967, as his time teaching at Iowa was drawing to a close, he garnered a three-book contract from Seymour Lawrence, which led to the publication of his most important novel, *Slaughterhouse-Five,* in 1969, as well as the reissuing of all his previous novels in hardcover.

As is the case with most literary careers, events beyond the control of the author play a significant role in determining contemporary notoriety, as well as a place in the literary canon posthumously. This is certainly true for Vonnegut. Up until the publication of *Slaughterhouse-Five,* he was relatively unknown, a paperback hack, even, by some standards. But with the tumultuous events of the 1960s – which included the assassination of President John F. Kennedy, the Reverend Dr. Martin Luther King Jr., and Malcolm X, among other political icons; the escalation of the Vietnam War; the movement toward countercultural values; race riots in major cities; feminism and shifting sexual mores; and the experimentation with psychedelic drugs by such noted cultural icons as Timothy Leary – readers were positioned perfectly for a novelist who would combine a critique of establishment ideas with a pacifistic rallying cry.

Certainly, *Slaughterhouse-Five* was not a radical departure from Vonnegut's previous novels. *Cat's Cradle* tendered a satiric send-up of religion – both the human desire for religious institutions at the center of our communities and the myths that serve as organizing principles for them – as well as cold war science and nuclear escalation in the form of Ice-9, a substance that ultimately destroys the world. Similarly, in *Mother Night* (1962), Vonnegut played with the popular tropes of espionage fiction to call into question the idea of an essential, innocent self that might remain unsullied, despite the acts of deception and murder a spy must perform in service to his or her country. In the introduction to that novel, Vonnegut issued one of his strongest moral pronouncements: "We are what we pretend to be, so we must be careful about what we pretend to be."[5] Likewise, in *God Bless You, Mr. Rosewater*, Vonnegut proffered a solution to so many of the problems raging about him by having his rotund and ridiculously flatulent protagonist utter one of the oddest baptismal pronouncements on record: "God damn it, you've got to be kind."[6]

Vonnegut contends that "the function of an artist is to respond to his own time" and points out that "Voltaire, Swift, and Mark Twain did it."[7] In writing *Slaughterhouse-Five* Vonnegut unmistakably set out to respond to his own time by traveling into both a personal and a public past in order to bear witness to the firebombing of Dresden, Germany, in the context of the Vietnam War and the radical cost to innocent life all wars consistently demand.

The novel intentionally breaks the formal barriers of fiction by including in the first and last chapters an account of Vonnegut's struggle to write the book. Rather than calling the first chapter a preface, Vonnegut suggests that the boundaries between nonfiction and fiction are slippery at best. All acts of creation for Vonnegut are in a sense "fictional," and for the first time in his career he places himself into his created world as a character, sharing a cameo in a scene with the novel's protagonist Billy Pilgrim. As he suggests in an interview, "Everything is a lie, because our brains are two-bit computers, and we can't get very high-grade truths out of them. But as far as improving the human condition goes, our minds are certainly up to that. That's what they were designed to do. And we do have the freedom to make up comforting lies. But we don't do enough of it."[8]

While the content of *Slaughterhouse-Five* includes some of the grimmest details of war, Vonnegut uses black humor, or what is often referred to as gallows humor, to help the reader swallow his bitter pill. He describes this form of humor as the predicament of "intelligent people in hopeless situations" and acknowledges that he has "customarily written about powerless people who felt there wasn't much they could do about their situations."[9] Billy Pilgrim fits such a description flawlessly, and his story of internment in Dresden is told through a series of flashbacks and flash-forwards, which Vonnegut explains are the result of coming "unstuck in time." This time-traveling device affords the author a range of absurdly funny and despairingly ironic juxtapositions. It also suggests that no one can make "sense" out of war. As he says to his editor, Sam Lawrence, "There is nothing intelligent to say about a massacre. Everybody is supposed to be dead, to never say anything or want anything."[10]

In the prologue to a later novel, *Slapstick* (1976), Vonnegut suggests why these uses of humor in the face of despair are so vitally important to him not only as a novelist but as a human. As he tells it, he was "perpetually intoxicated and instructed by Laurel and Hardy" during his childhood in the Great Depression. What made these early comedic screen actors so important is that they "bargained in good faith with their destinies and were screamingly adorable and funny on that account."[11]

And so Billy Pilgrim does not question the fact that *Slaughterhouse-Five*'s aliens look ridiculously similar to plumber's helpers; nor does he balk at the idea that they might snatch from earth a soft-core porn starlet named Montana Wildhack to mate with him in a zoo on the planet Tralfamadore in order to understand better the human characteristics of love.

Vonnegut admits that as an author he is "in the business of making jokes" and describes his own novels as "mosaics made up of a whole bunch of tiny little chips; and each chip is a joke."[12] This coping mechanism allows Vonnegut to move from judgment to acceptance of his character's plight and attendant shortcomings. As he explains, "It strikes me as gruesome and comical that in our culture we have an expectation that a man can always solve his problems," and as his own experience as a prisoner of war taught him, at times we are at the mercy of forces far larger than we are. It is for this reason that Vonnegut, in the book's initial chapter, acknowledges that writing antiwar books is as useless as writing antiglacier books; yet despite such a pronouncement he proceeds to do just that.

In 1964, while he was still floundering to make some kind of narrative sense of what he had experienced during the war, Vonnegut drove from Cape Cod to Pennsylvania to visit Bernard V. O'Hare, an old war buddy. He hoped that such a trip would jog memory from its foggy perch and that O'Hare would not only confirm his recollections but add to them. Mary O'Hare, Bernard's wife, had set a table for the two veterans but was clearly agitated by Vonnegut's presence. This scene, which Vonnegut recreates in the novel but which literally happened and which he recounts in several interviews, plays out to a dramatic conclusion.

In an uncharacteristic outburst, Mary harangues Vonnegut for the book she thinks he will write: "Well, I know," she says. "You'll pretend you were men instead of babies, and you'll be played in the movies by Frank Sinatra and John Wayne or some of those other glamorous, war-loving, dirty old men. And war will look just wonderful, so we'll have a lot more of them. And they'll be fought by babies like the babies upstairs."[13]

As literary and film history documents, no such thing occurred. In fact, Vonnegut writes in the first chapter that "I have told my sons that they are not under any circumstances to take part in massacres, and that the news of massacres of enemies is not to fill them with satisfaction or glee. I have also told them not to work for companies which make massacre machinery, and to express contempt for people who think we need machinery like that."[14]

With the unprecedented success of *Slaughterhouse-Five*, Vonnegut was launched into the position of cultural icon, landing him bit parts in movies and advertising campaigns. It also led to his decision to turn away from writing novels in order to pursue a career as a playwright. This decision was relatively short-lived, although it did produce the play *Happy Birthday, Wanda June* (1970), which had a brief run in New York, as well as the television play, *Between Time and Timbuktu, or Prometheus-5* (1972), which was produced by National Educational Television. During this same period his father died, his marriage ended, and he began a relationship with the renowned photographer Jill Krementz, who would become his second wife in 1979.

Perhaps not surprisingly given the tepid reception of his work as a playwright, by 1973 Vonnegut returned to writing novels and published *Breakfast of Champions*, a metatextual romp that included a large number of the author's pen and ink drawings. Vonnegut performs an even more significant role as a character in *Breakfast of Champions* than he had in *Slaughterhouse-Five*, including the penultimate scene in which he is instructed by his own character, the abstract expressionist painter Rabo Karabekian, about how he might understand the value of all life-forms and better embrace the sanctity of life.

Ever the populist writer, Vonnegut describes Karabekian's paintings as a sham: "I thought Karabekian with his meaningless pictures had entered into a conspiracy with millionaires to make poor people feel stupid."[15] But what Vonnegut discovers when confronted with Karabekian's painting *The Temptation of St. Anthony*, which consists of a vertical stripe of orange reflecting tape on a field of green wall paint, is

> everything about life which truly matters, with nothing left out. It is a picture
> of the awareness of every animal. It is the immaterial core of every animal –
> the "I am" to which all messages are sent. It is all that is alive in any of us – in
> a mouse, in a deer, in a cocktail waitress. It is unwavering and pure, no matter
> what preposterous adventure may befall us. A sacred picture of Saint Anthony
> alone is one vertical, unwavering band of light. If a cockroach were near him,
> or a cocktail waitress, the picture would show two such bands of light. Our
> awareness is all that is alive and maybe sacred in any of us.[16]

And in this way Vonnegut finds healing, making a leap of faith to believe in the sacred awareness in all living things, which affords him the courage to go on writing.

And write he does. After the popular success of *Breakfast of Champions* – the critics were not nearly as kind to this novel as the reading public, and it remains a top seller among high school and college students – Vonnegut produced two more novels before the end of the decade – *Slapstick* and *Jailbird* (1979) – as well as a work of nonfiction – *Wampeters, Foma, & Granfalloons* (1974).

Although Vonnegut, like Mark Twain, struggled with an increasingly dark pessimism about the future of humanity – even attempting suicide in 1984, which he speaks candidly about in *Fates Worse than Death* (1991) – writing appeared to be his best form of therapy. "I've worried some about why write books when Presidents and Senators and generals do not read them," Vonnegut explains, "and the university experience taught me a very good reason: you catch people before they become generals and Senators and Presidents, and you poison their minds with humanity. Encourage them to make a better world."[17]

To this end, during the 1980s Vonnegut wrote and published five books, including the children's story *Sun Moon Star* (1980), which is an orthodox retelling of Christ's birth; *Palm Sunday* (1981), which Vonnegut refers to as an autobiographical collage, offering a detailed account of his family's history in Indianapolis; *Deadeye Dick* (1982), which is a send-up of the dangers inherent in a culture addicted to firearms; *Galapagos* (1985), which was born out of a trip Vonnegut took with his wife Jill Krementz to the Galapagos Islands and explores the idea of human devolution into seal-like creatures that can no longer destroy one another; and finally *Bluebeard* (1987), in which Vonnegut reintroduces the character Rabo Karabekian in order to ponder the value of art and the role of women, deciding that "Now it's the Women's Turn!"

Vonnegut would go on to write and publish two more novels in his career, *Hocus Pocus* (1990), the story of a Vietnam veteran, and *Timequake* (1997), which he called a failed novel and which featured a return to Vonnegut himself as the main protagonist of his fiction. In addition to these imaginative forays, Vonnegut produced several more works of nonfiction, including *Fates Worse than Death* (1991); *God Bless You, Dr. Kevorkian* (1999); *A Man without a Country* (2005); and *Armageddon in Retrospect* (2008), which was published posthumously. Before his death in 2007, a work of short fiction, *Bagombo Snuff Box*, was published in 1999, and since his death two more collections of short fiction have appeared, *Look at the Birdie* (2009) and *While Mortals Sleep* (2011).

As his generation's supreme moralist, Vonnegut has a legacy as an American novelist that might best be characterized by his persistent belief in the best humanity might aspire to, while laughing at the ridiculousness of such a thought. His use of metatextual and metafictional techniques afforded him this dual vision and allowed him to pull back the veil on establishment hierarchies.

The impish delight he took in such ethical mischief continues to captivate audiences, and his persistence in the face of a future he described as hopeless serves as a powerful example. As he wrote in *God Bless You, Dr. Kevorkian*, "If it weren't for the message of mercy and pity in Jesus' Sermon on the Mount, I wouldn't want to be a human being. I would just as soon be a rattlesnake,"[18] a sentiment that echoes the advice he gave to Bennington College graduates in a speech: "I beg you to believe in the most ridiculous superstition of all: that humanity is at the center of the universe, the fulfiller or the frustrator of the grandest dreams of God Almighty. If you can believe that, and make others believe it, then there might be hope for us. Human beings might stop treating each other like garbage, might begin to treasure and protect each other instead."[19] And in such an idealistic and earnest request rests the legacy of Vonnegut's vision for a better world.

## FURTHER READING

Boon, Kevin Alexander (ed.), *At Millennium's End: New Essays on the Work of Kurt Vonnegut*, Albany, State University of New York Press, 2001.

Davis, Todd, *Kurt Vonnegut's Crusade, or How a Postmodern Harlequin Preached a New Kind of Humanism*, Albany, State University of New York Press, 2006.

Klinkowitz, Jerome, *Vonnegut in Fact: The Public Spokesmanship of Personal Fiction*, Columbia, University of South Carolina Press, 1998.

Merrill, Robert (ed.), *Critical Essays on Kurt Vonnegut*, Boston, Mass., G. K. Hall, 1990.

Mustazza, Leonard (ed.), *The Critical Response to Kurt Vonnegut*, Westport, Conn., Greenwood Press, 1994.

Rackstraw, Loree, *Love as Always, Kurt: Vonnegut as I Knew Him*, New York, Da Capo Press, 2009.

Reed, Peter J. and Marc Leeds (eds.), *The Vonnegut Chronicles: Interviews and Essays*, Westport, Conn., Greenwood Press, 1996.

Shields, Charles J., *And So It Goes: Kurt Vonnegut: A Life*, New York, Henry Holt, 2011.

Simmons, David (ed.), *New Critical Essays on Kurt Vonnegut*, New York, Palgrave Macmillan, 2009.

## NOTES

1  William Rodney Allen (ed.), *Conversations with Kurt Vonnegut* (Jackson, University Press of Mississippi, 1988), p. 34.

2  Kurt Vonnegut, *Slaughterhouse-Five* (New York, Dell, 1969), p. 2.

3  Allen, *Conversations with Kurt Vonnegut*, p. 104.

4  Allen, *Conversations with Kurt Vonnegut*, p. 103.

5  Vonnegut, *Mother Night* (New York, Dell, 1966), p. v.

6  Vonnegut, *God Bless You, Mr. Rosewater* (New York, Dell, 1965), p. 110.

7  Allen, *Conversations with Kurt Vonnegut*, p. 64.

8  Allen, *Conversations with Kurt Vonnegut*, p. 77.

9  Allen, *Conversations with Kurt Vonnegut*, p. 91.

10  Vonnegut, *Slaughterhouse-Five*, p. 19.

11  Vonnegut, *Slapstick* (New York, Delacorte, 1976), p. 1.

12  Allen, *Conversations with Kurt Vonnegut*, p. 69.

13  Vonnegut, *Slaughterhouse-Five*, p. 14.

14  Vonnegut, *Slaughterhouse-Five*, p. 19.

15  Vonnegut, *Breakfast of Champions* (New York, Dell, 1973), p. 219.

16  Vonnegut, *Breakfast of Champions*, p. 221.

17  Allen, *Conversations with Kurt Vonnegut*, p. 5.

18  Vonnegut, *God Bless You, Dr. Kevorkian* (New York, Seven Stories Press, 1999), p. 10.

19  Vonnegut, *Wampeters, Foma, and Granfalloons* (New York, Dell, 1976), pp. 163–4.

# 25
# John Updike

JAMES SCHIFF

John Updike (1932–2009) has stood as a major figure in the American literary landscape since the 1950s – of his contemporaries, only Philip Roth has been there as long. Updike emerged in his early twenties as the Wunderkind from Shillington, Pennsylvania, a gifted stylist with a lyric love of the surface world. As one reviewer wrote in 1960, "Updike frequently gives the impression that he has six or seven senses, all of them operating at full strength."[1] The early writing, which covered a Pennsylvania boyhood and early married life, was marked by keen visual detail, a mastery of image and metaphor, and revelation of how significance resides within the ordinary. The words also poured out rapidly. Short stories, poems, and articles by Updike were appearing in the *New Yorker* every few weeks.

By age forty Updike had published sixteen books, including *Rabbit, Run* (1960), *The Centaur* (1963), and *Couples* (1968), and he was already the subject of multiple volumes of literary criticism, something unheard of for such a young writer. A resident of Massachusetts since 1957, he had become a New Englander, as was increasingly reflected in settings and characters found in his work. His subject matter, most often aligned with family life, marriage, and domesticity, had turned more explicitly to sexuality and adultery, as well as the ways in which American culture and politics shape one's domestic existence.

By age sixty, Updike had added to his oeuvre *The Coup* (1978), *Rabbit Is Rich* (1981), *Roger's Version* (1986), and *Rabbit at Rest* (1990); had collected most of the literary prizes; and was heralded by fellow novelists and critics as one of the major literary figures of his time.[2] *Rabbit Angstrom*, his series of novels about a former basketball star who becomes an American Everyman, was collectively singled out as one of America's most significant postwar novels.[3] Updike's writings continued to explore domestic America yet increasingly demonstrated greater variety and range, with settings in fictionalized Africa and Brazil and characters that included an exiled dictator, a computer scientist, and contemporary witches. The new writings also revealed an increasingly erudite Updike, who had mastered and integrated into his novels a wealth of difficult information from such fields as particle physics, computer science, Buddhism, and Hinduism.

Updike's output, along with critical interest in his writings, remained consistent until his death in 2009, though his reputation dipped slightly during the last decade or two of his life. The fiction he published after *Rabbit at Rest* (1990) was not as strong as earlier work, and his treatment of gender, race, and sexuality suggested to some critics that he was a throwback to an earlier generation. That said, interest in his work increased after his death, and he continues at present to draw the same level of significant critical attention that began in the late 1960s. His supporters regard him as a brilliant and gifted stylist, with remarkable range and versatility, who, as William H. Pritchard wrote in 1973, "is putting together a body of work which in substantial intelligent creation will eventually be seen as second to none in our time."[4] His detractors, sometimes more vehement than his champions, view him as an overly precious stylist, a conventional realist, "the Great Male Narcissist," and "one of a group of contemporary novelists who are somewhat victimized aesthetically by their conventional religious yearnings."[5]

Because Updike has been a fixture for so long on the American literary landscape, it can become surprisingly difficult to see him clearly or through fresh eyes. It is too easy to adopt the thinking and terminology of one of these two critical camps: that he is either a vastly intelligent, ambitious, and gifted writer, on a level with Proust and Joyce, or a self-indulgent stylist whose traditional methods and patriarchal vision stifle any potential greatness. Updike's prolificacy does not make this any easier. His sixty-five volumes can be intimidating to a reader hoping to see him clearly and fully. Further, his best known work of fiction, *Rabbit Angstrom*, is five volumes and more than eighteen hundred pages.

One approach to understanding Updike's writings has been to link him to earlier American writers, particularly Hawthorne, James, Howells, and Salinger, as well as traditions, such as realism. A slightly different approach, which may be more fruitful, is to consider how Updike *differs* from other writers within the American tradition. It is curious how often Updike is pegged as a known commodity – for example, a conventional realist, a blatant sexist, a writer consumed with sex and self – when the reality is that his writing is more nuanced and ambiguous. For instance, while realism is at the core of Updike's art, several of his novels could just as easily be described as works of naturalism, modernism, or postmodernism. Because his writing is more complex and varied than is commonly acknowledged – novels like *A Month of Sundays* (1975) and *The Coup* (1978) provide ample evidence – it pays to study him more carefully, particularly in regard to how he differs from his peers and predecessors. The French may have sniffed this out first; as Sylvie Mathé points out, the leftist journal *Marianne*, in a piece of homage after his death, spoke of Updike, in her words, as "the unique representative of a totally original fictional form."[6]

Among American writers, Updike is unique in several respects, of which at least four seem worthy of examination. First, consider Updike's relationship to his culture. American writers have often written from the margins, positioned – either because of gender, race, class, ethnicity, education, politics, fashion, religion, or psychological makeup – as outsiders. Some, of course, have had no choice in the matter and find themselves to be outsiders for reasons beyond their control: the color of their skin, their ethnicity, gender, or class. Examples are legion: Frederick Douglass, Zora Neale Hurston, Leslie Marmon Silko, Toni Morrison. Others, however, are outsiders by choice, playing some variation on the role of exile, objector, artiste, recluse, victim, rebel, or social critic. Dickinson, Salinger, and Pynchon all sought varying forms of reclusiveness in order to live and harvest their work in relative isolation or anonymity. Stein, Hemingway, James, Henry Miller, and Djuna Barnes found American culture provincial, so they traveled to foreign shores, in some cases remaining there permanently. Others turned to political resistance: Thoreau earned his legacy through civil disobedience and solitude; Richard Wright joined the Communist Party and wrote protest novels. Even writers who stuck around and sought to absorb America, such as Kerouac, Mailer, Ken Kesey, and Robert Stone, charted a more resistant course away from mainstream bourgeois society toward counter- or alternative cultures. In contrast, Updike did not seek isolation or exile, did not feel mistreated or marginalized by his country or culture, did not feel inclined to protest politically or personally, and was not interested in pursuing the romantic persona of the solitary, troubled artist. Rather, Updike generally embraced and celebrated his culture and nation, finding a comfortable place near the center from which he could witness domestic, local, and national events. As a white heterosexual male who quickly rose from humble roots to fame and wealth, Updike may have had less to rebel against, yet other writers with similar profiles – Hemingway, Fitzgerald, DeLillo, Roth – did not embrace middle America and popular culture as Updike did.

As James Atlas wrote, Updike "followed Flaubert's advice that in order to be a great writer, one must live like a bourgeois."[7] A resident of small towns nearly all his life, Updike grew up in a family of modest means in Shillington, Pennsylvania, where as an only child he lived with his parents and grandparents. After receiving scholarships to both Harvard and the Ruskin School of Drawing and Fine Arts in Oxford (his earliest ambition was to be a cartoonist), Updike and his young family (he married in college and soon after began having children) arrived in New York, where he had been offered a job as a "Talk of the Town" reporter at the *New Yorker*. Given his deep infatuation with that magazine, one could easily have imagined for Updike a long career in Manhattan. Yet after two years in the city, Updike and his family left for the small New England town of Ipswich, Massachusetts, where they resided between 1957 and 1974, becoming part of the small-town middle class: "I felt that I had to hatch my books in a nest of relative quiet, and also I felt that the kind of life that I would witness in a small town would be more representative of American life than what I would see in Manhattan, had I stayed."[8]

In Ipswich, Updike, along with his wife and friends, "joined committees and societies, belonged to a recorder group and a poker group, played volleyball and touch football in season, read plays aloud and went Greek-dancing and gave dinner parties and attended clambakes and concerts and costume balls, all within a rather narrow society, so that everything resonated."[9] Except for brief stays of a year in London and two in Boston, Updike would spend the final fifty-two years of his life on Boston's North Shore, living in Ipswich, Georgetown, and Beverly Farms. There he found both the environment and the material needed to produce an art that closely examines the domestic and familial. Whereas many of his predecessors and peers would have rebelled against a small-town middle-class existence, Updike embraced and celebrated the lifestyle, delighting in its textures and surfaces, its objects and gestures. This sense of delight and celebration of the world is very much part of Updike's writing and being. Further, while many of his literary predecessors suffered from depression, financial problems, alcohol and drug addiction, or various strains of psychological disease – Hemingway once famously said that the first thing a writer needs is an unhappy childhood – Updike, perhaps more than any writer of his time, gave the impression of having a relatively happy life. Not that his life was saccharine or mindlessly placid – he endured a spiritual crisis in his twenties; his first marriage, marred by infidelity, was often in crisis and ended in divorce – but he generally gave the impression of being more content with his life and with the world than most writers.

Because he lived among and embraced the American middle class, it is natural that Updike chose to write about this world, which provides a second example of his uniqueness among American writers – namely, his subject matter. Whereas other writers have again been drawn more to the margins and extremes – Salinger depicted a gifted family of geniuses and brilliant performers; Cormac McCarthy wrote of men on the run, facing bleak, threatening circumstances; Wharton depicted the wealthy; Faulkner, the poor and idiosyncratic; Hemingway, the wounded and adventurous;

Wright and Morrison, the disenfranchised and abused – Updike was drawn
to the center, turning to what he called "the whole mass of middling, hidden,
troubled America."[10] Setting his fiction mostly in small towns and suburbs,
Updike depicted and closely examined the social and domestic lives of relatively ordinary middle-class characters: a car salesman and his family, an
adulterous contractor and his circle of friends and lovers, a North Shore
housewife seeking an independent life, a minister who loses his faith. As
he explained, "Something quite intricate and fierce occurs in homes, and it
seems to me without doubt worthwhile to examine what it is."[11] While the
American middle class has most often been the object of satire or parody –
consider, say, Sinclair Lewis's *Babbitt* (1922), which critiques the vacuity
and conformity of middle-class existence – Updike treated this world as
vital and interesting, his purpose being "to give the mundane its beautiful
due."[12] Perhaps more than any other American writer, Updike took everyday
domestic life seriously, endowing it with a depth, mystery, and lyrical beauty
that make it worthy of great literature.

The best example of this can be found in *Rabbit Angstrom*, a meganovel
that consists of four separate novels and one novella, written at ten-year
intervals: *Rabbit, Run* (1960), *Rabbit Redux* (1971), *Rabbit Is Rich* (1981),
*Rabbit at Rest* (1990), and "Rabbit Remembered" (2000). These books
collectively chronicle, amid America's declining grandeur, the life of Harry
"Rabbit" Angstrom, a former high school basketball star from small-town
Pennsylvania who sells Toyota automobiles while striving for spiritual and
material success. When Updike composed his first Rabbit novel in 1959, he
had no sense of its becoming a multivolume work about a single character,[13]
yet *Rabbit, Run* turned out to be one of his most successful novels. Ten years
later, after failing to produce a novel about President James Buchanan and
unsettled by what he called "the most dissentious American decade since
the Civil War," he returned to his former character, using him as "a recep-
tacle for my disquiet and resentments, which would sit more becomingly on
him than on me."[14] Each of the Rabbit books, "composed at the end of a
decade and published at the beginning of the next one," became, in Updike's
words, "a kind of running report on the state of my hero and his nation."[15]
Each also integrates into its pages a range of historical and cultural information pertaining to such events as the cold war, Vietnam, Ted Kennedy's fatal
automobile accident in Chappaquiddick, the *Apollo* moon shot, the 1979
Organization of Petroleum Exporting Countries– (OPEC)-induced gasoline
shortage, and the Iranian hostage crisis. As Updike pointed out, "My fiction
about the daily doings of ordinary people has more history in it than history
books"; thus, the novels stand as the story not only of a man but of a nation,
which, like its hero, is in decline.[16]

The great achievement of *Rabbit Angstrom* is the creation of Updike's eponymous protagonist, who exists not on the margins but near the center of American culture. Although he evolves over time, Rabbit is for the most part a large man (6'3" and 230 pounds at one point), who is optimistic, crude and culturally unsophisticated, fairly amiable and well-liked, self-indulgent, sexually obsessed, keenly aware of his own mortality, impulsive, and continually yearning for more. Like Hester Prynne, Huck Finn, Holden Caulfield, and Jay Gatsby, Rabbit Angstrom has become an icon in American literature, a mythical protagonist whose identity is familiar from just a single moniker – Huck, Hester, Gatsby, Rabbit – and whose story speaks eloquently to and reveals much about his national culture. Rabbit's standing is such that his death, at the conclusion of *Rabbit at Rest,* was of enough importance that both the *New York Times* and *Washington Post* addressed it not only in their book review sections but on their editorial pages. Rabbit provided for Updike a sensibility through which the author could observe, examine, and provide commentary on a range of subjects, including death, money, food, race, sex, materialism, and the fate of American culture. Although DeLillo, McCarthy, Morrison, and Roth wrote novels that, one could argue, are as important as *Rabbit Angstrom*, none created a character as familiar or as iconic as Rabbit.

The genius of *Rabbit Angstrom* is that Updike was able to create a compelling narrative from mundane material. Though there are crises in Rabbit's life – he and his wife, Janice, have extramarital affairs and live temporarily with their lovers; their newborn daughter dies tragically in an accidental bathtub drowning; their house burns to the ground – the bulk of the narrative, particularly in the latter two novels, is composed of quotidian scenes: Rabbit interacting with family and friends, Rabbit thinking about his life while driving through town listening to the car radio. The tenor of this may sound trivial, but that is hardly the case. Updike generates narrative activity and sustains interest, at least in part, through a free indirect style of narration, which moves effortlessly between first and third persons. We see Rabbit depicted from a god's eye view, or from the perspective of his wife, Janice, or his son, Nelson, then Updike takes us directly inside Rabbit's head, where at close range we experience his urges, fears, and desires. This narrative movement can be stimulating. It can also become uncomfortable. As we move into Rabbit's thoughts, some readers find him appealing and comically sympathetic, yet others see him as immensely unlikable and disgusting. George Will referred to Rabbit as an "emotionally stunted, intellectually barren, morally repulsive egoist"; on the other hand, Ralph Wood stated, "Rabbit Angstrom is one of us: the average sensual man, the American Adam, the carnally minded creature whom our moralistic religion and politics cannot encompass."[17] That Rabbit has elicited such a range of polarized responses makes him all the more intriguing as a character.

While Rabbit sustains our interest for much of this meganovel's eighteen hundred pages, the project itself, with its focus on everyday domestic life, could never have succeeded were it not for Updike's prose style – which marks a third example of how he stands unique among American novelists. Updike was not a brilliant constructor of plot or narrative design (he wrote his novels quickly and without extensive revision); nor was he a literary innovator like Melville or Pynchon. But what he could do better than any American writer of his era was write sentences. Even a formidable detractor like Harold Bloom admitted that Updike possessed "a major style" and was "perhaps the most considerable stylist among the writers of fiction in his American generation."[18] Although longer passages best illustrate his genius, a sentence or phrase can at least approximate: "[M]aybe God is in the universe the way salt is in the ocean, giving it a taste"; "That a marriage ends is less than ideal; but all things end under heaven, and if temporality is held to be invalidating, then nothing real succeeds."[19] Updike's style builds upon lush descriptive language, keen visual detail and clarity of expression, extraordinary intelligence, and a mastery of metaphor. Alert to the textures and beauty of the world, Updike could see what others could not, and his sentences, while singing the ordinary, often rise to a state of exuberance and delight; the writing becomes a performance, with language taking precedence over action and scene. This could at times be a liability – the writing runs the risk of becoming overly precious, so as to rob scenes of their emotional resonance. Yet when he was clicking on all cylinders, Updike could write as well as any American writer ever has.

Because he could do almost anything with language, in any form or genre, Updike was a writer of extraordinary range and versatility, the fourth and final example of how he differs from his peers. Many of his contemporaries represented in this volume, such as Morrison, Pynchon, McCarthy, and Roth, excelled at one genre, the novel, and are known almost exclusively as novelists. Updike, however, excelled at three genres: the novel, short fiction, and criticism. Immensely prolific, Updike published not only twenty-three novels but seventeen collections of short fiction, including more than two hundred stories; eight volumes of poetry; ten volumes and more than five thousand pages of essays and criticism; a memoir and a play; and several children's books. Although his poetry and lone effort in drama pale considerably beside the novels, his achievements in short fiction and criticism are significant as well as comparable. In this respect, Updike stands, like James, Howells, and Nabokov before him, as a major "man of letters"; in fact, given the scope, range, intelligence, and virtuosity of his oeuvre, he may be the most significant such figure in American literary history. Yet the tag *man of letters* carries a scent of old-fashioned patriarchy, suggesting the jacketed male writer in his study, surrounded by leather-bound volumes. Such an image does not accurately characterize Updike; nor does the term *man of letters* suggest what a playful, funny writer he was, or how artistic and sexually charged his writing could be. Updike seemed capable of writing exquisitely about anything, in any form or genre. As Martin Amis remarked, Updike was "a master of all trades, able to crank himself up to Ph.D. level on any subject he fancies; architecture, typography, cave painting, computers, evolution … and Gospel scholarship."[20] In a given week, one could find one of his short stories in the *New Yorker,* an art exhibition review in the *New York Review of Books,* and essays on, say, Kierkegaard, golf, Mickey Mouse, and seventeenth-century New England homes in various specialized journals and magazines. Updike's versatility and talent were so extraordinary that a novelist as talented as Philip Roth, upon finishing Updike's *Rabbit Is Rich,* lamented, "He knows so much, about golf, about porn, about kids, about America. I don't know anything about anything. His hero is a Toyota salesman. Updike knows everything about being a Toyota salesman. Here I live in the country and I don't even know the names of the trees. I'm going to give up writing."[21]

For nearly half a century now, Updike has been recognized as an important American writer. His novels and short stories depicting middle-class domesticity have resonated with readers and inspired a generation of younger fiction writers, including Ian McEwan, Julian Barnes, Martin Amis, Lorrie Moore, Ann Beattie, and Nicholson Baker. Because he was drawn to the ordinary and middling and wrote frequently in a mimetic style, he is sometimes tapped, albeit inaccurately, as a conventional writer. However, by resisting paths set down by his literary predecessors, and finding a position and territory all his own, Updike was a more original and unique writer than is commonly acknowledged, and that in many ways makes him, indeed, a particularly American writer.

## FURTHER READING

Baker, Nicholson, *U and I: A True Story*, New York, Random House, 1991.
De Bellis, Jack (ed.), *John Updike: The Critical Responses to the "Rabbit" Saga,"* Westport, Conn., Praeger, 2005.
Greiner, Donald J., *John Updike's Novels*, Athens, Ohio University Press, 1984.
Newman, Judie, *John Updike*, New York, St. Martin's Press, 1988.
Olster, Stacey (ed.), *The Cambridge Companion to John Updike*, Cambridge, Cambridge University Press, 2006.

Pritchard, William H., *Updike: America's Man of Letters*, South Royalton, Vt., Steerforth Press, 2000.

Schiff, James A., *John Updike Revisited*, New York, Twayne, 1998.

Yerkes, James (ed.), *John Updike and Religion: The Sense of the Sacred and the Motions of Grace*, Grand Rapids, Mich., William B. Eerdmans, 1999.

## NOTES

1 Whitney Balliett, "The American Expression," review of *Rabbit, Run*, by John Updike, *New Yorker,* November 5, 1960, p. 222.

2 Updike won the National Book Critics Circle Award on three occasions, the Pulitzer Prize twice, the National Book Award, the American Book Award, the Howells Medal, le Prix du Meilleur livre étranger, the Rea Award, as well as other prizes. In a survey conducted by the [London] *Sunday Times* in March 1994, in which notable writers and critics were asked to name "the greatest living novelist writing in English," Updike finished second only to Saul Bellow, Nicolette Jones, "The Order of Merit," March 13, 1994, pp. 8–9. On October 18, 1982, Updike appeared on the cover of *Time* magazine for the second time, an honor accorded to only Faulkner, Hemingway, Joyce, and Sinclair Lewis.

3 In a 2006 survey conducted by the *New York Times*, in which novelists and critics were asked "What is the best work of American fiction of the last 25 years?" *Rabbit Angstrom* placed third, behind Toni Morrison's *Beloved* and Don DeLillo's *Underworld*. See A. O. Scott, "In Search of the Best," *New York Times*, May 21, 2006, pp. 17–19.

4 William H. Pritchard, "Long Novels and Short Stories," review of *Museums and Women*, by John Updike, *Hudson Review* 26.1 (Spring 1973): 240.

5 David Foster Wallace, "Certainly the End of *Something* or Other, One Would Sort of Have to Think," *Consider the Lobster and Other Essays* (New York, Back Bay, 2006), p. 51; Harold Bloom, "Introduction," *John Updike* (New York, Chelsea House, 1987), p. 1.

6 Sylvie Mathé, "Under Gallic Eyes: The Case of John Updike's Ambivalent Reception in France," *John Updike Review* 1.1 (Fall 2011): 26.

7 James Atlas, "John Updike Breaks Out of Suburbia," *New York Times Magazine*, December 10, 1978, p. 69.

8 Dick Cavett, "A Conversation with John Updike (1992)," *Conversations with John Updike,* ed. James Plath (Jackson, University Press of Mississippi, 1994), p. 236.

9 John Updike, *Self-Consciousness* (New York, Knopf, 1989), pp. 51–2.

10 Updike, *Self-Consciousness*, p. 103.

11 Jane Howard, "Can a Nice Novelist Finish First? (1966)," *Conversations with John Updike,* ed. James Plath (Jackson, University Press of Mississippi, 1994), p. 11.

12 John Updike, "Foreword," *The Early Stories 1953–1975* (New York, Knopf, 2003), p. xv.

13 Updike's original intention was for *Rabbit, Run* and *The Centaur* to be two novellas bound into a single volume, so as to demonstrate the differences between running and plodding, yet the planned novellas eventually emerged as separate novels.

14 John Updike, "A 'Special Message' to Purchasers of the Franklin Library Limited Edition, in 1981, of *Rabbit Redux,*" *Hugging the Shore* (New York, Knopf, 1983), p. 858; John Updike, "Introduction," *Rabbit Angstrom* (New York, Knopf/Everyman's Library, 1995), p. xv.

15 Updike, "Introduction," p. ix.

16 John Updike, "One Big Interview," *Picked-Up Pieces* (New York, Knopf, 1975), p. 501.

17 George F. Will, "Updike, America, Mortality," *Washington Post,* October 28, 1990, p. C7; Ralph C. Wood, "Rabbit Runs Down," review of *Rabbit at Rest,* by John Updike, *Christian Century* 107 (November 21–28, 1990): p. 1099.

18 Bloom, "Introduction," pp. 7, 1.

19 John Updike, *Rabbit Is Rich* (New York, Knopf, 1981), p. 462–63; John Updike, "Foreword," *The Maples Stories* (New York, Knopf/Everyman's Pocket Classics, 2001), p. 11.

20 Martin Amis, "Magnanimous in a Big Way," review of *Odd Jobs,* by John Updike, *New York Times Book Review,* November 10, 1991, p. 12.

21 David Plante, "Conversations with Philip," interview, *New York Times Book Review,* January 1, 1984, p. 3.

# 26

# Thomas Pynchon

DAVID SEED

Thomas Pynchon (1937–) is a leading member of those American novelists who began their careers in the 1960s whose subsequent output not only garnered major awards but has gained recognition as making a unique commentary on recent American culture and history. In his introduction to his collection of short fiction, *Slow Learner* (1984), Pynchon explains how the writings of the Beats helped him to break free from the literary decorum stifling expression in late-1950s America and to create fiction containing a range of different voices, however profane. From the same period, the decade following Hiroshima, Pynchon dates "one of the most remarkable flowerings of literary talent … in our history," namely, that of science fiction.[1] Pynchon himself has incorporated a number of science fiction tropes in his fiction: moon rockets in *Gravity's Rainbow*, extraterrestrials in *Vineland*, a hollow earth voyage in *Against the Day*, among other examples. In a 2006 letter in support of Ian McEwan, who had been accused of plagiarism in his novel *Atonement*, Pynchon found common cause with "most of us who write historical fiction."[2] A diversity of voices and a concern to investigate different historical moments have been two of the main characteristics of Pynchon's fiction together with a skill at moving the reader to and fro between high seriousness and low farce.

Pynchon's first novel, *V.* (1963), alternates episodes from 1898 up to the 1930s with sections taking place in late 1955 and 1956. The latter approach the Suez crisis but cut off just before it breaks. Similarly the first episode in the historical sequence, originally published as a stand-alone story set in Egypt, "Under the Rose," is set on the eve of the Fashoda crisis of 1898, which almost brought France and Britain to war over rival imperial claims in Africa. This story establishes one of Pynchon's main historical themes – empire – whose ideology he was challenging when he incorporated the story into *V.* by multiplying perspectives to include those of the local functionaries blanked out in the guidebooks of the period that were his source for locations.

The chronological and textual discontinuity between the historical chapters of *V.* tacitly encourages the reader to construct a historical narrative in order to make sense of the connections between these chapters. However, the novel carries a warning embodied in the character of Herbert Stencil, a figure whose very name suggests that he is fitting his data into a preconceived pattern. Stencil is the amateur historian of the novel, attempting to keep track of the appearances of V. throughout the recent past. Like a parodic version of Henry Adams, Stencil finds connections everywhere. Pynchon's choice of an initial letter for his title tantalizingly hints to the reader at hidden identities that might be revealed later, but Stencil's obsessive quest reveals the potentially absurd nature of our search for meaning. Tony Tanner has argued that "Pynchon's concerns are usually related in one way or another to problems of decipherment," and Stencil's activities are only the first example in Pynchon's novels of characters pursuing their own attempts to understand the data before them.[3] Pynchon holds on to a basic premise throughout his work that no one can stand outside history, with the result that his characters to varying degrees are always embedded within the situations they are trying to understand. One exception to this in *V.* is Benny Profane, an antihero who drifts between contemporary situations mainly set in 1950s New York.

Stencil is accused by one character of having paranoia, and critics have rightly stressed the importance of the latter throughout Pynchon's work. Paranoia could best be understood as the direction taken by his characters' cognitive mapping, frequently involving the fear of conspiracies at work behind the visible. Its attraction lies in the connections posited between events, evoking an order, albeit a malign one. Pynchon's frequently playful evocations of paranoia implicitly recognize its long American pedigree. Thus his fiction constantly leads the reader toward hypothetical connections while warning against facile conspiracy theory. Pynchon's use of different writing styles to evoke different periods reflects his conviction that history consists of a medley of discourses, all with their different ideological coloring. In that sense his novels belong with those of E. L. Doctorow, Ishmael Reed, and Robert Coover in a form of postmodernism described by Linda Hutcheon as "historiographic metafiction," that is, novels that incorporate historical data while dramatizing the difficulties of their assimilation.[4]

Pynchon's second novel, *The Crying of Lot 49* (1966), drew on Marshall McLuhan's *Understanding Media* (1964), which argues that contemporary media actually affect the way we perceive the world through the nature of the media themselves rather than through the content of their messages. The novel traces out the exposure of its protagonist, Oedipa Maas, to these media once she leaves the enclosure of her suburban home. The action starts with a telephone message, and from that point on the media proliferate so extensively that an information overload propels Oedipa to the verge of breakdown. Called to execute the will of Pierce Inverarity, a "California real estate mogul," Oedipa embarks on a search that takes her into offbeat bars; Yoyodyne, a company loosely resembling Boeing; and a performance of a pastiche-seventeenth century tragedy in an arena theater. She gradually comes to realize that, far from shedding light on earlier messages, each new revelation simply adds to her expanding field of interconnected data, which she proves unable to process. In that respect the novel anticipates the cyber-punk fiction of the 1980s. The final scene of *Lot 49* shows Oedipa still wait-ing for the ultimate revelation that would make everything clear.

*Vineland* (1990) develops the attention to the media in *Lot 49*, this time focusing primarily on television. The ubiquitous Tube connects with vir-tually every aspect of the action, and indeed the narrative resembles an extended TV program in its use of flashbacks, dissolves, and breaks between episodes. In one of the first scenes, a character jumps through a window, realizes that it is made of simulated glass, and later watches his action on the TV. In short, TV induces self-consciousness throughout the action. In a novel containing multiple references to drugs it is the Tube that induces the most widespread addiction, especially in a quasi-hippie group called the Thanatoids, who make a cult out of their death-oriented obsession.

The novel is punctuated by countless references to older films being shown on TV and opens in the Redwood National Park in northern California where the 1983 film *Return of the Jedi* was shot. Pynchon's allusions to *Star Wars* implicitly connect film with one of the novel's major themes: the growth of government surveillance in Reagan's America. *Vineland* is set in 1984 and steadily unfolds its Orwellian dimension through its many refer-ences to surveillance of American citizens. *Vineland* describes the experiences of a number of characters still living off their memories of being hippies in the 1960s, long after their age and the conditions of American life justify it. Pynchon presents the Nixon and Reagan years following that period as The Repression. In particular Reagan's war on drugs emerges as one of the most visible signs of a general government clampdown on illegal activities. Just as the novel's landscape is historically layered from the original Yurok mythical land through hippie farms to contemporary housing complexes, so the action and even the characters operate on two levels: memories of a lost period of innocence and commercial and political compromise with the present. The character Frenesi Gates, for instance, was formerly a rev-olutionary filmmaker at Berkeley exploiting her conviction that "a camera is a gun" to record cases of police brutality. Now in the present, however, she has lost this revolutionary fervor to such an extent that she is carrying on a long-standing affair with a federal agent and acting as an informant to the Federal Bureau of Investigation (FBI). Pynchon's depiction of the loss of sixties idealism is so thorough that the novel amounts to a satire on what is sometimes presented as an indirect longing for security by extending childhood indefinitely and by ignoring history in favor of the pleasures of the present moment. Among the many meanings to the title of the novel, surely one of the most ironic must be its echo of the nineteenth-century agricultural utopia in Vineland, New Jersey.

The relation between the media and political power had long concerned Pynchon. As early as 1958 he collaborated with his Cornell friend Kirkpatrick Sale on a musical called *Minstral Island*, set in 1998, when IBM has come to dominate the world. In his introduction to Jim Dodge's 1990 novel *Stone Junction* Pynchon gives a negative view of the "cyberworld" with its "threat of control without mercy that lay in wait down the comely vistas of freedom that computer-folk were imagining then."[5] If this sounds Orwellian, Pynchon confirmed the connection in his foreword to the Centennial Edition of *Nineteen Eighty-Four* (1949), where he sees the present-day United States as exploiting a more complex but equally sinister process of manipulation like that of Orwell's Ministry of Truth: "It has become a commonplace circa 2003 for government employees to be paid more than most of the rest of us to debase history, trivialize truth, and annihilate the past on a daily basis."[6]

*Inherent Vice* (2009) returns to the Californian landscape of *Lot 49*, this time set in the years 1969–70 against the background of the Manson murders and the election to president of Richard Nixon. Although there are complexities in the action, *Inherent Vice* remains one of Pynchon's most accessible works, partly because the reader can recognize many of the generic features of the noir crime narratives on which the novel draws. Its protagonist is a private eye, Larry "Doc" Sportello, maneuvering his way between a Mafia-like secret organization named the Golden Fang and the forces of law and order embodied in Lieutenant "Bigfoot" Bjornsen of the Los Angeles Police Department. Pynchon skilfully evokes the era of psychedelia with its paranoid hinterland of covert Central Intelligence Agency (CIA) activities. One of the most striking features of the landscape is the secret military installations, which Pynchon would have known at first hand since he worked as a writer for Boeing between 1960 and 1962. *Inherent Vice* is packed with references to film, to evoke not merely the period but also film noir. Indeed, the narrative is repeatedly phrased in filmic terms as if we were watching a script unfold before our eyes.

Of Pynchon's historical fiction, *Gravity's Rainbow* (1973) takes place in late 1944 through mid-1945. The action first occurs in London during its attack by the Nazi V-2 rockets and then moves gradually across Europe with the Allied troops until they reach central Germany. The protagonist, U.S. Lieutenant Tyrone Slothrop, discovers an embarrassing congruence between his erections and the V-2 strikes, a correspondence that introduces the theme of behaviorism. Throughout the novel Pynchon juxtaposes different forms of exploitation with sporadic examples of kindness and intimacy, all the more rare in that sexuality is one of the fields of conditioning being explored by all sides. The cause of behaviorism is championed by the British scientist Edward Pointsman, who uses Pavlov's study of conditioned reflexes as scientific scripture. Throughout the first part of the novel this work – "The Book" – is quoted to evoke a scientific desire for rational explanation so extreme that it shades constantly into dreams of power and control. Pitted against Pavlov, Pynchon drew on Norman O. Brown's *Life against Death* (1959), which argues that humans are so unaware of their true motivation that ultimately they are in love with their own death. Brown helped Pynchon to link the Nazi rocket program with Pavlov's experiments as exercises in self-mystification screening fantasies of power of transcendence through death. The true opposition in the novel emerges as a contrast between the powerful and their victims. Slothrop, for example, discovers that he has been sold as a small child for behavioral experiments and probably has become the subject of unconscious conditioned reflexes. His shocked loss of autonomy is simply the most foregrounded example of related cases of victimization running all through the novel, and his loss ultimately results in his dispersal throughout the Zone – the limbo area of liberated Germany.

When he was researching material for *V.* Pynchon discovered the Herero, a South West African people who almost suffered extinction at the hands of their German imperial rulers in 1904.[7] Empire and race were to function as two sides of the same coin throughout Pynchon's subsequent fiction. Even in the essay that he wrote in the aftermath of the 1965 Watts riot in Los Angeles, Pynchon describes the area as one under white occupation.[8] In *V.* the Herero are briefly identified as a victimized people. They return in *Gravity's Rainbow* as a quasi-Nazi militarized group called the Schwarzkommando, who have entered the Zone to enact their ultimate fate at the hands of their imperial masters in seeking death. The novel situates this desire for death within its larger exploration of the symbolic connections within the Western psyche between blackness and death.

Cutting across these grim themes of exploitation and manipulation Pynchon deploys an anarchic comedy that intermittently converts the local subject into a performance. A slapstick sequence where Pointsman staggers around a bomb site with one foot stuck in a toilet bowl, a sequence of ribald limericks, the articulation of Slothrop's discovery of being conditioned in a song called "The Penis He Thought Was His Own," his masquerade in a Rocketman costume, and many similar cases drain off the gravity in the novel's title and give the reader temporary relief from the action's focus on manipulation and death. The novel's narrative segments are separated by lines of squares, which several critics have compared to the sprocket holes in films, and indeed Pynchon weaves into the action extensive allusions to German cinema, especially the latter's romantic tradition. These allusions blur the distinction between film and reality and at the same time remind the reader that film, like the other media, was put under government control by the Nazis. This blurring reaches its climax in the final montage of scenes from a rocket launch alternating with those from the Orpheus Theatre in Los Angeles, where the audience is waiting for the performance to start.

In his first novel Pynchon drew on the famous red Baedeker guide books to evoke a world of tourism where the traveler's routes were prescribed in advance and where European ethnocentrism displayed itself in the suppressed presence of the functionaries the tourist would have to deal with. *Lot 49* continues this theme by showing how Oedipa becomes an internal tourist exploring the part of California she thought she already knew. In these early narratives the street takes on a special significance not only as an avenue for travel but as a means of exploring the shared public life of a region. However, the imperial theme has remained one of Pynchon's main themes, manifesting itself through tourism and even the layout of cities. In *Gravity's Rainbow* he contrasts the rectangular grid of American cities with the circular layout of Herero townships, taking the latter as a holistic image of a unified culture and the other as a physical demonstration of how Western culture appropriates and structures space. Mapping thus was to become his central subject in *Mason & Dixon* (1997).

This novel describes the survey of 1763–7 that produced the famous dividing line marking boundaries among Pennsylvania, Maryland, Delaware, and Virginia. The undertaking was originally designed to identify areas of territory, but the Mason-Dixon Line took on a later historical significance by marking the boundary between the northern and southern states in the American Civil War. Like John Barth's *The Sot-Weed Factor* (1960), which takes place in seventeenth-century London and Maryland, Pynchon incorporates pastiche versions of the discourses circulating in his chosen historical period, whether religious, scientific, or picturesque. Through these he refracts a narrative that presents surveying as playing a crucial part in American expansion into the wilderness and in the rise of eighteenth-century commerce. Preliminary sections describing Mason and Dixon's visits to Cape Town and St. Helena, the latter administered at the time by the East India Company, establish the imperial terms of reference to be pursued throughout the novel. The finite spaces mapped out in those locations are contrasted with the "other worlds" of unexplored space. In America a surveyor named Shelby articulates the ideology of the new land as empty space: "Pure Space waits the Surveyor, – no previous Lines, no fences, no streets to constrain polygony however extravagant."[9] This evocation of America as a "virgin land" blanks out its earlier inhabitants and implicitly licenses white settlers to seize as much land as they can. The novel frequently alludes to resulting conflicts between the Europeans and Native Americans. The imperial rivalry between Britain and France for North America and the imperatives of trade both suppress the presence in the novel of the slaves (representing part of the infrastructure of imperial commerce) and Native Americans, cumulatively evoked as the Other in the "civilizing" mission of the settlers. Pynchon never allows the official ideology of the Europeans to blank out these presences by having a series of minor characters remind us of the routine violence in the settlers' actions.

Surveying throughout *Mason & Dixon* is an act inseparable from property ownership and the expansion of those property rights westward. The geometrical (literally "land-measuring") simplicity of their lines, forced across an uneven and hostile terrain, symbolizes for Pynchon a complex process of appropriation that combines discovery, investigation, designation of property, and ultimately commercial use. The famous line thus reflects a change in Philadelphia that Pynchon identified in an essay of 1993, written while he was researching the novel: "The city was becoming a kind of high-output machine, materials and labour going in, goods and services coming out, traffic inside flowing briskly long a grid of regular city blocks."[10] At the end of this passage Pynchon tacitly identifies a verbal nexus that was to become central to his novel, namely, the identification of cultural and moral values with geometrical simplicity. Thus "orthodoxy" and "rectification" etymologically signify straightness of opinion and rendering something straight. Again and again Pynchon hints that a rigid polarized mind-set is coming into being through the process of surveying that is eroding William Penn's original utopian plan to found a city of brotherly love. Pynchon's deep suspicion of linearity is reflected in the segmented narrative structure of *Mason & Dixon*, which jumps from episode to episode, challenging the reader to trace out connections between them.

Surveying in *Mason & Dixon* represents the main scientific activity in a novel evoking the transition in America from a religious to a secular culture. The second activity described is a series of experiments with clocks, reflecting the new attempts to measure time with regularity; other scientific devices here include Benjamin Franklin's glass harmonica and Vaucanson's Digesting Duck, both attempts to extend the range of mechanical contrivance. But the pursuit of science by no means excludes the transcendental.

Mason feels haunted by his dead wife and Dixon names one of his optical instruments a "cryptoscope" because it reveals "powers hidden and waiting the needles of Intruders."[11] The paranoia evoked in *Gravity's Rainbow* resurfaces here as a fear of secret conspiracies by the Jesuits and others. From the very beginning of the novel astronomy has blurred into astrology with the construction of natal charts, and virtually the last scene to focus on Mason describes his yielding to a visionary "procession of luminous Phantoms" despite his realization that this involved a "conscious Denial of all that Reason holds true."[12]

This juxtaposition of the scientific and the spiritual also informs *Against the Day* (2006), whose action spans the period from the 1893 Chicago World's Fair up to the immediate aftermath of the First World War. A secret organization is named the True Worshippers of the Ineffable Tetractys (or TWIT). Like *Gravity's Rainbow*, this novel makes constant reference to crossing over boundaries, whether man-made or transcendental limits to time and place. Haunting many of the narratives is the faith in a "hidden place" whose "geography is as much spiritual as physical."[13] The experiments into electricity by Nikola Tesla, who appears in the novel, are symptomatic of the explosion of scientific discoveries in Pynchon's period and in their combination with more fanciful possibilities in that Tesla was convinced he could record messages from other planets. *Against the Day* contains multiple plotlines linked by the theme of exploration. Thus an airship voyage to the Arctic is motivated by the desire to understand rays in the upper atmosphere and to discover lost races; travel to Colorado is fed by a desire for gold; and a trek across Siberia is conducted in order to investigate the massive Tunguska explosion of 1908. On one level exploration reflects imperial rivalries signaled in the fact that a Russian airship is called *The Great Game,* and Pynchon lingers over the Balkan wars of the 1910s, which reveal the imminent breakup of the Austro-Hungarian Empire.

However, territorial exploration is only part of a broader activity described in the novel. Pynchon alludes several times to H. G. Wells's *The Time Machine* (1895) as a key work of the period in its optimism that technology could carry humanity beyond the present. In *Against the Day* time travel is only one example of characters' recurring desire to move beyond known limits, whether through occult pilgrimage, along light "conduits," or through "bilocation"(simultaneously occupying two locations). This means that the landscape of the novel is constantly shifting into speculative dimensions – toward the end of the novel characters even believe in an alternative "Counter-Earth" – and a key medium for experimentation is light, transmitted by the ether. The latter is tied to the visionary, sometimes imagined by characters as offering a conduit to other realms.

The opening episode of *Against the Day* describes the activities of the Chums of Chance aboard an airship, and the novel continues a practice that Pynchon had begun in *V.* of refracting the action from a given period through the writing styles of that time. Thus *Against the Day* assembles pastiches of spy thrillers, westerns, and boys' adventure stories, among other genres. The Chums of Chance have already had their exploits converted into narrative form, as we learn early in the novel. Pynchon here has in mind stories like those of Frank Reade Jr., boy mechanic and adventurer, which began to appear in the 1890s, stories characterized by two-dimensional villains, stylized dialogue, and rapid action. By alluding to the popular series Pynchon draws the reader's attention to the sudden growth of the popular press in this period and to the emergence of radio and film, in other words, to the proliferation of the media themselves, whose interaction he has already dramatized in *The Crying of Lot 49*. *Against the Day* collects in one volume many of the key concerns of his earlier works, including Baedekerland and empire, transcendental dimensions to reality, and mapping out of intellectual and geographical terrains.

In the preface to his collection of short stories *Slow Learner* (1984) Pynchon admits a tendency in his writings to deflect subjects away from the autobiographical and to locate them in different periods. Throughout his career he has consistently practiced a kind of writing that evokes historical moments not only through topical events and artifacts but also through the narrative practices that were characteristic of those moments. He singled out for particular praise in *Nineteen Eighty-Four* Orwell's satirical depiction of the schizophrenic rhetoric of the 1940s Left as "double-think," and to date every work by Pynchon has evoked its subjects through pastiches of rhetoric ranging from cold war polarities in *Lot 49* to the assembly of styles in *Against the Day*, so complex that they resemble "thick" description in social anthropology. The intricacies of Pynchon's stylistic play have frequently led critics to understate the comic dimension to his writing, where ludicrous twists and exaggerations are often placed strategically to distance readers from his texts and encourage us to examine the ideological implications of these narratives.

## FURTHER READING

Abbas, Niran (ed.), *Thomas Pynchon: Reading from the Margins*, London, Associated University Press, 2003.

Copestake, Ian D. (ed.), *American Postmodernity: Essays in the Recent Fiction of Thomas Pynchon*, Bern, Peter Lang, 2003.

Hinds, E. J. W. (ed.), *The Multiple Worlds of Pynchon's "Mason & Dixon": Eighteenth-Century Contexts, Postmodern Observations*, Rochester N.Y., Camden House, 2009.

Mattessich, Stefan, *Lines of Flight: Discursive Time and Countercultural Desire in the Novels of Thomas Pynchon*, Durham N.C., Duke University Press, 2002.

Plater, William M., *The Grim Phoenix: Reconstructing Thomas Pynchon*, Bloomington, Indiana University Press, 1978.

Schaub, Thomas H., *Pynchon: The Voice of Ambiguity*, Urbana, University of Illinois Press, 1981.

Severs, Jeffrey and Christopher Leise (eds.), *Pynchon's "Against the Day": A Corrupted Pilgrim's Guide*, Newark, University of Delaware Press, 2011.

Smith, Shawn, *Pynchon and History: Metahistorical Rhetoric and Postnarrative Form in the Novels of Thomas Pynchon*, London and New York, Routledge, 2005.

Tanner, Tony, *Thomas Pynchon*, London, Methuen, 1982.

Thomas, Samuel, *Pynchon and the Political*, London and New York, Routledge, 2007.

Weisenburger, Steven C., *A Gravity's Rainbow Companion: Sources and Contexts for Pynchon's Novel*, 2nd ed., Athens, University of Georgia Press, 2006.

## NOTES

1 Thomas Pynchon, "Is It O.K. to Be a Luddite?" *New York Times Book Review*, October 28, 1984, p. 41.

2 Thomas Pynchon, "Words for Ian McEwan," *Daily Telegraph* December 6, 2006, available online. URL: http://www.themodernword.com/pynchon/pynchon_essays_mcewan.html

3 Tony Tanner, *Thomas Pynchon* (London and New York, Methuen, 1982), p. 41.

4 Linda Hutcheon, *A Poetics of Postmodernism* (London and New York, Routledge, 1988), pp. 105–23.

5 Pynchon, "Introduction," *Stone Junction* by Jim Dodge (Edinburgh, Canongate, 2004), p. viii.

6 Pynchon, "Foreword," *Nineteen Eighty-Four* by George Orwell (New York, Penguin, 2003), p. xxi.

7 In a letter of 1969 Pynchon details his reading in this area: David Seed, *The Fictional Labyrinths of Thomas Pynchon* (Iowa City, University of Iowa Press, 1988), pp. 240–3.

8 Pynchon, "A Journey into the Mind of Watts," *New York Times Magazine*, June 12, 1966, pp. 34–5, 78, 80–2, 84.

9 Pynchon, *Mason & Dixon* (London, Jonathan Cape, 1997), p. 586.

10 Pynchon, "The Deadly Sins/Sloth: Nearer, My Couch, to Thee," *New York Times Book Review* June 6, 1993, p. 3; also available at http://www.pynchon.pomona.edu/uncollected/sloth.html.

11 Pynchon, *Mason & Dixon*, p. 301.

12 Pynchon, *Mason & Dixon*, p. 769.

13 Pynchon, *Against the Day* (London, Jonathan Cape, 2006), p. 165.

# 27
# Toni Morrison

VALERIE SMITH

Toni Morrison (1931–) ranks among the most highly-regarded and widely-read fiction writers and cultural critics in the history of American literature. Novelist, editor, playwright, essayist, librettist, and children's book author, she has won innumerable prizes and awards and enjoys extraordinarily high regard both in the United States and internationally.[1] Her work has been translated into many languages, including German, Spanish, French, Italian, Norwegian, Finnish, Japanese, and Chinese, and is the subject of courses taught and books and articles written by scholars all over the world. It speaks to academic and mass audiences alike; four of her novels have been Oprah's Book Club selections. She invites frequent comparison with the best-known writers of the global canon: Virginia Woolf, William Faulkner, Zora Neale Hurston, James Joyce, Thomas Hardy, Gabriel Garcia Marquez, Wole Soyinka, Chinua Achebe, and others. Because of her broad appeal, throughout her career readers and critics alike have sought to praise Morrison by calling her work "universal."

The adjective "universal" has typically been applied to work in any medium that speaks to readers, viewers, or audience members whatever their race, ethnicity, gender, sexual orientation, age, or socioeconomic status. Art that achieves the status of "universality" is contrasted implicitly or explicitly with work that is labeled "provincial," that is, more explicitly grounded in the culture, lore, or vernacular of an identifiable group. But for all its "universality," Morrison's writing is famously steeped in the nuances of African-American language, music, everyday life, and cultural history. Even more precisely, most of her novels are concerned with the impact of racial patriarchy upon the lives of black women during specific periods of American history, such as the colonial period or the eras of slavery, Reconstruction, Jim Crow, and civil rights. By exploring the impact of historical and socioeconomic factors and processes upon the lives of black women, Morrison uses her fiction to mine the unexplored depths of American culture.

In her first two novels, Morrison holds up racialized and gendered cultural norms to scrutiny. *The Bluest Eye* (1970), Morrison's first novel, juxtaposes two moments in twentieth-century U.S. culture. The novel centers on a set of traumatic events in the life of Pecola Breedlove, a young African-American girl, in the 1940s. Claudia MacTeer, Pecola's friend and the principal narrator, reflects upon these events both from her childhood point of view and from her adult perspective in the late 1960s. In its heightened attention to the politics of aesthetics, *The Bluest Eye* is certainly born out of the racial self-consciousness of the 1960s. But the novel also evokes the advantages and liabilities black migrants from the South encountered as they adapted to their new lives in the North (in this case, Lorain, Ohio) during the post-war era. In seeking wider opportunities for themselves and their children, they escaped the most virulent forms of racial oppression. But they risked becoming alienated from the values and practices that had sustained previous generations of African Americans.

In the novel, Morrison explores processes through which the pursuit of idealized standards of beauty leads to self-loathing and victimizes the most vulnerable members of an already marginalized community. Many of the characters have internalized the effects of the selfsame hegemonic social and political policies and practices that brutalized them; they display not only a contempt for African features and social practices associated with black culture, but also a reverence for standards of beauty associated with whiteness. Furthermore, the roots of their self-disgust lie so deep that they do not recognize them for what they are. Instead, they project those feelings upon the most vulnerable members of their community, in this case, the young Pecola. By the end of the novel, Pecola has been destroyed psychologically not only by her rape at the hands of her father, but by the abuse that members of her community heap upon her as well.

In *Sula* (1973), her second novel, Morrison delves more deeply into the means by which social norms are produced in order to interrogate the binary logic upon which they are based and from which they derive their force. The relationship between Shadrack, the shell-shocked World War I veteran, and the town of Medallion, on the one hand, and the friendship between Nel and Sula (the two principal characters), on the other hand, suggest that notions such as madness and sanity, innocence and guilt, respectability and rebelliousness are mutually dependent and inextricable constructions, not polar opposites. Individuals and communities may need to demonize "the other" in order to shore up their own systems of belief, but their very survival depends upon the existence of that other, and the distinctions between them are less stable and evident than they may appear initially.

When *Song of Solomon* was published in 1977, it was enthusiastically received and widely reviewed. Its publication catapulted Morrison into the ranks of the most highly-acclaimed contemporary writers. As Morrison herself has observed, *Song* reflects an expansion of her artistic vision and range. A pivotal text in her body of work, it takes up several of the concerns central to her earlier novels (such as the deleterious effects of American cultural norms – especially capitalism and patriarchy – upon African Americans). But rather than focusing on a pair or a trio of young girls or women, this novel centers on several generations of the Deads, an African-American family, and considers the toll that dominant cultural practices and assumptions have taken on women and men alike. Moreover, with its multigenerational view of the impact of slavery, migration, and racial and economic injustice upon African Americans, it anticipates the breadth and preoccupations of her later work. Covering the period from slavery until the height of the civil rights era, *Song of Solomon* calls our attention to ways in which African Americans sought to articulate and express their identities within the context of historical change and diverse manifestations of social injustice.

Much of the early criticism of *Song of Solomon* addressed the implications of the mystical, supernatural aspects of the novel – Pilate Dead's absent navel, the apparently immortal figure of Circe, the recurrent motif of flight, the oblique ending, for example – reading *Song* as a site of critique of the destructive power of mainstream American cultural values. More recent criticism has emphasized the significance of the novel's use of its historical and political context. And indeed, with its liberal references to specific institutions such as the Freedmen's Bureau; events such as the First and Second World Wars, the murder of Emmett Till, the Montgomery bus boycott, and the bombing of the Sixteenth Street Baptist Church; or historical figures such as Malcolm X and Martin Luther King Jr., the novel is clearly situated in the period between Emancipation and the height of the modern civil rights movement. This shift in critical focus has opened up the novel to more complicated and subtle interpretations that view the mythical elements of the novel as symbolic expressions of ways in which African Americans have survived in the spaces within and between the institutions, practices, movements, periods, and grand events that punctuate the official historical record. These more historically-inflected readings have helped to draw thematic, rhetorical, and ideological connections between *Song of Solomon* and Morrison's later work.

In several ways, *Tar Baby* (1982) might seem to represent a radical departure from the rest of Morrison's oeuvre. The only one of her novels to be set largely outside the United States, other than *A Mercy* (2008), it is also the only one in which white characters feature prominently. These differences notwithstanding, *Tar Baby* shares many of the thematic concerns and preoccupations of the novels that precede and follow it. Like *The Bluest Eye, Sula,* and *Song of Solomon,* it explores the residual impact of slavery upon later generations of African Americans and illuminates the deleterious impact of hegemonic cultural values. Like *Song of Solomon* and *A Mercy,* it is sensitive to the destructive impact of capitalistic forces and enterprises upon the natural world. Moreover, like many of Morrison's novels, it features several characters who have been displaced voluntarily or involuntarily from their homes and suggests that a return to their literal or symbolic place of origin may be the only way for them to achieve a sense of personal, if not cultural self-knowledge.

Between 1987 and 1997, Toni Morrison published three novels to which she and many of her critics have referred collectively as a trilogy: *Beloved* (1987), *Jazz* (1992), and *Paradise* (1998). These novels are considered a trilogy for a variety of reasons. Some critics have argued that they are connected by their shared focus on the relationship between excessive love and violence: *Beloved* on maternal love, *Jazz* on romantic love, and *Paradise* on religious or communal love. They have been called a trilogy because of their historical reach: read chronologically, the novels span one hundred years of African-American life and cover a broad geographic area. *Beloved* is set during the 1870s outside Cincinnati, Ohio, with flashbacks to a plantation in Kentucky and a chain gang in Alfred, Georgia. *Jazz* is set in 1920s Harlem with flashbacks to Reconstruction era Virginia. *Paradise* is set mostly in the 1970s in the all-black town of Ruby, Oklahoma, but the text is flooded with memories of the ancestors, the "Old Fathers" who left Louisiana and Mississippi and founded Haven in the 1870s after the failure of Reconstruction. All three novels are set against the backdrop of a war – the Civil War, World War I, the Vietnam War. Perhaps most significantly, all three offer revisions of critical periods in U.S. history by foregrounding the underacknowledged experiences of African Americans.

Published in 1987, *Beloved* is widely considered to be Morrison's greatest literary achievement, the most celebrated contemporary novel of the slave experience, and one of the most highly acclaimed novels of the twentieth century. Winner of the 1988 Pulitzer Prize for fiction, in 2006 it was selected as the best work of U.S. fiction published in the previous twenty-five years.[2] The novel focuses on the story of an actual fugitive slave mother, Margaret Garner, who killed her two-year-old daughter rather than allowing her to be captured and returned to slavery. Morrison explores the nuances of this account to illuminate the factors that would enable a mother to murder her child. Moreover, she considers how the memory of that child and others lost to the ravages of slavery haunts the mother and all whose lives touch hers.

As a representation of the traumatic effects of slavery, memory, and forgetting upon the African-American individual, familial, and collective consciousness, it is most obviously a novel about the past. But it has also been read as a novel about the present.³ Furthermore, in a recent article Dennis Childs argues convincingly that the novel looks to the future as well.⁴ *Beloved* has been interpreted from diverse critical perspectives, including feminist, psychoanalytic, neo-Marxist, and critical race theory. It has been read as a text about slavery and freedom, motherhood, the body, the word, history, and memory. The widespread esteem in which *Beloved* is held confirms Morrison's belief that culturally specific narratives can convey universal truths.

The plot of *Jazz* is essentially summarized in its first pages. In the opening lines of the novel, we read of a woman named Violet whose husband murdered the eighteen-year-old woman with whom he was having an affair. At the young woman's funeral, Violet tried to slash the dead girl's face as she lay in her coffin, and the ushers ejected her; upon her return home, she opened her windows to let her pet birds fly away. But *Jazz* is about much more than these events. Like *The Bluest Eye, Sula, Song of Solomon*, and *Tar Baby*, it is concerned with the impact of migration from the South to the North upon African-American individuals and communities. As *Beloved* considers underacknowledged aspects of the institution of slavery, *Jazz* revises received ideas about African-American migration. Moreover, the novel explores the role of jazz music in the lives of the characters and the community in which they live. The sound and the form of jazz, a musical genre that constituted at least part of soundtrack of the urban streetscape of Harlem in the early decades of the twentieth century, inform the narrative voice. Not only does the sound of jazz infuse the characters' inner lives and leisure activities, but it shapes the aesthetic of the novel as well. In her experimentation with narrative voice, Morrison revises prevailing notions about the Jazz Age and demonstrates the complexity and multifariousness of African-American lives in the North.

In the Judeo-Christian tradition, paradise is another name for the Garden of Eden, where God's first creations resided until their fall from grace. *Paradise* (1997), the title of Morrison's seventh novel, invokes that ideal world and the myth of origins it contains, deploying it as a metaphor for the quest to create and maintain a protected, homogeneous world. Morrison's paradise is the all-black town of Ruby, Oklahoma, where the novel is primarily set. Established by a core group of men and their families in 1949, it recalls a number of all-black towns formed during the Jim Crow era to consolidate African-American resources and protect their residents from the threat of white violence. Few of these all-black towns remain, but they are often recalled nostalgically as places where black people worked in harmony for the common good.

In *Paradise* Morrison grapples with the implications of one question in particular: Why do our notions of utopia depend upon separation and exclusion? Why is the idea of paradise as much about those we include as it is about those we keep out? Ruby, Oklahoma descended from the town of Haven, which was founded by the patriarchs of nine black families who led more than a hundred formerly enslaved black people from Louisiana and Mississippi to the Oklahoma Territory after they were expelled from positions of power – generally in government – in the years following Reconstruction. By 1889, several such all-black towns had been established in the Oklahoma Territory, and these towns advertised for settlers. But the eager, dark-skinned black folks known as "8-Rock" who eventually settled Haven soon discovered that the other towns were inhabited by light-skinned blacks who wanted nothing to do with them.[5]

In its representation of the uses to which the townspeople put Christianity, the novel points to the ways in which a community forged in opposition to the exclusionary practices of a dominant culture replicates and legitimates its own exclusionary practices. If the national myth of American exceptionalism and belief in its origins in a city on a hill are linked inextricably to and dependent upon the exploitation of black, brown, and native peoples, *Paradise* explores how analogous myths of the sacredness of their origins both underlie and legitimate Ruby's own racial hierarchies. As Lucille P. Fultz and others have noted, even more specifically, the novel invites us to consider the town of Ruby in relation to the New England Puritans. Like the Puritans, the founders of Haven and Ruby "see their mission as a divine calling to establish an inviolate and inviolable … community."[6] When those norms are violated they find it all too easy to scapegoat women they brand as outlaws, even going so far as to call them witches.

In the foreword to *Love* (2003), Morrison considers the role of betrayal during the era of the long civil rights revolution. Typically, the narrative of the civil rights era is understood as a triumph over white supremacy, a political ideology enacted through a system of laws and cultural practices designed to relegate nonwhites to a second-class status, thus withholding from them their rights as citizens. But that narrative also depends upon the illusion, if not the fact, of intraracial loyalty and consensus. It presupposes a shared sense of unity among African Americans in the face of white oppression. In *Love*, however, Morrison provides a counternarrative, turning her readers' attention to the network of allegiances and deceptions, trust and duplicity, that shaped the relationships among black people – especially between black men and women – throughout the years of the freedom struggle. From the perspective of a cluster of economically, sexually, and psychically vulnerable women, the novel explores the connection between love and betrayal at the levels of cultural, political, and personal experience.

The plot of *Love* revolves around a character named Bill Cosey, the wealthy African-American owner of a hotel and night club in a seaside town called Up Beach that catered to black guests during the era of segregation. A savvy, entrepreneurial figure, Cosey is generous to his poor and working-class African-American neighbors while keeping them at a social distance, and solicitous of the wealthy whites who live in his community. The action of the novel flows from his 1942 marriage to Heed the Night Johnson, his granddaughter Christine's best friend, when Heed is only eleven. This marriage destroys the girls' relationship and triggers a rivalry between them that lasts until the moments before Heed's death as an elderly woman at the end of the novel. Not only do they compete for Cosey's love, but they also fight over the right to his home located at One Monarch Street in the town of Silk.

Rumor has it that either Christine or Heed poisoned Cosey, but by the end of the novel we learn that the real murderer is L, the cook at Cosey's restaurant, whose posthumous, italicized narration haunts the text. L reveals that she poisoned Cosey to prevent him from executing his legitimate will, in which he bequeathed his house to his longtime lover, the prostitute Celestial.

The structure of *Love* would seem to suggest that the novel is about Cosey and his charismatic power. Each of the nine sections into which the book is divided is named for a role Cosey occupies in the minds of others – Portrait, Friend, Stranger, Benefactor, Lover, Husband, Guardian, Father, and Phantom. Moreover, to varying degrees, the women characters – Heed, Christine, Junior Viviane, Celestial, May, Vida, and L – are enthralled by the literal and symbolic force of his personality. As the novel unfolds, it becomes increasingly clear that *Love* is more concerned with the destructive impact of patriarchal power upon the women and their relationships with each other than it is with Cosey himself. The figure of L and the secret that is only revealed in the final pages refocus the reader's attention on the buried story, the powerful girlhood friendship between Heed and Christine. By the end of the novel, we understand that by betraying that relationship, Cosey has relegated both women to a lifetime of trauma and despair.

Although *A Mercy*, Morrison's ninth novel, is set in a much earlier historical period than any of her other novels, it has much in common with several of her other works. Centering on a household of women characters, it reminds us of *Song of Solomon, Paradise, Jazz,* and *Love.* With its focus on the consequences of a slave mother's sacrifice, it invites comparison with

*Beloved.* Like *Love,* it addresses the consequences of the protagonist's early experience of abandonment and loss.

Set in the Atlantic colonies during the late seventeenth century, *A Mercy* focuses on a group of people drawn together into a common household through a series of commercial transactions. The characters are multiethnic and multiracial; they include an Anglo-Dutch farmer, his English wife, a Portuguese Catholic plantation owner, and a workforce of native, black, white, and mixed-race slaves, and indentured servants and a freedman. In the early years of their life together, the principal characters coexist in a state of mutual dependency, working together with great efficiency in order to create a world out of the wilderness. But greed sustained by powerful racial, gender, and class hierarchies contaminates their universe; greed is symbolically responsible for the death of Jacob Vaark, the farmer, and the tragic upheaval of the lives of the women who depend upon him. Like most of Morrison's novels, *A Mercy* is told from multiple narrative perspectives; the meanings of the narrative emerge out of the interconnections among the different points of view. In this instance, through the convergence of her characters' stories, Morrison interrogates the meaning of freedom and enslavement, wilderness and civilization.

Morrison's insistence throughout her career that our common humanity can be found in the specificity of our individual and cultural differences seems strikingly prescient from the vantage point of the second decade of the twenty-first century. In recent years, pundits and many average Americans alike have been quick to declare that the United States has entered the era of "postracialism." Not only is it naïve to assume that the election of an African-American president would mean the end of racism when so many markers of racial inequality still exist,[7] but the urge to cloak oneself (or the nation) in the "postrace" mantle also betrays an eagerness, if not a desperation, to run from the history and the current state of racial formations in the nation. Those who cling to the "postrace" notion fail to distinguish between racism, on the one hand, and, on the other hand, discursive practices that acknowledge, analyze, and resist the mechanisms through which processes of racialization are enacted. Moreover, they fail to acknowledge that the history and experience of race and racialization processes can yield more than racist language or a discourse of blame and victimization; they imply that there is something inherently shameful in the very language of racial specificity itself.

Throughout her writing, Morrison shows us that however violent, exploitative, and dehumanizing, the history and experience of racial formations have led to complex and rich emotional, cultural, and artistic responses, responses that artists are uniquely positioned to explore, illuminate, preserve, and represent. In words that recall the late Audre Lorde's essay "The

Master's Tools Will Never Dismantle the Master's House,"[8] Morrison observes that in writing about race she is not bound to "reproduce the master's voice and its assumptions of the all-knowing white father." Rather, drawing on the metaphor of the nation as a house, she remarks that her challenge is to transform the structure from a prison, out of which "no cry can be heard," to "an open house, grounded, yet generous in its supply of windows and doors."[9]

## FURTHER READING

Andrews, William L. and Nellie Y. McKay (eds.), *Beloved: A Casebook*, New York, Oxford University Press, 1999.

Christian, Barbara, "'The Past Is Infinite': History and Myth in Toni Morrison's Trilogy," *Social Identities* 6.4 (2000): 411–23.

Conner, Marc C. (ed.), *The Aesthetics of Toni Morrison: Speaking the Unspeakable*, Jackson, University Press of Mississippi, 2000.

Denard, Carolyn (ed.), *Toni Morrison: What Moves at the Margin, Selected Nonfiction*, Jackson, University Press of Mississippi, 2008.

Duvall, John N., *The Identifying Fictions of Toni Morrison*, New York, Palgrave, 2000.

McKay, Nellie Y. (ed.), *Critical Essays on Toni Morrison*, Boston, G. K. Hall, 1998.

Morrison, Toni, *Playing in the Dark: Whiteness and the Literary Imagination*, Cambridge, Mass., Harvard University Press, 1992.

Morrison, Toni (ed.), *Race-ing Justice, En-gendering Power: Essays on Anita Hill, Clarence Thomas, and the Construction of Reality*, New York, Pantheon Books, 1992.

Morrison, Toni and Claudia Brodsky Lacour (ed.), *Birth of a Nation'hood: Gaze, Script and Spectacle in the O. J. Simpson Trial*, New York, Pantheon Books, 1997.

Peterson, Nancy J., *Toni Morrison: Critical and Theoretical Approaches*, Baltimore, Johns Hopkins University Press, 1997.

Schreiber, Evelyn Jaffe, *Race, Trauma, and Home in the Novels of Toni Morrison*, Baton Rouge, Louisiana State University Press, 2010.

Tally, Justine, *The Cambridge Companion to Toni Morrison*, Cambridge, Cambridge University Press, 2008.

Taylor-Guthrie, Danille (ed.), *Conversations with Toni Morrison*, Jackson, University Press of Mississippi, 1994.

Treherne, Matthew. "Figuring In, Figuring Out: Narration and Negotiation in Toni Morrison's *Jazz*," in *Narrative* 11.2 (May 2003): 199–212.

Wyatt, Jean. "Love's Time and the Reader: Ethical Effects of Nachtraglichkeit in Toni Morrison's *Love*," in *Narrative* 16.2 (May 2008): 193–221.

## NOTES

1  A partial list of her many prizes and awards includes the National Book Critics Circle Award, the American Academy and Institute for Arts and Letters Award, the Robert F. Kennedy Book Award, the American Book Award, the Anisfield-Wolf

Book Award in Race Relations, the Pulitzer Prize, the MLA Commonwealth Award in Literature, the Nobel Prize for literature, the Condorcet Medal (Paris), and the National Humanities Medal.

2 A. O. Scott, "In Search of the Best," *New York Times*, May 21, 2006. http://www. nytimes.com/2006/05/21/books/review/scott-essay.html. May 18, 2010.

3 See James Berger, "Ghosts of Liberalism: Morrison's *Beloved* and the Moynihan Report," *PMLA* 111 (May 1996): 408–20.

4 Dennis Childs, "'You Ain't Seen Nothin' Yet': *Beloved*, the American Chain Gang, and the Middle Passage Remix," *American Quarterly* 61 (June 2009): 271–97.

5 The nine founding families call themselves "8-rock" because they are dark-skinned. "A deep deep level in the coal mines. Blue-black people, tall and graceful, whose clear, wide eyes gave no sign of what they really felt about those who weren't 8-rock like them." Toni Morrison, *Paradise* (New York, Knopf, 1998), p. 193.

6 Lucille P. Fultz, *Toni Morrison: Playing with Difference* (Urbana and Chicago, University of Illinois Press, 2003), p. 93.

7 I have in mind such factors as persistent gaps in black and white educational achievement and wealth and racially disparate incarceration rates, to mention but a few examples.

8 Audre Lorde, *Sister Outsider: Essays and Speeches* (Berkeley, Calif., Crossing Press, 1984), pp. 110–13.

9 Toni Morrison, "Home," *The House That Race Built: Black Americans, U.S. Terrain*, ed. Wahneema Lubiano (New York, Pantheon, 1997), p. 4.

# 28

# Philip Roth

### DEBRA SHOSTAK

I was a Jewish child, ... but I didn't care to partake of the Jewish character.... I wanted to partake of the national character.... You flood into history and history floods into you. You flood into America and America floods into you.

Philip Roth, *I Married a Communist*, 1998[1]

Philip Roth's (1933–) recurrent narrator, the novelist Nathan Zuckerman, writes these words as he nostalgically recalls his youth in the late 1940s. Then, all of America lay before him like a golden promise, and he was innocent of the tragedy that would fell his heroic subject, Ira Ringold, a Jew destroyed by his blithe confidence in the American myth of self-invention. Zuckerman exemplifies Roth's engagement with an enduring preoccupation of American literature: how history floods into – or washes away – the Emersonian self engaged in its own making.

Roth's contribution to American literature over the course of more than fifty years and thirty books lies in his scrutiny of American selfhood from the vantage point of a late twentieth-century postimmigrant Jewish sensibility. During the postwar period, numerous writers in the United States charged themselves with redefining the category of "American novelist," teasing out "American" as an indeterminate, pluralistic identity and "novelist" as a maker of many forms. Those writers, Roth among them, did not stray far from their nineteenth-century forebears, such as Hawthorne, Twain, or Melville, who wrested a literary culture from the unique landscape and history by seeking an American idiom and subject matter. To that end, Roth's fiction asks: Who or what is an American, especially one whose pedigree goes back no more than a generation or two? What is the nature of American manhood? How is desire lodged in the civilized self? What, for that matter, is the "self"? How flexible is the American novel's shape to capture the interdependence of self and world? In pursuing these questions, Roth embraces contradictions, formal and thematic. He reveals the

American landscape of the self as both ideal and empty, in tones both ironic and nostalgic and narrative modes both realistic and metafictional. His striving protagonists, poised painfully between opposing choices, alternately pursue and reject erotic fulfillments, ethnic subject positions, and determinate identities. Roth peoples his narratives with the voices and aspirations of his own history: his protagonists are Jews, voluble and hypersensitive, typically male, and often writers or intellectuals whose self-consciousness complicates their ability simply to *be*.

Roth's restless sampling of fictional modes, forms, and styles follows in rough sequence, with much overlap as his career gathers force. He begins in the 1950s and 1960s with social and psychological realism, alternating earnestness with raw comedy. The 1970s see him experimenting with genre, from satire, fable, and parody to multilayered reflexive narrative, in prose ranging from raucous exaggeration to pained delicacy. Having developed a preference for the first-person voice, Roth devotes the books of the 1980s and early 1990s to the alter ego Nathan Zuckerman and to autobiographical or faux-autobiographical writing. In his subsequent work, he recommits himself to realism. The American trilogy of the 1990s makes plain what was always tacit: the individual's inextricable position in cultural history. With the twenty-first century, Roth's comedy, whose influences range from Borscht Belt comedians to Kafka, recedes, replaced by bitter yearning, bleak realism, condensed forms, and austere prose. Throughout, Roth probes challenges to autonomous selfhood – to the possibility of crafting the individuality and agency promised by the American democratic ideal. His portraits shift from the expansive, egocentric, anxious selfhood of youth; to the mature self under pressure of personal and national histories; to the aging self reduced by the terrifying facts of mortality.

Roth's prose style likewise shifts over the course of his career, from a cool, free indirect style, for example, in *When She Was Good* (1967), to the crude, Yiddish-inflected vernacular and hilarious one-liners of *Portnoy's Complaint* (1969), through generous, translucent periodic sentences in *American Pastoral* (1997), to monosyllabic, clipped sentences in the late novels. Roth's ear for voices in extended dialogue or monologue is typically balanced by radiant passages of intensely rendered memory or precise material and sensory description. With Proustian immediacy, such passages describe, for example, the sights and smells of a New York delicatessen purveying "the bitter fragrance ... of everything pickled, peppered, salted, smoked, soaked, stewed, marinated, and dried," in *Operation Shylock* (1993);[2] or, in *Everyman* (2006), a boy's "ecstasy" while swimming in the ocean, where "the taste and the smell intoxicated him so that he was driven to the brink of biting down with his teeth to tear out a chunk of himself and savor his fleshly existence."[3]

Like his literary ancestors, Roth begins by staking out a territory, the largely Jewish Weequahic section of Newark, New Jersey, where he was born in 1933. Roth's novels express longing for – and repudiation of – a mythic ideal of moral and material fulfillment rooted in midcentury liberal ideologies promising the American Dream to the American Everyman. His novels thus, whether satirically or tragically, convey disgust at the country's failings. Roth's work often springs from autobiographical particulars, including the configuration of his family – father, mother, brother – but he ridicules readings of his work as untransformed fact, the very readings he slyly encourages: "'I write fiction and I'm told it's autobiography, I write autobiography and I'm told it's fiction,'" protests a novelist figure in *Deception* (1990), teasingly named "Philip."[4] With few exceptions, his work mines Jewish American experience for its concrete histories, its prescriptions for selfhood, and its moments of both cultural belonging and estrangement – a condition captured in his autobiography, *The Facts* (1988): "Though I never doubted that this country was mine..., I was not unaware of the power to intimidate that emanated from ... gentile America."[5] That Roth defines himself as an American first and a Jew second, however, determines his line of sight, provoking him to expose all such identifying categories as contingent and intertwined, and opening him to the charge of being a "self-hating" Jew from members of the Jewish community at the publication of his first book, *Goodbye, Columbus* (1959).

Stunned by that early blow, Roth seemed to counterattack, relishing controversy well into midcareer. Having marveled in 1960 that "American reality" beat any writer's "meager imagination,"[6] he appeared bent on outdoing it once he broke through to his mature voice in his fourth book, *Portnoy's Complaint*. This resembles the voice Roth later praises in the young Zuckerman of *The Ghost Writer* (1979): "something that begins at around the back of the knees and reaches well above the head"[7] – a voice, that is, intelligent, authentic, and visceral. *Portnoy's Complaint* brushes aside the influence of Roth's Jewish American elders – Saul Bellow, engaging in "struggles of ethical Jewhood," and Bernard Malamud, portraying "innocent, passive, virtuous" Jews[8] – for the outrageous sexual exploits, whining narcissism, and self-lacerating Jewish comedy of Alexander Portnoy's rant. *Portnoy's Complaint* likewise moves past the refined American masters, especially Henry James, inflecting Roth's first novels, *Letting Go* (1962) and *When She Was Good*, and returns for its locale to New Jersey from the vaguely deracinated Midwest.

With *Portnoy*, Roth expands on the material of *Goodbye, Columbus*, highlighting twin anxieties: how to forge an American identity from ethnic origins, and how to be a virile man, unencumbered by Jewish guilt and desexualized stereotypes of Jewish masculinity. Aiming to make Jewish diasporic experience *writable* as American life, Roth conveys a distinct sense of place, in the blunt vernacular of his eastern, middle-class, Jewish subjects. *Portnoy's Complaint*'s transgression against manners flouts postwar Jewish American fears that to represent Jews as embodied and desirous might provoke anti-Semitism. Such is apparent when Alex notoriously masturbates into the raw liver intended for the Portnoy table, or when he desires women as polymorphously perverse sex objects, like the image he fantasizes as "Thereal McCoy," or when he expresses his feverish wish to put "the id back in Yid."[9] Sex, for Portnoy, is at once the realm of physical pleasure denied by his superego – figured in his suffocating mother and his constipated, distracted father – and a metaphor for pursuing an American self he glimpses faintly in the distance. Explaining his penchant for non-Jewish women, for example, he admits his wan hope that "through fucking I will discover America. *Conquer* America" (265). Beholden in his early career to Freudian psychoanalysis, Roth conceives of the novel's form as a confession on the psychiatrist's couch. The inventive first-person voice, embedded in an associative rather than fully linear narrative structure, frees Roth to create a brutally comic oral idiom, screaming of desire and its repression and founded upon the whole history of Jewish civilization and its discontents: "LET MY PETER GO!" becomes Portnoy's anguished "slogan" (283).

If *Portnoy's Complaint* is Roth's most indecorous text, with the exception, perhaps, of the furious satire of President Richard Nixon in *Our Gang* (1971), it may also be the most liberating for him and his readers. A best seller, the novel signaled a tectonic cultural shift, opening American fiction to plain speaking, profanity, and sexual explicitness with scarce precedents. Following *Portnoy*'s narrative innovations, Roth experimented with fictional form for more than twenty years. He tried out a Kafkaesque fable of metamorphosis in *The Breast* (1972), for example, and a baggy comic epic in *The Great American Novel* (1973), which insouciantly adapts Melville in its first line ("Call me Smitty")[10] and generally presumes to speak for American culture, high and low, by interweaving the American canon with the great American pastime of baseball.

Roth's scope is more intimate, however, in *My Life as a Man* (1974), where he delves into his recurrent midcareer subject: the contradictory, often counterintuitive, relationship between "the written and the unwritten world,"[11] fundamental to metafictional narrative. Roth's exploration of referentiality typically focuses on indeterminate subjectivity, where the word, for good or ill, displaces and erases the stable, determinate selfhood promised by liberal humanism. Roth invents forms to tell the uncanny postmodern story of fugitive subjectivity, deploying writer figures who struggle to construct coherent selves through the process of narrating alternative life stories. The three novels that bracket this project are *My Life as a Man*, *The Counterlife* (1986), and *Operation Shylock* (1993). Each focuses on the protagonist's threatened masculinity, and the latter two gather energy specifically from the problem of maintaining a Jewish identity in the Diaspora. Most important, each dramatizes theoretical questions about fictiveness, developing a unique narrative structure in which the writer character attempts to understand his troubled biography, perhaps to work through his traumas, in the ordering medium of narrative prose.

*My Life as a Man* takes as its subject the narrator's efforts to grapple with his disastrous marriage. The details of Peter Tarnopol's marriage draw directly on Roth's first marriage, to Margaret Martinson Williams. Roth lures readers to see his biography lurking wholesale under the surface of his fiction, confounding the written with the unwritten world much as Tarnopol does when he tries to write his life story. The novel's interest lies in two features: Roth's inquiry into form through the novel's structure of embedded fictions, which imply that the self is a textual product, and his insight into the artist's problem of "aesthetic detachment"[12] from his material. Take, for example, Roth's note to the reader in the front matter. Normally such a note earns truth value outside the diegetic frame of the novel, but here Roth claims that the narrative's components "are drawn from the writings of Peter Tarnopol" – as if Tarnopol exists in the world outside the fiction that constructs his existence. Roth emphasizes the *textuality* of what follows, offering two of Tarnopol's short "Useful Fictions" before having his writer protagonist abandon the effort to "transform low actuality into high art" (210) and "forsake the art of fiction" for autobiography (100). In pledging himself to fact, in his own voice, Tarnopol hopes to gain agency, to become an "'I' owning up to its role as ringleader of the plot" (113) rather than its victim. In Tarnopol's vain wish "to be humanish: manly, a man" (174), Roth exposes the character's dread that he does not exist at all outside his words – and, like Pirandello, readers know that he does not. In Tarnopol's desperation, Roth intimates the emptiness of the signifier "I" and thus the autobiographical project, as well as the free-floating referentiality of fiction itself.

After Roth introduces Nathan Zuckerman as the subject and narrator of Tarnopol's "Useful Fictions," he arrives full-fledged as a writer figure in 1979 in *The Ghost Writer*, the künstlerroman initiating the *Zuckerman Bound* tetralogy (*Zuckerman Unbound* [1981], *The Anatomy Lesson* [1983], *The Prague Orgy* [1985]). Representing a paradigmatic self as if for dissection on the pathologist's table, Zuckerman exemplifies Tarnopol's insight that "his *self* is to many a novelist ... the closest subject at hand demanding scrutiny, a problem for his art to solve" (*My Life* 242). The tetralogy follows the writer's artistic and erotic life, from young obscurity through celebrity and the pain of mature self-renunciation and, like the subsequent *The Counterlife*, insistently draws readers to conflate the surrogate with Roth himself. *Operation Shylock* pretends to remove the mask altogether to write about "Philip Roth" directly. The latter two novels, teetering between realism and metafictional play, take to comic heights the recognition that artists cannibalize their own lives, and each finds different narrative strategies in which to inscribe alternative selfhoods. To test the premise that the American self is legitimately a project of free self-invention, both begin from the perception underlying Tarnopol's existential anxiety: that, according to *The Counterlife*, no "irreducible self" exists.[13]

Roth's explorations of the void of self in these two novels travel in opposing directions but reach similar destinations. *The Counterlife* rejoices that "in the absence of a self, one impersonates selves" (320), and the narrative revels in multiple impersonations over five mutually self-cancelling chapters, in each of which the fundamental "facts" of the characters are rewritten. In breaking the contract of narrative coherence with the reader, Roth urges a postmodern metaphysics, in which the transcendentally whole, humanistic *self* is replaced by the *subject*, a fleeting construction of language and cultural positioning. Roth has Zuckerman delight in his fluidity – an existence accomplished in words alone – which enables him to speak even from beyond the grave. *Operation Shylock*, however, presents a "Philip Roth" in existential vertigo and shock, his identity appropriated by illness and an impersonator. In breaking another contract with the reader – the conventional distinction between fiction and autobiography questioned in *My Life as a Man* – *Operation Shylock* undercuts the exhilaration of Zuckerman's indeterminacy. The novel presents "Philip Roth," like Tarnopol, in flight from a psychic breakdown, desperately asking, "Where is Philip Roth?" (*Shylock* 22) – his unstable condition exacerbated when he confronts the usurping double who claims, "I AM THE YOU THAT IS NOT WORDS" (87). The writer, nothing but words, finds himself superseded by the "uncontrollability of real things" (237).

The argument of each novel hinges on reinvigorating the question of Jewish identity in the Diaspora. Roth contrasts American and Israeli Jews, and the matter of ethnic or historical identity ultimately trumps each novel's gestures toward postmodern subjectivity. In *The Counterlife*, Zuckerman, who disdained his brother for redefining himself in Israel as a militant Jew, is brought up short in the final pages with the fact of reified cultural differences – with his ineradicable if indefinable identity as a Jew, a tribal identity imprinted on his body by the mark of circumcision. *Operation Shylock* begins with the troubling identity of the Jew, as "Philip" confronts his "counterself" (*Shylock* 29), another "Philip Roth," disseminating in Israel a wild program of "Diasporism" to return Jews to Europe. The dizzying plot that spins from this premise forces "Philip" – like Roth – to face the ethical and political consequences of identity; the project of self-invention is inevitably circumscribed by "Philip's" "Jewish conscience" (398).

When Roth turns to the fraught histories of Israel in *The Counterlife* and *Operation Shylock*, he changes course, underscoring that any individual subject is inextricably embedded in layers of cultural reality and national history. By the 1990s, however, his subject matter is no longer strictly the Jew embroiled in contest and controversy. Instead, Jewishness anchors his imaginative excursions into the disappointments wrought by historical circumstances on American dreams. Roth signals such disappointment when he wraps Mickey Sabbath, the mordantly funny, permanently outraged satyr of *Sabbath's Theater* (1995), in his dead brother's American flag to weep at the "monstrous purity of the suffering"[14] that is the wages of being alive. *The Counterlife* pinpoints one cause of such grief when Zuckerman acknowledges that the "pastoral genre" offering "desire's homeland" is a "womb-dream of life," existing only in a "beautiful state of innocent prehistory" (322–3). In Zuckerman's insight that the pastoral ideal lies outside history, Roth delineates the guiding metaphor of his forthrightly "American" books – the trilogy of *American Pastoral* (1997), *I Married a Communist*, and *The Human Stain* (2000), as well as *The Plot against America* (2004). Roth demolishes the unwitting dreamers of these novels with the historical consequences, social, political, and ethical, of their doomed projects to invent unfettered selves – as if to suggest that Fitzgerald's *Great Gatsby* (1925) is, after all, the essential American story.

The focus in these novels on specific historical moments from the second half of the twentieth century demands Roth's return to realism as a narrative mode. He reverts to psychological and social determinism for the mechanics of character and plot and punishes postmodern flights into indeterminate selfhood, as when Coleman Silk, the African American passing as a white Jew in *The Human Stain*, reenacts Sophoclean tragedy: "The man who decides to forge a distinct historical destiny, who sets out to spring the historical lock" is "ensnared by the history he hadn't quite counted on … the stranglehold of history that is one's own time."[15] Roth's faithful deputy, Zuckerman, narrates the American trilogy, now in a historiographic voice, often nostalgic. That the newly reclusive narrator speaks from the periphery of the action rather than its center correlates with Roth's own gradual withdrawal from the teeming world after the breakdown he suffered in 1987, revealed in *The Facts*, and his divorce from his second wife, the British actress Claire Bloom, in 1994. In keeping with this detached position, Roth displaces the anguished introspections of the earlier novels outward from self to others. Zuckerman's inability to fill gaps of knowledge except through imagination undercuts the illusion of an intimate perspective and the realistic mode of telling to which Roth commits him. Zuckerman cannot unknot the mysteries of self that the principals themselves fail to understand when they are destroyed by events only partly of their own making.

Seymour "the Swede" Levov of *American Pastoral* is a case in point. The blond, athletic hope of the Weequahic Jews, who fancies himself a benevolent new Johnny Appleseed, seems to live in America "the way he lived inside his own skin."[16] The Swede promises to shed his Jewish identity, assimilating seamlessly into America, but Roth instead blasts him with the "indigenous American berserk" (86) of 1960s political violence when his daughter shatters Seymour's model household and the pastoral dream he has sought materially. The Swede's fall from innocence – caused by his blind faith that he is not answerable to the history of differences in the United States – exposes the trauma at the heart of the great experiment in American democratic individualism. Roth likewise uncovers that trauma in *The Plot Against America*. Narrated by the adult "Philip," the novel poignantly recalls the confrontation of the young "Philip" and the rest of the "Roth" family with an uncanny counterhistory at the time of World War II. As fascism is unleashed in the United States and anti-Semitism becomes public policy, the Roths' pristine faith in their homeland is deeply shaken when they are forced to define themselves as irremediably *different*, as Jews who do not belong. Roth ultimately backs away from the fear he names in the novel's opening line, however, comfortingly reinserting the Roths into the history that really happened. He seems unwilling to embrace the consequences of his dystopian imagination, but its resonance lingers. He cannot, it seems, decide whether to love or loathe America.

The tensions in Roth's representation of American culture and its impingement on the individual are neatly captured in a verbal echo. Whereas *Sabbath's Theater* concludes with Sabbath's ironic rejection of suicide – "How could he go? Everything he hated was here" (*Sabbath* 450) –*American Pastoral*'s perpetually innocent Swede thinks, "Everything he loved was here" (*Pastoral* 213). Contradictorily balanced between an idealizing love and an energizing contempt for illusory ideals, Roth's fiction of the twenty-first century focuses on loss, as his protagonists confront their mortality. Although Roth shifts from scatology to eschatology, the central fact of human desire remains undimmed among his mortified and death-obsessed characters. From the aging figures whose physical or mental powers diminish in *The Dying Animal* (2001), *Everyman* (2006), *Exit Ghost* (2007), and *The Humbling* (2009) to youths destroyed by folly or chance in *Indignation* (2008) and *Nemesis* (2010), Roth peers unsparingly at the paltry gestures humans make against our common biological end. The many "nemeses" his characters face in these novels – illness, memory loss, sexual and professional incapacity, small-minded conservatism, warfare – all lead to the same conclusion: memento mori. These later works expose the stubborn human will to resist, or at least understand, the arbitrariness of our inexplicable fates. The narrator of *Nemesis*, for example, both honors and disparages his protagonist, Bucky Cantor, who, victim and silent carrier of polio, must "convert tragedy into guilt" in order to discern his agency in his fate; he is compelled to "find a necessity for what happens" rather than accept that events are "pointless, contingent, preposterous." Bucky, that is, like the rest of these late figures, is a "maniac of the why."[17]

And so is a novelist, of course. Roth's tone and narrative form have changed in these later books, which are alternately tender and severe, yearning and acerbic, with few of the sardonic laughs at the human comedy evident in the earlier decades of his career. He also writes them in short forms – closer to the novella than the novel – tailored to the morality tales they tell. But the American self remains his great subject. His fascination with probing desire, self-consciousness, self-centeredness, and Jewishness has, without doubt, laid him open to charges of narcissism. Roth has offended sensibilities, refusing to court the reader, but he has also repeatedly reinvented his fictional forms, and he has taken artistic risks that have paid off richly. On canvases large and small, in prose at times so transparently apt that its beauty may go unrecognized, Roth has been a "maniac of the why," uncompromising in exposing unlovely truths and welcoming unresolved contradictions concerning American history, the national character, and the American subject.

## FURTHER READING

Brauner, David, *Philip Roth*, Manchester, Manchester University Press, 2007.
Cooper, Alan, *Philip Roth and the Jews*, Albany, State University of New York Press, 1996.
Gooblar, David, *The Major Phases of Philip Roth*, New York, Continuum, 2011.
Halio, Jay and Ben Siegel (eds.), *Turning up the Flame: The Later Works of Philip Roth*, Newark, University of Delaware Press, 2005.

Masiero, Pia, *Philip Roth and the Zuckerman Books: The Making of a Storyworld*, Amherst, N.Y., Cambria, 2011.

Milbauer, Asher and Donald G. Watson (eds.), *Reading Philip Roth*, New York, St. Martin's, 1988.

Morley, Catherine, *The Quest for Epic in Contemporary American Fiction: John Updike, Philip Roth and Don DeLillo*, New York, Routledge, 2009.

Parrish, Timothy (ed.), *The Cambridge Companion to Philip Roth*, Cambridge, Cambridge University Press, 2007.

Posnock, Ross, *Philip Roth's Rude Truth: The Art of Immaturity*, Princeton, N.J., Princeton University Press, 2006.

Pozorski, Aimee, *Roth and Trauma: The Problem of History in the Later Works (1995–2010)*, New York, Continuum, 2011.

Royal, Derek Parker (ed.), *Philip Roth: New Perspectives on an American Author*, Westport, Conn., Praeger, 2005.

Safer, Elaine, *Mocking the Age: The Later Novels of Philip Roth*, Albany, State University of New York Press, 2006.

Searles, George J. (ed.), *Conversations with Philip Roth*, Jackson, University Press of Mississippi, 1992.

Shechner, Mark, *Up Society's Ass, Copper: Rereading Philip Roth*, Madison, University of Wisconsin Press, 2003.

Shostak, Debra, *Philip Roth – Countertexts, Counterlives*, Columbia, University of South Carolina Press, 2004.

## NOTES

1 Philip Roth, *I Married a Communist* (New York, Houghton Mifflin, 1998), p. 39.

2 Roth, *Operation Shylock: A Confession* (New York, Simon & Schuster, 1993), p. 378.

3 Roth, *Everyman* (New York, Houghton Mifflin, 2006), p. 127.

4 Roth, *Deception* (New York, Simon & Schuster, 1990), p. 190.

5 Roth, *The Facts: A Novelist's Autobiography* (New York, Farrar, Straus & Giroux, 1988), p. 20.

6 Roth, "Writing American Fiction," *Reading Myself and Others* (New York, Farrar, Straus & Giroux, 1975; rev. ed., New York, Penguin, 1985), p. 176.

7 Roth, *The Ghost Writer*, in *Zuckerman Bound* (New York, Farrar, Straus & Giroux, 1985), p. 72.

8 Roth, "Imagining Jews," *Reading Myself and Others*, pp. 286–7.

9 Roth, *Portnoy's Complaint* (New York, Fawcett Crest, 1985), pp. 147, 236.

10 Roth, *The Great American Novel* (New York, Penguin, 1986), p. 1.

11 Roth, "Author's Note," *Reading Myself and Others*, p. ix.

12 Roth, *My Life as a Man* (New York, Vintage, 1993), p. 231.

13 Roth, *The Counterlife* (New York, Penguin, 1989), p. 100.

14 Roth, *Sabbath's Theater* (New York, Houghton Mifflin, 1995), p. 403.

15 Roth, *The Human Stain* (New York, Houghton Mifflin, 2000), pp. 335–6.

16 Roth, *American Pastoral* (New York, Houghton Mifflin, 1997), p. 213.

17 Roth, *Nemesis* (New York, Houghton Mifflin Harcourt, 2010), p. 265.

# 29

# Don DeLillo

THOMAS HEISE

Near the conclusion of Don DeLillo's (1936–) first novel, *Americana* (1971), the twenty-eight-year-old New York television executive David Bell thumbs a ride "somewhere in Missouri" from a "paleolithic lavender Cadillac" that will drive him over the hardscrabble hills and deserts of the Southwest to a makeshift commune of free-love hippies living with a breakaway tribe of Apaches in a shallow valley of sagebrush.¹ "We want to cleave to the old things. The land. The customs. The words. The ideas," they tell Bell, who in the weeks since he left the city is unshaven and bedraggled (*A*, 358). Bell's westward journey is a well-traveled road in American literature, a flight from the trappings of civilization made famous by Huckleberry Finn's promise at the end of Twain's iconic novel to "light out for the Territory" for "howling adventures amongst the Injuns."² Dissatisfied with the petty affairs and cubicle conformity of corporate life, Bell is the latest in a long line of restless American seekers, though he does not know exactly what he is looking for except a way to formulate "links" that will lead him to the "nation's soul."³ But he knows he ultimately will not find them in the earnest but conspiratorially minded community of societal castoffs for whom the Apaches are a romantic metaphor for life lived off the "big government" grid (*A*, 358). With its huts "arranged in no discernible pattern" and no "village square or center" to speak of, the commune is an unwitting example of – rather than a solution for – the post-1960s' social disorder in a wounded country that has lost its bearings and its sense of national purpose (*A*, 354). The eerie disquietude that suffuses *Americana*, which is endemic to much of the post-modern fiction that DeLillo would go on to publish over the next thirty-five years, is finally exhaled in a technological primal scream on the final page of the novel. Driving a rented car at "insane speeds" into Dallas, Bell blares his horn as he steers his way "through Dealey Plaza," where only a few years prior on November 22, 1963, Lee Harvey Oswald's bullet shattered JFK's skull and in "seven seconds," as DeLillo would later write, "broke the back of the American century."⁴

*Americana* is a loose, wobbly novel whose multiple parts – a satire of New York City office culture, a flashback to the emotionally brittle Bell household, and the narrative of a road trip into the heartland – do not entirely hold together, but in retrospect, it can be understood as DeLillo's initial attempt to map out a literal and thematic territory that continues to preoccupy and define the diverse body of literature that he has written. This alone makes *Americana* a useful introduction for the student who has yet to discover *White Noise* (1985), *Libra* (1988), *Mao II* (1991), and *Underworld* (1997), the core texts that have established DeLillo's reputation as a major American novelist.[5] "It's no accident that my first novel was called *Americana*," he has declared, adding, it was "a statement of my intention to use the whole picture, the whole culture."[6] From Mark Twain to Jack Kerouac, the archetypal journey to the West in American letters has held out the possibility for personal and national renewal, but in DeLillo's fiction there is no such promise. The search that Bell embarks upon turns out to be a circular one, routing him back to New York, but not before he uncovers at every step more of what he had hoped to escape: insidious social paranoia, traumatic legacies of political violence, and rampant consumerism that has transformed remaining pockets of indigenous culture into mere simulations beneath which the bones of an older society appear to be missing. Beginning with *Americana*, DeLillo has shown himself to be an unflinching chronicler of the whole of the American scene, a writer of difficult fiction at the edge of mystery and despair whose novels charting familial breakdown, spiritual crises, compromised privacy, terrorism, assassination, and war are made more rich by the fact that they do not lose sight of the redemptive qualities of art and language that provide consolation, order, and dignity to a precarious national life whose shared consensus is only, ironically, its uncertainty.

DeLillo has garnered many accolades – the American Book Award, the PEN/Faulkner Award, the Jerusalem Prize – that have further established his standing as a leading writer of his generation. But for many scholars, the more unsettled question of his position in twentieth-century American literary history is tied not to how they assess his talent, but to how they assess the function of the contemporary artist more generally. A central debate in literary studies since the 1970s has revolved around the question of the late twentieth-century novelist's capacity to stake out critical distance from contemporary social, political, and economic relations. With their formidable, high formalism, the great experimental modernist writers, artists, and composers of the early twentieth century – James Joyce, Henri Matisse, Arthur Schoenberg, to name only a few – made a strong claim for an irrefutably unique, authentic style. Their bold reinventions of language, color, and compositional technique contrasted with a crass world of commodity production and consumption that defined middlebrow culture. One way scholars have understood the utopian undertaking of modernism has been to see its rarefied aesthetics as offering an alternative to a world of mass entertainment and marketplace values, a sphere of high art where personal and social redemption might be found.

Among theorists of postmodern art – notably Fredric Jameson and Linda Hutcheon – there has been little consensus regarding the ability of contemporary writers to establish an oppositional position to current economic and political realities.[7] In an era dominated by global finance capitalism and invidious media saturation, the notion of aesthetic distance from which an effective critique might be lodged is increasingly antiquated. For Jameson, the "cultural logic of late capitalism" operates by relentlessly commodifying and incorporating into the market resistant and alternative aesthetic practices.[8] The problem is compounded by the proposition that former reserves of authenticity (the private life, nature, the unconscious) from which an artist of DeLillo's generation might draw inspiration have been infiltrated and superseded by omnipresent visual technologies (photography, television, film, video) that no longer report upon reality but actively create it. If postmodern fiction is to formulate an antihegemonic cultural politics – a question that remains up in the air for Jameson – it must do so in the guise, Hutcheon argues, of a complicitous critique, a critical position from within the web-enshrouding world system of capitalist production and consumption. In Hutcheon's view postmodern writers have been able to articulate a necessary internal distance through techniques of irony and narrational self-reflexivity that underscore for readers not only the artificially constructed quality of the literary object, but also of the social, economic, and political structures that accrue power by passing themselves off as natural, universal, and immutable.

Not surprisingly, DeLillo's controversial work has been at the center of disagreements over the fraught status of the contemporary artist. Scholars have variously described DeLillo's writing as in the tradition of modernism, as acutely postmodern, as pessimistic in its assessment of the unchallengeable reach of consumer capitalism, as paranoid like much of postwar American culture, and, conversely, as oppositional to the dominant ideologies of the current era.[9] This range of scholarly assessment speaks to his work's refusal to be pigeonholed into premade categories or offer up reassuring solutions or platitudes. Rebuffing the cultural imperative for therapeutic closure, DeLillo calls his novels "unresolvable," while placing himself in the middle of the conversation over the plight of the contemporary artist by pondering the very questions that have vexed scholars.[10] In *Americana, Great Jones Street* (1973), *Libra, Mao II, Underworld,* and *Falling Man*

(2007), artists struggle for relevance in a culture that is hypnotized by endless entertainment and product options and simultaneously paralyzed by spectacular acts of violence and destruction. Two defining aspects of DeLillo's work – a preoccupation with visual technologies and a tendency to integrate corporate brand names into his prose – testify to the inescapably mediated nature of consumer culture. In *White Noise*, the sleeping daughter of Jack Gladney murmurs the phrase "Toyota Celica" in an "ecstatic chant."[11] The brand's identity has wormed its way into her young mind, literally becoming the stuff of dreams. Bucky Wunderlick, the rock-and-roll hero of *Great Jones Street*, abandons his fame, disappearing from the spotlight into a shabby building in the East Village in order to escape the reach of Transparanoia, the shady corporation that controls his music. The ironic lesson that Wunderlick learns is that "the more time you spend in isolation, the more demands are made on the various media to communicate some relevant words and pictures."[12] Similarly, the reclusive author Bill Gray of *Mao II* is more famous after his withdrawal from public life, a fruitless action he undertakes to prevent him from becoming, in his words, "incorporated."[13] "They control the language, you have to improvise and dissemble," DeLillo will later advise in *Underworld*.[14]

While literary scholars have debated the ability of the postmodern novelist to formulate a critical purchase on his or her culture, DeLillo has been unequivocal in his assertion that the writer by necessity be an outsider. "The writer is the person who stands outside society," DeLillo has stated, adding that "we need the writer in opposition, the novelist who writes against power, who writes against the corporation or the state or the whole apparatus of assimilation."[15] Though he has been forthright in asserting that he does not harbor "any political program," this has not prevented DeLillo's work from being characterized as an act of "bad citizenship," as the conservative commentator George Will in the *Washington Post* termed *Libra* for speculating upon the motivations of Oswald.[16] DeLillo should not be conflated with the artists who populate his novels, a mistake Will made in aligning DeLillo with his fictionalized version of Oswald (himself a would-be writer). He should be seen as an author of engagement, rather than withdrawal, a writer who has assiduously worked to expand the terrain of the literary novel to voice existential and political anxieties about the limitations of human knowledge, nuclear annihilation, and the emotionally deadening effects of wealth. In the lineage of Melville, Joyce, and Nabokov, DeLillo's ambition has been to deploy the capacious possibilities of his chosen form to think through "large themes and whole landscapes of experience" during our "enormously complex period ... filled with danger and change."[17]

In the midst of the fragile calm of the Eisenhower years, *Americana*'s fast-talking ad executive Clinton Bell, David's father, gathers his young suburban family in the basement several nights a week to watch – not home movies or even films – but commercials, while their mother, suffering from bouts of depression and soon to die of cervical cancer, sleeps curled in her bed. The Bell household is beset with its pretenses, sexual tensions, and family secrets, but the specter that lurks in its basement is of an altogether different order. Advertising has usurped in importance the programming it supports, the first coup of many for the commodified image. With a soft spot for "Western saddles" and books about "the American West," Clinton fashions himself in the lineage of a cowboy, but DeLillo implies that these are merely products propping up a personality that is more performative than authentic (*A*, 152). David intuits as much when on his odyssey he stops at a "frontier-style restaurant" that is a "replica" of "the famous Cattleman on Forty-fifth Street in New York City" (*A*, 348). Even the "real" is a copy of a copy. David grows up to be a third-generation Bell in the American dream factory, but his relationship with his medium is ambivalent. As an adult, he stumbles upon a revelatory scene at "an exhibit of prize-winning war photographs" where a man in the lobby is "photographing the photograph":

> The effect was unforgettable. Time and distance were annihilated and it seemed that the children were smiling and waving at him. Such is the prestige of the camera, its almost religious authority, its hypnotic power to command reverence from subject and bystander alike. (*A*, 86)

In the midst of his rumination, David recognizes how the instant nearly arrests him with its spell. The moment marks the beginning of DeLillo's career-long endeavor to unveil the power of the camera to record history, by providing documentary evidence of the century's worst traumas, and obliterate it, by collapsing time and space into a self-referential circle.

*White Noise*, DeLillo's eighth, pursues similar themes through the life of the Gladneys, who like the Bells gather around a screen, this one a television, to partake in a Friday ritual of silently absorbing an unending display of pixelated destruction – "floods, earthquakes, mud slides, erupting volcanoes" (*WN*, 64). "Every disaster made us wish for more," Jack admits (*WN*, 64). What is at work here is the logic of a postmodern culture that is entranced by spectacles of theatrical violence, death, and natural catastrophe and simultaneously desensitized to them by dint of their repeatability as images. The problem facing the novelist, whose task is to "confront realities," is more daunting than finding an audience in the midst of media-generated clamor.[18] It is a problem regarding the very redefinition of reality. In this regard, *White Noise* dramatizes the sociologist Jean Baudrillard's central claim about postmodern visuality. Two years before DeLillo's novel, Baudrillard theorized what he saw as a troubling new condition: "signs of the real" have been substituted "for the real itself," so now images conceal "nothing at all" and reveal nothing except radiance "with their own fascination."[19] His proposition is tested by Murray Siskind, a professor of popular culture, who takes Jack to see "THE MOST PHOTOGRAPHED BARN IN AMERICA" (WN, 12). Numerous signs along the road advertise its singular status, preempting one's ability to view it in any original or nonmediated way. Predictably the structure is surrounded by camera-toting curiosity seekers whose presence perpetuates its claim of being famous. The bemused Siskind remarks that the barn can no longer be seen – tellingly, DeLillo never describes it – because the fabric of its existence has disappeared under its simulated version.

DeLillo does not disagree with Murray's statement, but he does not capitulate to the terms of its argument either. In his later novel *Cosmopolis* (2003), our postmodern media-generated reality has been amplified and accelerated by advanced computer technologies to the point of causing surreal distortions of time and space, which come to be inextricably associated with death. Eric Packer, who has made billions by outmaneuvering equity and currency markets by a nanosecond, discovers that his limousine's light-emitting diode (LED) screens begin displaying his movements in advance of his actions. Cause and effect have become sundered, and by implication, conventional concepts of history, narrative, or human motivation have broken down. Packer eventually glimpses his own death at the hands of a mentally unstable former employee, Richard Sheets, who has rejected the globally destructive enterprise of cybercapitalism for a bunkered-down existence offline where he plots revenge. DeLillo's novels transform amorphous, often inchoate cultural ailments, by giving them shape, structure, and texture so that we can better see and understand our own era. To this end, he offers Sheets's nihilism not as a solution to the pathologies of his age, but as a symptom of them. For Sheets, like Oswald in *Libra* or the terrorist George Haddad in *Mao II*, extreme violence has a shattering effect whose purpose is to propel the individual back into history or to pierce through the simulation to a reality beneath it. But it does so in the service of a reductive, life-killing ideology or a paranoid, all-encompassing conspiracy that denies what DeLillo terms "the rich, dense, and complex weave of actual experience."[20]

In *Libra*, Oswald's murderous violence fuses the individual with history, conflating a personal and national identity in a manner that knits the wayward drifter into the tragic story of America.[21] At heart, *Libra* is a novel about story making, about the structuring properties of the narratives people write for themselves and the larger social and political narratives that are braided into them, often with overpowering effects. Beneath Oswald's radical individualism, DeLillo reveals a subjectivity that is not autonomous but multiply determined by external forces: government social service agencies, the Marine Corps, the KGB, and rogue elements within the Central Intelligence Agency (CIA), each with its own role for Oswald to play. Though Oswald's life is extraordinarily exceptional for the bloodstain it has left on the American psyche, in DeLillo's novel it functions as an allegory of postmodern selfhood that originates not so much from within, as from without, a product of dominant social scripts that construct Oswald's identity, or the identity of any individual, for that matter. Driven to reignite anti-Castro fervor, the CIA agent Win Everett devises a plan for a fake assassination attempt on JFK that eventually will be traced back to Cuba. Everett's scheme necessitates a gunman, so he begins "script[ing] a person ... out of ordinary pocket litter," a fabricated, but fully documented subject who is real and fictional (*L*, 28). Enter Oswald, who unbeknown to himself stands at the center of a plot that he feels is self-authored, but that by twists and turns will lead to his own death, on television no less. What the formal qualities of DeLillo's novel imply is that human subjectivity is borne out of nested and intertwined narratives. Around Oswald's plot is Everett's, and wrapped around both is the story of Nicholas Branch's fifteen-year effort to write the official version of Kennedy's murder from proliferating boxes of evidence. Framing Oswald's and Branch's stories is the story of *Libra* itself, DeLillo's sprawling yet interconnected labyrinth that he devised out of the cultural incoherency and national heartbreak of Dallas. As DeLillo himself has said, his work "could probably not have been written in the world that existed before the assassination," and in some sense, his writing since *Americana*'s ending has been haunted by the tragedy that demanded the full maturity of his intellect and imagination.[22]

Oswald's ferocious act spawns – in the novel and in the world beyond it – conspiracy narratives that tell a thousand other stories that discount the plausibility of the lone gunman and instead speculate upon the machinations of much larger organizations. Numerous postwar American writers – Ishmael Reed, Thomas Pynchon, David Foster Wallace – have evinced a fascination with cultural paranoia, but "the chief shaman of the paranoid school" is DeLillo (*AF*, 86). Nearly every one of his novels contains a web of conspiracy theories that puzzle over the killing of JFK, government cover-ups at Area 51, mind-control activities of corporations, the Vietnam War, terrorist networks in New York City, and the acquired immunodeficiency syndrome (AIDS) epidemic in inner-city America. *Underworld*, DeLillo's most ambitious novel to date, represents the continuation and culmination of his analysis of American paranoia. *Underworld* is about many things – the rise of the military-industrial complex, the devastating urban crises of the 1970s and 1980s, the political uses of art, the global dominance of capitalism with the fall of the iron curtain – but its emotive center is the story of Nick Shay and Albert Bronzini, and the strategies they use to cope with the "sense of displacement and redefinition" caused by the myriad upheavals since the start of the cold war (*U*, 786). Shay and Bronzini either cling to the past or flee from it, but orbiting around them is a paranoid citizenry – composed of Sister Edgar, Eric Deming, a fictionalized J. Edgar Hoover, and others – who respond to the half-century of change in another manner. They do so by knitting arbitrary and coincidental events and data into conspiracies, luminous constellations of fact and rumor that render an opaque and bewildering world into a persuasive and lucid narrative that provides them with a reassuring sense of order. DeLillo's Hoover is the most pure practitioner of this logic and the most dangerous because of the power at his fingertips. Sitting in the stands for the 1951 Dodgers-Giants pennant race, Hoover fixates on "a hundred plots" that "go underground, to spawn and skein," corroding the nation internally (*U*, 51). "What is the connection between Us and Them," he ponders, "how many bundled links do we find in the neural labyrinth?" (*U*, 51).

For DeLillo's other characters, who do not haunt the halls of power, conspiracy theory's "bundled links" are a means of salvaging agency and self-reliance, which have been besieged by the mounting complexity of postmodern life, the invasive reach of unyielding governments and corporations, and technologies that compromise the autonomy of the human subject.[23] "Conspiracy offers coherence," DeLillo has remarked, but coherence marked by contradictions.[24] Beneath the random welter of events, it provides a secret truth that invisible forces are at work, a truth that is comforting and yet alienating, empowering and yet enfeebling, one that connects the atomized citizen to the world of others and yet holds him or her at bay in a specious fantasy.

What does DeLillo offer as an alternative to this paranoid logic or to the physical violence of the desperate and determined individuals we find in his pages? DeLillo's writing provides what in *Underworld* is described as "another kind of history," not a furtive history of conspiracy, but the ordinary and underacknowledged story of American life that "lives in the spaces of the official play-by-play" (*U*, 59, 82). At one level, DeLillo's novels contemplate large public issues – from the geopolitical struggles between superpowers to the ecological ravages of capitalist development – but at another level they are about people making do, struggling to hold together their families, working in embattled communities, and suffering from economic or racial exclusions.

In *Underworld*, DeLillo returns to where he left off in *Americana*, only this time the wanderer is Marvin Lundy, the basement-dwelling widower, baseball collector, and all-around terribly lonely old man. Lundy is on the hunt for Bobby Thomson's lost home-run ball that won the Giants the pennant. His journey takes him into the nooks and crannies of everyday American life, which DeLillo records in a series of haunting and elliptical lists. They are, in essence, narratives waiting to be formed, links waiting to be made. One reads:

1. The mother of twins in what's that town.
2. The man who lived in a community of chemically sensitive people, they wore white cotton shirts and hung their mail on clotheslines.
3. The woman named Bliss, which he was younger then, Marvin was, and maybe could have, with eyes as nice as hers, done a little something, in Indianola, Miss.
4. The shock of lives unlike your own. Happy, healthy, lonely, lost. The one-eighth Indian. Lives that are blunt and unforeseen even when they're ordinary.
5. Who knew a Susan somebody who spoke about a baseball with a famous past. Marvin forgets the tribe.
6. Stomach acting up again. (*U*, 317)

Lundy's quest for the homer inspires "people to tell him things, to entrust family secrets and unbreathable personal tales," which then become "exalted, absorbed by something larger, the long arching journey of the baseball itself" (*U*, 318). Through Lundy's search, DeLillo excavates "the people's history" – stories of discarded lives that are "blunt and unforeseen even when they're ordinary" – that have been unrecorded in the "single narrative sweep" of postwar history (*U*, 27, 318, 82). The "official" story of the nation, the narrative of American suburban affluence, the rise of the middle class, and the triumph over communism have no place for the ordinary voices that emerge from the woodwork when Lundy comes knocking to ask about the ball. By way of his "weary traipse" to complete his collection of memorabilia, Lundy ends up collecting stories that are a counterrmemory of America (*U*, 175).

"I think we need to invent beauty, search out some restoring force. A writer may describe the ugliness and pain in graphic terms but they can also try to find a dignity and significance in ruined parts of the city," DeLillo once said about *Great Jones Street* (*AF*, 94). In much of his work, the "ruined parts" are national, even international, and yet there is in his patent attentiveness to language – "the sheer pleasure of making it and bending it and seeing it form on the page" – a minor restoration to those ruins and perhaps a consolation as well, as he says, "for having lived in the world" (*AF*, 107).

## FURTHER READING

Boxall, Peter, *Don DeLillo: The Possibility of Fiction*, New York, Routledge, 2006.

Cowart, David, *Don DeLillo: The Physics of Language*, Athens, University of Georgia Press, 2003.

Dewey, Joseph, *Beyond Grief and Nothing: A Reading of Don DeLillo*, Columbia, University of South Carolina Press, 2006.

LeClair, Tom, *In the Loop: Don DeLillo and the Systems Novel*, Chicago, University of Illinois Press, 1988.

Lentricchia, Frank (ed.), *Introducing Don DeLillo*, Durham, N.C.: Duke University Press, 1991.

Osteen, Mark, *American Magic and Dread: Don DeLillo's Dialogue with Culture*, Philadelphia, University of Pennsylvania Press, 2000.

Schneck, Peter and Philipp Schweighauser (eds.), *Terrorism, Media, and the Ethics of Fiction: Transatlantic Perspectives on Don DeLillo*, London, Continuum, 2010.

Simmons, Ryan, "What Is a Terrorist? Contemporary Authorship, the Unabomber, and Mao II," *Modern Fiction Studies* 45.3 (1999): 675–95.

Tabbi, Joseph, *Postmodern Sublime: Technology and American Writing from Mailer to Cyberpunk*, Ithaca, N.Y., Cornell University Press, 1995.

Tanner, Tony, *The American Mystery: American Literature from Emerson to DeLillo*, Cambridge, Cambridge University Press, 2000.

Willman, Skip, "Art after Dealey Plaza: DeLillo's Libra," *Modern Fiction Studies* 45.3 (1999): 621–40.

Wilcox, Leonard, "Don DeLillo's Underworld and the Return of the Real," *Contemporary Literature* 43.1 (2002): 120–37.

## NOTES

1 Don DeLillo, *Americana* (New York, Penguin, 1971), 348. Hereafter cited parenthetically as *A*.

2 M. Twain, *Mississippi Writings: Tom Sawyer, Life on the Mississippi, Huckleberry Finn, Pudd'nhead Wilson* (New York, Library of America, 1982), pp. 911–12.

3 DeLillo, *Americana*, p. 349.

4 Ibid., 377; DeLillo, *Libra* (New York, Viking, 1988), p. 181. Hereafter cited parenthetically as *L*.

5 In the opinion of the influential scholar Harold Bloom, DeLillo is grouped alongside Thomas Pynchon, Philip Roth, and Cormac McCarthy as one of the four most important living American novelists. See Harold Bloom, "Dumbing Down American Readers," *Boston Globe*, September 24, 2003, www.boston.com/news/globe/editorial_opinion/oped/articles/2003 /09/24/dumbing_down_american_readers.

6 A. Begley, "The Art of Fiction CXXXV: Don DeLillo," *Conversations with Don DeLillo*, ed. Thomas DePietro (Jackson, University Press of Mississippi, 2005), p. 88. Hereafter cited parenthetically as *AF*.

7 See F. Jameson, *Postmodernism; or the Cultural Logic of Late Capitalism* (Durham, N.C., Duke University Press, 1991), and L. Hutcheon, *A Poetics of Postmodernism: History, Theory, Fiction* (New York, Routledge, 1988).

8 Jameson, *Postmodernism*, 1.

9  See F. Lentricchia, "Tales of the Electronic Tribe," *New Essays on "White Noise*," ed. F. Lentricchia (Cambridge, Cambridge University Press, 1991); P. Nel, "DeLillo and Modernism," *The Cambridge Companion to Don DeLillo*, ed. J. N. Duvall (Cambridge, Cambridge University Press, 2008), pp. 13–26; P. Knight, "DeLillo, Postmodernism, Postmodernity," in *Cambridge Companion*, pp. 27–40.

10  Quoted in W. Goldstein, "PW Interviews: Don DeLillo," *Conversations with Don DeLillo*, ed. Thomas DePietro (Jackson, University Press of Mississippi, 2005), p. 49.

11  DeLillo, *White Noise* (New York, Penguin, 1985), p. 155. Hereafter cited parenthetically as *WN*.

12  DeLillo, *Great Jones Street* (New York, Penguin, 1973), p. 128.

13  DeLillo, *Mao II* (New York, Viking, 1991), p. 41.

14  DeLillo, *Underworld* (New York, Scribner, 1997), p. 444. Hereafter cited parenthetically as *U*.

15  Quoted in A. Arensberg, "Seven Seconds," in *Conversations with Don DeLillo*, ed. Thomas DePietro (Jackson, University Press of Mississippi, 2005), p. 45. Quoted in Begley, "Art," p. 97.

16  Quoted in K. Connolly, "An Interview with Don DeLillo," *Conversations with Don DeLillo*, ed. Thomas DePietro (Jackson, University Press of Mississippi, 2005), p. 38.

17  Quoted in G. Howard, "The American Strangeness: An Interview with Don DeLillo," *Conversations with Don DeLillo*, ed. Thomas DePietro (Jackson,University Press of Mississippi, 2005), p. 124.

18  Quoted in R. Harris, "A Talk with Don DeLillo," *Conversations with Don DeLillo*, ed. Thomas DePietro (Jackson, University Press of Mississippi, 2005), p. 18.

19  J. Baudrillard, *Simulations*, trans. P. Foss, P. Patton, and P. Beitchman (New York, Semiotext(e), 1983), pp. 4, 8–9. For additional consideration of Baudrillard in relation to DeLillo see S. Olster, "*White Noise*," *Cambridge Companion*, pp. 79–93, and R. Helyer, "DeLillo and Masculinity," *Cambridge Companion*, pp. 125–36.

20  Quoted in Howard, "American Strangeness," p. 124.

21  For an extended consideration of conspiracy theory and literary narratives see P. O'Donnell, *Latent Destinies: Cultural Paranoia and Contemporary U.S. Narrative* (Durham, N.C., Duke University Press, 2000).

22  Quoted in Goldstein, "PW," p. 49.

23  For an extended consideration of paranoia and American literature see T. Melley, *Empire of Conspiracy: The Culture of Paranoia in Postwar America* (Ithaca, N.Y., Cornell University Press, 2000).

24  Quoted in Goldstein, "PW," p. 51.

# 30

# Cormac McCarthy

## BRIAN EVENSON

Cormac McCarthy's (1933–) significance, particularly in his pre–Border Trilogy writings, lies in the refusal of his fiction to be significant, to be meaningful, in the way that American literature generally has intended. His work shies away from depictions of thought or interior mental space, leaving his readers to sort out the motivations of the characters on their own. His language is at times baroque (most notably in *Blood Meridian* [1985]), at other times stripped back and minimal (*Child of God* [1973] or *The Road* [2006]). At the same time, McCarthy is remarkably expert at appropriating the traditions of American fiction in a way that acknowledges them even as he employs them to new effect. He does this sometimes by simply pushing a mode or genre to its extreme. His novel *Outer Dark* (1968), for instance, toys with the traditions of southern gothic but does so as if the South were actually hell. *Blood Meridian* imitates the western even as McCarthy cross-pollinates this genre with the spirit of intense viciousness and gnostic philosophy. McCarthy seems both to be bringing one era of American literature – an era tied to more stable notions of character, self, genre, ethics, and order – to a close and to be opening another, this one more interested in the possibilities of pushing the forms and styles to which we are accustomed in new directions.

There is little to suggest this will be the case in McCarthy's first novel, *The Orchard Keeper* (1965), which, when it appeared was described as "sorely handicapped" by its "humble and excessive admiration for William Faulkner,"[1] a writer to whom McCarthy is often compared for better or for worse. The first of four novels set in Tennessee before McCarthy turned his gaze to the American West, *The Orchard Keeper* concerns three characters and a corpse. The corpse is that of young John Wesley Rattner's father, killed by Marion Sylder and dumped on Rattner's uncle's property. Rattner's uncle, living independently in a cabin beside a ruined apple orchard, has been watching over the corpse for years, unaware that it is that of his brother. With Sylder not knowing whom he has killed, and Young Rattner unaware of the circumstances of his father's death, and the corpse itself mute for obvious reasons, McCarthy manages to play out an elaborate dance of coincidence and chance in which only the reader has enough information to make the proper connections among the characters.

Equally important to *The Orchard Keeper* is the kind of attention that McCarthy pays to the natural world. His descriptions are less bucolic than affective, the sounds of the words resonating off the images being created and the language of the sentences often imbued almost with the rhythms and alliteration of poetry: "The oaks were black and stark and the leaves in the yard were frosted and snapped under his feet with thin glassy sounds."[2] This nonromantic attention to the natural world, and the way in which that world can be constructed anew linguistically, is something to be found throughout McCarthy's work.

Here, too, we see intimations of McCarthy's particular interest in lyrical violence, an interest that will reach its most intense expression in the most jubilantly aggressive passages of *Blood Meridian*. Consider, for instance, the meticulous verve with which McCarthy depicts Sylder's one-armed strangulation of Young Rattner's father. He first describes the complicated dynamics of trying to strangle someone one-handed and then progresses forward to the way "the jaw kept coming down not on any detectable hinges but like a mass of offal, some obscene waste matter uncongealing and collapsing in slow folds over the web of his hand."[3] For McCarthy, the line between being human and being dead, even being waste, is a very thin one indeed.

*Outer Dark*, McCarthy's second book, is a tale of incest between a brother and a sister, Culla and Rinthy Holme. When Rinthy gives birth to a child, Culla leaves the baby in the woods. When she discovers what he has done, she goes in search of her child, and Culla follows in search of her.

In many senses a typical southern gothic plot, *Outer Dark* stands out in the way this tale is impacted by three grim and mysterious strangers who shuttle back and forth across the landscape of the story, engaged in pillage and murder. They seem hardly human, are "like revenants that reoccur in lands laid waste with fever: spectral and palpable as stone."[4] They are never explained; instead, they seem palpable embodiments of evil. Culla crosses paths with them several times but manages to remain alive, perhaps because in his abandonment of the child he has established an affinity with them. The world itself seems too to fade back and forth between a realistic Appalachia and a kind of mythic space that may even be hell itself. There are echoes of biblical stories: a scene in which a herd of hogs plunge from a bluff recalls the story of the madmen and the pigs (Matthew 8: 28–34), though it does so quite irreverently. In *Outer Dark*, McCarthy erases our ability to make a distinction between different generic modes: the fantastic and the realistic mix in an unresolvable fashion. In addition, he has little interest in developing the characters or in resolving the plot completely. Little is done to explain the nature of the three strangers, for instance. They might be seen as a demonic inversion of the Holy Trinity, but knowing this does little to make sense of them. Instead, the characters begin to seem almost like tokens in a dark game, in which randomness and chance play a major role.

*Child of God* is the story of Lester Ballard, a man who by chance stumbles into necrophilia and then begins to collect a bevy of corpses. At once comic and horrifying, the novel explores the existence of a troubled man living on the edge of society and progressively moving farther and farther out into its fringe. Both the shortest and stylistically most spare of McCarthy's novels, it is also the funniest.

Lester Ballard, one of the townspeople suggests, is "a child of God much like yourself perhaps."[5] But the novel itself seems set on complicating this claim, by either reducing it to pabulum or ironizing it. Although the towns-people and others offer ample speculation for why Ballard is the way he is and the book ends with his body being dissected, McCarthy offers little by way of answer that would allow us to categorize Lester Ballard and file him and his crimes neatly away. The novel deliberately fails to explain Lester Ballard, and if he is a "child of God much like yourself perhaps," that is perhaps merely to say that all human nature exceeds logic or rational explanation.

Probably his most Faulknerian book after *The Orchard Keeper*, *Suttree* (1979) is the story of Cornelius Suttree, who has disowned a privileged life to live in a houseboat on the Tennessee River. As in *Child of God*, the focus is on the edges of the community, on the space in the boundaries where the outcasts and misfits reside, but here the community of people, although often troubled or confused, is more endearing than Lester Ballard. As an adopted member of this community, Suttree finds himself distracted from his fishing and life on the river by their individual needs. Among the out-casts, tramps, prostitutes, criminals, and misfits is Gene Harrogate, whom Suttree meets in a prison workhouse. Harrogate is naïve and bumbling, on the one hand, but with a natural inclination toward criminality, on the other. Saving Harrogate becomes a sort of project for Suttree, despite his own bet-ter judgment.

Moments of *Suttree* seem to respond directly to another river novel, *Huckleberry Finn* (1885), though Suttree's own journey seems much more meandering, and he has very little success either with Harrogate or with himself. Ultimately he abandons the river to hitch a ride in a car, ready to wander on elsewhere, an act that can be read as McCarthy's acknowledg-ment of the lineage existing between the river novel and the Kerouac-style road novel. Full of comic moments, the novel is also imbued with lyrical passages, as well as occasional moments that seem almost too burdened with meaning. Consider this part of his conversation with the corpse of a ragpicker: "A man is all men. You have no right to your wretchedness." In gestures such as these, we see McCarthy beginning to reach toward a philosophical universalism that the rest of his early work, and *Suttree* as a whole, tends to belie.

*Suttree* does for Knoxville what James Joyce's *Ulysses* (1922) did for Dublin. It brings the river into a particular and peculiar life in which place becomes almost as much of a protagonist as the characters themselves. A kind of baggy and various monster, the novel wanders and roams as much as the river that lies at its heart. Says Jerome Charyn, "The book comes at us like a horrifying flood. The language licks, batters, wounds – a poetic, troubled rush of debris. It is personal and tough, without that boring neatness and desire for resolution that you can get in any well-made novel."[6]

That lack of "boring neatness and desire for resolution" typifies McCarthy's next novel as well, his masterpiece: *Blood Meridian*. In it, McCarthy moved from the Appalachian settings that had characterized his early novels into the American West. Based loosely on Samuel Chamberlain's *My Confession: Recollections of a Rogue* (1996), the novel is the story of "the kid," a runaway from Tennessee who falls in with a gang of ruthless scalp hunters who progress from scalping marauding Apaches to butchering anybody whose scalp might pass for that of an Indian and thus earn them money. From there they move on to outright mayhem. The captain of the group is John Joel Glanton; the rest of the group consists of seasoned criminals, an ex-preacher, and other hard cases.

Perhaps the most intriguing character is Judge Holden, a strange pale and hairless man who resembles nothing so much as a giant baby or "some great pale diety."[7] He appears suddenly, sitting on a rock in the middle of nowhere, and seems almost magical in his ability to survive nearly anything. He is a draftsman and a recorder, intrigued by the natural world and seemingly well educated, but no less vicious or violent than any of the other members of the gang. As the novel develops, he seems to take a particular interest in the kid, observing him, judging him, and eventually becoming his nemesis. Their enmity is almost mythic: says the judge, "Our animosities were formed and waiting before ever we two met."[8]

Curiously, any time there is a scene of intense violence in the novel, the kid drops out, gradually disappearing as a recognizable entity and only reappearing after the scene is over. When fighting Indians with a group of army irregulars early in the novel, the kid is at first present but then quickly seems to dissolve.[9] We see his horse shot out from under him. We find that he has already fired his rifle but are not given the moment of shooting. Very quickly he is reduced from a fighting entity to a passive, observing one: six times we are told that "he saw," and then he simply disappears, only reappearing at the beginning of the next chapter as "one soul" who "rose wondrously from among the new slain dead and stole away in the moonlight" (55), a living soul born out of a pile of corpses.

Throughout the novel the kid remains largely unimplicated in the acts of violence, as if to suggest he is absent from them in spirit if not to body. It is perhaps this that the judge faults him for when, near the end of the novel, he approaches the kid when the latter is under arrest. "Why lurk there in the shadows?" the judge asks, upon which the narrator describes the kid as "Hardly more than a shadow himself."[10] Both statements can be read back into the kid's character as depicted in the book as a whole. The judge goes on to accuse: "Each was called upon to empty out his heart into the common and one did not. Can you tell me who that one was?"[11] Called upon to empty his heart out and turn himself over to violence, the kid instead hangs back in the shadows, observes. The judge condemns this refusal, in language appropriated from Christianity.

> "You came forward, he said, to take part in a work. But you were a witness against yourself. You sat in judgment of our own deeds. You put your own allowances before the judgments of history and you broke with the body of which you were pledged a part and poisoned it in all its enterprise. Hear me, man. I spoke in the desert for you and you only and you turned a deaf ear to me. If war is not holy man is nothing but antic clay."[12]

This alternative, between war's – and by implication, violence's – being holy or man's being capering clay, is thematically at the heart of a number of McCarthy's books. From the anxiety Sylder experiences feeling a body collapse into a corpse in a way that makes it resemble offal, to Lester Ballard's attempts to reanimate the corpses of the dead through his necrophilia, to the tension between Culla's antic wandering and the "grim triune's" deadly mayhem, the question is whether violence should be seen as holy and redemptive, a kind of communion, or whether there is any meaning in our lives at all. McCarthy's approach to this is less to choose one or the other than to create a tension and balance between the two mutually exclusive possibilities.

Stylistically, *Blood Meridian* is written as if a nineteenth-century dime store western, complete with the chapter summaries one might find in a book of the period. It avoids the use of apostrophes and seems at once to be a response to nineteenth-century typography and a pastiche of it. It does not fit smoothly into any literary camp and is, as Timothy Parrish has suggested, speaking of history (but in a way that I would extend to genre and literary history as well) "neither postmodern nor premodern,"[13] but rather serving as a kind of parenthetical whose tongs touch both the beginnings and the endings of American literature. The language is exceptionally dense, with McCarthy's employing a number of outdated and outmoded words (awap, spanceled, spartled, thrapple, etc.). It is a book awash in both violence and gnostic philosophy, a book full of "bald and flyspecked mountains," killers, of a sun described as "the head of a great red phallus," minor and major apocalypses, and every manner of extremity. Says Steven Shaviro of the novel, "In the entire range of American Literature, only *Moby-Dick* (1851) bears comparison to *Blood Meridian*. Both novels are epic in scope, cosmically resonant.... Both manifest a sublime visionary power."[14] It is McCarthy's greatest achievement.

McCarthy's next book, *All the Pretty Horses* (1992), the first book in his Border Trilogy, appeared seven years later. It has neither the baggy playfulness of *Suttree* nor the mad power of *Blood Meridian*, but it was McCarthy's first commercial success, going through seven printings in its first month. It is the story of John Grady Cole, a teenaged Texan cowboy who travels with his friend Lacey Rawlins south into Mexico, where they hope to work as cowboys. Once employed at a ranch, Cole falls in love with Alejandra, the daughter of the ranch owner. He has an affair with her, eventually ending up in jail because of it, along with Rawlins. After he is wounded in a knife fight, eventually his and Rawlins's release is arranged by Alejandra's aunt, on condition that Cole does not see Alejandra again. After an abortive encounter with Alejandra, the two cowboys return to the United States.

*All the Pretty Horses* is much more traditionally plot driven than any of McCarthy's previous works. Whereas his earlier work is uncompromising and rather bleak, *All the Pretty Horses* is almost romantic in feel and tone. One of the paradoxes of McCarthy's writing is that his earlier books seem more contemporary, genre-disruptive, and innovative than many of the later ones, as if, in his later books, he is recoiling into the tradition that he initially fought.

Having said that, however, there is still a great deal to recommend *All the Pretty Horses*. It is well written and complex, full of beautiful moments of language and vividly described scenes. The knife fight, for instance, has the same sort of raw power and confusion found in McCarthy's earlier work. Ultimately, however, this literary western about frustrated love does less to push at the boundaries of its category than McCarthy's earlier books. It is a prime and refined example of a particular type more than a transformation of it.

*The Crossing* (1994), the second book in the Border Trilogy, takes place as well near the border of the United States and Mexico. In it, young Billy

Parnham makes three trips across the border, sometimes with his younger brother, Boyd. In the first, he traps a pregnant wolf that has been preying on his father's cattle and determines to take it back to Mexico. In doing so, he establishes an intense bond with the wolf, identifying with its way of being in the world. When the wolf is confiscated, Billy pursues it to where it is being made to fight in a circus and shoots it to put it out of its misery.

He returns home to find his parents murdered and their horses missing and sets off in pursuit. In the attempt they manage to rescue a girl, whom Boyd falls in love with, and Boyd is shot but survives, later fleeing with the girl. Years later, Billy crosses into Mexico in search of him but only finds his bones.

There is here still the appreciation of chance found in McCarthy's other work, as well as several seemingly random and even motiveless encounters that are reminiscent of earlier gestures, but there is a different sort of philosophy motivating them. This philosophy is more reflective and less visceral than that found in the earlier novels and is more tied to a sense of mythologizing, almost Plotinian unity. As an ex-Mormon within the book suggests, "Things separate from their stories have no meaning. They are only shapes. Of a certain size and color. A certain weight. When their meaning has become lost to us they no longer have even a name. The story on the other hand can never be lost from its place in the world for it is that place." Or as he suggests later, "So everything is necessary. Every least thing. This is the hard lesson. Nothing can be dispensed with. Nothing despised.... I say again all tales are one. Rightly heard all tales are one." [15] Though one might argue that the notion that nothing can be dispensed with or despised goes a long way toward providing a motivation for the almost balefully uninhibited narrative gaze of McCarthy's earlier work, the comforting sense of oneness is something new.

The final book of the trilogy, *Cities of the Plain* (1998), is also the least effective. It is about the death of the Old West and unites John Grady Cole from *Horses* with Billy Parnham from *The Crossing*, each a few years older. They work as cowboys in southern New Mexico, living a life they love in a tradition that is rapidly ending. Cole falls in love with a prostitute named Magdalena, but her brothel owner has her killed rather than allowing her to leave with Cole. Cole has a knife fight with the brothel owner, whom he kills, but not before being fatally wounded himself. In an epilogue that takes place fifty years later, Parnham is left to grow old alone, watching the life that he loves die out. Again, there is much that is masterful about the novel, and its lack of much exposition gives it a strangely flattened effect, but there is little to surprise or amaze readers familiar with McCarthy's earlier work.

*No Country for Old Men* (2005) began as a screenplay before being transformed into a novel, with seemingly minimal modifications. It contains long runs of dialogue and meticulous but fairly flat descriptions of character actions, with short first-person reflections interspersed. It is the closest thing McCarthy has written to a thriller, the action beginning when Llewelyn Moss stumbles onto a drug deal gone wrong in the desert and takes a satchel containing $2.4 million. For the rest of the novel he is pursued by people who want the money, among them Anton Chigurh, a psychotic killer who believes himself an instrument of fate and a servant of chance. Indeed, he lets the toss of a coin determine the fate of those he might kill. Pursuing all of them is Sheriff Ed Tom Bell, a laconic westerner shocked by the trail of carnage the stolen money seems to have caused.

Largely third-person, there are several short sections of the novel in the sheriff's voice, in which he reflects on his sense of the world, on his role in the war, on his dreams, and so forth. Here McCarthy balances the relentlessness of Chigurh's violence, which is reminiscent of that of the trio in *Outer Dark*, against the sheriff's sense that something is wrong with the world. "I think I know where we're headed," he suggests at one point. "We're bein' bought with our own money."[16] For the somewhat dated but likeable sheriff the problem starts "when you begin to overlook bad manners."[17] McCarthy acknowledges the ineffectiveness of this philosophy even as he remains fond of it: the sheriff has the last word at the beginning and end of the novel, and even if Chigurh remains on the loose and the sheriff has recognized his inadequacy and his need to retire, his voice is still one of the few of the original ones remaining by the novel's end. Yet, his perspective cannot comprehend the violence of Chigurh, and thus the novel replays the tension in *Blood Meridian* wherein violence and redemption are posed as two mutually exclusive possibilities.

McCarthy's most recent novel, *The Road* (2006), continues to try to pursue this path of balancing two different philosophies of the world against one another. On the one hand, it is a postapocalyptic novel about how bad things might get in a semidestroyed world in which everyone is potentially out for himself. It explores the way the collapse of an infrastructure might lead to mistrust, fear, and even cannibalism. On the other hand, the novel explores the development of a relationship between a father and son within this ruined world, suggesting a kind of hope and faith in human nature despite the destruction of a social infrastructure. The novel is McCarthy's most decorated, having received the Pulitzer Prize and the James Tate Black Memorial Prize for Fiction, and was chosen for Oprah's Book Club. Though it does not have the range or scope of either *Blood Meridian* or *Outer Dark*, it does have some of those novels' unflinchingness. It is a sobering, clear-headed account of an unspecified disaster and the attempt to keep one's humanity intact in the face of it, and as such it has a great emotional span, moving through destruction and despair to achieve finally a tenuous hope in its concluding pages. By doing so, however, it enters more fully into the tradition of American literature than much of McCarthy's other work; indeed, it is perhaps his most accessible work. But what it lacks in innovation it makes up for in the delicacy of its narrative arc and its willingness, to borrow from the *Crossing*, neither to dispense with anything nor to despise it – something that all of McCarthy's best novels share.

Throughout his career, from his early stylistic engagement with Faulkner, to the response to *Huckleberry Finn* and anticipation of the road novel to be found in *Suttree* and fulfilled in *The Road*, to the reworkings of the eminently American form that is the western in *Blood Meridian* and the Border Trilogy, McCarthy remains seriously engaged with the history of American literature. *Blood Meridian* in particular seems a book that straddles different literary traditions, connecting the novel back to the epic of Homer, reworking these traditions even as it moves beyond them. His engagement with violence is particularly American as well, a clear-eyed acknowledgment of the bloodshed and violence that are at the heart of our own society rather than an apology for it. In that sense McCarthy's best books function almost as the subconscious of American literary history, raising to the surface aspects of our culture and our past that many other writers have shied away from. Of course, there is violence in the classic American tradition of Cooper, Melville, Twain, Faulkner, and even Cather, but McCarthy excludes from this tradition the comfort of a reliable moral perspective. By so doing he serves to round out a certain mode of American literature but does so in his own particular and peculiar fashion, in a way that leaves him beholden to no contemporary school or tradition. McCarthy has pursued his own unique path, even while drawing on the various possibilities of the writers who have come before him.

## FURTHER READING

Arnold, Edwin T. and Dianne C. Luce (eds.), *A Cormac McCarthy Companion: The Border Trilogy*, Jackson, University Press of Mississippi, 2001.

Arnold, Edwin T. and Dianne C. Luce (eds.), *Perspectives on Cormac McCarthy*, Jackson, University Press of Mississippi, 1993; rev. ed. 1999.

Bloom, Harold (ed.), *Modern Critical Views: Cormac McCarthy*, Philadelphia, Chelsea, 2002.

Hall, Wade and Rick Wallach (eds.), *Sacred Violence: A Reader's Companion to Cormac McCarthy*, El Paso, Texas Western Press, 1995.

Parrish, Timothy, "Cormac McCarthy's *Blood Meridian*: The First and Last Book of America." *From the Civil War to the Apocalypse: Postmodern History*

# GUIDE TO FURTHER READING

Adams, Rachel. *Continental Divides: Remapping the Cultures of North America.* Chicago: University of Chicago Press, 2009.

Ammons, Elizabeth. *Conflicting Stories: American Women Writers at the Turn into the Twentieth Century.* Oxford: Oxford University Press, 1991.

Arac, Jonathan. *The Emergence of American Literary Narrative, 1820–1860.* Cambridge, Mass.: Harvard University Press, 2005.

Armstrong, Nancy. *How Novels Think: The Limits of Individualism from 1719–1900.* New York: Columbia University Press, 2006.

Bahktin, M. M. *The Dialogic Imagination.* Translated by Caryl Emerson and Michael Holquist. Austin: University of Texas Press, 1981.

Baym, Nina. "Melodramas of Beset Manhood: How Theories of American Fiction Exclude Women Authors." *The New Feminist Criticism: Essays on Women, Literature, and Theory,* ed. Elaine Showalter. New York: Pantheon, 1985. 63–80.

Bell, Bernard W. *The Contemporary African American Novel: Its Folk Roots and Modern Literary Branches.* Amherst: University of Massachusetts Press, 2004.

Berlant, Lauren. *The Female Complaint: The Unfinished Business of Sentimentality in American Culture.* Durham, N.C.: Duke University Press, 2008.

Bloom, Harold. *How to Read and Why.* New York: Scribner, 2001.

Bradbury, Malcom. *The Modern American Novel.* 2nd rev. ed. Oxford: Oxford University Press, 1992.

Chase, Richard. *The American Novel and Its Tradition.* Garden City, N.Y.: Doubleday Anchor Books, 1957.

Cowley, Malcolm. *After the Genteel Tradition: American Writers, 1910–1930.* Carbondale: Southern Illinois University Press, 1964.

*Exile's Return: A Literary Odyssey of the 1920s.* New York: Viking Press, 1951.

Davidson, Cathy N. *Revolution and the Word: The Rise of the Novel in America.* New York: Oxford University Press, 1986, rpt. 2004.

Dickstein, Morris. *Leopards in the Temple: The Transformation of American Fiction 1945–1970.* Cambridge, Mass.: Harvard University Press, 1999.

Dimock, Wai Chee, and Lawrence Buell, eds. *Shades of the Planet: American Literature as World Literature.* Princeton, N.J.: Princeton University Press, 2007.

Douglas, Ann. *The Feminization of American Culture.* New York: Avon Books, 1977.

Edgar, Christopher, and Gary Lenhart, eds. *The Teachers and Writers Guide to Classic American Literature.* New York: Teachers and Writers Collaborative 2001.

Elliott, Emory et al., eds. *The Columbia History of the American Novel*. New York: Columbia University Press, 1991.

Ellison, Ralph. *The Collected Essays of Ralph Ellison*. Ed. John F. Callahan. New York: Modern Library, 1996.

Evans, Brad. *Before Cultures: The Ethnographic Imagination in American Literature, 1865–1920*. Chicago: University of Chicago Press, 2005.

Fabi, Guilia M. *Passing and the Rise of the African American Novel*. Urbana: University of Illinois Press, 2001.

Fabre, Genevieve, and Michel Feith, eds. *Temples for Tomorrow: Looking Back at the Harlem Renaissance*. Bloomington: Indiana University Press, 2001.

Feidleson, Charles. *Symbolism and American Literature*. Chicago and London: University of Chicago Press, 1953.

Ferraro, Thomas J. *Ethnic Passages: Literary Immigrants in Twentieth-Century America*. Chicago: University of Chicago Press, 1993.

Fetterley, Judith. *The Resisting Reader: A Feminist Approach to American Fiction*. Bloomington: Indiana University Press, 1978.

Fiedler, Leslie A. *Love and Death in the American Novel*. New York: Criterion Books, 1960.

Fishkin, Shelley Fisher. *Was Huck Black? Mark Twain and African American Voices*. New York: Oxford University Press, 1993.

Foreman, P. Gabrielle. *Activist Sentiments: Reading Black Women in the Nineteenth Century*. Urbana: University of Illinois Press, 2009.

Gardner, Jared. *Master Plots: Race and the Founding of an American Literature, 1787–1845*. Baltimore: Johns Hopkins University Press, 2000.

Giles, Paul. *Transatlantic Insurrections: British Culture and the Formation of American Literature, 1730–1860*. Philadelphia: University of Pennsylvania Press, 2001.

Hall, David D., ed. *A History of the Book in America*. Vols. 1–5. Chapel Hill: University of North Carolina Press, 2010.

Hicks, Granville. *The Great Tradition*. New York: Macmillan, 1933.

Hungerford, Amy. *Postmodern Belief: American Literature and Religion since 1960*. Princeton, N.J.: Princeton University Press, 2010.

Hunter, J. Paul. *Before Novels*. New York: Norton, 1990.

Hutcheon, Linda. *A Poetics of Postmodernism: History, Theory, Fiction*. London: Routledge, 1988.

James, Henry. *Literary Criticism: Essays on Literature, American Writers, English Writers*. Ed. Leon Edel. New York: Library of America, 1984.

*Literary Criticism: French Writers, Other European Writers, The Prefaces of the New York Edition*. Ed. Leon Edel. New York: Library of America, 1984.

Jehlen, Myra. *American Incarnation: The Individual, the Nation, and the Continent*. Cambridge, Mass.: Harvard University Press, 1986.

Kazin, Alfred. *On Native Grounds*. New York: Harcourt, Brace & World, 1942.

Klein, Marcus. *Foreigners: The Making of American Literature*. Chicago: University of Chicago Press, 1981.

Kolodny, Annette. *The Lay of the Land: Metaphor as Experience and History in American Life, and Letters*. Chapel Hill: University of North Carolina Press, 1975.

Kundera, Milan. *The Art of the Novel*. Trans. Linda Asher. New York: Grove Press, 1986.

Lawrence, D. H. *Studies in Classic American Literature*. New York: Thomas Seltzer, 1923.

Lewis, R. W. B. *The American Adam: Innocence, Tragedy and Tradition in the Nineteenth Century*. Chicago: University of Chicago Press, 1955.

Marx, Leo. *The Machine in the Garden: Technology and the Pastoral Ideal in America*. New York: Oxford University Press, 1964.

Matthiessen, F. O. *American Renaissance: Art and Expression in the Age of Emerson and Whitman*. New York: Oxford, 1941.

McGurl, Mark. *The Novel Art: Elevations of American Fiction after Henry James*. Princeton, N.J.: Princeton University Press, 2001.

McHale, Brian. *Postmodernist Fiction*. 2nd ed. London: Routledge, 1991.

Moretti, Franco, ed. *The Novel*. Vol. 1, *History, Geography, Culture*. Princeton, N.J.: Princeton University Press, 2007.

Moretti, Franco, ed. *The Novel*. Vol. 2, *Forms and Themes*. Princeton, N.J.: Princeton University Press, 2007.

Nadel, Alan. *Invisible Criticism: Ralph Ellison and the American Canon*. Iowa City: University of Iowa Press, 1988.

Parrish, Timothy. *From the Civil War to the Apocalypse, Postmodern History and American Fiction*. Amherst: University of Massachusetts Press, 2008.

Phillips, Dana. *The Truth of Ecology: Nature, Culture, and Literature in America*. New York: Oxford University Press, 2003.

Poirier, Richard. *A World Elsewhere: The Place of Style in American Literature*. New York: Oxford University Press, 1966.

Reynolds, David S. *Beneath the American Renaissance: The Subversive Imagination in the Age of Emerson and Melville*. Cambridge, Mass.: Harvard University Press, 1988.

Showalter, Elaine. *A Jury of Her Peers: American Women Writers from Anne Bradstreet to Annie Proulx*. New York: Alfred A. Knopf, 2009.

Smith, Henry Nash. *Democracy and the Novel: Popular Resistance to Classic American Writers*. New York: Oxford University Press, 1978.

Spillers, Hortense J. *Black, White, and in Color: Essays on American Literature and Culture*. Chicago: University of Chicago Press, 2003.

Stepto, Robert B. *From behind the Veil: A Study of Afro-American Narrative*. Urbana: University of Illinois Press, 1979.

Sundquist, Eric. *To Wake the Nations: Race in the Making of American Literature*. Cambridge, Mass.: Harvard University Press, 1993.

Tabbi, Joseph. *Postmodern Sublime: Technology and American Writing from Mailer to Cyberpunk*. Ithaca, N.Y.: Cornell University Press, 1995.

Tanner, Tony. *The American Mystery: American Literature from Emerson to DeLillo*. Cambridge and New York: Cambridge University Press, 2000.

Tocqueville, Alexis de. *Democracy in America*. 2 vols. New York: Vintage Books, 1945.

Trilling, Lionel. *The Liberal Imagination*. New York: Viking, 1950.

Vidal, Gore. *United States: Essays 1952–92*. New York: Random House, 1993.

Wall, Cheryl. *Worrying the Line: Black Women Writers, Lineage, and Literary Tradition*. Chapel Hill: University of North Carolina Press, 2005.

Wertheimer, Eric. *Imagined Empires: Incas, Aztecs, and the New World of American Literature*. Cambridge: Cambridge University Press, 1999.

Williams, William Carlos. *In the American Grain*. New York: New Directions, 1925.

Wilson, Edmund. *Patriotic Gore: Studies in the Literature of the American Civil War*. New York: Atheneum, 1962.

Wirth-Nesher, Hana. *Call It English: The Languages of Jewish American Literature*. Princeton, N.J.: Princeton University Press, 2006.

Wood, James. *How Fiction Works*. London: Jonathan Cape, 2008.

# INDEX

# Index

# Index

# Index

# Index

# Cambridge Companions to...

*Mary Wollstonecraft* edited by Claudia L. Johnson

*Virginia Woolf* edited by Susan Sellers (second edition)

*Wordsworth* edited by Stephen Gill

*W. B. Yeats* edited by Marjorie Howes and John Kelly

*Zola* edited by Brian Nelson

TOPICS

*The Actress* edited by Maggie B. Gale and John Stokes

*The African American Novel* edited by Maryemma Graham

*The African American Slave Narrative* edited by Audrey A. Fisch

*Allegory* edited by Rita Copeland and Peter Struck

*American Crime Fiction* edited by Catherine Ross Nickerson

*American Modernism* edited by Walter Kalaidjian

*American Novelists* edited by Timothy Parrish

*American Realism and Naturalism* edited by Donald Pizer

*American Travel Writing* edited by Alfred Bendixen and Judith Hamera

*American Women Playwrights* edited by Brenda Murphy

*Ancient Rhetoric* edited by Erik Gunderson

*Arthurian Legend* edited by Elizabeth Archibald and Ad Putter

*Australian Literature* edited by Elizabeth Webby

*British Literature of the French Revolution* edited by Pamela Clemit

*British Romantic Poetry* edited by James Chandler and Maureen N. McLane

*British Romanticism* edited by Stuart Curran (second edition)

*British Theatre, 1730–1830*, edited by Jane Moody and Daniel O'Quinn

*Canadian Literature* edited by Eva-Marie Kröller

*Children's Literature* edited by M. O. Grenby and Andrea Immel

*The Classic Russian Novel* edited by Malcolm V. Jones and Robin Feuer Miller

*Contemporary Irish Poetry* edited by Matthew Campbell

*Creative Writing* edited by David Morley and Philip Neilsen

*Crime Fiction* edited by Martin Priestman

*Early Modern Women's Writing* edited by Laura Lunger Knoppers

*The Eighteenth-Century Novel* edited by John Richetti

*Eighteenth-Century Poetry* edited by John Sitter

*English Literature, 1500–1600* edited by Arthur F. Kinney

*English Literature, 1650–1740* edited by Steven N. Zwicker

*English Literature, 1740–1830* edited by Thomas Keymer and Jon Mee

*English Literature, 1830–1914* edited by Joanne Shattock

*English Novelists* edited by Adrian Poole

*English Poetry, Donne to Marvell* edited by Thomas N. Corns

*English Poets* edited by Claude Rawson

*English Renaissance Drama* edited by A. R. Braunmuller and Michael Hattaway (second edition)

*English Renaissance Tragedy* edited by Emma Smith and Garrett A. Sullivan, Jr.

*English Restoration Theatre* edited by Deborah C. Payne Fisk

*The Epic* edited by Catherine Bates

*European Modernism* edited by Pericles Lewis

*European Novelists* edited by Michael Bell

*Fantasy Literature* edited by Edward James and Farah Mendlesohn

*Feminist Literary Theory* edited by Ellen Rooney

*Fiction in the Romantic Period* edited by Richard Maxwell and Katie Trumpener

*The Fin de Siècle* edited by Gail Marshall